KT-382-570

Barcelona.

Damien Simonis

LONELY PLANET PUBLICATIONS
Melbourne • Oakland • London • Paris

Barcelona
3rd edition – October 2002
First published – April 1999

Published by
Lonely Planet Publications Pty Ltd ABN 36 005 607 983
90 Maribyrnong St, Footscray, Victoria 3011, Australia

Lonely Planet offices
Australia Locked Bag 1, Footscray, Victoria 3011
USA 150 Linden St, Oakland, CA 94607
UK 10a Spring Place, London NW5 3BH
France 1 rue du Dahomey, 75011 Paris

Photographs
Many of the images in this guide are available for licensing from
Lonely Planet Images.
w www.lonelyplanetimages.com

Front cover photograph
Dorg i Ocell, sculpture by Joan Miro at Parc Joan Miro - Barcelona,
Cataluna (Damien Simonis)

ISBN 1 74059 341 3

Printed through Colorcraft Ltd, Hong Kong
Printed in China

Contents – Text

2 Contents

PLACES TO STAY   147

PLACES TO EAT   155

ENTERTAINMENT   170

SHOPPING   186

EXCURSIONS   192

LANGUAGE   212

GLOSSARY   220

INDEX   230

Contents – Maps

The Author

Damien Simonis

With a degree in languages and several years' reporting and sub-editing on Australian newspapers (including the *Australian* and the *Age*), Sydney-born Damien left the country in 1989. He has since lived, worked and travelled extensively throughout Europe, the Middle East and North Africa. Since 1992, Lonely Planet has kept him busy in *Jordan & Syria*, *Egypt & the Sudan*, *Morocco*, *North Africa*, *Italy*, *Tuscany*, *Florence*, *Venice*, *Spain*, *The Canary Islands*, *Madrid* and *Catalunya*. In addition he has penned other guidebooks and written and snapped for publications in Australia, the UK and North America. When not on the road, Damien resides in splendid Stoke Newington, deep in the heart of north London.

FROM DAMIEN

As usual, a coterie of friends kept me sane on this excursion through the Big B. In no particular order thanks go to the following for their company and tips: Maria Barbosa Pérez, Silvia Folch, Susan Kempster, Michael van Laake and Rocio Vázquez, Susana Pellicer, Teresa Moreno Quintana, Armin Teichmann, Nicole Neuefeind and Anna Torrisi. Although we didn't manage to meet up often, various members of SCIJ España, such as Ita Fabregas and Antonio Campaña, had some useful nuggets to offer.

Edith López García converted herself into a special advisor on the Food Front – the assistance is much appreciated. Sergi Ferrer-Salat kindly offered to revise the foodie text for me.

At home in London, brother Des helped keep things ticking over when I wasn't around to deal with problems.

Finally, the sweat, blood and tears of this latest edition of *Barcelona* is dedicated to Janique LeBlanc. I would walk one thousand miles...

This Book

Damien Simonis has written this and the two previous editions of Lonely Planet's *Barcelona* guidebook.

FROM THE PUBLISHER

This edition of *Barcelona* was produced in Lonely Planet's Melbourne Office. Evan Jones was the coordinating editor, Mark Griffiths was responsible for the mapping, Anna Judd for the colour pages and Tamsin Wilson for the layout. Elizabeth Swan, Anne Mulvaney and Isabelle Young assisted with the editing, while Jarrad Needham and Sarah Sloane assisted with the mapping. The cover was designed by Annika Roojun and the climate chart was produced by Paul Edmunds; both are from the London office. Lonely Planet Images supplied the photographs and the illustrations were drawn by Mick Weldon and Jane Smith. Many thanks to Emma Koch for supplying the Language chapter. Overseeing the various aspects of the book were Adriana Mammarella, Brigitte Ellemor, Bruce Evans, Celia Wood and Heather Dickson. A special thanks goes to the author, Damien, for his hard work.

Grateful acknowledgement is made for permission to reproduce the TMB: *Barcelona Metro Map* © 2002.

THANKS

Many thanks to the travellers who used the last edition and contacted us with helpful hints, advice and interesting anecdotes.

Sabine Agena, Ellen Anker-Kofoed, Jens Augustinsson, Tony Bellette, Tony Benfield, Peter Binfield, Tamas Biro, Sylvia Campbell, Rachel Cane, Mollie Churchill, Moira Coleman, Lonnie Croal, Leann Currie-McGhee, Merel de Boer, Dawn de Kock, Jordi Dols, Bec Eddington, Blake Eddington, Ben Edmunds, Nick Elliott, Marleen Enschede, M Fairmont, Chris Fleming, Chris Foster, Maxine Gere, Marcus Hadley, Jeff Haire, Judith Hammerle, Judith Hargraves, Martha Harssema, Otto Hermkens, Adrian Hervey, Meagan Hess, Dr H Hope-Stone, Kimberly Huie, Eva Jilken, Joonas Kaarnametsa, Liz Kao, Moshe Katzanek, Patricia Keays, Sukey Kielman, Phillip Kinkelis, David Lofting, Robert Mahoney, Sermont Marmot, Aviva Mayers, Rob Megens, Naomi Mitchell, Frank Muller, Eija Narvanen, Miguel Nunes, Paul O Brien, Arnout den Ouden, Susan Park, Ilan Peri, Maria Ralph, R David Rangely, Laura Rice, Ed Sawford, A J Scheffer, Deborah Schubert, Rebecca Scott, Gary Scowcroft, Sue Sedwell, Omer Sela, Mark Stallings, Tim Stubbs, Julia Stueeken, Clayton Trapp, Jo Ubags, Othmar Ulrich, Mariska van Eck, Mieke van Marissing, Dee Varney, Dirk Wellens, Tim White, Kyle Whiting, Roy Wiesner, Fiona Wilson, Stella Wood, Lucy Woodward, Carlo Zevi, Katie Zuzek

Foreword

ABOUT LONELY PLANET GUIDEBOOKS

The story begins with a classic travel adventure: Tony and Maureen Wheeler's 1972 journey across Europe and Asia to Australia. There was no useful information about the overland trail then, so Tony and Maureen published the first Lonely Planet guidebook to meet a growing need.

From a kitchen table, Lonely Planet has grown to become the largest independent travel publisher in the world, with offices in Melbourne (Australia), Oakland (USA), London (UK) and Paris (France).

Today Lonely Planet guidebooks cover the globe. There is an ever-growing list of books and information in a variety of media. Some things haven't changed. The main aim is still to make it possible for adventurous travellers to get out there – to explore and better understand the world.

At Lonely Planet we believe travellers can make a positive contribution to the countries they visit – if they respect their host communities and spend their money wisely. Since 1986 a percentage of the income from each book has been donated to aid projects and human rights campaigns, and, more recently, to wildlife conservation.

Although inclusion in a guidebook usually implies a recommendation we cannot list every good place. Exclusion does not necessarily imply criticism. In fact there are a number of reasons why we might exclude a place – sometimes it is simply inappropriate to encourage an influx of travellers.

UPDATES & READER FEEDBACK

Things change – prices go up, schedules change, good places go bad and bad places go bankrupt. Nothing stays the same. So, if you find things better or worse, recently opened or long-since closed, please tell us and help make the next edition even more accurate and useful.

Lonely Planet thoroughly updates each guidebook as often as possible – usually every two years, although for some destinations the gap can be longer. Between editions, up-to-date information is available in our free, quarterly *Planet Talk* newsletter and monthly email bulletin *Comet*. Information in Lonely Planet's website (W *www.lonelyplanet.com*) is also regularly updated by authors and editors, and the site's *Scoop* section covers news and current affairs relevant to travellers. Lastly, the *Thorn Tree* bulletin board and *Postcards* section carry unverified, but fascinating, reports from travellers.

Tell us about it! We genuinely value your feedback. A well-travelled team at Lonely Planet reads and acknowledges every email and letter we receive and ensures that every morsel of information finds its way to the relevant authors, editors and cartographers.

Everyone who writes to us will find their name listed in the next edition of the appropriate guidebook, and will receive the latest issue of *Comet* or *Planet Talk*. The very best contributions will be rewarded with a free guidebook.

We may edit, reproduce and incorporate your comments in Lonely Planet products such as guidebooks, websites and digital products, so let us know if you don't want your comments reproduced or your name acknowledged.

How to contact Lonely Planet:
Online: e talk2us@lonelyplanet.com.au, W www.lonelyplanet.com
Australia: Locked Bag 1, Footscray, Victoria 3011
UK: 10a Spring Place, London NW5 3BH
USA: 150 Linden St, Oakland, CA 94607

Introduction

Location, location, location. If Barcelona were up for sale, it would pull a fortune for position alone. You are never more than a few hours' drive from: southern France; the Pyrenees (skiing in winter, hiking in summer); the seaside lunacy of Sitges (the gay capital of the *costas*); Romanesque and Gothic monasteries and churches; the Penedès wine country; and the rugged splendours of the northern Costa Brava. Old rivals such as medieval Girona (to the north) and Roman Tarragona (south) are easily accessible.

Barcelona is one of the most exciting cities to visit on the western Mediterranean seaboard – sedulously promoting itself as a European metropolis, a link between the sub-Pyrenean peninsula and the heartland of Western Europe.

At its worst over the centuries, it has been a parochial and smugly self-satisfied bourgeois town. At its best, it displays a zest for life, artistic genius and sense of style few cities can rival.

Barcelona is and isn't Spain. The second city after Madrid, it is capital of the autonomous region of Catalunya, only fully incorporated into the state after defeat in battle in 1714. The Catalans speak their own language, and not just literally. Viewed with suspicion and envy by some from more southern parts, the *polacos* ('Pollacks') are to Spain what the Scots are to the UK.

It was during Barcelona's medieval period that left it with one of the most impressive and varied Gothic legacies in all Europe. True, the city's fortunes slid as its Mediterranean empire crumbled and Madrid enforced tighter central rule, and artistically the city stagnated.

But then came the Modernistas. Led by Antoni Gaudí, they cast across Barcelona an Art Nouveau splash unparalleled anywhere else. Some of the greatest artists of this century put in time here – Picasso and

Miró make an impressive duo, and Dalí was born and lived much of his life just up the coast.

Barcelona is not just monuments and paintings. The city that shot into the limelight with the 1992 Olympic Games provides all sorts of entertainments, starting with the palate. Catalan cuisine is among Spain's best, so you're in for a treat. Traditional old restaurants will welcome you from the cool of winter and you can spend long summer afternoons over al fresco seafood meals. The wine you drink will probably come from the nearby Penedès area, home to *cava*, the prized local bubbly.

If you thought it was time to head for bed after a meal that might not have begun before 10pm, think again. You've barely begun. The city centre and several *barris* heave to the joyous rhythms of bar-hoppers. Barcelona leaves much of the rest of Europe for dead for its sheer concentration of bars, cafés and clubs.

In summer especially, various parts of the city seem to lose their sanity, giving themselves over to week-long *festes*. These outdoor parties feature bands, competitions, and traditional parades of giants, dwarfs and demons *(gegants, capgrossos* and *dimonis)*. Not to mention the madness of fire-running *(correfoc)* through the narrow lanes of the old city with fire-breathing dragons during the September Festes de la Mercè.

New bars, cafés and restaurants continue to spring up all over town as the city council keeps up a cracking pace to clean up its most rundown quarters, especially in Ciutat Vella (old city). Fortunately Barcelona retains some of its rough-diamond flavour, with even a grunge-chic inner-city set that appears here to stay.

As soaring rent and home-buying prices attest, people are flocking to this Mediterranean jewel. Come to 'Barna' and you'll soon see why!

Facts about Barcelona

HISTORY

The history of the second city of Spain, although far longer than that of its brasher Castilian rival Madrid, could be dismissed as that of an also-ran, a wannabe that at various moments was clearly on the brink of greatness but whose hopes and pretensions were all too often dashed by events.

For centuries Barcelona shrank in the shadow of greater cities and powers. When finally it emerged from the Dark Ages as the successful headquarters of a burgeoning mercantile empire across the Mediterranean, Barcelona still failed – just – to attain the grandeur of some of its major competitors.

Absorption into unified Spain at the close of the Middle Ages meant Barcelona not only was relegated to second place behind Madrid, the newly established centre of the Spanish empire, but frequently languished well behind other cities of greater imperial weight, such as Seville in the south.

Civil conflicts, revolts against Madrid and the disaster of defeat in 1714 contributed little to the city's happiness, but a tenacious optimism helped to fuel repeated sparks of growth and activity. By the end of the 19th century, Barcelona was probably *the* leading economic light in an otherwise vexed and gloomy country, shackled by poverty, inept government and incessant infighting.

Republican defeat in the Spanish Civil War again meant relegation. General Franco's rigid distaste for the devolutionist desires of the Catalans was most eloquently expressed by the official suppression of their language. Unsurprisingly, little love was lost between the diminutive dictator and the bulk of Barcelonins (as residents of Barcelona are called) – his demise in 1975 was greeted with palpable relief. Since the political devolution process began in 1978, Barcelona has sparkled back to life.

Early Barcelona

The area around present-day Barcelona was certainly inhabited prior to the arrival of the Romans in Spain in 218 BC. By whom, and whether or not there was an urban nucleus, is open to debate.

Pre-Roman coins found in the area suggest the Iberian Laietani tribe may have settled here. As far back as 35,000 BC the tribe's Stone Age predecessors had roamed the Pyrenees and begun to descend into the lowlands to the south. In 1991 the remains of 25 corpses were found in Carrer de Sant Pau in El Raval – they had been buried around 4000 BC. It has been speculated that, in those days, much of El Raval was a bay and that the hillock that is Plaça de Sant Jaume may have been home to a Neolithic settlement.

Other evidence hints at a settlement established around 230 BC by the Carthaginian conqueror (and father of Hannibal), Hamilcar Barca. It is tempting to see in his name the roots of the city's own name. Archaeologists believe that any pre-Roman town must have been built on the hill that is current-day Montjuïc.

In the centre of old Barcelona is Carrer d'Hèrcules (Hercules Street). Among the many feats attributed to this figure from Greek mythology is the actual founding of Barcelona – a claim that's not taken terribly seriously by anyone.

The Romans

The heart of the Roman settlement of Barcelona lay within what would later become the medieval city – now known as Barri Gòtic. At its core was a low rise known as Mont Taber, where the temple was raised. Remains of city walls, temple pillars and graves all attest to what would eventually become a busy and lively town. Barcino (as the Romans knew it) was not a major centre, however. Tarraco (Tarragona) to the south and the one-time Greek trading centre of Empúries to the north were both regarded as being more important. In fact, Tarraco became capital of the Roman province of Hispania Citerior.

It took the Romans some two centuries to fully subjugate the peninsula but the area around Barcelona enjoyed a mostly peaceful occupation, and in 15 BC Caesar Augustus was magnanimous enough to grant the town the title of Colonia Julia Augusta Faventia Pia. Evidence from sources such as the Latin poet Ausonius suggests a picture of contented prosperity – Roman Barcelona lived well off the agricultural produce in its hinterland and from fishing. Oysters, in particular, seem to have appeared regularly on the Roman menu in ancient times.

Barbarian Invasions

All good things come to an end and, as the Roman Empire began to wobble, Hispania (as the Iberian Peninsula was known to the Romans) felt the effects. It is no coincidence that the bulk of the Roman walls, vestiges of which remain today, went up in the 4th century AD. Marauding Franks had visited a little death and destruction on the city in a prelude to what was to come – several waves of invaders flooded across the country like great Atlantic rollers. By 415 the comparatively Romanised Visigoths had arrived and, under their leader Athaulf, made a temporary capital in Barcelona before moving on to Toletum (Toledo). In all Hispania there were probably never more than a few hundred thousand Visigoths, but they remained the ruling class – much aided by Hispano-Roman nobility and the emerging Christian clergy.

Islamic Blitzkrieg

In 711 the Muslim general Tariq landed an expeditionary force in present-day Gibraltar (Arabic for Tariq's Mountain). After the death in 632 of the prophet Mohammed in distant Arabia, Muslims had swept across Asia Minor and all of North Africa, conquering and converting as they went in an unprecedented spate of divinely inspired ad-hoc empire building.

In Spain, Tariq found the Visigothic 'state' so rotten and divided that he had no trouble sweeping across the peninsula all the way into France, where he and his army were only brought to a halt in 732 by the Franks at Poitiers.

Barcelona fell under Muslim sway but this situation was short-lived. Little is known about the period. The town is mentioned in Arabic chronicles but it seems the Muslims resigned themselves early on to setting up a defensive line along the Riu Ebro to the south. Whatever the thinking at the time, Barcelona was taken by Louis the Pious, the future Frankish ruler, in 801.

The counts *(comtes)* who were installed here as Louis' lieutenants hailed from local tribes roaming on the periphery of the Frankish empire. Barcelona was a frontier town in what was known as the Frankish or Spanish March – a rough-and-ready buffer zone south of the Pyrenees designed to keep the Muslims and other undesirables at arm's length, and to be used as a springboard for later offensives.

A Hairy Beginning

The history of Barcelona, in one sense, only truly began at this point. The plains and mountains to the northwest and north of Barcelona were populated by the people who by then could be identified as 'Catalans' (although surviving documentary references to the term only date from the 12th century). Catalan, the language (and its many dialects) of these people, was closely related to the *langue d'oc*, the post-Latin lingua franca of southern France (of which Provencal is about the only barely surviving reminder). It is definitely not a dialect of Castilian Spanish.

The March was under nominal Frankish control but the real power lay with local potentates (themselves often of Frankish origin, however) who ranged across the territory. One of these rulers went by the curious name of Guifré el Pelós, or Wilfred the Hairy. This was not a reference to uneven shaving habits: According to legend, old Guifré had hair in parts most people do not (exactly which parts was never specified!).

Through Holy Roman imperial decree and a dash of intrigue, Guifré and his brothers managed to gain control of most of the Catalan counties. These included Barcelona (something of a glorified country town at the time).

This task was completed by 878 and Guifré entered the folk mythology of Catalunya. A great funder of religious foundations in Barcelona (none of which survive) and across Catalunya (some of which do), he astutely won for himself the benevolence of the only people who could write in those days – the clergy. They began a tradition of eulogy that has never really died since. If Catalunya can be called a nation, then its 'father' was the hirsute Guifré.

Guifré and his immediate successors continued, at least in name, to be vassals of the Franks. In reality, his position as 'Comte de Barcelona' (Count of Barcelona; even today many refer to Barcelona as the *ciutat comtal*, or city of counts) was assured in his own right.

The Comtes de Barcelona

By the late 10th century, the Casal de Barcelona (House of Barcelona) was the senior of several counties (whose leaders were all related by family ties) that would soon be a single, independent principality covering most of modern Catalunya except the south, plus Roussillon (which today lies across the border in France).

This was the only Christian 'state' on the Iberian Peninsula not to fall under the sway of Sancho III of Navarra in the early 11th century. One last Muslim assault came

Born in Blood

Guifré el Pelós founded the Casal de Barcelona (House of Barcelona) more or less with the consent of his Frankish overlords. But what's a new political entity without a flag of some sort? Scribblers of history and other tall tales soon hit upon a particularly gratifying account for the existence of Catalunya's national colours (the following story and several other versions began to circulate sometime around the 16th century).

Called upon to join the holy fight against the wicked Muslims with an army of Frankish good guys, the gutsy Guifré fell wounded in hair-raising style on the field of battle. The Frankish emperor, Charles the Bald (this is not a joke), was so touched by his vassal's loyalty that he wanted to reward him in some way. No, not with an all-expenses-paid holiday to Rome or a gold-plated letter-opener. Upon seeing Guifré's bright golden shield embarrassingly bereft of a coat of arms, old Charles dipped his fingers in a pool of Guifré's fresh, warm blood and drew four finger stripes, les quatre barres, down the shield.

So much for the story-telling. From this tale came the Catalan coat of arms, concrete evidence of which first appears in 1150 in a seal of Count Ramon Berenguer IV. The same heraldic sign (said to be the fourth oldest in all Europe) can also be made out on the coffin of Ramon Berenguer II (in the cathedral in Girona), who died in 1082. Its origins remain a mystery. The coat of arms went on later to become that of the so-called Corona de Aragón, the state formed in 1137 of a coalition comprising the principality of Catalunya, Aragón, Valencia, the Balearic Islands and Roussillon (in present-day France).

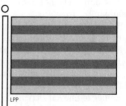

The Catalan flag (in which the stripes become horizontal) is first documented in the 13th century and became the official symbol of the modern, autonomous region of Catalunya in 1979. A similar symbol to the coat of arms, but oval in shape, was concocted in 1932 and now represents the Generalitat, or regional government. The same colour combination also appears in the heraldry of the former members of the Corona de Aragón.

when Al-Mansur raided Barcelona in 985. The city was torched and many of those citizens who were not slaughtered were marched off into slavery in Córdoba.

Calls for Frankish aid to repulse Al-Mansur had gone unheeded, so from this time on the counts implicitly refused to acknowledge Frankish suzerainty. The Franks never contested the new status quo and so a new entity – Catalunya – acquired tacit recognition across Europe.

Throughout Spain, a confusion of counties, principalities and kingdoms vied, jockeyed and fought for local or peninsula domination. It was as common for Muslim warlords to team up with Christian rulers in local spats as for Christians and Muslims to challenge one another. These were, to say the least, interesting times. Particularly so for the counts of Barcelona, who managed to pick up plenty of booty by judicious meddling in Muslim squabbles to the south.

This booty was put to good use. Count Ramon Berenguer I was able to buy the counties of Carcassonne and Béziers, north of Roussillon, with acquired Muslim bullion. Barcelona would maintain ambitions in France for two more centuries – at one point it held territory as far east as Provence. Under Ramon Berenguer III (1082–1131) sea trade developed and Catalunya launched its own fleet.

Marriage of Convenience?

In 1137 Ramon Berenguer IV clinched what must have seemed an unbeatable deal. He was betrothed to Petronilla, heiress to the throne of Catalunya's western neighbour Aragón, thus creating a joint state that set the scene for Catalunya's golden age. This state, known as the Corona de Aragón (Crown of Aragon), was ruled by *comtes-reis* (count-kings, ie, counts of Barcelona and kings of Aragón). The title enshrined the continued separateness of the two states, and both retained many (but not all) of their own laws. The arrangement was to have unexpected consequences as it tied Catalunya to the destiny of the rest of the peninsula in a way that ultimately would not appeal to many Catalans.

In the meantime, however, Don Ramon wasn't content to lie about with Petronilla. In the course of the 1140s he wrested control of southern Catalunya from the Muslims. This southwards expansion heralded a major shift in policy, which until then had been concerned with the north. Defeat by the French at the Battle of Muret and the subsequent loss to France of most Catalan possessions north of the Pyrenees would confirm the change of direction.

Mediterranean Empire

Not content to leave all the glory of the Reconquista to the Castilians, Jaume I (1213–76) set about on his own spectacular missions.

Although Barcelona's shallow, silty harbour was hardly ideal, the city's importance by now should have made it a logical launchpad for Mediterranean sea trade, at this time largely the preserve of Italian city states such as Genoa, Pisa and Venice, and their North African counterparts. Indeed, when prevailing winds were favourable, sailing vessels often zipped across from Barcelona to the Balearic Islands. There was just one problem: the islands were occupied by Muslim North Africans who were making a nice living by using them as a customs staging post and as a base for piracy.

Jaume I set off in 1229 with fleets from Tarragona, Barcelona, Marseilles, and other ports. His object was Mallorca, which he won. Six years later he had Ibiza and Formentera in hand. Things were going so well that, prodded by the Aragonese, for good measure he took control of Valencia (on the mainland) too. This was no easy task and was only completed in 1248 after 16 years of grinding conquest. All this activity helped fuel a boom in Barcelona and Jaume raised new walls that increased the size of the enclosed city ten-fold.

The empire-building program shifted into top gear in the 1280s. Jaume I's son Pere II (1240–85) took Sicily in a virtually bloodless campaign in 1282. The easternmost part of the Balearics, Menorca, was not so lucky, falling to Alfons II in 1287 in a bloodbath. Most of its people were killed or enslaved and the island remained largely deserted throughout its occupation. Malta, Gozo and Athens were also briefly taken. A half-hearted attempt was made on Corsica but the most determined and ultimately fruitless assault began on Sardinia in 1324. The island became the Corona de Aragón's Vietnam. As late as 1423 Naples also came under the influence of the Catalo-Aragonese.

In spite of the carnage and the expense of war, this was Barcelona's golden age. The grandest city in the Catalo-Aragonese coalition, Barcelona was the base for what was now a thriving mercantile empire. The western Mediterranean had been turned virtually into a Catalan lake and trade proceeded apace, not only among the occupied territories but also with North Africa (through which Barcelona dominated the African gold trade) and to a lesser extent in the Levant.

The Rise of Parliament

The rulers of the Casal de Barcelona and then the count-kings of the Corona de Aragón had a habit of regularly absenting themselves from Barcelona. Initially, local city administration was in the hands of a viscount, but in the course of the 12th century local power began to shift.

Citizens of senior rank already had some say in the running of city affairs and, in 1249, Jaume I authorised the election of a committee of key citizens to advise his officials. The idea developed and, by 1274, the Consell dels Cent Jurats (Council of the Hundred Sworn-In) formed a kind of electoral college from which an executive body of five *consellers* (councillors) was nominated to run city affairs.

In 1283 the Corts Catalanes met for the first time. This new legislative council for Catalunya (equivalent bodies sat in Aragón

The Usatges de Barcelona

Under the Casal de Barcelona a system of feudal government and law evolved that had little to do with the more centralised and absolutist models that would emerge in subsequent centuries in the Castile, reconquered from the Muslims.

A hodgepodge of Roman-Visigothic laws combined with emerging feudal practice found its way into the written bill of rights called the *'Usatges de Barcelona'* from around 1060. Although aimed in part in providing the lower classes with some minimal rights and giving them greater security, the main aim of the Usatges appears to have been to rein in a frequently headstrong nobility under the *casal*, through the Comtes de Barcelona, who became the supreme arbiter.

Some articles of the code could not spell out more clearly the intention of the Comte de Barcelona: '…let none of the magnates hereafter presume in any way to either punish criminals…or to build a new castle against the prince (Comte)…' (article 73).

Justice in those days may seem a little rough for modern tastes: '…let them (the rulers) render justice as it seems fit to them: by cutting off hands and feet, putting out eyes, keeping men in prison for a long time and, ultimately, in hanging their bodies if necessary.' Was there an element of misogyny in the Usatges? 'In regard to women, let the rulers render justice by cutting off their noses, lips, ears and breasts, and by burning them at the stake if necessary…'

Where evidence and witnesses were in short supply, the only options left for some cases were 'judicial battle' or trial by ordeal. The former involved duelling (oneself or by proxy) while the latter involved what was tantamount to torture with boiling and freezing water. Adultery was usually handled in this way, the ordeal of boiling water being common for peasants. 'If the wife is victorious, let her husband honourably keep her and make compensation to her…'! One can only wonder what would compensate for a prolonged bath in boiling water.

The Usatges remained at the heart of Catalan law-making until defeat at the hands of King Felipe in 1714 ended the War of the Spanish Succession and Catalan autonomy.

and Valencia) was made up of representatives of the nobility, clergy and high-class merchants to form a counterweight to regal power. The Corts Catalanes met at first annually, then every three years, but had a permanent secretariat known as the Diputació del General or Generalitat. Its home was, and remains, the Palau de la Generalitat.

The Corts and Council increased their leverage as trade grew and their respective roles in raising taxes and distributing wealth became more important. As the count-kings required money to organise wars and other enterprises, they increasingly relied on Barcelonin and Catalan impresarios who were best represented through these two oligarchic bodies.

Those citizens not considered of high enough quality to break into these clubs, but who increasingly contributed a good amount of wealth to the city and state, became restless. Occasional uprisings and riots were fomented in the streets of Barcelona and the city was roughly divided into two factions: the dominant Biga and the opposition Busca (who at times appeared to get a nudge and a wink from regal sources, just to keep a little pressure on the institutions, while not precipitating unbridled power struggles that might have slipped out of control). Barcelona was as violent as any other average medieval city but the trouble was always contained.

The Corts and Council lasted until all local rights were abrogated by the Bourbon king, Felipe V, in 1714.

Meanwhile, Barcelona's trading wealth paid for the great Gothic buildings that still bejewel the city. The cathedral, the Capella Reial de Santa Àgata and the churches of Santa Maria del Pi and Santa Maria del Mar were all built in the late 13th or early 14th centuries. King Pere III (1336–87) created the breathtaking Reial Dressiness (royal shipyards) and extended the city walls again, this time to include the El Raval area west of La Rambla.

Decline & Castilian Domination

Preserving the empire began to exhaust Catalunya. Sea wars with Genoa, resistance in Sardinia, the rise of the Ottoman Empire and the loss of the gold trade all drained the coffers. Commerce collapsed. The Black Death and famines killed about half of Catalunya's population in the 14th century. Barcelona's Jewish population suffered a pogrom in 1391.

After the last of Guifré el Pelós' dynasty, Martí I, died heirless in 1410, a special council elected Fernando (Ferran to the Catalans) de Antequera, a Castilian prince of the Trastámara house, to the Aragonese throne. This, the so-called Compromiso de Caspe (Caspe Agreement) of 1412 was engineered by the nobility in Aragón, who saw a chance to reduce Catalan influence over their affairs. Indeed, Fernando and his successors were soon at daggers drawn with their Catalan subjects, who felt they were being exploited for Castilian interests. In 1462 the Catalans rebelled against King Juan II, who in 1473 reduced Barcelona after a grinding siege.

Juan II's son, Fernando, succeeded to the Aragonese throne in 1479 and his marriage to Isabel, queen of Castile, united Spain's two most powerful monarchies. Just as Catalunya had been hitched to Aragón, now the combine was hitched to Castile.

Catalunya effectively became part of the Castilian state, although it jealously guarded its own institutions and system of law. Juridically, Catalunya had never ceased to be a distinct entity within the Catalo-Aragonese arrangement. Rather than attack the problem head on, Fernando and Isabel side-stepped it, introducing the hated Inquisition to Barcelona. The local citizenry implored them not to do so as what was left of business life in the city lay largely in the hands of *conversos* (Jews at least nominally converted to Christianity) who were a particular target of Inquisitorial attention. The pleas were ignored and the *conversos* packed their bags and shipped out their money. Barcelona was reduced to penury.

To make matters worse, the Catholic Monarchs banned the Catalans from trading directly with the newly established American colonies. Instead, everything had to go through the recently enriched Castilian ports of Seville and Cádiz. As Spain hit a high point under Carlos I (or Karl V of the Habsburg empire) and his successor Felipe II, Catalunya's fortunes, now brought further to heel under a viceroy from Madrid, continued to sink.

Impoverished and disaffected by ever growing financial demands from the crown, Catalunya revolted again in the 17th century and declared itself to be an independent 'republic', under French protection, in the Guerra dels Segadors (Reapers War; 1640–52). Countryside and towns were devastated, and Barcelona was finally besieged into submission. The French protection was less than convincing (and in the end largely resented), however, and seven years later, when France and Spain concluded hostilities, Louis XIV and Felipe IV signed a peace treaty that cost Spain chunks of Catalan territory – in particular Roussillon and also parts of Cerdanya.

War of the Spanish Succession

By now Spain itself was on the skids, and Catalunya was going down with it. When the last of the Habsburgs, Carlos II, died in 1700, he left no successor. France imposed the investiture of a Bourbon, Felipe V. Although the Catalans preferred the Austrian candidate, Archduke Carlos, they did not at first actively oppose Felipe's enthronement. Schooled in French-style absolutism and centralism, Felipe soon proved vexatious to the Catalans, who threw in their lot with England, Holland, some German states, Portugal and the House of Savoy in their decision to bat for Austria. In 1702 the War of the Spanish Succession broke out. Catalans thought they were onto a winner. They were wrong, however, and in 1713 the Treaty of Utrecht left Felipe V in charge in Madrid.

Felipe had already taken control of Valencia and Aragón anyway. Barcelona had little to hope for from Felipe V and decided to resist. The siege began in March 1713 and ended on 11 September 1714.

There were no half measures. Felipe V abolished the Generalitat, built a huge fort (the Citadels) to watch over Barcelona, and banned writing and teaching in Catalan.

What was left of Catalunya's possessions were farmed out to the great powers: Menorca had gone to the British in 1713, Naples and Sardinia went to Austria, and Sicily to the House of Savoy.

A New Boom

After the initial shock, Barcelona found the Bourbon rulers to be comparatively lighthanded in their treatment of the city. Indeed, its prosperity and productivity was in the country's interest. Throughout the 18th century the Barcelonins concentrated on what they do best – industry and commerce.

The big break came in 1778 when the ban on American trade was lifted. Some enterprising traders had already sent vessels across the Atlantic to deal directly in the Americas – although this was still technically forbidden. Their early ventures were a commercial success and the lifting of the ban stimulated business. In Barcelona itself, growth was modest but sustained. Small-scale manufacturing provided employment and profit. Wages were rising and city fathers even had a stab at town planning, creating the grid-based workers' district of La Barcelonese.

Before the industrial revolution, based initially on the cotton trade with America, could really get underway, Barcelona and the rest of Spain had to go through a little more pain. A French revolutionary army was launched Spain's way (1793–95) with limited success, but when Napoleon turned his attentions to the country in 1808 it was another story. Barcelona and Catalunya suffered along with the rest of the country until the French were expelled in 1814 (Barcelona was the last city in the hands of the French, who left in September).

By the 1830s Barcelona was beginning to ride on a feel-good factor that would last for most of the century. Wine, cork and iron industries developed. From the mid-1830s onwards, steamships were launched off the slipways . In 1848 Spain's first railway line was opened between Barcelona and Mataró.

Well, not everyone was feeling so good. Creeping industrialisation and prosperity for the business class did not work out so well down the line. Wages were higher than in Madrid, but working-class families lived in increasingly putrid and cramped conditions. Poor nutrition, bad sanitation and disease were the norm in workers' districts, and riots, predictably, resulted. As a rule they were put down with little ceremony – the 1842 rising was bombarded into submission. Some relief came in 1854 with the knocking down of the medieval walls but the pressure remained acute. The population then was increasing by up to 28% per year.

In 1869, a revolutionary plan to expand the city was begun. Ildefons Cerdà designed L'Eixample (The Enlargement) as a grid, broken up with gardens and parks and grafted on to the old town, beginning at Plaça de Catalunya.

It became (and to a large extent remains) the most sought-after chunk of real estate in Barcelona – but the parks were mostly sacrificed to an insatiable demand for housing. The flourishing bourgeoisie paid for lavish, ostentatious buildings, many of them in the unique, Modernista (Catalan Art Nouveau) style.

There seemed to be no stopping this town. In 1888 it hosted a Universal Exhibition. It did so in spite of going almost broke in the process, partly due to lack of funding from Madrid. Little more than a year before, work on the exhibition buildings and grounds had not even begun, but they were all completed only 10 days late. Although the Exhibition attracted more than two million visitors, it did not get the international attention some had hoped for.

Still, changing the cityscape had become habitual in modern Barcelona. La Rambla de Catalunya and Avinguda del Paral.lel were both slammed through in 1888. The Monument a Colom and Arc de Triomf, rather odd monuments in some respects (Columbus had little to do with Barcelona and triumphs were in short supply) also saw the light of day that year.

Renaixença

Barcelona was comparatively peaceful for most of the second half of the 19th century. The city wasn't politically inert, though.

The relative calm and growing wealth that came with commercial success helped revive interest in all things Catalan.

The so-called Renaixença (Renaissance) reflected the feeling in Barcelona of renewed self-confidence. The mood was both backward- and forward-looking. Politicians and academics increasingly studied and demanded the return of former Catalan institutions and legal systems. The Catalan language was readopted by the middle and upper classes and a new Catalan literature emerged as well.

In 1892 the Unió Catalanista (Catalanist Union) was formed and demanded the re-establishment of the Corts in a document known as the Bases de Manresa. In 1906 the suppression of Catalan news-sheets was greeted by the formation of Solidaritat Catalana (Catalan Solidarity, a nationalist movement). Led by Enric Prat de la Riba, it attracted a broad band of Catalans, not all of them nationalists.

Perhaps the most dynamic expression of the Catalan Renaissance occurred in the world of art. Barcelona was the home of Modernisme, the Catalan version of Art Nouveau. While the rest of Spain largely stagnated, Barcelona was a hotbed of artistic activity. It was an avant-garde base with close links to Paris. The young Picasso spread his artistic wings here and drank in the artists' hang-out, Els Quatre Gats.

1898

This was a very bad year. While textiles and mills formed the backbone of local industry in Barcelona, a good chunk of the wealth was generated in Spain's remaining possessions abroad, Cuba and Puerto Rico in particular. A push for home rule in Cuba became a militant independence movement and proved fatal to what remained of Spain's 'empire'.

Rather than meet the claims halfway, Madrid chose the heavy (and ham-fisted) approach. The USA had had its eye on these territories for some time and it was not too hard for it to pose as guardian angel to independence movements. Trouble had also been brewing in the Philippines. To cut a long story short, virtually the entire ill-equipped Spanish navy was sunk in two ignominious battles in Cuba and the Philippines, and the colonies were lost to the USA.

For Barcelona, the news was disastrous. Many families with considerable business interests in the overseas possessions lost everything. The ragtag Spanish army was slowly transported home and, at the turn of the 20th century, the most common sight on Barcelona's once bustling docks was near-starving, despondent and disease-ridden returned conscripts. They had nothing to do and nowhere to go. Storm clouds once again gathered on the horizon.

Mayhem

Barcelona's proletariat was growing fast. The total population grew from 115,000 in 1800 to over 500,000 by 1900 and over one million by 1930 – boosted, in the early 19th century, by poor immigrants from rural Catalunya and, later, from other regions of Spain. All this made Barcelona ripe for unrest.

The city became a swirling vortex of anarchists, Republicans, bourgeois regionalists, gangsters, police terrorists and hired gunmen *(pistoleros)*. Madrid could not resist introducing a meddling hand into this dangerous cocktail. (Read Gerald Brenan's *The Spanish Labyrinth* or Eduardo Mendoza's novel *City of Marvels* for a taste of some of the unbelievable things that went on: In one episode related by Brenan, gangsters in police pay planted 2000 bombs at or near the bourgeoisie's factories to provide the police with an excuse for arresting a number of anarchists.) One genuine anarchist bomb at the Liceu opera house on La Rambla in the 1890s killed 20 people. Anarchists were also reckoned to be behind the Setmana Tràgica (Tragic Week) in 1909 when, following a military call-up for Spanish campaigns in Morocco, rampaging mobs wrecked 70 religious buildings and workers were shot on the streets in reprisal.

The political front was also active. In 1914 Solidaritat Catalana launched the Mancomunitat de Catalunya, which was a kind of shadow parliament that demanded a Catalan state within a Spanish federation.

In the post-WWI slump, unionism took hold. This movement was led by the anarchist Confederación Nacional del Trabajo (CNT), or National Confederation of Work, which embraced as many as 80% of the city's workers. During a wave of strikes in 1919 and 1920, employers hired assassins to eliminate union leaders. The 1920s dictator General Miguel Primo de Rivera opposed both bourgeois-Catalan nationalism and working-class radicalism, banning the CNT and Mancomunitat and even closing Barcelona football club, a potent symbol of Catalanism. But he did support the staging of a second world fair in Barcelona, the Montjuïc World Exhibition of 1929.

A Taste of Nationhood

Rivera's repression only succeeded in uniting, after his fall in 1930, the pent-up fervour of Catalunya's radical elements. Within days of the formation of Spain's Second Republic in 1931, leftist Catalan nationalists – ERC (Esquerra Republicana de Catalunya) – led by Francesc Macià and Lluís Companys, proclaimed Catalunya a republic within an imaginary 'Iberian Federation'. Soon after, Madrid pressured them into accepting unitary Spanish statehood. However, in 1932 Catalunya got a new regional government, with the old title of Generalitat.

Francesc Macià, its first president, died in 1933 and was succeeded by Lluís Companys who, in 1934, tried again to achieve near-independence, proclaiming the 'Catalan State of the Spanish Federal Republic'. The Madrid government responded with an army bombardment of the Generalitat offices and Barcelona's town hall. The Generalitat was closed and its members given 35-year jail terms. They were released and the Generalitat restored when the leftist Popular Front won the Spanish general election in February 1936. Now, briefly, Catalunya gained genuine autonomy. Companys, its president, carried out land reforms and planned an alternative Barcelona Olympics to the official 1936 games in Nazi Berlin.

But things were racing out of control. The left and the right across Spain were shaping up for a showdown. Anarchists (and their trade union, the CNT) and socialists (embodied in the Unión General de Trabajadores; General Workers' Union) lined up on the left, the former of the two the most vocal advocate of revolt.

Ranged against them were disgruntled sectors of the armed forces (among whom General Francisco Franco was a key figure), a mixed bag of royalists and conservatives routed in the 1936 polls, and the Falange movement of José Antonio Primo de Rivera (the ex-dictator's dapper son), all of whom were moving closer to forming a single front.

The Civil War

On 17 July 1936, just one day before the Barcelona games were due to start, an army uprising in Morocco kick-started the Spanish Civil War. Barcelona's army garrison attempted to take the city for Franco but was defeated by armed anarchists and police loyal to the government.

Franco's forces quickly took hold of most of southern and western Spain. Galicia and Navarra in the north were also his. Most of the east and industrialised north stood with Madrid and the Republic. Initial rapid advances on Madrid were stifled and the two sides settled in for almost three years of misery.

Most of the army backed the coup. Franco's forces soon had the upper hand economically, occupying much of the country's grain and grazing country. By the end of 1936, Hitler's Germany and Mussolini's Italy had recognised Franco and supplied him with arms, troops and cash.

The Republican side had most of the airforce and navy (the latter proved unbelievably ineffectual), and much of the country's industry. Although France was sympathetic, the West decided to keep out and even blocked military supplies in the interests of 'neutrality'. The only help came from Stalin's Soviet Union – in the form of military advisers and hardware. But this assistance was never enough and was bought at the price of the nation's entire gold reserves. Ideology was ultimately what killed the Republicans' chances. While radical anarchists wanted to pursue social revolution at all costs, the increasingly tough communists ostensibly set winning the war as their primary goal, all the while devoting considerable energy to suppressing anarchists and even moderate socialists – their own allies! Their infighting was one of Franco's greatest allies.

The War in Barcelona

The civil war broke the Catalan class alliance. For nearly a year Barcelona was run by anarchists and the POUM (Partido Obrero de Unificación Marxista; the Marxist Unification Workers' Party) Trotskyist militia, with Companys as president only in name. Factory owners and rightists fled the city. Unions took over factories and public services, hotels and mansions became hospitals and schools, everyone wore workers' clothes, bars and cafés were collectivised, trams and taxis were painted red and black (the colours of the anarchists), private cars vanished from the streets, and even one-way streets were ignored as they were seen to be part of the old system.

The anarchists were a disparate lot ranging from gentle idealists to hardliners who drew up death lists, held kangaroo courts, shot priests, monks and nuns (over 1200 of whom were killed in Barcelona province during the civil war), and also burnt and wrecked churches – which is why so many of Barcelona's churches are today oddly plain inside.

The revolutionary atmosphere waned as anarchists began to join the Catalan and Spanish Republican governments and, under Soviet influence, the PSUC (Partit Socialista Unificat de Catalunya; Catalan communist party) grew more powerful. In May 1937 Companys ordered police to take over the anarchist-held telephone exchange on Plaça de Catalunya. After three days of street fighting, chiefly between anarchists and the PSUC, in which at least 1500 died, the anarchists asked for a cease-fire. They and the POUM were soon disarmed.

Barcelona became the Republicans' national capital in autumn 1937. The city was first bombed from the air in March 1938. In the first three days 670 people were killed; after that, the figures were kept secret. In the end, after the Republicans' defeat in the Battle of the Ebro around Tortosa in southern Catalunya in summer 1938 – the last big set-piece clash of the civil war – Barcelona was left undefended. Combatants and the Catalan and Spanish Republican governments joined the civilians who were fleeing to France – around 500,000 in all – and the city fell to the Nationalists on 25 January 1939.

Up to 35,000 people were shot in the ensuing purge, and the executions continued into the 1950s. Lluís Companys was arrested in France by the Gestapo in August 1940, handed over to Franco, and shot in secret on 15 October on Montjuïc. He is reputed to have died with the words 'Visca Catalunya!' ('Long live Catalunya!') on his lips.

The Franco Era

Franco didn't hang about waiting for the war to end before he abolished the Generalitat yet again. This symbolic act was carried out in 1938. Companys was succeeded as the head of the Catalan government-in-exile by Josep Irla, a former ERC MP who remained in charge until May 1954. Irla was succeeded by the charismatic Josep Tarradellas after the parliament-in-exile met in Mexico. Tarradellas remained at the head of the government-in-exile until after the death of Franco.

Franco, meanwhile, embarked on a programme of Castilianisation in Catalunya. He banned public use of Catalan and had all town, village and street names rendered in Spanish. Book publishing in Catalan was allowed from the mid-1940s, but education, radio, TV and the daily press remained in Spanish.

In Barcelona, the Francoist Josep Maria de Porcioles became mayor in 1957, a post he would hold until 1973. That same year he obtained for the city a 'municipal charter', which expanded the mayor's authority and the city's capacity to raise and spend taxes, manage urban development and, ultimately, widen the city's metropolitan limits to absorb neighbouring territory.

In response, the occasional anarchist bombing or shooting took place in the 1940s, but by the 1950s opposition had turned to peaceful mass protests and strikes. In 1960 an audience at the city's Palau de la Música Catalana concert hall sang a banned Catalan anthem in front of Franco. The ringleaders included a young Catholic banker, Jordi Pujol, who spent two years in jail as a result. Pujol was to become Catalunya's president in the post-Franco era.

The big social change under Franco was a flood of immigrants from poorer parts of Spain, chiefly Andalucía, attracted by economic growth in Catalunya. Some 750,000 came to Barcelona in the 1950s and '60s, and almost as many to the rest of Catalunya. Many lived in appalling conditions. While some made the effort to learn Catalan and integrate as fully as possible into local society, the majority came to form great Spanish-speaking pockets in the poorer working-class districts of the city. In the earlier days, many lived in shanty towns or even caves, worked extraordinary hours for very low pay and generally struggled along. Spain as a whole suffered in the post-war years, but when economic take-off began in the 1960s many of Barcelona's newcomers reaped at least some of the benefits.

After Franco

Two years after Franco's death in 1975, Josep Tarradellas was invited to Madrid by the newly elected Adolfo Suárez to hammer out the Catalan part of a regional autonomy policy. Shortly afterwards, Barcelonins celebrated the Diada, which marks the 1714 defeat, on 11 September, with a huge pro-autonomy march across the city – some say as many as a million people marched.

Eighteen days later, King Juan Carlos I decreed the re-establishment of the Generalitat and recognised Josep Tarradellas as its president. When Tarradellas finally returned to Barcelona he announced simply: 'Ja soc aquí' ('I am finally here').

The new Spanish constitution promulgated in 1978 included a policy of autonomy not only for Catalunya but for all the regions. In Catalunya, a commission of experts had already cobbled together an autonomy statute in 1977. This got the royal seal of approval in 1979. The Catalan nationalist, Jordi Pujol, was elected Tarradellas' successor in April 1980 and he has remained at the helm of the Generalitat ever since.

Pujol has waged a constant war of attrition with Madrid, eking out ever more powers. Catalunya has made considerable advances on this front, controlling a range of areas including local police, education, trade, tourism, agriculture, hospitals, social security, culture and so on. In 1996 Catalunya and other regions won the right to collect one-third of national income tax.

Politics aside, the big event in post-Franco Barcelona was the successful 1992 Olympics, which spurred a burst of public works and brought new life to areas such as Montjuïc, where the major events were held. The once-shabby waterfront has been transformed with promenades, beaches, marinas, restaurants, leisure attractions and new housing.

The games may be receding from the public mind but the impetus created has hardly slowed. Enormous projects to 'rehabilitate' vast tracts of rundown central Barcelona continue and the city's profile continues to rise. One recent study placed it behind only New York, Paris and Amsterdam as UK holiday-makers' favourite city-break destination – Barcelona needs no introduction.

Barcelona in the New Millennium

Although not everyone is enamoured of Barcelona's mayor, Joan Clos, no-one could say that his Ajuntament (local council) is inactive. Development plans are on the table or already in progress for huge tracts of the city.

Minds are also concentrated on the World Cultural Forum 2004 project. A somewhat ill-defined international culture fest, the forum has been used as a vehicle to promote continued development of the city, particularly in the area where Avinguda Diagonal reaches the sea (see Architecture later in this chapter).

If Mayor Clos has his way, skyscrapers will, in the coming years, flourish in what he has dubbed the 22@ area of El Poblenou. Clos hopes to transform the rundown heart of 19th-century Barcelona's industrial zone into a 21st-century hi-tech haven. Several big projects are already underway, so the idea may well catch on and attract further international investment.

Urban renewal plans, including a big hotel project, are on the drawing board for El Raval. Further waterfront development is planned for the cargo port area. Indeed, the scope of the plans rivals the frenetic architectural activity that accompanied the run-up to the 1992 Olympic Games. Nature sometimes gets in the way, and massive storms in late 2001 wrecked much of the city coastline, causing more than €10 million damage that still hadn't been completely repaired by early summer 2002.

A growing pole of interest beyond Spain, Barcelona has not been left untouched by international events. The World Bank had planned a meeting in the city in May 2001 but cancelled in the face of threatened violence by antiglobalisation groups. In March 2002 the city got another chance to test its mettle with the European Union (EU) heads-of-government summit. Thousands of police and military were mobilised for the event. More than 300,000 demonstrators joined an antiglobalisation march through the city, which happily went off without incident.

GEOGRAPHY

Barcelona spreads southwest to northeast along the Catalan coast in what is known as the Pla de Barcelona (Barcelona Plain), roughly midway between the French border and the regional frontier with Valencia. The plain averages about 4m above sea level. Mont Taber, the little elevation upon which the Romans built their town, is 15m above sea level. To the southwest, Montjuïc is 173m high.

Urban sprawl tends to be channelled along the coast in either direction, as the landward side is effectively blocked off by the Serralada Litoral mountain chain, which between the Riu Besòs and Riu Llobregat is known as the Serra de Collserola. Tibidabo is the highest point of this chain at 512m, with commanding views across the whole city. As is typical for any large and growing metropolis, surrounding villages have tended to have been swallowed up in the expanding conurbation.

Badalona to the northeast and l'Hospitalet to the southwest mark the municipal boundaries of the city – although, as you drive through them, you'd never know where any began and ended. To the north, the Besòs in part marks the northern limits of the city. The Riu Llobregat, which rises in the Pyrenees, empties into the Mediterranean just south of l'Hospitalet. Just over the southern side of the river is El Prat de Llobregat and Barcelona's airport.

CLIMATE

Barcelona enjoys a Mediterranean climate, with cool winters and hot summers. July is the most torrid month, with August just behind. Highs at this time of year can reach 37°C. The seaside location also promotes humidity, but sea breezes can bring relief (especially if you happen to be sitting in a seaward apartment room a few floors up). A hotel room with air-conditioning or a fan can make all the difference to having a good night's sleep.

In the depths of winter (especially in February) it gets cold enough (average lows of 6.7°C) for you to wish you had heating in your room but by March, with a little luck,

things begin to thaw out. Oddly enough, you can get lucky with the weather in January, which has a tendency to be quite sunny if not terribly warm.

As a rule, rainfall is highest in autumn and winter. In September and into October, Barcelona often gets a washdown from cracking, late-summer thunderstorms.

As Barcelona is downwind from the Pyrenees, cold snaps are always on the cards and the April-May period is changeable. At its best, though, May can be the most pleasant month of the year – clear and fresh.

ECOLOGY & ENVIRONMENT

Problems of air pollution are typical of a crowded Mediterranean conurbation such as Barcelona. Although some restrictions apply to parking and driving through the centre of town, the city is generally full to bursting. Cars jostle and the air is none too clean. Sea breezes occasionally manage to shift the smog around a bit. The city has not remained indifferent to the problem, introducing 35 buses that run on natural gas in late 2001. By the end of 2004 almost a third of the city's buses will run on natural gas.

The water at the beaches is not the most inviting you will see on the Catalan coast but, compared with the way the beaches once were, it is, in the most part, remarkably clean and perfectly OK to swim in.

The disposal of garbage remains a fairly unecological affair. True, large brightly coloured containers have been scattered about the city for the separated collection of paper, glass and cans, but use of them depends entirely on the citizens. Discouragingly, it is not unusual to see mounds of rubbish piling up around these and other general refuse containers – the stuff is eventually hauled off, but it is hard to escape the feeling that recycling is not a big priority. You will also no doubt notice that many Barcelonins have a love affair with canine pets. This is never clearer than in the narrow lanes of Barri Gòtic, where sticky poochy waste products can make unpleasant close encounters with your shoes.

Barcelona, as with so many Spanish cities, is justly acclaimed for its nightlife.

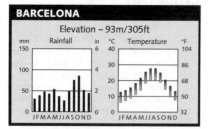

BARCELONA

Elevation – 93m/305ft

Rainfall   Temperature

J F M A M J J A S O N D   J F M A M J J A S O N D

Those long summer nights are perfect for sitting at open-air cafés and bars *(terrasses/terrazas)*, sipping away into the wee hours. To the general hubbub are added the dubious pleasures of impromptu street entertainment and busking. Fantastic. But spare a thought for the poor sods who live on the squares and streets where all the fun is going on. Noise pollution is a big problem throughout the city. Rowdy traffic, late-night garbage collection, lusty use of sirens by the emergency services and a trigger-happiness with car horns all help to keep nerves well jangled.

GOVERNMENT & POLITICS

The Generalitat de Catalunya, the regional parliament of Catalunya, was resurrected by royal decree in 1977. Its power as an autonomous government is enshrined in the statutes of the national Spanish constitution of 1978, and by the Estatut d'Autonomia (devolution statute), which got the royal green light in 1979. The Govern, as the government is also known, is housed in the Palau de la Generalitat on Plaça de Sant Jaume in central Barcelona.

The Generalitat has wide powers over matters such as education, health, trade, industry, tourism and agriculture. Education is now nearly all in Catalan which, at the time of Franco's death, had been in some danger, not only because of the immigration of Castilian-speakers but also because many Catalans, although they spoke Catalan, could no longer read or write it.

Since the first post-Franco regional elections in March 1980, Jordi Pujol's nationalist, right-of-centre Convergència i Unió (CiU) coalition has been at the controls in the Palau de la Generalitat. CiU does not want full independence from Spain but constantly seeks to strengthen Catalan autonomy. Indeed, only a few Catalans seriously contemplate the idea of independence. The pro-independence party Esquerra Republicana de Catalunya (ERC; Republican Left of Catalonia) has won only 8% to 10% of the vote in recent elections. The ERC is avowedly nonviolent and there's no Catalan equivalent of the Basque ETA.

Pujol came close to defeat by the Catalan Socialist leader Pascual Maragall in the 1999 regional elections, but it seems he is destined to never lose. He will instead bow finally out in 2003, leaving his designated successor, Artur Mas, to battle it out with Maragall in that year's elections.

The Ajuntament stands opposite the Palau de la Generalitat and has traditionally been a Socialist haven. The Partit Socialista de Catalunya (PSC) is as prodevolution as anyone else in Catalunya but moderate in its approach. The CiU gets a lot of its support from the Catalan provinces. Barcelona, the one-time haven of anarchist revolution, is unsurprisingly less tolerant of nationalist rigidity of any kind. The PSC, aligned with the main Spanish socialist party, the Partido Socialista Obrero Español (PSOE), has a younger leadership than the CiU, which probably also helps to explain its appeal to Barcelonin voters.

Until 1997, the highly popular Pascual Maragall was *alcalde* (mayor) at the head of the Ajuntament. Much of the go-ahead feeling of Barcelona today is attributed to his forward-looking vision. He was succeeded by Joan Clos who, although less charismatic, seems equally set on maintaining the momentum. He continues to push grandiose urban redevelopment schemes across the city and is agitating for greater control over municipal affairs. A charter signed with the Generalitat in 1986, transferring powers from the region to the city, still had not been fully implemented in 2002 when the central right-wing Partido Popular government intervened to block its application. In the end it appears Clos will get his way, and the application of the charter will, among many practical measures (greater responsibility for traffic, police and town planning), will mean the city is officially recognised as the capital of Catalunya and granted its own flag and coat of arms.

Elections to both the Ajuntament and Generalitat take place every four years. They are free and by direct universal suffrage. The members of each house thus elected then vote to appoint the president of the Generalitat and the mayor.

For administrative purposes Barcelona is divided into 10 *districtes*, each with its own ajuntament.

ECONOMY

Barcelona has a reputation for being a hard-working industrial and mercantile city. The roots of its trading culture lie in the days of Mediterranean empire-building, but industry first stirred to life in the small-scale textiles factories that began to emerge during the 18th century.

Industry took off in the mid-19th century and metallurgy and engineering became sources of pride to prosperous Barcelona. Steamships were launched here and Spain's first trains were 'made in Barcelona'.

But business relied on heavy protection, meaning that with the loss of the last American possessions in 1898, Barcelona had to rely almost exclusively on selling inside Spain. With few raw materials of its own, Barcelona played second fiddle to Bilbao (País Vasco) and Oviedo (Asturias) in mining and secondary industry, especially iron and other metals.

In the 1950s and '60s, hundreds of thousands of immigrants in search of work converged on Barcelona from the rest of a largely impoverished Spain. The conditions they encountered were often miserable, but most were absorbed eventually into the local industrial workforce.

With all its ups and downs, Barcelona is today an economic powerhouse. About a quarter of all Spanish exports come from Catalunya and three-quarters of the region's industry is in or near Barcelona. Although Barcelona is increasingly concerned by the rise of Madrid as the senior hub of finance and business in Spain, with a higher level of inward investment, statistics released in 2001 show that Barcelona and the surrounding metropolitan area (with a population nearing five million) export more than Madrid, Zaragoza and Valencia put together!

Textiles remain big business in Barna alongside leather goods, chemicals, pharmaceuticals and cosmetics. The heart of the city's metal and other heavy industries was La Barceloneta and then El Poblenou, but in the past couple of decades it has shifted further from the city centre. The so-called 22@ area of El Poblenou has been ear-marked with a view to creating a new hub of hi-tech industry in the capital.

It was just outside Barcelona (in Martorell) that the national car manufacturing company, Seat, came into being. The company is still turning out cars, although it is now part-owned by the German company Volkswagen.

Across Catalunya about 60% of the working population is employed in the service sector, 36% in industry and 4% in agriculture. Tourism represents 14% of the city's Gross Domestic Product (GDP), with as many as 3.5 million visitors coming to the city each year.

By national standards, Catalunya is not doing too badly in the employment stakes. According to statistics, 13% of the entire Spanish population is out of work, but in Catalunya the figure is 9%. Inflation in Catalunya (3%) is in line with that across the nation. Wage-earners have a tough time though. Salaries increase 2% on average each year but rent and house prices in the city have been rocketing since the late 1990s – rising 50% to 75% in the past four to five years. On average, salaries in Spain are third from the bottom in the EU (only in Portugal and Greece are people paid less). In 2001-2002 Catalunya, like the rest of Spain, found its economy slowing considerably as a knock-on effect of the recession in the USA.

POPULATION & PEOPLE

The city of Barcelona is home to 1.5 million people, although the greater Barcelona area (Barcelona metropolitana), considered to extend as far southwest to Vilanova i la Geltrú and inland to Granollers and Terrassa, counts another 3.3 million people. Indeed, many people are leaving the city centre to live in cheaper areas of the surrounding conurbation. In total, the greater metropolitan area of Barcelona accounts for three-quarters of Catalunya's population of 6.3 million (Spain's is 40.5 million).

The average age in Catalunya is 39.5 – almost two years above that for the rest of Spain. Indeed, Catalunya is one of the fastest ageing regions in Spain, which itself holds the world record with 22% of the nation being aged over 60.

Most of the growth in Barcelona came this century, particularly in the decades following the civil war when up to 750,000 people migrated to Barcelona and its surrounding areas in search of work (see History for more details). It is estimated that, at the height of this exodus in the late 1960s, a quarter of those flocking to the city were from rural Catalunya. Roughly 30% came from Andalucía, 11% from the two Castiles, 7% from Extremadura and about 6% each from Galicia and Aragón. In all, it is estimated that from 1950 to 1975, 1.4 million migrants from the rest of Spain moved to Catalunya. For this reason alone you are just as likely to hear Castilian as Catalan spoken in Barcelona.

Whether the city's populace likes it or not, Barcelona is rapidly acquiring a multicultural air unthinkable a decade ago. The registered foreign population of the city grew by 54% in 2001, and official estimates point to 7.6% of the city's population being foreign. The breakdown of this figure is roughly one half from Latin America (especially Peru, the Dominican Republic and Argentina), 20% of 'European origin' (mostly Brits, Germans, French and Italians), followed by 16% Asians (mostly Filipinos and Pakistanis) and another 12% from Africa, mostly Morocco. A 2002 study revealed that 42% of school children aged up to 16 in Ciutat Vella are of non-Spanish origin.

Studies have found that this migrant population makes a considerable financial contribution to the regional economy, flatly contradicting fears that foreigners would take local jobs and drain the coffers. Indeed, foreigners *do* take local jobs, usually ones that locals don't want.

On the other hand, police statistics (and anecdotal evidence from Lonely Planet readers) attribute much of the large rise in crime (especially robbery and muggings) of more than 10% across all Spain to the arrival of jobless illegal migrants.

EDUCATION
Each region in Spain administers its own education system, although overall guidelines are similar throughout the country. In Catalunya, about 1.3 million people are enrolled in some kind of educational institute, from preschool to university.

The Generalitat's drive to encourage the use of Catalan has meant that it is increasingly becoming the standard language of education in schools. Some fear Castilian is being pushed onto the back seat.

University education is in some respects a more complex issue. Some classes are still held in Castilian, but ideally the Generalitat would like to change that too. Making the speaking of Catalan a prerequisite for lecturing would exclude the rest of the country's academics from teaching in Catalunya, something that ultimately might do more harm than good.

Illiteracy is still an issue in Catalunya, as it is in the rest of Spain – and, contrary to popular belief, in many Western countries. Some 3.3% of the Catalan population is illiterate (the national average is 3.9%). Since the bulk of these people are in older age groups, it is to be supposed that the problem will gradually diminish.

ARTS
From the splendours of Barcelona's grand Gothic monuments to the genius of Picasso, Barcelona basks in a rich artistic heritage.

Painting & Sculpture
Medieval Painting A great many anonymous artists left their work behind in medieval Catalunya, mostly in the form of frescoes, altarpieces and the like in Romanesque and Gothic churches. But a few leading lights managed to get some credit. Ferrer Bassá (c.1290–1348) is considered to be one of the region's first masters. Influenced by the Siennese school, his few surviving works include murals with a slight touch of caricature in the Monestir de Pedralbes. The style of which he is commonly

considered to be the originator is also known as Italo-Gothic.

This style soon displayed a more international flavour, best expressed in the work of Bernat Martorell (1400–52), a master of chiaroscuro who was active in the mid-15th century. As the Flemish school gained influence, painters such as Jaume Huguet (1415–92) adopted its sombre realism and lightened it with Hispanic splashes of gold, as can be seen in Huguet's *Sant Jordi* in the Museu Nacional d'Art de Catalunya (Map 7). Another of his paintings hangs in the Museu Frederic Marès (Map 6; see the Things to See & Do chapter for details).

While in that museum you will be overwhelmed by the collection of medieval wood sculpture. Mostly anonymous sculptors were busy throughout Catalunya from at least the 12th century, carving religious images for the growing number of churches. Although saints and other characters sometimes figured, by far the most common subjects were Christ crucified and the Virgin Mary with the Christ child sitting on her lap. Romanesque churches were largely bereft of stone sculptural decoration, although this gradually changed as the style gave way to Gothic. Some of the most exquisite sculpture is to be found in the sarcophagi of important persons.

There are a few clues to enable you to distinguish between the Romanesque and the Gothic. Firstly, much Romanesque work was done al fresco on church walls and the like; by the Gothic period, such mural painting had largely ceased in Catalunya. Gothic figures are more lifelike than the intentionally two-dimensional didactic representations of the Romanesque period. The latter served to convey the other-worldliness of their subject, far removed from the grubby earthly reality in which their admirers toiled. That distinction was maintained in Gothic paintings and sculpture but artists began to inject *feeling* into their portraits.

Decline & the 19th Century It is fair to say that little of greatness was achieved in the field of Catalan painting or sculpture from the end of the Middle Ages to the 19th

century. Barcelona neither produced nor attracted any El Grecos, Velázquezs, Goyas, Zurbaráns or Murillos.

By the mid-19th century, Realisme was the modish medium on the canvas, reaching something of a zenith with the work of Marià Fortuny (1838–74). You can see some of his stuff, and that of his contemporaries, in the Museu Nacional d'Art Modern de Catalunya. The best known (and largest) of his paintings is the 'official' version of the *Batalla de Tetuán* (1863), when the Spanish managed a rousing victory over a ragtag Moroccan enemy in North Africa.

Modernisme As the years progressed, painters developed a greater eye for intimate detail and less for epic themes and this led painters into Anecdotisme, out of which emerged a fresher generation of artists – the Modernistas of the turn of the century. Influenced by their French counterparts (Paris was seen as Europe's artistic capital), the Modernistas allowed themselves greater freedom in interpretation than the Realists. They sought not so much to portray observed 'reality' as to interpret it subjectively and infuse it with flights of their own fantasy. But neither Barcelona nor any other place in Spain was exactly at the forefront of innovation. Ramón Casas (1866–1932) and Santiago Rusiñol (1861–1931) were easily the most important exponents of the new forms of art in Barcelona. The former was a wealthy dilettante of some talent, the latter perhaps a more earnest soul who ran a close second. Although both were the toast of the bohemian set in turn-of-the-20th-century Barcelona, neither was to be destined for greatness.

Noucentisme From about 1910, as Modernisme was fizzling out, the more conservative cultural movement Noucentisme sought, in general, to advance Catalunya. In the next 20 years, illiteracy was attacked with force, generalised education spread rapidly and telecommunications were extended across the region. Artistically speaking, Noucentisme claimed to be looking back to more classical models. A return to clarity and 'Mediterranean light' were favoured over what by some were seen as the obscure symbolism of the Modernistas.

From about 1917, a second wave of Noucentistas challenged such notions, which had began to feel like an artistic straitjacket. Some of their work was clearly influenced by the likes of Cézanne. Joaquim Sunyer (1874–1956) and Isidre Nonell (1876–1911) are among the better known of a gaggle of Noucentista painters who, just as had happened to their Modernista predecessors, were soon to be largely overshadowed and forgotten by true genius.

Pablo Picasso Born in Málaga in Andalucía, Pablo Ruiz Picasso (1881–1973) was already sketching by the age of nine. After a stint in La Coruña (Galicia), he landed in Barcelona in 1895. His father had obtained a post teaching art at the Escola de Belles Artes de la Llotja (the stock exchange building) and had his son enrolled there too. It was in Barcelona and Catalunya that Picasso developed his famous style, spending the next 10 years there ceaselessly drawing and painting.

Although schooled in an academic style, his paintings soon showed a diversity of style and an unusual verve of brushstroke movement. His father sent him to the Escuela de Bellas Artes de San Fernando in Madrid for a year in 1897, but the precocious Picasso was bored with school and took himself to the Prado to learn from the masters and to the streets to depict life as he saw it.

Back in Catalunya he spent six months with his friend Manuel Pallarès in bucolic Horta de Sant Joan – he would later claim that it was here he learned everything he knew. In Barcelona Picasso lived and worked in Barri Gòtic and got an introduction to the underside of life in Barri Xinès. By 1900 he was a young regular of Els Quatre Gats, the Modernistas' tavern and lair of the avant-garde in Barcelona. He exhibited here and in the same year made his first trip to Paris.

By the time Picasso moved to France in 1904, he had explored his first personal style. In this so-called Blue Period, his canvases have a melancholy feel heightened by the trademark dominance of dark blues. This was followed by the Pink (or Rose) Period, in which the subjects became merrier and the colouring leaned towards light pinks and greys.

Picasso was a turbulent character and gifted not only as a painter but as a sculptor, graphic designer and ceramicist, and his work encompassed many different style changes. With *Les Demoiselles d'Avignon* (1907), Picasso broke with all forms of traditional representation, introducing a deformed perspective that would later spill over into cubism. By the mid-1920s he was dabbling with surrealism. His best-known work is *Guernica*, a complex painting portraying the horror of war inspired by the German aerial bombing of the Basque town, Gernika, in 1937.

Picasso was prolific during and after WWII and he was still cranking out paintings, sculptures, ceramics and etchings until the day he died in 1973.

Joan Miró By the time the 13-year-old Picasso arrived in Barcelona, his near contemporary, Joan Miró (1893–1983), was

MW

Miró's work is recognisable from his use of primary colours and just the essence of shape.

cutting his teeth on rusk biscuits in Barri Gòtic, where he was born and would spend his younger years. Indeed, he passed a third of his life in his home town. Later in life he divided his time between France, the Tarragona countryside and Mallorca, where he ended his days.

Like Picasso, Miró attended the Escola de Belles Artes de la Llotja. He was a shy man and initially less certain about his artistic vocation – in fact he studied commerce. Nevertheless, from 1915 he produced a series of panoramas that betrayed the influence of Cézanne and portraits reminiscent of the naivety of Romanesque frescoes.

His first trip to Paris came in 1920 but he was still deeply drawn to the Catalan countryside and coast. From 1919 to the early 1930s Miró wintered in Paris and spent the summers at his family's farmhouse at Montroig on the southern Catalan coast. In Paris he mixed with Picasso, Hemingway, Joyce and friends, and made his own mark, after several years of struggle, with an exhibition in 1925. The masterpiece from this, his so-called realist period, was *La Masia* (The Farmhouse).

In the early 1930s Miró went through an artistic crisis, temporarily rejecting painting in favour of collage and other techniques: 'Painting must be murdered' was his cry. The civil-war years provoked strong reactions from the painter, particularly with a series of lithographs entitled *Barcelona*.

But it was during WWII, while living in seclusion in Normandy, that his definitive leitmotivs finally emerged. Among Miró's most important images are women, birds (the link between earth and the heavens), stars (the unattainable heavenly world, source of imagination), and a sort of net entrapping all these levels of the cosmos. The Miró works that most people are acquainted with emerged from this time – arrangements of lines and symbolic figures in primary colours, with shapes reduced to their essence.

In the 1960s and '70s Miró devoted more time to sculpture and textiles. From 1956 he lived in Mallorca, home of his wife Pilar Juncosa, until his death in 1983.

Salvador Dalí Although he spent precious little of his time living in Barcelona, and nothing much of his can be seen here, it would be churlish to leave Salvador Dalí i Domènech (1904–89) out of the picture altogether. He was born and died in Figueres, where he left his single greatest artistic legacy, the Teatre-Museu Dalí.

Prolific painter, showman, shameless self-promoter or just plain weirdo, Dalí was nothing if not a character – probably a little too much for the conservative small-town folk of Figueres.

From the age of 13 he was taking drawing lessons and, by 1922, his name had appeared in Barcelona's press as an up-and-coming artist. His move to Madrid that year to study at the Escuela de Bellas Artes de San Fernando was important, not for what he studied (he no more liked the school than Picasso) but for his meetings with the poet Federico García Lorca and future film director Luis Buñuel.

Every now and then a key moment arrives that can change the course of one's life. Dalí's came in 1929 when the French poet Paul Eluard visited Cadaqués with his Russian wife Gala. The rest, as they say, is histrionic. Dalí shot off to Paris to be with Gala and plunged into the world of surrealism.

Salvador Dalí – prolific surrealist painter, showman and shameless self-promoter

In the 1930s, Salvador and Gala returned to live at Port Lligat on the north Catalan coast, where they played host to a long list of fashionable and art-world guests until the war years – the parties were by all accounts memorable. From the outbreak of war until his return to Port Lligat in 1948, Dalí spent time in France and the USA. Excluded by now from the surrealist movement, his painting style underwent something of an about-face, reaching back to classical roots – but it remained unmistakably Dalian. Hallucination seems always to have been its distinguishing hallmark.

Besides painting, Dalí collaborated in the theatre and cinema, mostly working on sets, and dabbled in writing. All he did seemed calculated to increase his prestige and income, and André Breton, poet and leading light of the surrealist movement, dubbed him Avida Dollars (an anagram of his name).

Back in Port Lligat, the international guest list again grew, as did the scope of the partying. The stories of sexual romps and Gala's appetite for young local boys are legendary. The 1960s saw Dalí painting pictures on a grand scale, including his 1962 reinterpretation of Marià Fortuny's *Batalla de Tetuán*. From 1979 things began to go rapidly downhill. Gala died and Dalí became a recluse, nearly dying in a fire at his property at Púbol. On his death in 1989 he was buried (according to his own wish) in the Teatre-Museu he had created in the old theatre in central Figueres, which now houses the single greatest collection of Dalí's work (see the Excursions chapter for more information).

Contemporary Artists After such a trio, all other artists and their work seem a little dull by comparison. But Antoni Tàpies (1923–) is one important contemporary artist who has often been overlooked in all the commotion over the big three. Much of his work can now be seen in the Fundació Antoni Tàpies (see the Things to See & Do chapter for more information). Early on in his career (from the mid-1940s onwards) he seemed very keen on self-portraits, but also experimented with collage using all sorts of materials from wood to rice. This use of a broad range of material to achieve texture and depth remains a feature of his work to this day. In his 1994 *Duat* he even attached window shutters to his 'canvas'. He is still producing prolifically and is considered one of country's leading artists.

Barcelona's Susana Solano (1946–) is a painter and above all sculptor, considered to be one of the most important at work in Spain today. Another interesting contemporary sculptor is Sergi Aguilar (1946–). Jordi Colomer (1962–) makes heavy use of audiovisual material in his artworks, creating highly imaginative spaces and three-dimensional images.

To get an idea of what is happening in Catalan art today, you should make for the Macba art gallery (Map 6; see the Things to See & Do chapter).

Avant-Garde in the Streets Barcelona hosts quite an array of street sculpture, from Miró's *Dona i Ocell* (Map 4), which stands in the park dedicated to the artist, to the *Peix* (Map 1) by contemporary architect Frank Gehry, which can be found on the Vila Olímpica waterfront.

Others you may want to keep an eye out for are *Barcelona's Head* by Roy Lichtenstein (Map 5; on Moll de la Fusta, the waterfront area by Maremàgnum) and Fernando Botero's characteristically tumes-cent *El Gat* at Carrer del Portal de Santa Madrona, behind the Drassanes (Map 6).

Perhaps the weirdest monument is what looks like a pile of square containers with windows leaning precariously, like so many dice, on La Barceloneta beach. Made in 1992 by Rebecca Horn, it is called *Homenatge a la Barceloneta* (Homage to La Barceloneta).

Architecture

When most people think of architecture and Barcelona, it is Gaudí's name that usually springs to mind. But the genius of that architect was in a sense the fruit of all that went before. The Romans built a modest town here and medieval Barcelona was at first full of Romanesque monuments. But if you were to sum up the city in a word, it would be Gothic. Barcelona is one of Europe's great Gothic treasure houses and it was largely on the legacy of this artistic dish that the Modernistas of the late 19th and early 20th centuries supped so keenly, adapting the old to fit their new ways of seeing and building.

Early Barcelona What Caesar Augustus and friends called Barcino was a fairly standard Roman rectangular job. The forum lay more or less where Plaça de Sant Jaume is today and the whole place covered little more than 10 hectares.

Today there remain some impressive leftovers of the 4th-century walls that once comprised 70 towers. In the basement of the Museu d'Història de la Ciutat you can inspect parts of a tower and the wall, as well as other Roman remains. Elsewhere in the immediate vicinity stand temple columns and, a little further north, a modest burial ground (in Plaça de la Vila de Madrid).

Romanesque Unfortunately, little remains of Barcelona's Romanesque past – it was torn down to make way for what were considered greater Gothic spectacles as the city moved into its golden age. If you have the opportunity, a tour through the northern reaches of Catalunya should more than satisfy your curiosity as to what form the Catalan version of this first great wave of Christian European architecture took.

It was Lombard artisans from northern Italy who first introduced this style of building to Catalunya. It is characterised by a pleasing simplicity. The exterior of most early Romanesque edifices that have not been tampered with is virtually bereft of decoration. Churches tend to be austere, angular constructions, with tall, square-based bell towers. There were a few notable concessions to the curve – almost always semicircular or semicylindrical. These included the barrel vaulting inside the churches, the apse (or apses – as the style was developed up to five might be tacked on to the 'stern' of a church) and arches atop all the openings.

The main portal and windows are invariably topped with straightforward arches. When builders got a little saucy, they might adorn the main entrance with several arches within one another. From the late 11th century, stonemasons began to fill the arches with statuary.

In Barcelona you can espy only a few Romanesque remnants. In the Catedral the 13th-century Capella de Santa Llúcia survives, along with part of the cloister doors. The 12th-century former Benedictine Monestir de Sant Pau del Camp is also a good example, especially the cloisters. There are a few other scattered reminders, but if Romanesque is your thing and you want to see a little more without really leaving Barcelona, catch the FGC train north to Sant Cugat del Vallès. Although much was incorporated into a later Gothic construction, the 12th-century cloister is fine and the Lombard bell tower is Romanesque.

The counterpoint to Romanesque architecture was the art used to decorate so many of the churches and monasteries built in the style. In this respect Barcelona is *the* place to be, as the best of Romanesque art from around Catalunya has been concentrated in the Museu Nacional d'Art de Catalunya.

Gothic This soaring form of architecture took off in France in the 13th century and spread across Europe. In Barcelona, its emergence coincided with Jaume I's march into Valencia and the annexation of Mallorca and Ibiza, accompanied by the rise and rise of a trading class and a burgeoning mercantile empire. The enormous cost of building the grand new monuments could thus be covered by the steady increase in the city's wealth.

The style of architecture reflected the development of building techniques. The introduction of buttresses, flying buttresses and ribbed vaulting in ceilings allowed engineers to raise edifices that were loftier and seemingly lighter than ever before. The pointed arch became a standard characteristic and the great rose windows were the source of light inside these enormous spaces. Think about the little hovels that most of the labourers on such enormous projects lived in, the precariousness of wooden scaffolding and the primitive nature of building materials available and you get some idea of the degree of awe the great cathedrals, once completed, must have inspired in people.

Catalan Gothic did not follow the same course, though. Decoration here tends to be more sparing than in northern Europe and the most obvious defining characteristic is the triumph of breadth over height. While some northern European cathedrals reach for the sky, Catalan Gothic has a tendency rather to push to the sides, stretching its vaulting design to the limit.

The Saló del Tinell, with a parade of 15m arches (among the largest ever built without reinforcement) holding up the roof, is a perfect example of Catalan Gothic. Another is the Drassanes, Barcelona's enormous medieval shipyards (and home today to the Museu Marítim). In their churches, too, the Catalans opted for a more robust shape and lateral space – step into Santa Maria del Mar or Santa Maria del Pi and you'll soon get the idea.

Another notable departure from what you might have come to expect of Gothic north of the Pyrenees is the lack of spires and pinnacles. Bell towers tend to terminate in a flat or nearly flat roof. Occasional exceptions prove the rule – the main facade of Barcelona's Catedral, with its three gnarled and knobbly spires, does vaguely resemble the outline that confronts you in cathedrals in Chartres or Cologne.

Perhaps the single-greatest building spurt came under Pere III. This is odd in a sense because, as Dickens might have observed, it was not only the best of times, but also the worst. As the Mediterranean empire had spread, Barcelona's coffers had been filled but, by the mid-14th century, when Pere III was in command, the city had been pushed to the ropes by a series of disasters: famine, repeated plagues, and pogroms.

Maybe the king didn't notice. He built, or began to build, much of the Catedral, the Drassanes shipyards, the Llotja stock exchange, the Saló del Tinell, the Casa de

la Ciutat (which now houses the Ajuntament) and numerous lesser buildings, not to mention part of the city walls. Along with the Catedral, the churches of Santa Maria del Pi and Santa Maria del Mar were completed by the end of the century. The last of these is considered by many to be the finest of Barcelona's great Gothic monuments.

Gothic had a longer use-by date in Barcelona than in many other European centres. It seemed that with this style the city had found the expression of its soul. Even several centuries later, architects still felt subject to it. By the early 15th century the Generalitat still didn't have a home worthy of the name and the architect Marc Safont set to work on the present building on Plaça de Sant Jaume. Even renovations carried out a century later were largely in the Gothic tradition, although some Renaissance elements eventually snuck in – the

Església de Santa Maria del Mar – Barcelona's finest example of Catalan Gothic

facade on Plaça de Sant Jaume is a rather disappointing result.

Carrer de Montcada, in La Ribera, was the result of a late medieval act of town planning – a street laid out by design rather than simply 'evolving'. Eventually, mansions belonging to the moneyed classes of 15th- and 16th-century Barcelona were erected along it. Many now house museums and art galleries. Although these former mansions appear quite austere and forbidding on the outside, their interiors often reveal another world altogether, of pleasing courtyards and decorated staircases.

The great bulk of Barcelona's Gothic heritage lies, predictably enough, within the boundaries of Ciutat Vella, but a few examples can be found beyond it, notably the Monestir de Pedralbes in the *barri* (district) of Sarrià, which until 1921 was a separate village.

Renaissance & Baroque The strong Barcelonin affection for Gothic, coupled with a decline in the city's fortunes that led to a decrease in urban development, seems to have largely closed Barcelona to the extravagances that elsewhere in Europe accompanied the Renaissance and baroque periods. Such modest examples of baroque as can be found in Barcelona are generally purely decorative rather than structural, and are usually additions to pre-existing Gothic structures.

Among the more important but restrained baroque constructions in Barcelona are the Església de la Mercè, home to the medieval sculpture of Mare del Déu de la Mercè (Our Lady of Mercy; Barcelona's copatron with Sant Eulàlia), the Església de Sant Felip Neri and the Jesuits' Església de Betlem (largely destroyed in the civil war and since rebuilt). Also worth a look is the courtyard of the Palau Dalmases, in Carrer de Montcada, which has been reworked from the original Gothic structure.

Modernisme This remarkable, if brief, flurry of fantasy-filled design and architecture in Barcelona took off in the 1880s and was already sputtering to a close by 1910.

For more information, see the colour special section 'The Modernistas' on pages 33 to 40.

After Modernisme Even before Gaudí died in 1926, Modernisme had been swept aside. In the aftermath of WWI especially, it seemed already stale, quite decadent and somehow unwholesome.

While other movements replaced it in fine arts and literature, architecture took a bit of a nose dive from here on. Between the two world wars a host of neoclassical and neobaroque edifices went up. In the aftermath of the civil war there was little money, time or willingness for architectural fancy work. Apartment blocks and offices, designed with a realism and utilitarianism that to most mortals seems deadly dull, were erected instead.

Barcelona Today The title of Llàtzer Moix's study of architecture and design in modern Barcelona, *La Ciudad de los Arquitectos* (The City of Architects), could just as well serve as an epithet for the city.

In the run-up to the 1992 Olympics, more than 150 architects were beavering away on almost 300 building and design projects! The Port Olímpic area (Map 1), dominated by the Hotel Arts and Mapfre towers, is a strange result – an improvement on the ramshackle state of affairs that preceded it, but somehow oddly characterless too.

Things have slackened off a little since then, but that doesn't mean Barcelona has lost its taste for building.

Ricard Bofill's team designed the Teatre Nacional de Catalunya – a mix of neoclassicism and the modern. Across the road, Rafael Moneo's L'Auditori has become one of the city's top venues for classical music. Moneo is now busy causing a storm in Madrid with his project to expand the Prado.

The World Trade Center, now largely completed and already operating, is touted as the biggest commercial centre in any European port and a building of the 'latest generation'.

As these projects wind up, Barcelona looks further ahead to the next big event –

the World Cultural Forum in 2004. It has provided an excuse to further spruce up the city. The area from Port Olímpic northeast to the Riu Besòs is set to be revamped as a new waterfront residential haven, and the so-called Front Marítim along the shore has been earmarked for gardens, a marine zoo, hotels, fair grounds, new housing and a marina. The Avinguda Diagonal will finally stretch uninterrupted from Pedralbes to the sea just short of the Riu Besòs. Around Plaça de les Glòries Catalanes several remarkable buildings are planned, including an extraordinary 142m phallic tower block.

Other areas singled out for development include El Raval and El Poblenou, in particular the streets around Carrer de Llacuna known as the 22@ area (see Barcelona in the New Millennium under History earlier). In El Raval, slum blocks are being swept away. Plans for the area, by the noted Barcelona architect Oriol Bohigas, include an oval-shaped hotel and shopping complex on the Rambla del Raval.

Not everyone is happy with all these projects (and a host of others) but a British town planner, Richard Rogers, declared in 2000 that Barcelona was 'perhaps the most successful city in the world in terms of urban regeneration'.

Literature

Beginnings The earliest surviving documents written in Catalan date from the 12th century. Most of them are legal, economic, historical and religious texts. The oldest of them is a portion of the Visigothic law code, the *Liber Iudicorum*, rendered in the vernacular. The oldest original texts in Catalan are the *Homilies d'Organyà*, which is a religious work.

The first great Catalan writer was Ramon Llull (1235–1315), who eschewed the use of either Latin or Provençal in literature. His two best-known works are perhaps *El Llibre de les Bèsties* and *El Llibre d'Amic i Amat*, the former an allegorical attack on feudal corruption and the latter a series of short pieces aimed at daily meditation – both inspired in part by Islamic works.

The count-king Jaume I was a bit of a scribbler himself and penned a rare autobiographical work called the *Llibre dels Feyts* (Book of Deeds), in the late 13th century. Ramon Muntaner (1265–1336), more of a propagandist than anything else, spent a good deal of his life eulogising various Catalan leaders and their deeds in his *Crónica*.

Segle d'Or Everyone seems to have a 'golden century', and for Catalan writers it was the 15th. Ausiàs March (1400–59), actually from Valencia, announced he had abandoned the style of the troubadours and went ahead to forge a Catalan poetic tradition. His style is tormented and highly personal, and continues to inspire Catalan poets to this day.

Most European peoples seem to feel it necessary to claim to have produced the first European novel. The Catalans claim it was Joanot Martorell's *Tirant lo Blanc*. Cervantes himself thought it the best book in the world. Martorell (c.1405–65) was also a busy fighting knight and his writing tells of bloody battles, war, politics and sex. Some things don't change. More obscure names of the epoch include Bernat Metge (who saw out the 14th century), Roís de Corella and Jaume Roig.

Renaixença Catalan literature declined rapidly after the 15th century and suffered a seemingly mortal blow when the Bourbon king, Felipe V, banned the language after his victory in 1714.

However, as Catalunya began to enjoy a burgeoning economy in the 19th century, there was sufficient leisure time for intellectuals, writers and artists to take a renewed interest in all things Catalan. The revival of Catalan literature is commonly dated to 1833 when the rather saccharine poem *A la Pàtria* was written in Madrid by Carles Aribau (1798–1862).

From 1859, when Catalan intellectuals reintroduced Catalan-language poetry competitions, the Jocs Florals, a steady stream of material that was generally fit to be ignored started to dribble out of the tap.

True quality in poetry came only with the appearance in 1877 of a country pastor, Jacint Verdaguer (1845–1902), whose *L'Atlantida* is an epic that defies easy description. To the writer's contemporaries, though, the poem confirmed Catalan's arrival as a 'great' language. Verdaguer soon inspired others, above all the novelist Narcís Oller (1846–1930) and also playwright Àngel Guimerà (1845–1924). The former's *La Febre d'Or* (1893) describes the shaky world of speculative finance that dominated much of boomtime Barcelona.

Modernisme & Noucentisme Modernisme's main literary voice of worth was the poet Joan Maragall (1860–1911). Also noteworthy is the work of Víctor Català (1873–1966), a pseudonym of Caterina Albert – why did women have to pretend to be men in order to get anywhere? Her principal work is *Solitud*, a mysterious novel charting the awakening of a young woman whose husband has taken her to live in the Pyrenees.

Eugeni d'Ors (1881–1954), more of a journalist, critic and social commentator than writer, was one of the leading figures of Noucentisme, which aimed in part to rid the cultural scene of Modernisme. Carles Riba (1893–1959) was the period's most notable poet.

To the Present Josep Pla (1897–1981) was a prolific writer who, after the victory of Franco in 1939, spent many years abroad. He wrote in Catalan and Castilian and his work ranged from travel writing to histories and fiction. His complete works total 46 volumes.

Mercé Rodoreda (1909–83) was one of the major writers in Catalan of the 20th century. Her first successful novel was *Paloma* (1938), which tells the story of a young girl who was seduced by her brother-in-law. After the civil war Rodoreda went into exile and, in 1962, published one of her best-known works, *Plaça del Diamant*, which recounts life in Barcelona seen through the eyes of a working-class woman. The book has been translated into English and several other languages.

Since the demise of Franco, the amount of literature being produced in Catalan has increased greatly, but some of the region's more noteworthy scribblers write in Castilian, too, and in some cases prefer to do so.

Juan Goytisolo (1931–) started off in the neo-Realist camp but his more recent works, such as *Señas de Identidad* and *Juan sin Tierra*, are decidedly more experimental. Goytisolo lives in Marrakesh. Goytisolo's pal, Jaime Gil de Biedma (1929–90), was one of the 20th century's most influential poets in Catalunya and indeed across Spain.

A highly accessible writer is José Luis Sampedro (1917–). A professor of structural economics (!) and one-time senator, his novels are wide-ranging and thought-provoking. He considers *Octubre, Octubre* his life testament.

Borges Bags Barcelona

As you wander around the bustling streets of modern Barcelona, you might find it hard to fathom how someone could hate the place.

The writer and sophisticate from Buenos Aires, Jorge Luis Borges, travelled with his family to Spain in 1920 and seems not to have been overly impressed with what he found. If his letters reveal disdain for Spain ('so rough...so sad'), they display a venomous dislike for Barcelona, where he ended up for a time in May. In one epistle he wrote: 'Barcelona is an unpleasant city. I'm tempted to add that it's the worst city in the peninsula: ugly, vulgar and strident.'

Modernista architecture reminded Borges of the kind of taste one might expect in brothels, and he was no less dismissive of Catalan intellectuals. He reserved particular dislike for writer Eugeni d'Ors: 'It may well be,' he wrote, 'that a ridiculous gentleman is best placed to explain the essence of something as artificial and absurd as neoclassical Catalanism...'.

[Continued on page 41]

The Modernistas

THE MODERNISTAS

Say Barcelona and most people instantly think 'Gaudí' (often pronouncing it 'gaudy', in some cases an expression of artistic judgement).

Antoni Gaudí (1852–1926; pronounced gow-dee) was born in Reus and initially trained in metalwork. He obtained his architecture degree in 1878. Gaudí personifies, and in large measure transcends, a movement in architecture that brought a thunderclap of innovative greatness to an otherwise only middle-ranking (artistically speaking) European city. This startling wave of creativity subsided just as quickly – the bulk of the Modernistas' work was done from the 1880s to about 1910.

What the Catalans call Modernisme emerged as a trend in all the arts in Barcelona in the 1880s. The avowed aims (especially in literature) of its followers were perhaps outlandish and pretentious, but the urge to seek innovation in expression coincided with a period of generalised optimism in Barcelona and throughout much of Western

Title Page: Tile work by Antoni Gaudí at Palau Güell, built in the late 1880s for his most important patron, Euset Güell (Photo by Christopher Groenhout)

Inset: Detail of one of the Passion Towers, La Sagrada Família (Photo by Dale Buckton)

Left: Wave-shaped window frames and balconies give Gaudí's Casa Batlló an underwater-castle effect

CHRISTOPHER GROENHOUT

MARK AVELLINO

Europe. In spite of the loss of Cuba and the Philippines in 1898 and the spread of violence in the city in the first decade of the 20th century, Barcelona experienced a *belle époque* to equal those that occurred elsewhere in Europe.

Modernisme did not appear in isolation in Barcelona. To the British and French the style was Art Nouveau; to the Italians it was *lo stile Liberty*; the Germans called it *Jugendstil* (Youth Style); and their Austrian confreres *Sezession* (Secession).

The curve implies movement, and hence vitality, and this idea informed a great deal of Art Nouveau thinking across Europe, in part inspired by long-standing tenets of Japanese art.

There is something misleading about the name Modernisme. It suggests the adoption of new means of construction and/or decoration and the rejection of the old. In a sense, nothing could be further from the truth. From Gaudí down, Modernista architects looked to the past for inspiration. Gothic, Islamic and Renaissance all had something to offer.

Top Right: Decorative capitals and railings atop Sala Hipostila in Parc Güell, designed by Gaudí

Bottom: Sunlit panorama of the rooftop at Gaudí's La Pedrera

CHRISTOPHER GROENHOUT

At its most playful, Modernisme was able to intelligently flout the rule-books on all these styles and create new and exciting cocktails. Even many of the materials used by the Modernistas were traditional – the innovation came in their application.

The search for a source or spirit was complemented by a desire to renew and transform those sources into a new expression, or re-expression, of timeless values in a contemporary universe. Those roots and their transformation are of course more readily observed in some Modernista constructions than in others.

As many as 2000 buildings in Barcelona and throughout Catalunya display at least some Modernista traces and Gaudí also undertook a handful of projects beyond Catalunya. It is one thing to have at hand an architect of genius – it is still more remarkable that several others of considerable talent should have been working at the same time. But the proliferation of their work was due, above all, to the availability of hard cash – as with most great artists down the centuries, genius required both a muse and a patron. Gaudí and friends had no shortage of orders. By happy coincidence, Modernisme picked up pace at the same time as Barcelona's urban expansion project in L'Eixample was gathering steam. And money for building was also available.

Modernisme also emerged within the context of the Catalan Renaixença, a rebirth or rediscovery of Catalan heritage by a certain

SIMON BRACKEN

Left: The smaller spires of La Sagrada Família, dedicated to Sant Josep patron saint of workers and the family, designed and built in part by Gaudí

intellectual elite. This rebirth expressed itself in many ways, from the founding of avowedly Catalan nationalist political pressure groups that sought the re-establishment of autonomous rights for the region through to the (self-) conscious resurrection of Catalan as an active literary language. The good and the great of Barcelona felt, too, that their town was emerging on the world stage. After all, it had been the first city in Spain to stage a Universal Exhibition (all the rage in Europe at that time), in 1888.

Three Geniuses

Gaudí, although a Catalan nationalist, does not appear to have been particularly vocal on the subject. The two architects who most closely followed him in talent, Lluís Domènech i Montaner (1850–1923) and Josep Puig i Cadafalch (1867–1957), were prominent nationalists. Puig i Cadafalch, in fact, was an important politician and president of the Catalan Mancomunitat (see Mayhem under History in the Facts about Barcelona chapter) from 1916 to 1923.

A quick comparison of some of the work by these three architects is enough to illustrate the difficulty in defining closely what is Modernisme. As Gaudí became more adventurous he increasingly appeared as a lone wolf. With age he became almost exclusively motivated by stark religious conviction and devoted much of the latter part of his life to what remains Barcelona's call sign – the unfinished La Sagrada Família church. His inspiration in the first instance here is clearly Gothic. But you don't have to take too close a look at the parts built in his lifetime to see that he is right out there by himself. Gaudí sought the perfection of harmony and perspective he observed in nature. Straight lines were out. Man was hard-pressed to emulate the works of nature, but he could try. Gaudí found his inspiration in the forms of plants and stones and used complex string models weighted with plumb drops to

PASCALE BEROUJON

Right: Sculptural cluster from the main facade of Palau de la Música Catalana

make his calculations (you can see examples in the upstairs mini-museum in La Pedrera). The architect's work is at once a sublime reaching out to the heavens and yet an earthy appeal to the sinewy movement – even in stillness – of nature's own constructs. For more details, see the boxed text 'Gaudí: God's Architect' in the Things to See & Do chapter.

Other key works by Gaudí show a similar preoccupation with the forms of nature, such as the Casa Milà (La Pedrera) and Casa Batlló (see the Things to See & Do chapter for more detail), where not a single straight line appears anywhere.

For contrast, just look from Casa Batlló to Puig i Cadafalch's Casa Amatller next door, where the straight line is much in evidence. This architect also looked to the past and to foreign influence (the gables are borrowed from the Dutch), and created a house of startling beauty and invention. Domènech i Montaner, too, clearly looked into the Gothic past but never simply copied, as shown by the Castell dels Tres Dragons (built as a café-restaurant for the Universal Exhibition in 1888 and now home to the Museu de Zoologia) or the Hospital de la Santa Creu i de Sant Pau. In these buildings, Domènech i Montaner put his own spin on the past, in both decoration and structure. In the case of the Castell dels Tres Dragons, the main windows are more of a neo-classical borrowing, and Islamic touches can be made out in the detail. Domènech i Montaner seems to come closest to Gaudí's ideas in the Palau de la Música Catalana. The structure may be largely linear, the decor is anything but.

DALE BUCKTON

Left: View of the Palau de la Música Catalana, built by Domènech i Montaner between 1905 and 1908

DAMIEN SIMONIS

Materials & Decoration

All three of the 'greats', and a whole gaggle of lesser-known figures of the Modernista style, relied heavily on artisanal skills that have been, by now, all but relegated to history. There were no concrete pours for these guys. Unclad brick, exposed iron and steel frames, and copious use of glass and tiles in decoration were all features of the new style – and indeed it is often in the decor that Modernisme is at its most flamboyant and identifiable.

The kinds of craftsmen required to execute these intricate tasks were the heirs of the guild masters, and had absorbed centuries of know-how about just what could and could not be done with these materials. Forged iron and steel were newcomers to the scene, but the approach in learning how they could be used was not dissimilar to that adopted for more traditional materials. Gaudí, in particular, relied on these old skills and even ran schools in La Sagrada Família workshops to keep them alive.

Iron came into its own in this period. Nowhere is this more evident than in Barcelona's great covered markets: Mercat de la Boqueria, Mercat del Born (now being excavated and with an uncertain future) and Mercat de Sant Antoni, just to name the main ones. Their grand metallic vaults not only provided shade over the produce for sale but were also a proclamation both of Barcelona's dynamism and the success of 'ignoble' materials in grand building.

Top Right: Detail from the Modernista Hospital de la Santa Creu, built by Domènech i Montaner

The Rome-trained sculptor Eusebi Arnau (1864–1934) was one of the most constant figures called up to decorate Barcelona's great Modernista buildings, both inside and out. The appearance of the Hospital de la Santa Creu i de Sant Pau is one of his legacies and he was heavily involved in the design and embellishment of monuments in the Parc de la Ciutadella. He also had a hand in the Palau de la Música Catalana, the Fonda Espanya restaurant in El Raval, and Casa Amatller among others.

Decorators of several less-grand establishments were quick to jump onto the Modernista bandwagon. Casa Quadros on La Rambla, with its Chinese dragon and impossible cladding of umbrellas, remains a dreamy example of daring shopfront design. Less obvious but just as clearly Modernista on a closer look are the many surviving shop fronts of, above all, pharmacies (for example, Carrer de València 256 and Carrer de Mallorca 312) and bakeries (for example, Antiga Casa Figueras, La Rambla 83).

Where to Look

Barcelona is full of Modernista traces. A separate guidebook would be needed to detail all of them. In the Walking Tours chapter there is a selective tour of the main Modernista sights (largely concentrated in L'Eixample or nearby, although there are some important exceptions). A number of lesser sights are also mentioned in passing. The main ones are discussed in more detail in the Things to See & Do chapter.

Tourist offices can also provide pamphlets and other material with detailed maps that cover a greater range of Modernista sights. Remember that many of these Modernista buildings are still private houses and/or offices so it is often difficult to see inside them.

Bottom: Sculptures of fans and umbrellas decorate Casa Quadros on La Rambla

GUY MOBERLY

[Continued from page 32]

Jorge Semprún (1923–), who lost his home and family in the civil war, ended up in a Nazi concentration camp for his activities with the French Resistance in WWII. He writes mostly in French. His first novel, *Le Grand Voyage*, is one of his best.

Eduardo Mendoza (1943–) is a fine Barcelonin writer, whose *La Ciudad de los Prodigios* (also published in English as The City of Marvels) is an absorbing novel set in the city in the period between the Universal Exhibition of 1888 and the World Exhibition in 1929. It was filmed, with disappointing results, in 1999.

Terenci Moix (1942–) is a successful columnist and writer who tends to write in Castilian (although not exclusively). His books are fairly lightweight, but highly popular, literature exploring Spanish society and often involving a lot of self-discovery. His recent *El Arpista Ciego* is a fantastical journey into the time of the pharaohs.

Enrique Vila-Matas (1948–) has won fans way beyond his native Barcelona. His novels have been translated into a dozen languages. In his latest effort, *Bartleby y Compañía*, a writer convinced that modern works are vapid enters a crisis, strongly attracted to nothingness.

Montserrat Roig (1946–91) crammed a lot of journalistic and fiction writing (largely in Catalan) into her short life. Her novels include *Ramon Adéu*, *El Temps de les Cireres* and *L'Hora Violeta*.

Manuel Vázquez Montalbán (1939–) is one of the city's more prolific writers, best known for his Pepe Carvalho detective novel series. However, he doesn't restrict his activity to Pepe and, in 2002, he published *Erec y Enide*, a modern love story inspired by the Chrétien de Troyes treatment of King Arthur.

On the detective theme, Xavier Moret (1952–) brings to life a quite different character, Max Riera, a 1970s hippy turned detective. In *Zanzíbar Pot Esperar*, written in 2002, Riera gets mixed up in a case of fraud that involves the eviction of a group of squatters.

One of Montalbán's pals, Juan Marsé (1933–), is another important figure on the Barcelona literature scene. Among his outstanding novels are *Motocicleta*, *Últimas Tardes con Teresa* and *El Embrujo de Shanghai*. The latter, set in Gràcia, was brought to the screen in a memorable picture by Fernando Trueba in 2002. The story revolves around characters struggling along in the wake of the civil war and a 14-year-old's timid discovery of love.

Ana María Moix (1947–) gained considerable acclaim with her prize-winning *Julia* in 1970, but then fell silent until 1985 when she resurfaced with a collection of short stories, *Las Virtudes Peligrosas*, which take a caustic look at society.

Quim Monzó (1952–) is a prolific writer of short stories, columns and essays (in Catalan). His wide-ranging work is marked by a mordant wit and an abiding interest in pornography. He revised the best of his stories and published them under one volume, *Vuitanta-sis Contes*, in 1999. His latest collection, *El Millor dels Mons*, appeared in print in 2001.

Nuria Amat is an emerging local talent, whose *Reina de América* (2002) plunges a young Spanish writer into the vortex of the narco-wars in Colombia.

Theatre

Barcelona rivals Madrid as a centre of theatrical production in Spain. Purely Catalan theatre was revived, amid the rhetoric of the Renaixença, in the late 19th century, with playwright and all-round Catalan nationalist Àngel Guimerà as its principal driving force. It went through some ups and downs in subsequent decades, and was kept fairly well under heel during the long Franco years. Today a raft of young directors and writers stage classics of Spanish and foreign theatre in Catalan, as well as promoting local productions.

Possibly one of the wackiest theatre companies is La Fura dels Baus. These guys turn theatre spaces (often warehouses) into a kind of participatory apocalypse – 60 minutes of, at times, spine-chilling performance. The audience becomes an integral part of the 'act', prodded and cajoled to contribute its own two cents' worth. The company grew out of Barcelona's street-theatre culture in the late 1970s and, although it has grown in technical prowess, it has not abandoned the rough-and-ready edge of street performances.

Tricicle is another big Barcelona name. It's a three-man mime team easily enjoyed by anyone – no need to understand Catalan. Els Comediants and La Cubana are two highly successful groups that also owe a lot to the impromptu world of street theatre.

Music

Traditional It is hard to know into what category to put the medieval troubadours. In many respects the verses they sang (largely the plaintive cries of courtly love inspired by French traditions) represent some of the earliest medieval literature in Mediterranean Europe. Provençal and not Catalan, however, remained the universal language for a long time.

The strongest musical tradition to have survived to some degree in popular form in Catalunya is that of the *havaneres*, nostalgic songs and sea shanties brought back from Cuba by Catalans who lived, sailed and traded there. Even after Spain lost Cuba in 1898, the *havanera* tradition continued and today they are enjoying a revival. In some coastal towns, such as Calella on the Costa Brava, you can turn up for an evening's *cantada de havaneres*.

Baroque The Catalan Jordi Savall (1941–) has assumed the task of rediscovering a Europe-wide heritage in music that predates the era of the classical greats. He and his wife, the soprano Montserrat Figueras, have been largely responsible, along with musicians from other countries, for resuscitating the beauties of medieval, Renaissance and, above all, baroque music. In 1987 Savall founded La Capella Reial de Catalunya and two years later he formed the baroque orchestra, Le Concert des Nations.

Classical Spain's contribution to the world of classical music has been comparatively modest, but Catalunya did produce a few exceptional composers.

Perhaps best known is Camprodon-born Isaac Albéniz (1860–1909), a gifted pianist who later turned his hand to composition. Among his best remembered works is the *Iberia* cycle.

Lleida's Enric Granados i Campina (1867–1916) came on to the scene in the early 20th century. Another fine pianist, he established Barcelona's conservatorium in 1901 and composed a great many pieces for piano, including *Danzas Españolas*, *Cantos de la Juventud* and *Goyescas*.

Other Catalan composers/musicians of some note include Eduard Toldrà (1895–1962) and Frederic Mompou (1893–1987).

Opera Montserrat Caballé is Barcelona's most successful voice. Born in Gràcia in 1933, the soprano made her debut in 1956 in Basel (Switzerland). Her home-town launch came four years later in the Gran Teatre del Liceu. In 1965 she performed at New York's Carnegie Hall to wild acclaim. She hasn't looked back and remains one of the world's top sopranos. Catalunya's other world-class opera star is the renowned tenor Josep (José) Carreras (1946–).

Contemporary A good deal of Spain's most representative modern music has grown out of the lively Barcelona *movida*, that post-Franco outburst of activity and nightlife that filled the streets of Spain in the early 1980s.

Lluís Llach, probably the best-known name in Catalan pop, is the Catalan Bob Dylan, a sing-songwriter who emerged as a voice of protest in the dying stages of the Franco era. He still produces and performs new work. Gossos is a four-man band that specialises in folk-rock much along the lines of Crosby, Stills and Nash.

Rock Català (Catalan rock) is not essentially different from rock anywhere else, except that it is sung in Catalan by local bands that appeal to local tastes. Among the most popular bands are: Els Pets (one of the region's top acts), Ja T'ho Diré, Sopa de Cabra (who broke up in late 2001), Lax'n'Busto,

Whiskyn's, Glaucs, No Nem Bé, Dr Calypso, Antònia Font, Dept, Pomada, Xavi Vidal and Glissando. Barcelona brothers David and José Muñoz (aka as Estopa), have enjoyed national success with their mix of rock, rumba and pop.

Since August 1998 the annual Senglar Rock concert has been *the* date for Catalan rock music. It was held in Montblanc at the end of June in 2000, but dates and location can change, so keep your eyes peeled from about June onwards.

Dance

Contemporary Barcelona is the capital of contemporary dance in Spain. This is not necessarily saying much, as dance does not thrive here as in other European cities such as Paris, Brussels and even London.

A Slow Number

The Catalan dance, par excellence, is the *sardana*; its roots lie in the far northern Empordà region of Catalunya. Compared with flamenco it is a sober sight indeed but is not unlike a lot of folk dances seen in various parts of the Mediterranean.

The dancers hold hands in a circle and wait for the 10 or so musicians to begin. The performance starts with the piping of the *flabiol*, a little wooden flute. When the other musicians join in, the dancers begin – a series of steps to the right, one back and then the same to the left. As the music 'heats up' the steps become more complex, the leaps are higher and the dancers lift their arms. Then they return to the initial steps and continue. If newcomers wish to join in, space is made in the circle for them as the dance continues and the whole thing proceeds in a more or less seamless fashion.

In Barcelona the best chance you have of seeing people dancing the *sardana* is at noon on Sunday in front of the Catedral. Other possibilities are at 6.30pm on Saturday and 7pm on Wednesday. You can also see them during some of the city's festivals.

Ramon Oller is one of the city's leading choreographers, working with one of the country's most solidly established companies, Metros. Its dance is rooted in a comparatively formal technique. Four other prominent dance companies worth keeping an eye out for are: Cesc Gelabert (run by the choreographer of the same name), Mudanzas (Àngels Margarit), Lanonima Imperial (Juan Carlos García) and Mal Pelo (Maria Muñoz and Pep Ramis). All four companies tend to work from a base of 'release technique', which favours 'natural' movement, working from the skeleton, over a reliance on muscular power.

Cinema

In December 1896, the Cinématographe Lumière was installed in the Salón Fotográfico Napoleón and the first brief movies were shown to an appreciative audience. Afterwards, the French brothers Lumière were roundly congratulated in the Barcelona press for their success – the Catalan city was, therefore, present at the earliest stages in the life of the 'seventh art'. Two years later, the first film theatre was opened on La Rambla.

In 1932, Francesc Macià, president of the Generalitat, opened Spain's first studios for making 'talkies' and a year later Metro-Goldwyn-Mayer had a dubbing studio in Barcelona. Prior to the civil war, *El Fava d'en Ramonet* was about the only cinematic hit in Catalan to make it to the screen.

In the wake of Franco's victory, pretty much all cinematic production happened in Madrid and was, in any case, a mix of propaganda and schmaltz. In 1952 a small group of Catalans made a film called *El Judes*, in Catalan, but it was banned.

In 1956 the so-called Escola de Barcelona began to produce a lot of experimental stuff, some of which did see the light of the day. Many film-makers such as Vicente Aranda (1926–) cut their teeth here. Aranda later gained fame for *Amantes* (1991), set in 1950s Madrid and based on the real story of a love triangle that ends particularly badly. He followed it three years later with the steamy *La Pasión Turca*.

War of Words

Catalan belongs to the group of Western European languages that grew out of Latin (Romance languages), including Italian, French, Castilian and Portuguese. By the 12th century, it was a clearly established language with its own nascent literature.

A Rocky History

The survival or predominance of a language is often closely linked to political and social events dating back centuries, and Catalan's history has certainly been a rocky one.

The language was most closely related to *langue d'oc*, the southern French derivative of Latin that long reigned supreme as the principal tongue in Gallic lands. The most conspicuous survivor of *langue d'oc* is the now little-used Provençal.

Until the disaster of the Battle of Muret in 1213 (see History earlier in this chapter), Catalan territory extended well across southern France, taking in Roussillon and reaching into Provence. Catalan was spoken, or at least understood, throughout these territories and in what is now Catalunya and Andorra.

In the following couple of hundred years, while the losses of French territory were being compensated by their Mediterranean empire building, the Catalans spread their language south into Valencia, west into Aragón and east to the Balearic Islands (Illes Balears/Islas Baleares). The language also reached Sicily and Naples, and the Sardinian town of Alghero is still a partly Catalan-speaking outpost today.

Dialects

Like most languages, Catalan has its dialects. The main distinction is between western and eastern varieties – the former is used in Andorra, western and far-southern Catalunya and the Catalan-speaking parts of Aragón and Valencia, the latter in the rest of the Catalan world. Linguistic experts further subdivide these into 12 subdialects!

Optimists count about 10 million speakers of Catalan today throughout Spain and in parts of France, but the reality is a little different. Many Valencianos actually prefer Castilian to Catalan and find the whole pan-Catalan phenomenon emanating from nationalist quarters in Barcelona profoundly irritating. Indeed, beyond Catalunya, inland northern Valencia and Andorra, you're as likely to hear Castilian spoken as Catalan.

In and around Barcelona itself, much of the population's origins lie in other parts of Spain and, although the second generation has grown up learning Catalan, Castilian is often still their first tongue. In Sardinia and France, Italian and French respectively have all but submerged Catalan.

Revival

From 1714 on, the use of Catalan was repeatedly banned. Franco was the last of Spain's rulers to clamp down on it.

Even post-Franco, Madrid has remained the centre of Spanish cinema and it has been slow going in the Catalan film world. José Juan Bigas Luna (1946–) is one of the region's better-known directors. He also directed the popular comedy *Jamón, Jamón* in 1992, which was his best effort in more than a decade.

Ventura Pons (1945–) is a veteran of Catalan theatre and film-making. His *Food of Love* (2001), the story of a young music student in the USA who finds he hasn't got what it takes to make the big time, won a lot of critical praise from cinamagoers around the world. Part of the film was shot in Barcelona. The prolific Pons has churned

War of Words

Renewed interest in the language first came from intellectual circles with the Renaixença at the end of the 19th century; in rural areas at least, its use had never really waned. Franco loosened the reins a little from the 1960s on, but all education in Catalan schools was to remain exclusively in Castilian until after the dictator's demise in 1975.

Since Jordi Pujol's nationalist Convergència i Unió (CiU) coalition took control of the Generalitat in 1980, it has waged a campaign to 'normalise' the use of Catalan. The Generalitat reckons that 93% of the population in Catalunya understand Catalan and 68% speak it. In Valencia, about half the population speak it, as do 67% in the Balearic Islands.

The big problem is that not nearly as many can write it – the true test of linguistic capacity. Even in Catalunya it's estimated that only 39% write Catalan satisfactorily.

If you find yourself watching chat programs on a local TV chanel, you'll occasionally strike comperes speaking Catalan and their interlocutors answering in Castilian.

Catalan Today

So tenacious has the CiU's campaign been that in Catalunya today it is virtually impossible to get a public-service job without fluency in Catalan. It's not so easy in the private sector either. And just as Franco had all signs in Catalan replaced, Castilian road signs, publicity and the like are now harder and harder to find, although both languages have equal legal status.

Pujol stirred the pot still more in 1998 with his *Llei de Política Lingüística* (Linguistic Policy Law). Socialists and conservatives in and outside Catalunya cried out that Pujol was attempting to impose Catalan monolingualism.

The result today is that in most areas of the public service and in a great deal of the private sector, Catalan is the dominant language. In school, about 80% of primary education is in Catalan, and about 50% of secondary. At university level, in spite of fairly strict language policies on some campuses, the situation remains fairly fluid, with professors lecturing as much in one language as the other.

Oddly, in spite of the rise in the use of Catalan at an official level, it is has lost ground outside the workplace. A 2002 study showed that while 44% of Barcelonins claimed their first language was Catalan in 1995, only 39% did so in 2000. Nevertheless, the process of 'linguistic normalisation' continues. And in 2002 the Institut Ramon Llull was born. It will, in the coming years, work with the national Instituto Cervantes (see the Facts for the Visitor chapter) to diffuse knowledge of the Catalan language and culture abroad.

Some aspects of Pujol's 1998 law have an almost Quixotic touch. The Second 'Additional Disposition' refers to the Generalitat's 'duty' to 'ensure the promotion, use and protection of the Catalan language and generalise and extend knowledge and use of it' in all Catalan territories (ie, all those listed here). One might well wonder what historical justification there could be for bolstering the use of Catalan in Alghero (Àlguer in Catalan), when it was virtually enforced on locals in the first place, an act of imperialism no less flagrant than any of those of which the Castilians might be accused!

out a feature film almost every year since he seriously got involved in film-making in 1989.

Sergi López (1965–), from Vilanova i la Geltrú (just down the coast from Barcelona) is one of Catalunya's best-known actors, with a long list of credits in both Spanish and French cinema. Among his better pic-tures are the suspenseful black comedy *With a Friend Like Harry* (2001) and *Une Relation Pornographique* (2000), in which two people get together for sex and find real lurve.

In 2000 Barcelona hosted the Goya awards, Spain's version of the Oscars, for the first time ever.

SOCIETY & CONDUCT

Catalans have a bit of a reputation for being reserved. That may or may not be true, but as a rule Barcelonins are tolerant and courteous. No-one really expects you to speak Catalan, but if you can stumble along good-humouredly in Castilian in shops and other situations you'll generally receive a friendly response.

Codes of good manners differ the world over, and what can sometimes seem brusque treatment to Anglos is not intended as anything of the sort. While the latter may be obsessed with 'please' and 'thank you', you'll find your average Barcelonins not overly fussed. Profusions of *'por favors'* (please) are not part of the local mindset. In bars and the like you are likely to hear the most respectable people simply say 'give me...' whatever it might be. But Catalans stand on ceremony in other ways. It is common to wish all and sundry *'bon dia/buenos días'* when entering a shop or bar and to say *'adéu/adiós'* on the way out. It's not mandatory, but common.

Spaniards, in general, are individualistic and Catalans are not much of an exception to that rule. That is not to say they are lone wolves. Although not as party conscious as some of their more southern neighbours, Barcelonins love to hang out in bars and open-air cafés. Invitations to people's homes are more of an exception than the rule.

Dos & Don'ts

The standard form of greeting between men and women (even when meeting for the first time) and between women is a kiss on each cheek, right then left. Now, we're not talking about big sloppy ones – a light brushing of cheeks is perfectly sufficient. Men seem to be able to take or leave handshakes on informal occasions, but they are pretty much standard in a business context.

In some older bars the locals chuck their rubbish – paper, toothpicks, cigarette butts and so on – on to the floor. At the end of the day it's all swept up. This does not apply everywhere so don't start indulging your deeply buried urges to be a litterbug unless you are quite sure you are in a sufficiently grungy bar. Be sure to check the floor and other customers' behaviour first!

Treatment of Animals

Although bullfighting does not have the same appeal in Barcelona as elsewhere in Spain, it is still a popular sport with some. There is little doubting its cruelty and the subject can generate animated debate.

For the *aficionados* (enthusiasts) it is an art, a virtuoso display of courage that generally ends in the honourable death of the bull – a better fate than the abattoir they will tell you. Its opponents are simply sickened by the spectacle.

If you feel revulsion for the fight, you can contact the organisations listed below for further information and suggested action:

People for the Ethical Treatment of Animals (PETA)
UK: (☎ 020-8870 3966, fax 8870 1686) PO Box 3169, London SW18 4WJ
USA: (☎ 757-622 7382, fax 622 0457, w www.peta.org) 501 Front St, Norfolk, VA 23510

World Society for the Protection of Animals (WSPA)
UK: (☎ 020-7587 5000, fax 7793 0208, e wspa@wspa.org.uk) 81 Albert Embankment, London SE1 7TP
USA: (☎ 508-879 8350, fax 620 0786, e wspa@wspausa.com) 34 Deloss St, Framingham, MA 01702
Canada: (☎ 416-369 0044, fax 369 0147, e wspa@wspa.ca, w www.wspa.org.uk) 90 Eglinton Ave East, Suite 960, Toronto, Ontario M4P 2Y3

For more information about the bullfight, see Spectator Sports in the Entertainment chapter.

RELIGION

Barcelona, like the rest of Spain, is largely Catholic, at least in name. But a strong anarchist and socialist tradition, which historically has almost always meant anticlericalism, has left an indelible mark here and many Barcelonins pay little more than lip service to their faith. According to a 2002 study, 29% of Catalans claim to profess no faith and only 27% attend Mass regularly.

From the end of the 19th century through to the end of the civil war, church-burning was a popular pastime. The two worst waves came in 1909 during the Setmana Tràgica and at the outbreak of the Spanish Civil War in 1936. Under Franco, Catholicism was again made a state religion and the Church played a preponderant role in society, although less markedly so in Barcelona where vast sections of the populace remained essentially 'red'.

Many Spanish theologians, much as their counterparts elsewhere in Europe and the USA has, have criticised the Church for its conservatism on issues such as sex, abortion and divorce, warning that it will lose even further ground with Spaniards if it does not 'modernise'. In early 2002, a group of Catalan priests, with considerable popular support, called for an end to the obligation of celibacy in the priesthood.

LANGUAGE

Catalan and Spanish (the latter is more appropriately known as *castellano*, or Castilian) have equal legal status in Barcelona. Given the city's history of immigration from other parts of Spain, you'll probably hear the latter spoken as much as, if not more than, the former. This may change in the coming years but generally the foreigner will be well enough received just for trying their luck in Spanish. English is not as widely spoken as you might expect in such a city and French even less so, although among younger people you are likely to have more luck with the former. In some hotels and restaurants (even at budget level) you may also be able to make yourself understood. An effort on your part to come to grips with some of the basics of Catalan or Spanish will be a useful investment, though. To get you started, turn to the Language chapter.

Facts for the Visitor

WHEN TO GO

Spring and early summer is the best time to be in Barcelona. The weather is usually pleasant, the number of other tourists manageable and the city humming. High summer (particularly mid-July to late August) is asphyxiating – many locals get the hell out and leave it to the *guiris* (foreigners).

September is not a bad month either, when the city recovers its normal rhythms, the heat eases off and tourist numbers drop, but the weather can be dodgy. For *real* rain, hang about in October.

Winter is not especially distressing. Things are more subdued, but at least you can get around in peace. It can get nippy (you will want a room with heating), so come prepared.

ORIENTATION

Barcelona's coastline runs northeast to southwest and many streets are parallel or perpendicular to this.

Major arteries include: Gran Via de les Corts Catalanes, running parallel to the coast right across the city; Avinguda Meridiana, which cuts a (nearly) straight path north out of the city; Avinguda del Paral.lel (according to tradition, the road was built along parallel 41°, 44') and its continuation under other names, which runs west from Port Vell, and Avinguda Diagonal, which cuts across the city from Pedralbes to the coast.

The city is divided into 10 municipalities, themselves subdivided (by tradition if not officially) into *barris/barrios* (districts). The areas of most interest to visitors can be broken down as follows.

La Rambla & Plaça de Catalunya

The focal axis of the city is La Rambla, a 1.25km-long boulevard running northwest and slightly uphill from Port Vell (the old harbour) to Plaça de Catalunya. The latter marks the boundary between the Ciutat Vella (old city) and the more recent parts further inland.

Ciutat Vella

The Ciutat Vella, a warren of narrow streets, centuries-old buildings and a lot of bottom-end and mid-range accommodation, spreads either side of La Rambla. Its heart is the lower half of the section east of La Rambla called the Barri Gòtic (Gothic quarter), which is where the medieval core of the city grew on the site of the Roman settlement. West of La Rambla is the, at times, seedy El Raval, while northeast of Barri Gòtic, across Via Laietana, is La Ribera.

Waterfront

Port Vell has an excellent modern aquarium and two marinas. At its northeastern end is La Barceloneta, the old fishermen's quarter, from where beaches and a pedestrian promenade stretch 1km northeast to Port Olímpic, which was built for the 1992 Olympic Games.

L'Eixample

Plaça de Catalunya at the top of La Rambla marks the beginning of L'Eixample (el Ensanche in Spanish), the grid of straight streets into which Barcelona spread in the 19th century. This is where you'll find most of Barcelona's Modernista architecture – including La Sagrada Família – as well as its glossiest shops and many expensive hotels. The main avenues are Passeig de Gràcia and, running parallel to it, Rambla de Catalunya, which goes northwest from Plaça de Catalunya. The part to the west of Passeig de Gràcia is known as L'Esquerra (the Left) de l'Eixample, while to the east it's La Dreta (the Right) de l'Eixample.

Gràcia

Beyond the wide Avinguda Diagonal on the northern edge of central L'Eixample, Gràcia is a net of narrow streets and small squares with a distinct feel from that of the core of Barcelona. With something of a bohemian past and a strong Catalan stamp, it is a lively place to spend a Friday or Saturday night. Just to the north of Gràcia is Gaudí's remarkable Parc Güell.

Montjuïc & Tibidabo

Two good pointers to indicate which way you're facing are the hills of Montjuïc and Tibidabo. Montjuïc, the lower of the two, begins about 700m southwest of La Rambla. Tibidabo is 6km northwest of the top of La Rambla. It's the high point of the range of wooded hills that form a backdrop to the whole city.

Main Transport Terminals

The airport is 14km southwest of the centre at El Prat de Llobregat. The main train station is Estació Sants (Map 4), 2.5km west of La Rambla and southwest of L'Eixample. Catalunya station is at the top end of La Rambla. The main bus station, Estació del Nord (Map 1), is 1.5km further northeast.

MAPS

Tourist offices hand out free city and transport maps that are OK, but better is Lonely Planet's *Barcelona City Map* (1:24,000 with a complete index of streets and sights). If you can't find it, try the Michelin No 40 *Barcelona* map (€5.50). You can buy it with a comprehensive street index (Michelin No 41), bringing the price to €6. Plenty of stalls on La Rambla sell maps.

If you intend to hang about for a while and want a handy map book, Editorial Pamias' *Guía Urbana Barcelona* (€10.57) is a compact and complete guide to city streets and is packed with information. More complete still for long-termers is *Guía Barcelona i Poblacions Limítrofes* (€16), published by Oceano. Handier for the backpack is Michelin's ringbound *Barcelona*, scaled at 1:12,000 (€5).

TOURIST OFFICES
Local Tourist Offices

The **Oficina d'Informació de Turisme de Barcelona** *(Map 6; ☎ 906 30 12 82; from abroad ☎ +34 93 368 97 30/1; Plaça de Catalunya 17-S – underground; open 9am-9pm daily)* concentrates on city information and can help book accommodation, make reservations at restaurants, and sell tickets for some shows. It also offers a money exchange service. Information can also be obtained by telephoning this tourist office on ☎ 93 304 32 32 or at the website W www .barcelona-on-line.es.

There is another **information office** *(Map 6; open 9am-8pm Mon-Fri, 10am-8pm Sat, 10am-2pm Sun & holidays)* in the town hall (Ajuntament) on Plaça de Sant Jaume.

The **regional tourist office** *(Map 2; ☎ 93 238 40 00; Passeig de Gràcia 107; open 10am-7pm Mon-Sat, 10am-2pm Sun)* is in the late-19th-century neo-classical Palau Robert. It has a host of material, audio-visual stuff, a bookshop and a branch of Turisme Juvenil de Catalunya (where you can get Euro<26 cards – see Student, Teacher & Youth Cards later in this chapter). By the way, if you are feeling hot and bothered, you can retire out the back to the lovely gardens.

Turisme de Barcelona *(Map 4; open 8am-8pm daily June-Sept, 8am-8pm Mon-Fri, 8am-2pm Sat, Sun & holidays Oct-May)* in Estació Sants covers Barcelona only.

The **tourist office** *(☎ 93 478 05 65; open 9am-9pm daily)* in the airport's European Union (EU) arrivals hall has information on all Catalunya. The **tourist office** *(☎ 93 478 47 04)* at the international arrivals hall opens the same hours.

Another useful office for events information (and tickets) is the **Palau de la Virreina arts information office** *(Map 6; ☎ 93 301 77 75; La Rambla de Sant Josep 99)*.

From late June to late September, a temporary information booth is set up in Plaça de la Sagrada Família (Map 2). At the same time, you'll find information officers known as *casaques vermelles* ('red jackets') hanging around Barri Gòtic, La Rambla and also Passeig de Gràcia.

A couple of general information lines worth bearing in mind are ☎ 010 and ☎ 012. The first is for Barcelona and the second for all Catalunya (run by the Generalitat). You sometimes strike English speakers although for the most part operators are Catalan/ Castilian bilingual. They can often answer quite obscure questions.

Finally, there is a nationwide tourist information line in several languages, which can come in handy if you are calling from elsewhere in Spain. Call ☎ 901 30 06 00 from 8.30am to 10.30pm daily for basic information in Spanish, English and French.

Tourist Offices Abroad

Information on Barcelona is available from the following overseas branches of the Oficina Española de Turismo:

Canada (☎ 416-961 3131; e toronto@ tourspain.es) 2 Bloor St W, 34th Floor, Toronto M4W 3E2

France (☎ 01 45 03 82 57; e paris@tourspain .es) 43 Rue Decamps, 75784 Paris, Cedex 16

Germany (☎ 030-882 6543; e berlin@ tourspain.es) Kurfürstendamm 63, D-10707 Berlin. There are also branches in Düsseldorf, Frankfurt am Main and Munich.

Portugal (☎ 213 541 992; e lisboa@ tourspain.es) Avenida Sidónio Pais 28 3° Dto, 1050 Lisbon

UK (☎ 020-7486 8077; e londres@ tourspain.es) 22–23 Manchester Square, London W1U 3PX

USA (☎ 212-265 8822; e nyork@tourspain.es) 666 Fifth Ave, 35th Floor, New York, NY 10103. Branches can also be found in Chicago, Los Angeles and Miami.

TRAVEL AGENCIES

Barcelona is hardly one of Europe's best places for discount flights. That said, you can still find reasonable deals to major Western European destinations, and occasionally to the USA. You could start with contacting the following agents, but there is no substitute for shopping around – frequently small neighbourhood travel agents come up with surprising offers.

usit Unlimited (Map 5; ☎ 93 412 01 04; Ronda de l'Universitat 16) sells youth and student air, train and bus tickets. It has a branch in the office of Turisme Juvenil de Catalunya (Map 8) on Carrer de Rocafort 116–122. Another useful agent to contact is **Viatgi** (Map 4; ☎ 93 317 50 98; Ronda de l'Universitat 1).

Asatej (Map 6; ☎ 93 412 63 38; w www .asatej.com; Rambla 140) can organise anything from car rental to trips outside Spain.

Halcón Viatges (national phone reservations ☎ 902 30 06 00; branch: Map 2; Carrer de Pau Claris 108) is a reliable chain of travel agents that sometimes has good deals. The branch described here is one of 31 around town.

VISAS & DOCUMENTS
Visas

Spain is one of 15 member countries of the Schengen Convention, an agreement whereby all EU-member countries (except the UK and Ireland) plus Iceland and Norway abolished checks at internal borders in 2000. The other member countries are Austria, Belgium, Denmark, Finland, France, Germany, Greece, Italy, Luxembourg, the Netherlands, Portugal and Sweden.

EU, Norwegian and Icelandic nationals need no visa, regardless of the length or purpose of their visit to Spain. If they stay beyond 90 days they are required to register with the police, though. Legal residents of one Schengen country (regardless of their nationality) do not require a visa for another Schengen country.

Nationals of many other countries, including Australia, Canada, Israel, Japan, New Zealand, Switzerland and the USA, do not need a visa for tourist visits of up to 90 days in Spain, although some of these nationalities (including Australians and Canadians) may be subject to restrictions in other Schengen countries and should check with consulates of all Schengen countries they plan to visit. If you wish to work or study in Spain, you may need a specific visa to do so, so contact a Spanish consulate before you travel.

If you are a citizen of a country not mentioned in this section, check with a Spanish consulate whether you need a visa. The standard tourist visa issued by Spanish consulates is the Schengen visa, valid for up to 90 days. A Schengen visa issued by one Schengen country is generally valid for travel in all other Schengen countries.

Those needing a visa must apply *in person* at the consulate in the country where they are resident. You may be required to provide proof of sufficient funds, an itinerary or hotel bookings, return tickets and a letter of recommendation from a host in Spain. Issue of the visa does *not* guarantee entry.

You can apply for no more than two visas in any 12-month period and they are not renewable once in Spain. In the UK, single-entry visas for a 30-day stay cost UK£15.50. Multiple-entry visas valid for a 90-day stay cost UK£21.70. Visas are free for spouses and children of EU nationals. Various forms of transit visas also exist.

Visa Extensions & Residence Schengen visas cannot be extended. Nationals of EU countries, Norway and Iceland who want to stay in Spain longer than 90 days are supposed to apply during their first month for a residence card *(tarjeta de residencia)*. This is a lengthy procedure – if you intend to subject yourself to it, consult a Spanish consulate before you go to Spain as you will need to take certain documents with you.

People of other nationalities who want to stay in Spain longer than 90 days are also supposed to get a residence card, and for them it's a truly nightmarish process, starting with a residence visa issued by a Spanish consulate in your country of residence. Start the process aeons in advance.

Travel Insurance
Medical costs for some travellers might already be covered through reciprocal healthcare agreements (see Health later in this chapter) but you'll still need cover for theft or loss and for unexpected changes in travel plans (ticket cancellation etc). Check what's already covered by your local insurance policies and credit card – you might not need separate travel insurance. In most cases, however, this secondary type of cover is limited and its small print is laced with loopholes. For peace of mind, nothing beats straight travel insurance at the highest level you can afford.

Driving Licence & Permits
EU member states' pink-and-green driving licences are recognised in Spain. If you hold a licence from other countries you are supposed to obtain an International Driving Permit (IDP), too.

Hostel Cards
A valid HI (Hostelling International) card or youth hostel card from your home country is required at most HI youth hostels in Spain, including those in Barcelona. If you don't have one, you can get an HI Card, valid until 31 December of the year you buy it, at most HI hostels in Spain. You pay for the card in instalments of €3.01 each night (in addition to the cost of accommodation) you spend in a hostel, up to the total of €18.06 (people legally resident in Spain for at least a year can get a Spanish hostel card for €11, or €5 if under 30 years old).

The cards are also available from the **Xarxa d'Albergs de Catalunya** *(Map 4; ☎ 93 483 83 63, fax 93 483 83 50; W www .tujuca.com; Metro: Rocafort)*, which is in the office of the Turisme Juvenil de Catalunya on Carrer de Rocafort 116–122.

Student, Teacher & Youth Cards
These cards can get you worthwhile discounts on travel, and reduced prices at some museums, sights and entertainments.

The International Student Identity Card (ISIC), for full-time students (€4.20 in Spain), and the International Teacher Identity Card (ITIC), for full-time teachers and academics (€6), are issued by more than 5000 organisations around the world – mainly student-travel-related organisations that often sell student air, train and bus tickets, too. They include:

Australia
STA Travel (☎ 03-9207 5900) 224 Faraday St, Carlton, Melbourne, Victoria 3053
(☎ 02-9360 1822) 9 Oxford St, Paddington, Sydney, NSW 2021
Nationwide (☎ 1300 360 960; W www .statravel.com.au)

Canada
Travel CUTS (☎ 416-979 2406) 187 College St, Toronto, Ontario M5T 1P7
Nationwide (☎ 800-667 2887; W www .travelcuts.com)
Voyages Campus (☎ 514-398 0647) Université McGill, 3480 rue McTavish, Montreal, Quebec H3A 1X9

UK

Cards are best obtained from youth travel organisations such as STA Travel (see The UK under Air in the Getting There & Away chapter).

USA

Council Travel (☎ 212-822 2700) 205 East 42nd St, New York, NY 10017
(☎ 310-208 3551) 931 Westwood Blvd, Westwood, Los Angeles, CA 90024
(☎ 415-421 3473) 530 Bush St, San Francisco, CA 94108
Nationwide (W www.counciltravel.com)

Anyone aged under 26 can get a GO25 card or a Euro<26 card. Both give similar discounts to the ISIC and are issued by most of the same organisations. The Euro<26 is known as the Under 26 Card in England and Wales, and the Carnet Joven Europeo in Spain (or Carnet Jove in Catalunya).

As an example of the sorts of discounts you can expect in Spain, the better things on offer for Euro<26 card-holders include 20% or 25% off most 2nd-class train fares; 10% or 20% off many Trasmediterránea ferries and some bus fares; good discounts at some museums; and discounts of up to 20% at some youth hostels.

In Spain, the Euro<26 is issued by various youth organisations, including Barcelona's Turisme Juvenil de Catalunya office (see Hostel Cards earlier).

Copies

All of your important documents (passport data page and visa pages, credit cards, travellers cheque numbers, travel insurance policy, air/bus/train tickets, driving licence etc) should be photocopied before you leave home. Leave one copy with someone at home and keep another with you, separate from the originals.

There is another option for storing details of your vital travel documents before you leave – Lonely Planet's online Travel Vault. Storing details of your important documents in the vault is safer than carrying photocopies. It's the best option if you travel in a country with easy Internet access. Your password-protected Travel Vault is accessible online at any time. You can create your own Travel Vault for free at W www.ekno .lonelyplanet.com.

EMBASSIES & CONSULATES
Your Own Embassy

Embassies can generally do little for their citizens if they get themselves into trouble with the law. They can assist with replacement passports and perhaps with arranging an English-speaking lawyer if need be.

Spanish Embassies & Consulates

The following is a list of selected Spanish embassies and consulates in countries throughout the world:

Andorra (☎ 80 00 34; e embespad@ correo.mae.es) Carrer Prat de la Creu 34, Andorra la Vella
Australia (☎ 02-6273 3555; e embespau@ mail.mae.es) 15 Arkana St, Yarralumla, Canberra, ACT 2600
    Consulates: Melbourne (☎ 03-9347 1966) and Sydney (☎ 02-9261 2433)
Canada (☎ 613-747 2252; e spain@ docuweb.ca) 74 Stanley Ave, Ottawa, Ontario K1M 1P4
    Consulates: Toronto (☎ 416-977 1661) and Montreal (☎ 514-935 5235)
France (☎ 01 44 43 18 00; e ambespfr@ mail.mae.es) 22 Av Marceau, 75381 Paris, Cedex 08
Germany (☎ 030-254 0070; e embespde@ mail.mae.es) Schoenberger Ufer 89, 10785 Berlin
    Consulates: Düsseldorf (☎ 0211-43 90 80), Frankfurt am Main (☎ 069-959 16 60) and Munich (☎ 089-998 47 90)
Ireland (☎ 01-269 1640) 17A Merlyn Park, Ballsbridge, Dublin 4
Japan (☎ 03-3583 8533; e embesjp@ mail.mae.es) 1-3-29 Roppongi Minato-Ku, Tokyo 106
Morocco (☎ 07-26 80 00; e ambespma@ mail.mae.es) 3 Zankat Madnine, Rabat
    Consulates: Rabat (☎ 07-70 41 47), Casablanca (☎ 02-22 07 52) and Tangier (☎ 09-93 70 00)
Netherlands (☎ 070-302 49 99; e ambespnl@ mail.mae.es) Lange Voorhout 50, 2514 EG The Hague
New Zealand (The closest embassy is in Australia)
Portugal (☎ 01-347 2381; e embesppt@ mail.mae.es) Rua do Salitre 1, 1250 Lisbon
UK (☎ 020-7235 5555; e embesuk@mail .mae.es) 39 Chesham Place, London SW1X 8SB
    Consulates: London (☎ 020-7589 8989) 20 Draycott Place, London SW3 2RZ; Manchester

(☎ 0161-236 1262); and Edinburgh (☎ 0131-220 1843)

USA (☎ 202-728 2332) 2375 Pennsylvania Ave NW, Washington, DC 20037
Consulates: Boston (☎ 617-536 2506), Chicago (☎ 312-782 4588), Houston (☎ 713-783 6200), Los Angeles (☎ 213-938 0158), Miami (☎ 305-446 5511), New Orleans (☎ 504-525 4951), New York (☎ 212-355 4080) and San Francisco (☎ 415-922 2995)

Consulates in Barcelona

Most countries have diplomatic representation in Spain, but all the embassies are in the capital, Madrid. Consulates in Barcelona, including the following, are generally open 9am or 10am to 1pm or 2pm Monday to Friday. You can find them listed in the phone book under Consulat/Consulado.

Australia (Map 3; ☎ 93 490 90 13) 9th floor, Gran Via de Carles III 98
Belgium (Map 2; ☎ 93 467 70 80) Carrer de la Diputació 303
Canada (Map 1; ☎ 93 204 27 00) Carrer d'Elisenda de Pinos 10
Denmark (Map 4; ☎ 93 488 02 22) Rambla de Catalunya 33
France (Map 5; ☎ 93 270 30 00) Ronda de l'Universitat 22B 4rt
Germany (Map 2; ☎ 93 292 10 00) Passeig de Gràcia 111
Italy (Map 2; ☎ 93 467 73 05) Carrer de Mallorca 270
Japan (Map 3; ☎ 93 280 34 33) Avinguda Diagonal 662-664
Netherlands (Map 3; ☎ 93 410 62 10) Avinguda Diagonal 601
Sweden (Map 2; ☎ 93 488 25 01) Carrer de Mallorca 279
Switzerland (Map 3; ☎ 93 409 06 50) Gran Via de Carles III 94
UK (Map 3; ☎ 93 366 62 00) Avinguda Diagonal 477
USA (Map 1; ☎ 93 280 02 95) Passeig de la Reina Elisenda de Montcada 23-25

Embassies in Madrid

Embassies (*embajadas* in the phone book) in Madrid include:

Australia (☎ 91 441 60 25) Plaza del Descubridor Diego de Ordás 3-2, Edificio Santa Engrácia 120

Canada (☎ 91 423 32 50; W www.Canada-es.org) Calle de Núñez de Balboa 35
France (☎ 91 423 89 00) Salustiano Olózaga 9
Germany (☎ 91 557 90 00; W www.embajada-alemania.es) Calle de Fortuny 8
Ireland (☎ 91 436 40 95) Paseo de la Castellana 46
Morocco (☎ 91 563 10 90) Calle de Serrano 179
Consulate: (☎ 91 561 21 45) Calle de Leizaran 31
Netherlands (☎ 91 353 75 00) Avenida del Comandante Franco 32
New Zealand (☎ 91 523 02 26 or ☎ 91 531 09 97) Plaza de la Lealtad 2
Portugal (☎ 91 782 49 60) Calle del Pinar 1
Consulate: (☎ 91 577 35 38) Calle Lagasca 88
UK (☎ 91 700 82 72) Calle de Fernando el Santo 16
Consulate: (☎ 91 308 53 00) Calle del Marqués Ensenada 16
USA (☎ 91 587 22 00; W www.embusa.es) Calle de Serrano 75

CUSTOMS

People entering Spain from outside the EU are allowed to bring in duty-free one bottle of spirits, one bottle of wine, 200 cigarettes and 50mL of perfume.

Duty-free allowances for travel between EU countries were abolished in 1999. For *duty-paid* items bought at normal shops in one EU country and taken into another, the allowances are 90L of wine, 10L of spirits, unlimited quantities of perfume and 800 cigarettes. VAT-free shopping *is* available in the duty-free shops at airports for people travelling between EU countries.

MONEY

A combination of travellers cheques and credit or debit cards is the best way to carry your money.

Currency

On 1 January 2002, the euro (€) unseated the peseta and became the new currency of Spain as well as 11 other EU nations (Austria, Belgium, Finland, France, Germany, Greece, Ireland, Italy, Luxembourg, the Netherlands and Portugal).

The seven euro notes come in denominations of €500, €200, €100, €50, €20, €10 and €5, in different colours and sizes.

FACTS FOR THE VISITOR

The eight euro coins are in denominations of €2 and €1, then 50, 20, 10, five, two and one cents.

On the reverse side of the coins each participating state decorates the coins with its own designs, but all euro coins can be used anywhere that accepts euros.

Exchange Rates

country	unit		euros
Australia	A$1	=	(0.56
Canada	C$1	=	(0.66
Japan	¥100	=	(0.86
New Zealand	NZ$1	=	(0.49
Switzerland	Sfr1	=	(0.68
UK	UK£1	=	(1.57
USA	US$1	=	(1.01

Exchanging Money

You can change cash or travellers cheques at virtually any bank or exchange bureau, at bus and train stations and at the airport. The main-road border crossings also usually have exchange facilities. Banks tend to offer the best rates, with minor differences between them. Many banks have ATMs (automated teller machines), known as *(caixers automàtic/cajero automático)* in Catalan/Spanish.

Barcelona is crawling with banks, including several around Plaça de Catalunya and more on La Rambla.

Exchange bureaus (you'll see many along La Rambla and elsewhere in central Barcelona), usually indicated by the word *canvi/cambio* (exchange), generally offer longer opening hours and quicker service than banks, but often offer poorer exchange rates. American Express (AmEx) can be reliable, but in any case you should always shop around.

Travellers cheques usually get a better exchange rate than cash but often attract higher commissions than cash exchange.

Wherever you change money, ask about commissions first and confirm that the exchange rates are as posted. Commissions vary from bank to bank, may be different for travellers cheques and cash, and may depend on how many cheques, or how much in total, you're cashing. A typical commission

is 2.5% to 3%, with a minimum of €2 to €4. Places that advertise 'no commission' may offer poor exchange rates to start with.

American Express has an office *(Map 2; ☎ 93 415 23 71 or 93 217 00 70; Passeig de Gràcia 101, entrance on Carrer del Rosselló; open 9.30am-6pm Mon-Fri, 10am-1.30pm Sat)* and a **branch** *(Map 6; ☎ 93 301 11 66; La Rambla dels Caputxins 74; open 9am-midnight daily Apr-Sept, 9am-2pm & 3pm-8.30pm Mon-Fri, 10am-7pm Sat Oct-Mar)* that has a machine giving cash on AmEx cards.

Cash Don't bring wads of cash – travellers cheques and plastic are safer. If you wander around with pounds and dollars in your pockets you are inviting rubber fingers to make you instantly poor. It is, however, an idea to keep an emergency stash separate from other valuables in case you lose your travellers cheques and credit cards.

You will need euros in cash for many day-to-day transactions (many small pensiones, eateries and shops take cash only). Try not to carry around more than you need at any one time, though.

Travellers Cheques Most banks and exchange bureaus will cash travellers cheques. Keep in mind that travellers cheques can be replaced if lost (unlike cash). AmEx and Thomas Cook are widely accepted brands. For AmEx travellers-cheque refunds you can call ☎ 900 99 44 26 from anywhere within Spain.

It doesn't really matter whether your cheques are in euros or in the currency of the country you buy them in – Spanish exchange outlets will change most nonobscure currencies. Get most of your cheques in large denominations (say, the equivalent of €100) to reduce the number of per-cheque commission charges you pay.

It's vital to keep your initial receipt, and a record of your cheque numbers and the ones you have used, separate from the cheques themselves. You will need ID (such as your passport) when cashing travellers cheques.

Credit/Debit Cards You can use plastic to pay for many purchases (including meals and rooms at many establishments, especially from the mid-price range up, and long-distance trains), and you can use it to withdraw cash pesetas from banks and ATMs. Among the most widely useable cards are Visa, MasterCard, AmEx, Cirrus, Eurocard, Plus, Diners Club and JCB.

On the exchange-rate front you also generally get a better deal than with cash and cheques, even taking into account any charges levied on foreign transactions and cash advances (usually around 1.5%, but sometimes minimum charges for each withdrawal apply).

A high proportion of Spanish banks, even in small towns and villages, have an ATM that will dispense cash euros at any time (and no queues!) if you have the right piece of plastic. Some stop accepting foreign cards at midnight.

Check with your card's issuer before leaving home on how widely useable your card will be, on how to report and replace a lost card, on withdrawal/spending limits, and on whether your personal identification number (PIN) will be acceptable (some European ATMs don't accept PINs of more than four digits).

Always report a lost card straight away. Call these numbers: **AmEx** (☎ 902 37 56 37); **Visa** (☎ 900 97 44 45); **MasterCard/ Eurocard** (☎ 900 97 12 31); and **Diners Club** (☎ 91 547 74 00).

TravelMoney Visa TravelMoney comes in the form of a prepaid disposable credit card that you buy from selected banks or travel agencies for amounts from UK£100 to UK£5000. It works for ATMs wherever the Visa sign is displayed. Enquire at **Thomas Cook** (in the UK ☎ 01733-318900) or call Visa before you travel. Ask about charges and commissions made on withdrawals.

International Transfers To have money transferred from another country, you need to organise someone to send it to you (through a bank where they are or a money-transfer service such as Western Union or MoneyGram) and a bank (or Western Union or MoneyGram office) in Barcelona at which to collect it. If there's money in your bank account back home, you may be able to instruct the bank yourself.

For information on **Western Union** services and branches, call ☎ 900 63 36 33 free from anywhere in Spain. **MoneyGram** (☎ 900 20 10 10) is represented by AmEx and several other exchange outlets.

A bank-to-bank telegraphic transfer typically involves costs at either end, which depend largely on the individual banks. Fees of around €25 are not uncommon in Spanish banks for receiving money. Western Union and MoneyGram can supposedly hand money over to the recipient within 10 minutes of it being sent. The sender pays a fee in proportion to the amount sent. It's also possible to have money sent through AmEx.

Security

Keep only a limited amount of cash, with the bulk of your money in more easily replaceable forms such as travellers cheques or plastic. If your accommodation has a safe, use it. If you have to leave money in your room, divide it into several stashes and hide them in different places.

For carrying money on the street the safest thing is a shoulder wallet or under-the-clothes money belt. External money belts and 'bum bags' are like shining beacons. You may as well wear a neon sign saying 'Pick me: I'm a tourist'.

Costs

As Spain's second city, Barcelona is expensive by local standards, but northern Europeans generally find costs to be reasonable. Travellers from beyond the EU (such as the USA and Australia) tend to find anywhere in Europe pricey. Costs of accommodation, eating out and transport are lower than in Britain or France. If you are frugal, it's possible to scrape by on €30 to €40 a day. This would involve staying in the cheapest possible accommodation, not eating in restaurants or going to museums or bars, and not moving around too much.

A more comfortable budget would be €80 a day. This could allow you around €40 for accommodation; €3 for breakfast (coffee, juice and a pastry); €7 to €12 for a set lunch; €1.90 for public transport (two metro or bus rides); €10 a day for museums; and €15 to €18 for a simple dinner, with a bit over for a drink or two.

With €200 a day you can stay in good mid-range accommodation, splurge in Barcelona's better restaurants and even hire a car for a few days' touring outside town.

Ways to Save Two people can travel more cheaply (per person) than one by sharing rooms. You'll also save money by avoiding the peak tourist seasons (Christmas–New Year, Easter and June to September), when room prices can go up. A student or youth card, or a document such as a passport proving you're aged over 60 (or 65 in some cases), brings worthwhile savings on some travel costs and admission to some museums and sights (see Visas & Documents earlier in this chapter). Some museums and sights have free days now and then, and a few are cheaper for EU passport-holders.

Prolific letter-writers can save a few cents on mail to destinations outside Europe by sending aerograms instead of standard letters (under 20g) or postcards.

Tipping & Bargaining

In restaurants, the law requires that menu prices include service charges, so tipping is a matter of personal choice – most people leave some small change if they're satisfied and 5% is usually plenty. It's common to leave small change at bar and café tables. Hotel porters will generally be happy with €1.

In pensiones and hotels it can be worth asking about discounts for prolonged stays.

Taxes & Refunds

IVA ('ee-ba', Impuesto sobre el Valor Añadido) is the Spanish value-added tax (VAT). On accommodation and restaurant prices, IVA is 7% and is usually – but not always – included in quoted prices. On retail goods IVA is 16%. On vehicle hire it seems to fluctuate between 7% and 16%. To check whether a price includes IVA ask *'¿Está incluido el IVA?'* ('Is IVA included?').

Visitors are entitled to a refund of the 16% IVA on individual purchases costing more than €90.15, from any shop, if they take the goods out of the EU within three months. Ask the shop for a Cashback refund form showing the price and IVA paid for each item and identifying the vendor and purchaser. Then present the form at the customs booth for IVA refunds when you depart from Spain (or elsewhere from the EU). You will need your passport and a boarding card that shows you are leaving the EU. The officer will stamp the invoice and you hand it in at a bank at the departure point for the reimbursement.

At Barcelona airport, look for La Caixa bank in Terminal A, which hosts the Cashback refund desk. Otherwise you can use the envelope provided to have the tax paid back to your credit card or by cheque.

POST & COMMUNICATIONS
Post

Stamps are sold at most *estancos* (tobacconist shops with 'Tabacs/Tabacos' in yellow letters on a maroon background), as well as at Correus i Telègrafs/Correos y Telégrafos (post offices).

The **main post office** (Map 6; ☎ 902 19 71 97; Plaça d'Antoni López; open 8am-9.30pm Mon-Sat for stamp sales, poste restante at windows No 7 & 8) is opposite the northeastern end of Port Vell.

The post office also has a public fax service, as do many shops and offices around the city.

Another handy **post office** (Map 2; ☎ 93 216 04 53; Carrer d'Aragó 282; open 8.30am-8.30pm Mon-Fri, 9.30am-1pm Sat) lies just off Passeig de Gràcia. Other district offices tend to open 8am to 2pm Monday to Friday only.

Rates Sending a postcard or letter weighing up to 20g costs €0.25 within Spain, €0.50 to other European countries and €0.75 to the rest of the world. Three A4 sheets in an air-mail envelope weigh between 15g and 20g. You can speed up delivery by sending mail *urgente*, which costs €1.80/2.25/2.50. An aerogram costs €0.50 to any country in the world.

Getting Addressed

Just because you have an address in your hot sweaty palm doesn't mean you will have no trouble finding what you are after. If the pension you are looking for is at C/ de Montcada 23, 3°D Int, just off Av Marqués, you could be forgiven for scratching your head a little. Abbreviations contain a lot of information, and in Barcelona things are made worse by the fact that some people may give you the Catalan version of an address while others may give you the Castilian version. Here are some common abbreviations:

Av or Avda	Avinguda/Avenida
Bda	Baixada/Bajada
C/	Carrer/Calle
Cí or C°	Camí/Camino
Ctra, Ca or Cª	Carretera
Cró/Cjón	Carreró/Callejón
Gta	Glorieta (major roundabout)
Pg or P°	Passeig/Paseo
Ptge/Pje	Passatge/Pasaje
Plc/Plz	Placeta/Plazuela
Pl, Pza or Pª	Plaça/Plaza
Pt or Pte	Pont/Puente
Rbla	Rambla
Rda	Ronda
s/n	sense numeració/ sín número (without number)
Tr or Trav	Travessera
Trv	Travessia/Travesía
Urb	Urbanització/Urbanización

MW

The following are used where there are several flats, hostales, offices etc in one building. They're often used in conjunction, eg 2°C or 3°I Int:

Ent	Entresuelo (ground floor)
Pr	Principal (what Brits & Company would consider the 1st floor)
1°	1st floor (2nd floor to Brits & Co)
2°	2nd floor (3rd floor to Brits & Co)
C	centre/centro (middle)
D	dreta/derecha (right-hand side)
Esq, I or Izq	esquerra/izquierda (left-hand side)
Int	interior (a flat or office too far inside the building to look onto any street – usually has windows onto an interior patio or shaft – the opposite is Ext, exterior)

If someone's address is Apartado de Correos 206 (which can be shortened to Apdo de Correos 206 or even Apdo 206), don't bother tramping the streets in search of it – it is a post office box.

Street names often get short shrift too. Carrer de Madrid (literally 'Street of Madrid') will often appear simply as Carrer Madrid. In spoken exchanges the word Carrer is often dropped. Thus Carrer del Comte d'Urgell will be referred to simply as Comte d'Urgell.

Certificado (registered mail) costs €2.10 within Spain and €2.60/2.85 to Europe/rest of the world (for a normal letter up to 20g). To get registered mail delivered fast you pay €3/3.80/4.05, respectively.

A day or two quicker than the *urgente* service – but a lot more expensive – is Postal Exprés, sometimes called Express Mail Service (EMS). This uses courier companies for international deliveries. Packages weighing up to 1kg cost €28.80 to €34.40 to send to destinations in Europe, €46.90 to North America and €56.30 to Australia or New Zealand.

Sending Mail It's quite safe to post your mail in the yellow street postboxes *(bústies/buzones)* as well as at post offices. Ordinary mail to other Western European countries normally takes up to a week; to North America up to 10 days; and to Australia or New Zealand up to two weeks.

Receiving Mail Delivery times are similar to those for sending mail. Using the Spanish five-digit postcode (which goes *before* the name of the city) will help speed up the process.

Poste restante mail can be addressed to you at *lista de correos*. It will be delivered to the main post office unless another one is specified. Take your passport when you go to pick up mail. A letter addressed to poste restante in central Barcelona should look like this:

Jenny JONES
Lista de Correos
08080 Barcelona
Spain

AmEx or travellers-cheque holders can use the free client mail-holding service at its main office in Barcelona (see Money earlier in this chapter).

Couriers Most international courier services have representatives in Barcelona, including **United Parcel Service** *(UPS;* ☎ *900 10 24 10)* and **DHL** *(*☎ *902 12 24 24)*. Just call them to pick up or deliver.

Telephone
The ubiquitous blue pay phones are easy to use for international and domestic calls. They accept coins, phonecards *(tarjetas telefónicas)* issued by the national phone company Telefónica and, in some cases, various credit cards. Tarjetas telefónicas come in €6 and €12.02 denominations (the latter includes €0.60 free in extra credit) and, like postage stamps, are sold at post offices and tobacconists.

Public phones inside bars and cafés, and phones in hotel rooms, are nearly always a good deal more expensive than street pay phones.

There are **telephone** and **fax** offices *(open 8am-10pm Mon-Sat)* at Estació Sants (Map 4) and there are also offices at Estació del Nord (Map 1).

Costs As elsewhere in Europe, the cost of making a phone call is slowly falling in Spain. Within Spain you can make three types of call: *metropolitana* (local), *provincial* (a call within the same province) and *interprovincial* (national). Note that calls from pay phones cost about 35% more than calls from private phones.

The cost of a call within Spain also depends on when you make it. Two call bands operate; *normal* is the dearest and runs from 8am to 8pm (to 6pm for local calls) Monday to Friday. The rest of the time is *reducida* rate, the cheapest band.

A three-minute pay-phone call in the higher band costs about €0.09 within your local area, €0.16 to other places within the same province, and €0.28 to other provinces in Spain.

Although the two bands supposedly operate for international calls too, the national phone company has levelled call costs so that it makes no difference what time you call. A three-minute pay-phone call to Australia will cost €3.81. To the USA and EU countries you pay €0.73.

Calls to Spanish numbers starting with 900 are free. Calls to other special numbers starting with 901 to 906 vary. A common one is 902, which costs €0.08 a minute from a private phone. Calls to mobile phones –

telephone numbers starting with 6 – range from €0.13 to €0.26 a minute, depending on the mobile phone company and the time of day.

Cut-Price Phone Calls If you're arriving from the USA or the UK, you are probably already acquainted with the idea of buying cut-price phonecards. You buy the card, dial a toll-free number and then follow the instructions – it can bring savings on international calls if you are calling from a pay phone. Compare rates (where possible before buying).

Call centres *(locutorios)* are another option. Some are *not* a good deal, so check rates. The one on the corner of Carrer de la Riera Alta and Carrer de la Lluna is good (Map 6).

Mobile Phones

Spain uses GSM 900/1800, compatible with the rest of Europe and Australia but not with the North American GSM 1900 or the totally different system in Japan (although some North Americans have GSM 1900/900 phones that do work here). If you have a GSM phone, check with your service provider about using it in Spain, and beware of calls being routed internationally (very expensive for a 'local' call).

You can organise to rent a mobile phone by calling the Madrid-based **Cellphone Rental** (☎ 91 547 85 75 or 656-26 68 44; **w** *www .onspanishtime.com/web*). It will send it to your hotel and provide you with a postal bag to send it back when you're done. The basic service costs US$30 a week for the phone plus postal costs (except in Madrid). You pay a US$200 deposit to discourage scarpering with the phone. The whole operation is done on the Web.

You may be just as well off buying one, though. You can get phones that operate with prepaid cards from about €60. You may also be able to buy a SIM card to insert into your own mobile phone.

Domestic Calls All phone numbers have nine digits, including the area code (which must always be dialled). Dial ☎ 1009 to speak to a domestic operator, including for a domestic reverse-charge (collect) call *(una llamada por cobro revertido)*. To call directory enquiries dial ☎ 1003.

International Calls The access code for international calls from Spain is ☎ 00. To make an international call dial the access code, wait for a new dialling tone, then dial the country code, area code and the number you want.

Making international collect calls are simple: dial ☎ 900 followed by a code for the country you're calling. The following is a selection:

Australia	(☎ 99 00 61)
Belgium	(☎ 99 00 32)
Canada	(☎ 99 00 15)
Denmark	(☎ 99 00 45)
France	(☎ 99 00 33)
Germany	(☎ 99 00 49)
Ireland	(☎ 99 03 53)
Israel	(☎ 99 09 72)
Italy	(☎ 99 03 91)
Japan	(☎ 98 09 81, 98 08 11 or 98 08 12)
Netherlands	(☎ 99 00 31)
New Zealand	(☎ 99 00 64)
Portugal	(☎ 99 03 51)
UK	(☎ 99 00 44 for BT, 99 09 44 for Cable & Wireless)
USA	(☎ 99 00 11 for AT&T, 99 00 13 for Sprint, 99 00 14 for MCI, 99 00 17 for Worldcom)

The numbers will get you straight through to an operator in the country you're calling. The same numbers can be used with direct-dial calling cards.

If for some reason the above information doesn't work for you, in most places you can get an English-speaking Spanish international operator on ☎ 1008 (for calls within Europe) or ☎ 1005 (for the rest of the world).

For international directory enquiries you can dial ☎ 025.

Calling Barcelona from Abroad Spain's country code is ☎ 34. Follow this with the full nine-digit number you are calling.

ekno Communication Service

Lonely Planet's ekno global communication service provides low-cost international calls – for local calls you're usually better off with a local phonecard. ekno also offers free messaging services, email, travel information and an online travel vault, where you can securely store all your important documents. You can join online at W www .ekno.lonelyplanet.com.

Fax

Most main post offices have a fax service, and in the bigger cities there is no shortage of private fax services: sending one page costs about €1.50 within Spain, €2.70 to elsewhere in Europe and €3.70 to the USA. Subsequent pages can cost €0.60/1.20/ 2.40, respectively.

Email & Internet Access

You can keep in touch by email if you travel with a portable computer but most people elect to use cybercafés and similar Internet centres to log in to either their providers or one of several international free services.

Another option is to open a free Web-based email account such as **HotMail** (W *www.hotmail.com*) or **Yahoo! Mail** (W *www. mail.yahoo.com*). You can then access your mail from anywhere in the world at any Net-connected machine running a standard Web browser. Also see the ekno Communication Service earlier.

Have you brought your portable computer along? It's malfunctioning? You can find several ads for English-speaking computer technicians in the free English-language magazine, *Barcelona Metropolitan*, or *Business Barcelona* – see the Newspapers & Magazines section later in this chapter.

Cybercafés Dozens of places, ranging from cafés to computer stores, offer Internet access in Barcelona. Some options include

Bcnet (Map 6; ☎ 93 268 15 07; W www .bcnetcafe.com) Carrer de Barra de Ferro 3. This

is a laid-back little café with a sprinkling of terminals. It opens from 10am to 1am daily. An hour online costs €3.60 or you can buy a coupon for €18 (10 hours).

Café Insòlit (Map 5; ☎ 93 225 81 78) Maremàgnum shopping complex. It's open 1pm to 1am daily and going online here costs €3.60 an hour.

Café Interlight (Map 2; ☎ 93 301 11 80) Carrer de Pau Claris 106. This cybercafé opens from 8am to 11pm Monday to Friday and 2pm to midnight on weekends. It charges €2 an hour (€1 for students) or you can take out a card for 10 hours for €18.

Conéctate (Map 2; ☎ 93 467 04 43) Carrer d'Aragò 283. This is a similar place, open 24 hours and providing net time for as little as €1.20 an hour (it depends on usage at any given time).

Cybermundo (Map 5; ☎ 93 317 71 42) Carrer Bergara 3. It opens 9am to midnight daily. You pay €2.40 an hour basic rate. Or you can become a lifetime member for €6 and pay as little as €0.90 an hour. Students also pay €0.90 before 5pm. It has an international phone service and café, and another branch around the corner at Carrer de Balmes 8.

easyEverything (Map 5; ☎ 93 412 13 97) Ronda de l'Universitat 35. Open 24 hours and with 300 terminals and café, this is an Internet temple. €1 gets you about half an hour (it depends on demand). Or you can pay €5/7/12 for unlimited access for a day/week/month. There is another branch (Map 6; ☎ 93 318 24 35) at La Rambla 31.

Inetcorner (Map 2; ☎ 93 244 80 80; W www .inetcorner.net) Carrer de Sardenya 306. Just down the road from La Sagrada Família, this place opens from 10am to 10pm Monday to Saturday and noon to 8pm Sunday.

INTERNET RESOURCES

Scouring the Net for a few hours can lead you to some interesting tips about most aspects of the city, including practical information such as event listings. You could start a search at the **Lonely Planet** website (W *www.lonelyplanet.com*). Many of the sites are multilingual (eg, Castilian, English and French). Some sites to surf include:

Ajuntament This general website offers a wide variety of information on the city's many services and events.
  W www.bcn.es
All About Spain It's a varied site with information on everything from fiestas to hotels and a

yellow-pages guide to tour operators around the world that do trips in Spain.
W www.red2000.com

Autoritat de Transport Metropolità For everything you wanted to know, and probably plenty you didn't, on Barcelona's integrated public transport system, try this site.
W www.atm-transmet.es

Barcelona.de It's a German-language (also in English, Spanish and Catalan) information site on Barcelona, which also has a forum for message exchange.
W barcelona.de

Barcelona Hoy This is one of the better sites (Spanish only). It is comprehensive and gives broad listings, general news, links to white- and yellow-pages sites and more.
W www.barcelonahoy.com

Cities.Com Search for Barcelona on this site and it takes you to a list of other potentially interesting sites, some of which appear in this list.
W www.cities.com

Generalitat de Catalunya The Generalitat's website contains some curious pages dealing with various aspects of Catalunya's history and its culture.
W www.gencat.es

Renfe You can check out timetables, tickets and special offers on Spain's national rail network.
W www.renfe.es

Spanien.Com It is another German-language site, this time run by the big Spanish portal Ya.Com. Click on the Barcelona 'cityguide' for general information and listings.
W www.spanien.com

Turespaña This is the Spanish tourist office's official site, with lots of general information about the country and some interesting links.
W www.tourspain.es

Turisme de Barcelona Here you'll find information on sights, eateries and other aspects of interest in Barcelona, along with up-to-date details on what's on in the city. You can send an email requesting information from the site.
W www.barcelonaturisme.com

Viapolis.Com Pick a city (in this case Barcelona) on this Spanish site and you will end up in a busy listings site.
W www.viapolis.com

BOOKS

Most books are published in different editions by different publishers in different countries. As a result, a particular book might be a hard-cover rarity in one country and readily available in paperback in

another. Fortunately, bookshops and libraries search by title or author, so your local bookshop or library is the best placed to advise you on the availability of the following recommendations.

Bookshops Abroad

In London several good bookshops specialise in the business of travel. For guidebooks and maps, **Stanfords bookshop** (☎ 020-7240 3611; 12-14 Long Acre, London WC2E 9LH) is acknowledged as one of the better first ports of call. A well-stocked source of travel literature is **Daunt Books for Travellers** (☎ 020-7224 2295; 83 Marylebone High St, London W1U 4QW). For books in Spanish, one of the best options is **Grant & Cutler** (☎ 020-7734 2012; 55-57 Great Marlborough St, London W1V 7AY).

Still in the UK, **Books on Spain** (☎ 020-8898 7789, fax 8898 8812; **W** www.books-on-spain.com; PO Box 207, Twickenham TW2 5BQ) can send you mail-order catalogues of hundreds of titles on Spain.

In the USA, try **Book Passage** (☎ 415-927 0960; 51 Tamal Vista Blvd, Corte Madera, California) and **The Complete Traveler Bookstore** (☎ 212-685 9007; 199 Madison Ave, New York). For those in Australia, **Travel Bookshop** (☎ 02-9261 8200; 3/175 Liverpool St, Sydney) is worth a browse. In France, **L'Astrolabe rive gauche** (☎ 01 46 33 80 06; 14 Rue Serpente, Paris) is recommended.

Lonely Planet

If you're planning to travel extensively from Barcelona, check out Lonely Planet's companion titles, including *Catalunya & the Costa Brava*, *Spain*, *Walking in Spain*, *Andalucía*, *Madrid* and *France*. *World Food Spain* is a trip into Spain's culinary soul, while the *Spanish phrasebook* will enable you to fill some of the gaps between ¡hola! and ¡adiós!.

Guidebooks

An interesting walking guide to the city is *Dotze Passejades per la Història de Barcelona* (12 Strolls Through Barcelona's History), published by the Fundació de la Caixa. The only extant versions seem to be in Catalan but, as two of its co-authors were Anglos, you might get lucky and strike an English-language version kicking around.

A still more comprehensive street-by-street guide to the city is *50 Vegades Barcelona* (50 Times Barcelona), published by the Ajuntament.

History & People

Homage to Barcelona by Colm Tóibín (1990) is an excellent personal introduction to the city's modern life and artistic and political history, by an Irish journalist who has lived there.

Homage to Catalonia, on the other hand, is George Orwell's account of the 1936–39 civil war in Catalunya, moving from the euphoria of the early days in Barcelona to disillusionment with the disastrous infighting on the Republican side. If you want a good general history of the war, get *The Spanish Civil War* by Hugh Thomas.

The Usatges of Barcelona, translated by Donald J Kagay, is the Catalan equivalent of the Magna Carta. The document, as well as Kagay's commentary on it, gives the reader a fascinating insight into the historical backdrop for Catalunya's separateness from the rest of Spain.

A guidebook with a difference leads you on strolls around Barcelona while recounting the histories and stories of its women. Called *Guía de Dones de Barcelona*, it is by Isabel Segura and is also available in Castilian. An unevenly translated but accessible history of the city is Joan Castellar-Gossol's *Barcelona – A History*.

Arts & Architecture

It is no easy task to categorise Robert Hughes' *Barcelona*, a witty and passionate study of the art and architecture of the city through history. It is neither flouncing artistic criticism nor dry history, rather a distillation of the life of the city and people and an assessment of its expression.

A useful building-by-building account of architecture in the city is *Passejant per Barcelona – Art i Espais Urbans* (Strolling Around Barcelona – Art and Urban Spaces) by Núria Casas & Lourdes Mateo. If your Spanish is good you shouldn't have too much trouble deciphering at least some of the Catalan.

If you prefer English, *Barcelona Architecture Guide* by Antoni González Moreno-Navarro & Raquel Lacuesta Contreras, adopts a more technical approach to the same subject, but only covers the years 1929 to 1996. The same authors have also put out the *Guía de Arquitectura Modernista de Cataluña*.

Xavier Güell's *Gaudí Guide* (available in several languages) is poor in text but rich in black and white photography. In the handy Thames & Hudson series on artistic movements, *Romanesque Art* by Meyer Schapiro covers the pre-Gothic era that so sharply marked early Catalan architecture.

Cuisine

Several books have been published locally on Catalan cuisine. If you really want to test yourself you could try *Cuina Catalana* by Pere Sans – in Catalan. If English is more your thing, take a look at *Catalan Cuisine* by Colman Andrews.

General

If you can, grab a copy of Eduardo Mendoza's *La Ciudad de los Prodigios* (City of Marvels), a novel set in Barcelona between the Universal Exhibition of 1888 and the World Exhibition of 1929.

To put things in context, you may want to read a little more widely about Spain. The two best overall introductions to modern Spain are *The New Spaniards* by John Hooper, a former Madrid correspondent for the *Guardian*, and the more controversial and personal *Fire in the Blood* by Ian Gibson, based on a British TV series. Gibson has also written a weighty biography of Salvador Dalí.

FILM

The city hasn't been the focus of foreign cinematic interest all that often. One relatively recent exception was Whit Stillman's *Barcelona* (1994), which follows the loves and trials of two American cousins in post-Franco Barcelona.

Back in 1978 the French director Jacques Deray set his *Un Papillon sur l'Epaule*, a mystery thriller, partly in Barcelona.

In Susan Seidelman's *Gaudí Afternoon* (2000), Gaudí is present through his works alone. Judy Davis plays the part of Cassandra, a translator living rather poorly in Barcelona and helping a friend to look for her husband, who has left her.

One of the best films set in Barcelona is Pedro Almodóvar's Golden Globe award–winning 1999 hit, *Todo Sobre Mi Madre* (All About My Mother). In 2002, Fernando Trueba's *El Embrujo de Shanghai*, set in Barcelona's Gràcia district and based on the novel by Juan Marsé, was another local hit filmed on location.

NEWSPAPERS & MAGAZINES
You can find a wide selection of national daily newspapers from around Europe at newsstands all over central Barcelona and especially along La Rambla. The *International Herald Tribune*, *Time*, *The Economist*, *Le Monde*, *Der Spiegel* and other international magazines are also available.

Spanish National Press
The main Spanish dailies can be identified along roughly political lines, with the old-fashioned paper *ABC* representing the conservative right, *El País* identified with the PSOE (Spain's centre-left socialist party) and *El Mundo* being a more radicalised left-wing paper that prides itself on breaking political scandals. For a good spread of national and international news, *El País* is the pick. One of the best-selling dailies is *Marca*, devoted exclusively to sport.

Local Press
El País includes a daily supplement devoted to Catalunya, but Barcelona is home to a lively home-grown press too. *La Vanguardia* and *El Periódico* are the main local Castilian-language dailies. The latter also publishes an award-winning Catalan version. The more Catalan nationalist–oriented daily is *Avui*.

A free morning daily most likely to be found in many metro stations is *20 Minutos*

en Barcelona. A similar competitor that you can pick up is *Metro*.

Useful Publications
Barcelona's entertainment bible is the weekly Castilian-language magazine *Guía del Ocio* (€0.90), which comes out on Thursday and lists almost everything that's on in the way of music, film, exhibitions, theatre and more. You can pick it up at the newsstands.

The free monthly English-language *Barcelona Metropolitan* is a handy magazine with articles on the local scene and classifieds that will lead you to English-speaking doctors, dentists, baby-sitters and other useful information. It's aimed at long-term residents. You can pick it up at various bars and cafés (including Cafè de l'Òpera; Map 6), restaurants and shops (such as Come In bookshop; Map 2). Once you have a copy, keep the page at the back, which has a list of places where you can find next month's magazine.

Business Barcelona (€2), a monthly English-language business paper, is often full of insightful articles on the commercial life of the city, and more besides. It is on sale at the Come In bookshop. Other free rags you may see include the free monthly *Urban Rambler*, which covers local stories and minor listings, and the free weekly *Sports Matter*.

RADIO
You can pick up **BBC World Service** (**w** *www.bbc.co.uk*) broadcasts on a variety of frequencies. Broadcasts are directed at Western Europe on, among others, 6195 kHz, 9410 kHz and also 15,485 kHz (for short wave).

Voice of America (VOA) can be found on a host of short-wave frequencies, including 6040 kHz, 9760 kHz and 15,205 kHz, depending on the time of day. The BBC and VOA broadcast around the clock, but the quality of reception varies considerably and you may have to do a lot of dial twiddling (for instance from midnight to 5am).

The Spanish national network Radio Nacional de España (RNE) has several stations: RNE 1 (738 AM; 88.3 FM in Barcelona) has general interest and current affairs programs; RNE 3 (98.7 FM) presents a decent range of pop and rock music; and RNE 5 (576 AM) concentrates on sport and entertainment. Among the most listened to rock and pop stations are 40 Principales (93.9 FM), Onda Cero (94.9 FM) and Cadena 100 (100 FM).

Those wanting to get into Catalan can tune into Catalunya Ràdio (102.8 FM), Catalunya Informació (92 FM) and a host of small local radio stations.

TV

Most TVs receive seven channels – two from Spain's state-run Televisión Española (TVE 1 and La 2), three which are independent (Antena 3, Tele 5 and Canal Plus), the Catalunya regional government station (TV-3) and another Catalan station (Canal 33). Most TV sets will also get the local city stations, Barcelona TV and Citytv, and the music station Flaix. You may get a couple of other local Catalan stations.

News programs are generally decent and you can occasionally catch an interesting documentary or film (look out for the occasional English-language classic late at night on La 2). Otherwise, the main fare is a rather nauseating diet of soaps (many from Latin America), endless talk shows and almost ' vaudevillian variety shows (with plenty of glitz and tits). Canal Plus is partly a pay channel dedicated mainly to movies: you need a decoder and subscription to see the movies, but anyone can watch the other programs.

Many private homes and better hotels have satellite TV, serving up the usual diet of BBC World, CNN, Eurosport and the like.

VIDEO SYSTEMS

If you want to record or buy video tapes to play back home, you won't get a picture if the image registration systems are different. Spanish TVs, and nearly all prerecorded videos on sale in Spain (available in many photography stores), use the PAL (Phase Alternation Line) system common to most of Western Europe and Australia.

France uses the incompatible SECAM system and North America and Japan use the incompatible NTSC system. PAL videos can't be played back on a machine that lacks PAL compatibility.

PHOTOGRAPHY & VIDEO

Most main brands of film are widely available and processing is fast and generally efficient. APS films are also available.

A roll of print film (36 exposures, ISO 100) will cost you around €4.35 and can be processed for around €11 (more for same-day service), although there are often better deals if you have two or three rolls developed together. The equivalent in slide *(dia-positiva)* film is around €5.40 plus €5.20 for processing.

There are plenty of places to have films developed. **Panorama Foto** *(Map 5; Passeig de Gràcia 2)*, which has branches across town, will develop most photos, including slides, in an hour. It also sells standard blank video cassettes.

Some museums and galleries ban photography, or at least flash, and soldiers can be touchy about it. Video is also often not allowed. It's common courtesy to ask – at least by gesture – when you want to photograph people unless, perhaps, they're in some kind of public event such as a procession. The bright middle-of-the-day sun in Spain tends to bleach out your shots. You will get more colour and contrast earlier or later in the day whether you are using still or video film. For more hints, pick up a copy of *Travel Photography: A Guide to Taking Better Pictures* by Richard I'Anson and published by Lonely Planet.

Your camera and film will be passed routinely through airport X-ray machines. These shouldn't damage your film but you can ask for inspection by hand if you're at all worried. Lead pouches for film, available in some specialised camera stores, are another solution.

TIME

Spain (and hence Barcelona) is on GMT/UTC plus one hour during winter, and GMT/UTC plus two hours during the daylight-

STEPHEN SAKS

GUY MOBERLY

Had enough of sightseeing? You can always pop down to the beach (top); or stroll along Passeig Marítim in Vila Olímpica (bottom).

Contemporary structures in Barcelona (clockwise from top left): the Olympic Ring at sunset; detail from the *Peix* sculpture by Frank Gehry at Port Olímpic; the wave-shaped footbridge, La Rambla de Mar, which rotates to allow boats entry to the marina behind it

saving period from the last Sunday in March to the last Sunday in October. Most other Western European countries have the same time as Spain year-round, the major exceptions being Britain, Ireland and also Portugal, which are an hour behind.

When it's noon in Barcelona, it's 11am in London, 6am in New York and Toronto, 3am in San Francisco, 9pm in Sydney and 11pm in Auckland. During the daylight-saving period in Spain, when it is noon in Barcelona, it's 7pm in Sydney and 9pm in Auckland. Note that the changeover to/from daylight usually differs from the European setup by a couple of weeks in Australasia and North America.

ELECTRICITY

Electric current in Barcelona is 220V, 50Hz, as in the rest of continental Europe. Several countries outside Europe (such as the USA and Canada) have 60Hz, which means that appliances with electric motors (such as some CD and cassette players) from those countries may perform poorly. It is always safest to use a transformer.

Plugs have two round pins, again as in the rest of continental Europe.

WEIGHTS & MEASURES

The metric system is used in Spain. As with other continental Europeans, the Spanish indicate decimals with commas and thousands with points. You will sometimes see years written thus: 1.998 and decimals as 5,5 (for 5½). See also the conversion charts at the end of this book.

LAUNDRY

Self-service laundries are beginning to catch on in Barcelona, although they remain something of a rarity. One is **Lavomatic** *(Map 6; Carrer del Consolat de Mar 43-45 • Map 6; Plaça de Joaquim Xirau 1; open 9am-9pm Mon-Sat).* A 7kg load of washing costs €3.75, while drying costs €0.75 for five minutes.

Wash'N Dry *(Map 2; Cnr Carrer de Torrent de l'Olla & Carrer Ros de Olano, Gràcia; open 7am-10pm daily)* charges €4.50 for an 8kg load (€8 for 16kg) and €1 for 10 minutes'

drying time. There is another branch at Carrer Nou de la Rambla 19 *(Map 6).*

Laundry *(Map 2; Plaça del Sol 11-12; open 7am-11pm daily)* is the most recent wash centre to open up. An 8kg load costs €3.25 to wash and a 12kg load costs the same price to dry.

TOILETS

Public toilets are not particularly common in Barcelona but it's OK to wander into most bars and cafés to use their toilet, even if you're not a customer (although this writer prefers to do them the courtesy of having a quick coffee).

LEFT LUGGAGE

Consignas (left luggage) facilities can be found at the airport, Estació Sants, Estació de França and Estació del Nord. Turn to the Getting There & Away and Getting Around chapters for more details.

HEALTH

You should encounter no particular health problems in Barcelona. Your main risks are likely to be sunburn, dehydration or mild gut problems at first if you're not used to a lot of olive oil.

Spain has reciprocal health agreements with other EU countries. Citizens of those countries need to get hold of an E111 form from their national health bodies (in the case of the UK and Ireland, get one at the local post office). If you should require medical help you will need to present this, plus photocopies and your national health card. This is only valid for Spanish public health care.

Travel insurance is still a good idea. You should get it anyway to cover you for theft, loss and unexpected travel cancellations, so you will be covered for the cost of private health care as well.

No vaccinations are required for Spain unless you are coming from an infected area (this generally relates to yellow fever – you may be asked for proof of vaccination), but it is recommended that everyone keeps up-to-date with vaccinations such as tetanus, polio and diphtheria.

For minor health problems, you can head to your local *farmàcia* where pharmaceuticals tend to be sold more freely without prescription than in places such as the USA, Australia or the UK.

Medical Services & Emergency

Hospitals which have an emergency service include **Hospital Creu Roja** *(Map 1; ☎ 93 507 27 00; Carrer del Dos de Maig 301)* and **Hospital de la Santa Creu i de Sant Pau** *(Map 1; ☎ 93 291 90 00; Carrer de Sant Antoni Maria Claret 167)*.

If you need an ambulance call ☎ 061 or ☎ 93 300 20 20.

Of the city's several 24-hour pharmacies the following may be helpful: **Farmàcia Clapés** *(Map 6; ☎ 93 301 28 43; La Rambla 98)*; **Farmàcia Torres** *(Map 4; ☎ 93 453 92 20; Carrer d'Aribau 62)*; **Farmàcia Álvarez** *(Map 2; ☎ 93 302 11 24; Passeig de Gràcia 26)*; **Farmàcia Castells** *(Map 2; Passeig de Gràcia 90)*; and **Farmàcia Saltó** *(Map 1; ☎ 93 339 63 32; Avinguda de Madrid 222)*, which is somewhat out of the centre. Otherwise, for information on duty chemists call ☎ 010. Note that at some late-night pharmacies you have to knock at a small shutter for service; often they will only fill prescriptions or deal with urgent problems outside normal business hours – this is not the time to buy your shampoo.

HIV & AIDS

Although the spread of HIV/AIDS (SIDA/VIH in Castilian) has slowed over the past couple of years, it remains a big problem in Spain. Barcelona is no exception.

Hospital del Mar *(Map 5; ☎ 93 248 30 00)* in La Barceloneta has a special AIDS-testing clinic, but it is entirely probable that you will be first asked to visit your local public General Practitioner, or CAP (Centre d'Assistència Primària) to fill in forms. As nonresident foreign visitors won't have a CAP, they may be obliged to go to a private clinic for a test (which in turn may well *not* be covered by insurance).

For AIDS-related information you can call the service run by the **Generalitat** *(☎ 93 339 87 56; 9am-5.30pm Mon-Fri)*. Other

AIDS information lines include **900 Rosa** *(☎ 900 60 16 01)* and **Associació Antisida** *(☎ 93 317 05 05)*.

WOMEN TRAVELLERS

As visitors have flooded into Barcelona, the fascination of the local guys with foreign women has tended to diminish. In general terms, therefore, harassment is unlikely to be much more apparent here than in any other European metropole.

Since the death of Franco, women have surged into the workforce and become far more assertive, but the truisms that apply elsewhere in the world apply here too. More often than not, women are paid less than their male counterparts. Household duties still tend to fall onto the shoulders of women (even among younger people), and in many cases working women do most of the family raising too.

Organisations

The first stop for anyone seeking information on women's issues should be the **Institut Català de la Dona** *(Map 6; ☎ 93 317 92 91; Carrer de Portaferrissa 1-3)*. It can point you in the right direction for: information on rape/assault counselling; marriage, divorce and related issues for long-termers; and social activities, women's clubs and so on.

Ca la Dona *(Map 2; ☎ 93 412 71 61; Carrer de Casp 38)* is the nerve centre of Barcelona's feminist movement. It includes about 25 diverse women's groups and has been going since 1988. However, some women's groups will probably move into **Casa Bonnemaison** *(Map 6; Carrer de Sant Pere més baix 7)*, which was until 2002 a theatre school.

The **Centre Municipal d'Informació i Recursos per a les Dones** *(Map 1; ☎ 93 413 27 22; Avinguda del Diagonal 233)* is a local government-run information service. Among other things it publishes the *Guía de Grups i Entitats de Dones de Barcelona*, which is a comprehensive guide to all associations and groups connected with women and women's issues in the city.

On the subject of assault, the nationwide Comisión de Investigación de Malos Tratos a Mujeres (Commission of Investigation into the Abuse of Women) has a free 24-hour **national emergency line** (☎ 900 10 00 09) for victims of physical abuse.

Recommended reading is the *Handbook for Women Travellers* by M & G Moss.

GAY & LESBIAN TRAVELLERS

Gay and lesbian sex are both legal in Spain and the age of consent is 16 years, the same as for heterosexuals. Catalunya went a step further in October 1998 by introducing a law recognising gay and lesbian couples. A similar law at national level has been stalled in the Cortes by the ruling conservative Partido Popular (PP). The Catalan law does not yet sanction marriage of such couples, nor the adoption of children by them.

There are a few Spanish sites on the Internet. The Barcelona-based **Coordinadora Gai-Lesbiana** (W *www.pangea.org/org/cgl*) has a good site with nationwide links. Here you can zero in on information ranging from bar, sauna and hotel listings through to contacts pages. **GuíaGay** (W *www.guiagay.com*) is an interesting site – select Barcelona and search listings that range from sex shops to hairdressers. Other interesting national websites include W www.corazongay.com and W www.naciongay.com, which is oriented to news and views.

A couple of informative free magazines are in circulation in gay bookshops and gay and gay-friendly bars. One is *Shangay*. It comes out every two weeks and is jammed with listings and contact ads. It is aimed mostly at readers in Barcelona and Madrid, although information from other towns also appears. A companion publication, *Shangay Express*, is better for articles and a handful of listings and ads. Finally for news (in Spanish) on the gay community across Spain, look out for *Naciongay.com*, the printed version of the website.

If you want to pay for your information and contacts, you can pick up the monthly *Mensual* at newsstands for €3.61.

Organisations

Casal Lambda (*Map 6;* ☎ 93 319 55 50; *Carrer de Verdaguer i Callis 10, Barri Gòtic*) is a

gay and lesbian social, cultural and information centre. **Coordinadora Gai-Lesbiana** (*Map 1;* ☎ 900 60 16 01; e *ccogailes@pangea.org; Carrer de Finlàndia 45*) is the city's main coordinating body for gay and lesbian groups. Some of the latter are to be found at Ca la Dona (see Women Travellers above).

Sestienda (*Map 6; Carrer d'En Rauric 11, Barri Gòtic*), a gay sex shop, has a give-away map of gay Barcelona showing lesbian and gay bars, discos and restaurants.

DISABLED TRAVELLERS

Like most cities, Barcelona is a bit of an obstacle course for the disabled. Some museums and offices provide wheelchair access but many older buildings do not have lifts, so getting up to hostales and the like can be difficult. Some public transport (such as metro line 2, some buses and Radio Amic taxis) is equipped to cater to the disabled. All metro stations and buses should be wheelchair adapted by 2005–06. For information on public transport facilities for the disabled call ☎ 93 486 07 52.

The UK-based Royal Association for Disability and Rehabilitation (Radar) publishes a guide called *European Holidays & Travel Abroad: A Guide for Disabled People*. It is dating but can be a useful general guide. Contact **Radar** (☎ 020-7250 3222; W *www.radar.org.uk; Unit 12, City Forum, 250 City Rd, London EC1V 8AS*), or look at its website. You can also find accommodation listings on the **Disability World** website (W *www.disabilityworld.com*).

Another UK organisation worth calling is **Holiday Care** (☎ 01293-774535; *2nd Floor, Imperial Buildings, Victoria Rd, Horley, Surrey RH6 7PZ*). It produces an information pack on Spain for disabled people and others with special needs. Tips range from hotels with disabled access through to where you can hire equipment and tour operators that deal with the disabled.

Accessible Travel & Leisure (☎ 08702-416127; W *www.atlholidays.com; Avionics House, Quedgeley Enterprise Centre, Naas Lane, Gloucester GL2 4SN*) claims to be the biggest travel agent in the UK dealing with travel for the disabled. The company lays emphasis on accessibility rather than disability and encourages the disabled to travel independently.

Organisations

In Barcelona itself is **ECOM** *(Map 4; ☎ 93 451 55 50, fax 93 451 69 04; Gran Via de les Corts Catalanes 562, 08011 Barcelona)*, Spain's federation of private organisations for the disabled. It can provide information on accommodation with disabled-people's facilities, public- and private-transport options, as well as leisure-time and holiday possibilities in and around Barcelona.

You could also try the **Institut Municipal de Persones amb Disminució** *(Map 1; ☎ 93 413 27 75; Avinguda Diagonal 233)* for more city information.

The national blind people's organisation, **ONCE** *(Map 4; ☎ 93 325 92 00; Carrer de Calàbria 66-76)*, can help with information for the sight impaired, including lists of places such as restaurants where Braille menus are provided. It has also produced a guide to Barcelona in Braille.

SENIOR TRAVELLERS

People aged over 65 can get free or half-price admission to many museums and other attractions in Barcelona. For more details see the Things to See & Do chapter.

Price reductions are also possible on some long-distance transport, mainly trains. You usually need to provide proof of age. It is always worth asking if reductions apply.

You should also seek information in your own country on travel packages and discounts for senior travellers, through seniors' organisations and travel agencies.

BARCELONA FOR CHILDREN

You will generally have no problem taking your kids with you to restaurants, hotels, cafés and the like, although few locals are inclined to take their *peques* (little ones) out for a night on the tiles.

Kids can open doors where adults alone never would. This is especially so where a language barrier impedes communication – cute kids doing the cute things that cute kids sometimes do can be a great ice-breaker.

Catalans have fewer qualms about keeping their children up late than people from more northerly climes. In summer especially, you'll see them at the local *festes* until the wee hours. Taking children to cafés or snack bars that have outdoor tables (preferably in pedestrian zones) is no problem at all. Of course, your wee bairn's body clock may not quite be up to it.

What to Do with Ankle Biters

Some of the museums appear to have been thought out for kids as much as for adults. Museu Marítim (Map 6) and Museu d'Història de Catalunya (Map 5) fall into that category, the former with its audio-visual trek through time and the latter with its various hands-on gadgets.

Parc d'Atraccions up on Tibidabo is perfect for the kids and few young ones will turn up their noses at the beach or outdoor pools in summer. If you've been cruel enough to subject them to the Museu d'Art Modern in Parc de la Ciutadella, why not compensate with an ice cream and a stroll through the park, a trip to the zoo (Map 5) and/or a bit of a row on the little artificial lake? Still not satisfied? Try the Màgic BCN virtual train ride nearby.

The high-level *funicular aereo* (cable car) between Montjuïc and La Barceloneta might be the go, as indeed could be a harbour excursion on one of the *golondrina* boats (Map 5).

The watery tunnels of L'Aquàrium (Map 5), Europe's biggest fish 'zoo', should be a winner and you could also try the nearby Imax cinema.

In the early evening, the Teatre Nou Tantarantana (Map 5) sometimes puts on great children's shows.

Finally, even the most adventurous of children will at times feel nostalgia for toys back home. Bring a couple of favourites along to keep them occupied during dull moments, or when you're trying to take a rest yourself.

Before You Go

There are no particular health precautions you need to take, though kids tend to be more affected than adults by unaccustomed heat, changes in diet and sleeping patterns, and just being in a strange place. Nappies, creams, lotions, baby foods and so on are all easily available in Barcelona, but if there's some particular brand you swear by it's best to bring it with you.

Lonely Planet's *Travel with Children* has lots of practical advice on the subject and first-hand stories from many Lonely Planet authors, and others, who have done it.

USEFUL ORGANISATIONS

The **Instituto Cervantes** (W *www.cervantes .es*), with branches in over 30 cities around the world, exists to promote the Spanish language and the cultures of Spain and other Spanish-speaking countries. It's mainly involved in Spanish teaching, and in library and information services. The library at the London **branch** (☎ *020-7235 0353, fax 7235 0329; 102 Eaton Square, London SW1W 9AN*) has a wide range of reference books, books on history and the arts, periodicals, over 1000 videos including feature films, language-teaching material, electronic databases and music CDs. You can find more addresses on the institute's website.

UNIVERSITIES

Barcelona has five universities. Teaching is predominantly in Catalan, meaning that even Castilian speakers may have difficulties at first. European students in Barcelona are mostly on one-year programs on the Erasmus scheme. They do this as part of their undergraduate studies. You need to approach the Socrates and Erasmus council in your country for information.

Of the universities, the oldest and biggest is the **Universitat de Barcelona** (☎ *93 402 11 00;* W *www.ub.es*), with campuses at Gran Via de les Corts Catalanes 585 (Map 4) and the Zona Universitària (Map 1).

The remaining institutions are:

Universitat Autònoma de Barcelona (☎ 93 581 10 00; W uab.es) Bellaterra. This place is north of the city near Sabadell and an unlikely choice for foreigners.
Universitat Politècnica de Catalunya (Map 1; ☎ 93 401 62 00; W www.upc.es) Carrer de Jordi Girona 31 (metro Zona Universitària). As the name suggests, this is a technical and engineering university. It has several campuses located outside town.
Universitat Pompeu Fabra (Map 6; ☎ 93 542 20 00, fax 93 542 20 02; W www.upf.es) Plaça de la Mercè 10-12. Based in the old city, this university concentrates on social sciences and has faculties dotted about central Barcelona (eg, just off La Rambla on Plaça de Joaquim Xirau; Map 6).
Universitat Ramon Llull (Map 1; ☎ 93 602 22 00; W www.url.es) Carrer Claravall 1. Ramon Llull is a private institute for students with fat wallets. The faculty buildings are also spread across town.

Foreign students who are planning to live in Barcelona can get help on a range of information from lodgings to language tuition, how to organise work experience in local companies, cultural activities and so on, at **Punt d'Informació Juvenil** (*Map 4;* ☎ *93 483 83 84; Carrer de Calàbria 147*).

CULTURAL CENTRES

British Council (Map 3; ☎ 93 241 99 77) Carrer d'Amigó 83. The British Council provides English classes, library services, film seasons and other cultural events.
Goethe Institut (Map 4; ☎ 93 292 60 06) Carrer de Manso 24-28. Apart from German classes and library services, the institute organises lectures, exhibits, film seasons and the like.
Institut Français de Barcelona (Map 2; ☎ 93 209 59 11) Carrer de Moià 8. It puts on concerts, films and exhibitions.
Institute for North American Studies (Map 3; ☎ 93 240 51 10) Via Augusta 123. Library material is also available here.
Istituto Italiano di Cultura (Map 2; ☎ 93 487 53 06) Passatge de Méndez Vigo 5. The institute's main aim is to teach Italian. It also has a library and puts on lectures and film seasons.

LIBRARIES

The city's most important library is the **Biblioteca de Catalunya** (*Map 6;* ☎ *93 270 23 00, fax 93 270 23 04; Carrer de l'Hospital 56*), which is housed in part of the former medieval Hospital de la Santa Creu. Access, however, is for accredited students and researchers only. Otherwise, each city district has three or four local libraries that you can use.

FACTS FOR THE VISITOR

Fifty Ways to Lose a Wallet

The tales of woe from unlucky travellers who have been stung in Barcelona are remarkable most of all for the degree of fantasy employed by muggers and other crooks. If it's any consolation, this writer has been done too!

Try these for size. You're walking down a street and suddenly you feel a glob of what looks like bird shit on your shoulder. An obliging fellow with a tissue emerges from nowhere and helps you remove the mess. Then he removes himself and shortly thereafter you notice he has also removed the contents of your pockets – the 'shit' was a chocolate and milk mix dropped from a balcony.

Another fun one involves somebody bending over in front of you (say on an escalator to pick up something they have dropped). You are distracted and hey, presto, no more wallet. The variations on that theme are innumerable. 'Tourists' asking for directions are another common gag.

Pickpocketing happens on the streets, in the metro, at the bus stations...and even in clubs. Don't wear money belts and the like in clubs if you can help it (unless they are well hidden) as there have been cases of them being snipped.

Sadly, less inventive and more threatening incidents do occasionally take place. One reader reports having been grabbed in a headlock from behind while his trouser pockets were slashed and emptied. The reader was alone late at night in a dark street in Barri Xinès – not a good idea at the best of times.

In the same part of town you'll still see some fairly tawdry-looking damsels (some with remarkably deep voices) of the night lolling about. If you're male and particularly unlucky you may find one suddenly attaching their hand in vice-like fashion to your nether region and smiling gap-toothedly at you while suggesting some back alley frolics. While you engage in a delicate attempt to recover possession of your genitals and make your excuses, you can be fairly sure you are being relieved of your possessions.

Along La Rambla watch out for the *trilers*, or three-card tricksters. While you are busy betting (and losing), other members of the team will be keeping an eye on where you put your wallet.

Finally, if someone asks to see your passport, don't be too willing to whip it into view. The only people with a right to see it are hoteliers and police.

Don't panic, though, just don't let your guard down!

DANGERS & ANNOYANCES

Unfortunately, it appears petty crime, principally theft and muggings, are on the increase in Barcelona. Overall, it is not a city in which you are likely to feel threatened but you need to be aware of the danger. The city's visitors are prime targets.

Prevention

...is better than cure! Only walk around with the amount of cash you intend to spend that day or evening. Hidden money belts or pouches are a good idea. For more details, see Security under Money earlier in this chapter. You should be especially vigilant on the metro or when arriving at or leaving the train or bus stations or your hotel, as you are more vulnerable when encumbered by luggage.

As a rule, dark, empty streets are to be avoided. Luckily, Barcelona's most lively nocturnal areas are generally busy with crowds having a good time. But while there is safety in numbers, they are no guarantee of immunity. Among the worst offenders are street youths, many of whom are illegal immigrants, who know well that the police can do little even when they are caught. As minors, young offenders are soon released.

Before You Leave Home You can take a few precautions before you even arrive in Barcelona. Inscribe your name, address and telephone number *inside* your luggage and take photocopies of the important pages of your passport, travel tickets and other important documents. Travel insurance against theft and loss is another very good idea. For more details, see Copies under Visas & Documents earlier in this chapter.

Theft & Loss

You need to keep an eye out for pickpockets and bag-snatchers in the most heavily touristed parts of town, especially La Rambla and Ciutat Vella. Barri Xinès, the lower end of La Rambla and the area around Plaça Reial, although much cleaned up in recent years, remain dodgy.

Pickpocketing is rife in busy spots such as the area in front of the Catedral. Indeed the shopkeepers there have demanded greater policing. Increasingly, gangs not averse to violence are preying on hapless tourists and the occasional local. Even attractions as far from the centre as Parc Güell can be a problem.

In summer, the beach (especially at La Barceloneta) is a particularly popular playground for thieves – always keep your belongings guarded or within reach and in view. The beach theft problem is bad enough for local police to mount a special anti-theft operation on the beach each summer.

Never leave anything visible in your vehicle and preferably leave nothing at all. Temptation usually leads at least to smashed windows and loss – it happens in broad daylight too, so take this seriously. Foreign and hire cars are especially vulnerable. If you have a foreign or hire car, it might be an idea to leave the glovebox open to emphasise there is nothing of value inside.

In reputable hotels and hostels, use the safe if there is one. Try not to leave valuables in your room. If you must, then bury them deep in your luggage.

If anything does get lost or stolen, you need to report it to the police and get a written statement from them if you intend to claim on insurance. If your ID or passport disappears, you must also contact your nearest consulate as soon as possible, to arrange for a replacement.

Terrorism

Although you would have to be extraordinarily unlucky to be in the wrong place at the wrong time, ETA terrorists (seeking independence for the Basque Country) have occasionally struck in Barcelona and Catalunya. A bomb let off in the resort town of Salou in August 2001 was clearly part of a declared strategy of attempting to scare off tourists. Generally, though, the occasional bombs that the Basques have set off in Barcelona over the years have been aimed at specific political or judicial figures. Unfortunately, there's not much you can do in the line of prevention.

Lost & Found

The city's main **lost-and-found office** (*objectes perduts; Map 6;* ☎ *010; Carrer de la Ciutat 9*) is open from 9am to 2pm. If you leave anything in a taxi call ☎ 93 223 40 12. For things lost in the metro, try the **Centre d'Atenció al Client** (*Map 4;* ☎ *93 318 70 74*) at

If You Are a Victim

If you fall victim to the numerous pickpockets and bag-snatchers, try to remain calm and remember to do the following:

Cancel any stolen travellers cheques and credit cards (and arrange for replacements) by calling the emergency numbers you should have for this purpose (see also Money earlier in this chapter). You need to report the crime to the nearest Comisaría (national police station), which for many will be the one at Carrer Nou de la Rambla 80 (Map 5). You should get an English-speaking policeman to attend but be aware that, other than take a statement (which you will need for insurance purposes and to replace stolen passports), they can do little.

If your passport is taken contact your nearest consulate or embassy to arrange to have a new one issued. This can be the most aggravating procedure as it won't necessarily happen overnight and you generally may not travel without such documents.

the Universitat metro stop. If you lose anything at the airport try ☎ 93 298 33 49. The office is located between terminals B and C.

EMERGENCIES
The general EU standard emergency number is ☎ 112. You can reach all emergency services on this number and occasionally even get multilingual operators.

Barcelona abounds with different kinds of police. The **Guàrdia Urbana** (city police; Map 6; ☎ 092; La Rambla 43) has a station opposite Plaça Reial. They generally deal with traffic and minor offences.

The **Policía Nacional** (Map 5; ☎ 091; Carrer Nou de la Rambla 80) are the people you need to see in case of theft or other crime.

The **Mossos de Esquadra** (☎ 93 300 91 91) is a Catalan force that is replacing the national **Guàrdia Civil** (☎ 062) in some tasks (such as highway patrol). The latter are a military-style police force involved in everything from security to highway patrol.

If you have been a victim of a crime and are at a loss what to do next, you could try contacting the **Servei d'Atenció a la Víctima** (Map 6; ☎ 900 12 18 84 or ☎ 93 567 44 11; Via Laietana 4).

For the fire brigade call ☎ 080.

LEGAL MATTERS
If you're arrested you will be allotted the free services of a duty solicitor (abogado de oficio), who may speak only Catalan and/or Castilian. You're also entitled to make a telephone call. Your embassy or consulate, however, will probably be able to do no more than refer you to a lawyer who speaks your language. If you end up in court, the local authorities are obliged to provide you with a translator.

Drugs
The only legal drug is cannabis, and then only for personal use – which means very small amounts.

Public consumption of any drug is illegal, yet you may still come across the occasional bar where people smoke joints openly. In short, be discreet if you plan to use cannabis. It is unwise to smoke dope in

hotel rooms or guesthouses, and could be risky in even the coolest of public places.

BUSINESS HOURS
Generally, people work from about 9am to 2pm and then again from 4.30pm or 5pm for another three hours, Monday to Friday. Shops and travel agencies are usually open these hours on Saturday too, although some may skip the evening session. Big supermarkets and department stores such as El Corte Inglés often stay open from about 9am to 9pm Monday to Saturday. A handful of shops are open on Sunday. Many government offices don't bother with afternoon opening any day of the year.

See earlier sections of this chapter for bank and post office hours.

PUBLIC HOLIDAYS & SPECIAL EVENTS
The two main periods when Barcelonins go on holiday are Setmana Santa (the week leading up to Easter Sunday) and, more noticeably, the month of August. In Easter, incoming tourists make up the numbers for the leaving locals (accommodation is at a premium during this week), but in August the city is like a ghost town, even though in recent years the tendency has been to stagger departures and returns in two-week chunks over July and August.

Barcelona likes to party, and throughout the year there is no shortage of public holidays, colourful festes, arts and music festivals, and more. For a rundown on the most important events held here throughout the year, see the Holidays & Festivals special section.

DOING BUSINESS
The Barcelonins are often seen by their counterparts in Madrid as being rather dull workaholics and tightwads.

The image, while much exaggerated, does reflect the city's relatively business-like feel. From the Middle Ages, Barcelona thrived on foreign trade and, since manufacturing took off in the 19th century, the city has had (and indeed cultivated) an image of industriousness viewed with a mix of envy and scorn by much of the rest of Spain.

This activity has been in Barcelona's favour as Spain has integrated into the EU and the global market in the past 20 years, although Madrid is increasingly asserting itself as the economic and financial capital of the country. Still, Barcelona is viewed enthusiastically by the foreign business community and tourists.

Business Services

Business people who need to work in Barcelona temporarily or long term, and people hoping to set up new businesses here, should first contact the trade department of the Spanish embassy or consulate in their own country. The next port of call should be the **Cambra Oficial de Comerç, Indústria i Navegació** *(Map 2;* ☎ *93 416 93 00 or* ☎ *902 44 84 48, fax 93 416 93 01; Avinguda Diagonal 452)*. It has a business-oriented bookshop and documentation centre, the Llibreria de la Cambra.

Barcelona Activa *(Map 1;* ☎ *93 401 97 77; Gran Via de les Corts Catalanes 890)* aims to help with business start-ups. It is mainly aimed at locals, but could be a useful port of call if you want to start a business in Barcelona. Self-employed people or those running their own business (or wanting to) may want to contact **Autempresa** *(*☎ *902 20 15 20)* for information on bureaucracy and tax questions.

The Fira de Barcelona's information office (see Exhibitions & Conferences following) offers business services (communications etc), meeting rooms and other facilities for people working at trade fairs.

Exhibitions & Conferences

With more than 70 trade fairs a year and a growing number of congresses of all types, Barcelona is becoming an important centre of international business in Europe. It claims to rank fifth worldwide for the organisation of congresses, in part due to the lower costs involved – organisers of the city's trade fair, the Fira de Barcelona, claim that congresses cost 20% less to stage here than in other major European cities.

The nature of the fairs ranges from fashion to technology, from jewellery to book, and from furniture to recycling.

The main trade fair (Fira M1; Map 7) is located between the base of Montjuïc and Plaça d'Espanya, with 90,000 sq m of exhibition space (of a total area of 224,000 sq m). To cope with expansion in the past years, the Fira M2 (Fair No 2; Map 1), southwest of Montjuïc, has been expanded to about 40,000 sq metres of exhibition space. Under the Fira's 2000–10 plan, Fira M2 could be further expanded to 120,000 sq metres by the end of 2007. It is hoped a new metro line will link the two trade fair areas and the airport. The Palau de Congressos at Fira M1 can host up to 1650 people, and smaller conference halls abound. The Fira has an **information centre** *(Map 7;* ☎ *93 233 20 00; Plaça d'Espanya)*. It can provide limited communications facilities for business people and professionals who are involved in the fairs.

Another number you can try if you want advice on organising conventions within Barcelona is the **Barcelona Convention Bureau** *(*☎ *93 368 97 00, fax 93 368 97 01;* [e] *cbcb@barcelonaturisme.com; Rambla de Catalunya 123)*.

Hotel Rey Juan Carlos I's private **Palau de Congressos** *(*☎ *93 364 44 00; Avinguda Diagonal 661-671)* has a capacity of 2300.

Down at Port Vell, work continues on the World Trade Center (Map 1), already partly up and running. Further ambitious plans include a new congress centre with a capacity of 15,000 to be built for Fòrum 2004 near the northeastern waterfront of the city.

WORK

Although Catalunya has one of the lowest unemployment levels in Spain, this is hardly the ideal place to look for work. But there are a few ways of earning your keep (or almost) while you're here.

Bureaucracy

Nationals of EU countries, Norway and Iceland may work in Spain without a visa, but for stays of more than three months they are supposed to apply within the first month for a *tarjeta de residencia* (residence card). If you are offered a work contract, your employer will usually steer you through the labyrinth. See Visas & Documents earlier in this chapter for details.

Virtually everyone else is supposed to obtain, from a Spanish consulate in their country of residence, a work permit and, if they plan to stay more than 90 days, a residence visa. These procedures are well nigh impossible unless you have a job contract lined up before you begin to apply. Quite a few people, though, do work discreetly, without bothering to tangle with the bureaucracy.

Language Teaching

This is the obvious option, for which language-teaching qualifications are a big help (often indispensable). Be warned, though. English teaching is not the gold mine it was a few decades ago. Every English-speaking bum and his dog tries to get this type of work nowadays, so competition is fierce. English teachers are actually paid less today in Barcelona than prior to the Olympics in 1992. Classroom rates are around €10 to €15 per hour, depending on the school and your experience.

Predictably, Barcelona is loaded with 'cowboy outfits' that pay badly and often aren't overly concerned about quality. Still, the only way you'll find out is by hunting around. Schools are listed under Acadèmies de Idiomes in the yellow pages.

Sources of information on possible teaching work – school or private – include foreign cultural centres (the British Council, Institut Français etc), foreign-language bookshops (such as Come In), universities and language schools. Many of these have notice boards where you may find work opportunities, or where you can advertise your own services.

Bar Work & Waiting

If your Spanish (and preferably Catalan as well) are in reasonable shape, you can sometimes swing jobs waiting tables or, more easily, in bars. For English speakers the city's pseudo-Irish bars are the first obvious port of call.

Buskers & Street Artists

La Rambla is one of the great busking stages of Europe, so you could try your luck here. It's no easy road, though. Competition is fierce and the quality of some acts is surprisingly high, but if you have an original and well-rehearsed act to present, this could be the place to try it out.

Street artists may also find the going tough. The Ajuntament applies a quota (a maximum of 50 artists can work La Rambla) and hopefuls must apply for a permit if they do not want to be moved along by the local police.

Getting There & Away

After Madrid, Barcelona is Spain's biggest international transport hub. It's easy to reach by air from anywhere in Europe and North America. Regular train and bus links as well as a smooth super highway connect Barcelona into France and the rest of Europe, and there are plenty of air and land connections to destinations all over Spain.

AIR

A phalanx of airlines flies direct to Barcelona from the rest of Europe. It pays to shop around and, for short stays, you should consider flight/hotel packages. From North America, flights frequently entail a stopover en route (Madrid or another European centre). Travellers from more distant locales, such as Asia and Australasia, have fewer choices. Increasingly, travellers are turning to the Internet to look for flight deals and book tickets. Most airlines and many travel agencies operate interactive

websites. Several budget airlines, mostly operating out of London, encourage customers to purchase tickets online.

For information on airport facilities, see the Getting Around chapter.

Travellers with Special Needs

If they're warned early enough, airlines can often make special arrangements for travellers such as wheelchair assistance at airports or vegetarian meals on the flight. Children aged under two years travel for 10% of the standard fare (or free on some airlines) as long as they don't occupy a seat. They don't get a baggage allowance, though. 'Skycots', baby food and nappies should be provided by the airline if requested in advance. Children aged between two and 12 can usually occupy a seat for around two-thirds of the full fare, and they do receive a baggage allowance.

The disability-friendly website W www .allgohere.co.uk has an airline directory that provides information on the facilities offered by various airlines.

Departure Tax

Airport taxes are factored into ticket prices, although fares are generally quoted without the taxes. They can range from €20 to €70 depending on the destination. The passport formalities are minimal.

Other Parts of Spain

Flying within Spain is generally not economical. **Iberia** (☎ 902 40 05 00; W www .iberia.es) and the small subsidiaries Iberia Regional-Air Nostrum and Binter Mediterráneo cover all destinations and offer a range of fares.

Competing with Iberia are **Spanair** (☎ 902 13 14 15; W www.spanair.com) and **Air Europa** (☎ 902 40 15 01; W www.air-europa .com). Air Europa is the bigger of the two, with regular flights between Barcelona and Madrid, Palma de Mallorca, Málaga and other mainland Spanish destinations.

The cheapest return fare between Barcelona and Madrid with any of these airlines is €87, but it can range up to €260. What you pay depends on when you fly and the conditions attached to the ticket. The cheaper tickets are generally nonrefundable and do not allow changes.

Canary Islands From Barcelona, Iberia, Air Europa, Spanair and charter companies all fly to Santa Cruz de Tenerife and Las Palmas de Gran Canaria. Tourist-class return flights between Barcelona and Santa Cruz start at around €260 (and go up according to season, time of day and other factors). To get the cheapest scheduled flights you need to book at least two days in advance, stay a weekend and not more than 14 days. Such tickets are generally non-refundable and cannot be changed. Although there are many direct flights, you may find some of the cheapest flights involve a stop in Madrid. Charter flights occasionally cost less.

The UK

Discount air travel is big business in London. Most British travel agents are registered with the Association of British Travel Agents (ABTA) and all agents that sell flights in the UK must hold an Air Travel Organiser's Licence (ATOL). If you have paid for your flight with an ABTA-registered or ATOL agency that then goes bust, the Civil Aviation Authority will guarantee a refund or an alternative under the ATOL scheme. Unregistered travel agencies are riskier but sometimes cheaper.

Travellers are increasingly using the Internet to search for good fares and some airlines, particular the budget ones, encourage you to book online.

One of the more reliable, but not necessarily cheapest, agencies is **STA** (☎ 020-7361 6161 for European flights; W www.statravel.co.uk). STA has several offices in London, as well as branches on many university campuses and in cities such as Cambridge, Leeds, Bristol, Manchester and Oxford.

A similar agency is **Trailfinders** (☎ 020-7937 1234 for European flights; W www

.trailfinder.com). It has a short-haul **booking centre** (215 Kensington High St, London W8) and offices in Birmingham, Manchester, Bristol, Glasgow and Newcastle.

The two flag airlines linking the UK and Spain are **British Airways** (BA; ☎ 0845 773 3377; W www.british-airways.com; 156 Regent St, London W1B 5LB), and Spain's **Iberia** (☎ 0845 601 2854; W www.iberia.com; 10 Hammersmith Broadway, London W6 7AL). Of the two airlines, BA is more likely to have special deals below the standard scheduled fares (around UK£200 return in the high season).

Air Europa (☎ 0870 240 1501; W www.air-europa.com) flies once daily from London Gatwick to Barcelona, but the hitch is you change in Madrid. A return flight in late June costs UK£187.40.

Web-based budget airlines have become important players in the shorthaul European travel market.

easyJet (☎ 0870 600 0000, in Spain ☎ 902 29 99 92; W www.easyjet.com) has tickets from London's Luton and Gatwick airports to Barcelona for as little as UK£50 each way, plus UK£12 tax. In slow periods (such as winter weekdays), one-way prices have been known to drop as low as UK£20 plus tax! Once fares approach the UK£100 mark (one way), though, it is time for you to look elsewhere.

Go (☎ 0870 607 6543, in Spain ☎ 901 33 35 00; W www.go-fly.com) has departures from London Stansted (a 40-minute train ride from Liverpool St train station) and Bristol. If you comply with certain restrictions (easily done if you're planning to spend a week or more in Spain) you are looking at around UK£50 to UK£60 one way plus taxes to Barcelona.

British Midland (☎ 0870 607 0555; W www.flybmi.com) flies to several Spanish destinations from London Heathrow and other UK airports. In early 2002, in response to the competition from budget airlines, British Midland created a no-frills subsidiary, **BMI Baby** (☎ 0870 264 2229; W www.flybmi.com/bmibaby), with one daily flight to Barcelona (return fare in low season UK£79) from East Midlands airport.

Virgin Express (☎ 020-7744 0004; W www .virgin-express.com) flies to Barcelona via Brussels. It sometimes runs some cheap promotional fares for midweek travel.

Spanish Travel Services (STS) (☎ 020-7387 5337; W www.apatraveluk.com; 138 Eversholt St, London NW1 1BL) can get scheduled return flights with Iberia, BA, Air Europa and other airlines for as little as UK£89/149 in the low/high season (including taxes). It also organises city breaks, beach holidays, accommodation and a range of other services in Spain.

Several times a year, usually around Easter and again in autumn (September to November), STS and various charter companies offer low-price four- or five-day long-weekend fares, sometimes with accommodation thrown in, to Barcelona and other Spanish destinations.

The budget airlines' fare structure makes it easy to plan open-jaw flights, with which you fly into one destination and leave from another. With other airlines it is also possible, if sometimes a little more complicated, to make such arrangements.

You needn't fly from London, as many good deals are easily available from other centres in the UK.

From Ireland, **Aer Lingus** (☎ 01-868888; W www.aerlingus.ie) has direct flights daily from Dublin to Barcelona. Return fares can start at €160.

Continental Europe

Short hops can be expensive, but for longer journeys you can often find fares that beat overland alternatives on cost.

France Standard return flights from Paris to Barcelona with either Iberia or Air France frequently cost around €180.

Air Littoral (☎ 0825 834 834, in Spain ☎ 901 11 67 15; W www.air-littoral.fr) operates three daily flights from Nice (with incoming connections from other cities in France and Italy) to Barcelona. Its fares are not especially cheap.

The student travel agency **OTU Voyages** (☎ 0820 817 817, 01 44 41 38 50; W www .otu.fr; 39 Av Georges Bernanos) has an office in central Paris and another 30 offices around the country.

Germany In Berlin you could try **STA Travel** (☎ 030-311 09 50; W www.statravel .de; Goethestrasse 73). There are also offices in Frankfurt am Main (☎ 069-70 30 35; Bockenheimer Landstrasse 133), and in 16 other cities across the country.

A return trip from Frankfurt to Barcelona in May ranges in cost from €279 with Czech Airways to €365 with Iberia.

Italy A good place in Italy to look for cheap fares is **CTS** (Centro Turistico Studentesco e Giovanile; W www.cts.it), which has branches countrywide. Its head office is in Rome (☎ 06 462 04 31; Via Genova 16), but there are many other branches located across the country.

Netherlands & Belgium Transavia airline's budget subsidiary, **Basiq Air** (☎ 0900-227 4724; W www.basiqair.com) offers flights to Barcelona from Amsterdam for as little as €39 (one way in low season). The UK-based budget airline **easyJet** (☎ 023 568 4880; W www.easyjet.com) gives them some stiff competition on the same route.

Brussels is the main hub for **Virgin Express** (☎ 02 752 05 05), which has up to seven flights a day between Brussels and Barcelona. Fares vary wildly depending on the season, time of day and conditions. You might pay €150 return to Barcelona with various strings attached, but it could just as easily be €450 if you want a high degree of flexibility.

Portugal Flying between Barcelona and Lisbon is a costly business. Iberia, Air Europa and **TAP Air Portugal** (☎ 218 431 100, 808 205 700; W www.tap-airportugal.pt) do it for around €250 return in the high season.

The USA

Several airlines fly to Barcelona (usually with a stopover), including Iberia, BA and KLM-Royal Dutch Airlines. Delta flies direct from New York daily from about April to October, but not at all the rest of the year.

Standard fares can be expensive. Discount and rock-bottom options from the USA include charter flights, stand-by and courier flights.

Reliable travel agencies that you can check out include **STA** (☎ 1-800-781 4040; ⓦ www.statravel.com) and **Council Travel** (☎ 1-800-226 8624; ⓦ www.counciltravel.com); both have offices in major cities. Details of discount travel agencies, known as consolidators in the USA, can be found in the weekly travel sections of the *New York Times*, *Los Angeles Times*, *Chicago Tribune* and *San Francisco Examiner*.

Stand-by fares are often sold at 60% of the normal price for one-way tickets. **Airhitch** (☎ 1-800 605 HITCH; ⓔ info@airhitch.org; ⓦ www.airhitch.org) is a specialist agency that operates mostly online. You will need to give a general idea of where and when you need to go, and a few days before your departure you will be presented with a choice of two or three flights. One-way flights from the USA to Europe cost from US$165 (east coast) to US$233 (west coast), plus taxes.

Courier flights involve you accompanying a parcel to its destination. A New York–Barcelona return on a courier flight can cost under US$300 in the low season (more from the west coast). You may have to be a US resident and apply for an interview first. Most flights depart from New York. **Now Voyager** (☎ 212-431 1616; Suite 307, 74 Varrick St, New York, NY 10013) is a courier-flight specialist.

Regular fares fluctuate enormously. **Iberia** (☎ 212-644 8841) flies from New York to Barcelona (generally via Madrid), but often you can get better deals with other airlines via other European centres. Flights from New York can range from US$500 to US$900 in the low and high seasons, respectively. If you're lucky, it might work out much the same from the West Coast too, although frequently you are looking at about US$200 more.

Air Europa (☎ 212-921 2381) offers flights via Madrid from New York. From time to time it comes up with some low fares.

If you can't find a good deal, consider getting an inexpensive transatlantic hop to London and prowling around the discount travel agencies there.

Canada

Scan the travel agencies' advertisements in the *Toronto Globe & Mail*, *Toronto Star* and *Vancouver Sun*. **Travel CUTS** (☎ 800-667 2887; ⓦ www.travelcuts.com), called Voyages Campus in Quebec, has offices in all major cities in Canada.

Iberia has direct flights to Barcelona from Toronto and Montreal. Other major European airlines offer competitive fares to Barcelona via other European capitals. Typical low-season fares hover around the C$700 mark. In high season they can go to US$900 and as much as C$1400 if you're unlucky. Flights from Toronto cost much the same. From Vancouver, you are looking at around C$200 more.

Australia

STA Travel (☎ 1300 360 960 Australia-wide; ⓦ www.statravel.com.au) and **Flight Centre** (☎ 1310 362 665 Australia-wide; ⓦ www.flightcentre.com.au) are major dealers in cheap airfares, although heavily discounted fares can often be found at your local travel agency. The Saturday editions of Melbourne's the *Age* and the *Sydney Morning Herald* have many advertisements offering cheap fares to Europe.

As a rule, there are no direct flights from Australia to Spain. You will have to fly to Europe via Asia and change flights (and possibly airlines).

Return low-season fares from Australia to Barcelona start from around A$2025 going via Bangkok and Rome with Qantas/Alitalia or A$1958 with Qantas/Air France via Singapore and Paris.

For courier flights, try **Jupiter** (☎ 02-9317 2230; 3/55 Kent Rd, Mascot, Sydney 2020).

New Zealand

STA Travel (☎ 0508 782872; ⓦ www.statravel.co.nz) and **Flight Centre** (☎ 0800 243544; ⓦ www.flightcentre.co.nz) are popular agencies, with branches throughout the country.

The *New Zealand Herald* has a travel section in which travel agencies advertise deals on fares.

Low-season return fares from Auckland start from NZ$2349 with Thai International via Bangkok or NZ$2499 via Singapore with Singapore Airlines.

Asia

Although most Asian countries offer competitive fare deals, Bangkok, Hong Kong and Singapore are still the best places to shop around for discount air tickets. From Hong Kong expect to pay from HK$8480 to HK$10,850 with Thai International to Barcelona.

STA has branches in Bangkok, Hong Kong, Kuala Lumpur, Singapore and Tokyo.

Airline Offices in Barcelona

You can find airlines listed under Línias Aèries/Líneas Aéreas in the phone book. They include:

Air Europa (☎ 902 40 15 01) El Prat airport
Alitalia (Map 2; ☎ 902 10 03 23) Avinguda Diagonal 403
Delta Airlines (☎ 901 11 69 46, 93 478 23 00) El Prat airport
easyJet (☎ 902 29 99 92) El Prat airport
Iberia (Map 2; ☎ 902 40 05 00, 93 401 33 73) Carrer de la Diputació 258
Lufthansa Airlines (☎ 902 22 01 01) El Prat airport
Spanair (☎ 902 13 14 15) El Prat airport
Virgin Express (☎ 93 226 66 71) El Prat airport

BUS

Buses are generally cheaper than trains, but less comfortable for the long haul. Eurolines is the main international carrier throughout Europe, often working in tandem with national companies such as, in the case of Spain, Alsa-Enatcar. The website at **w** www.eurolines.com has links to all national Eurolines websites.

The main intercity bus station in Barcelona is the modern **Estació del Nord** *(Map 1; information desk* ☎ *93 265 65 08; Carrer d'Alí Bei 80; open 7am-9pm daily).* Left-luggage lockers are outside by the bus stands and cost €3 for 24 hours.

Some long-distance services – most importantly some international buses and some to Montserrat – use Estació d'Autobusos de Sants beside Estació Sants train station (Map 4).

The main international services are run by **Eurolines/Julià Via** (☎ 93 490 40 00) from Estació d'Autobusos de Sants, and by **Eurolines/Linebús** (☎ 93 265 07 00) from Estació del Nord and Estació d'Autobusos de Sants.

Other Parts of Spain

You can ride buses to most large Spanish cities from Barcelona. A plethora of bus companies operate to different parts of the country, although many come under the umbrella of **Alsa-Enatcar** (☎ *902 42 22 42;* **w** *www.alsa.es).* For schedule information call ☎ 93 245 88 56.

Daily departures from Estació del Nord include the following, with journey time and fare (where frequencies vary, the lower figure is usually for Sunday):

destination	no. of buses	duration (hrs)	fare (€)
Almería	5	11½-14	49.57
Burgos	3-4	7-8	32.29
Granada	5	12-14¼	54.51
Madrid	11-18	7-8	21.21
Salamanca	7	11½	37.72
Seville	1-2	16	61.16
Valencia	8-10	4¼-5½	24.67-38.23
Vigo	1-2	16	43.06
Zaragoza	11	4½	10.74

Note that a handful of regional services within Catalunya depart from other parts of town. If you are unsure, call the **tourist office** *(*☎ *906 30 12 82),* **Estació del Nord** *(*☎ *93 265 65 08)* or the ☎ 010 information line to find out about your destination.

The UK

Eurolines (☎ *0870 514 3219; 4 Cardiff Rd, Luton LU1 1PP)* – the London terminal is at Victoria Coach station on Buckingham Palace Rd – runs buses to Barcelona on Friday (late June to early September only),

Saturday, Monday (leaving at 11am; connection to Alicante) and Wednesday (10pm). The trip takes 24 to 26 hours. The one-way and return fares are UK£65 and UK£95 (10% less for those aged 13 to 25). You can get an Apex return fare of UK£59 if you book a week in advance and return within a month. Prices rise in the peak summer season (July and August) and in the week before Christmas.

France

Eurolines has offices in several French cities, including the **Paris bus station** (☎ 01 49 72 51 51; 28 Av du Générale de Gaulle) and a more central office (☎ 01 43 54 11 99; Rue St-Jacques 55) off Blvd St-Michel. From Paris, you pay €80/148 (€72/134 if aged under 26) one-way/return. There is one departure on most days.

Other International Services

Eurolines/Julià Via also has long-distance services at least three times weekly from Amsterdam, Brussels, Florence, Geneva, Milan, Montpellier, Nice, Perpignan, Rome, Toulouse, Venice and Zürich, and twice a week from Morocco.

TRAIN

The main international and domestic train station is **Estació Sants** (Map 4; Plaça dels Països Catalans), 2.5km west of La Rambla.

Only a handful of services, including one to Madrid, now use Estació de França, on Avinguda del Marquès de l'Argentera (Map 5). Since the discovery in 2002 of an archaeological site at the former Mercat del Born, which had been destined to house Barcelona's new provincial library, there is now talk of converting this seriously underused train station into the library.

Some long-distance and regional trains call at **Catalunya** (Plaça de Catalunya; metro Catalunya), and **Passeig de Gràcia** (Cnr Passeig de Gràcia & Carrer d'Aragó; metro Passeig de Gràcia), 10 minutes' walk north of Plaça de Catalunya.

Note that the entrance for Renfe (Red Nacional de los Ferrocarriles Españoles) long-distance trains is at the northern end of

Plaça de Catalunya and quite separate from the entrances to the metro and FGC lines. Similarly, the Renfe entrance at Passeig de Gràcia is three blocks north of the metro entrance. All this can be a little confusing for the harried traveller.

Information

It's advisable to book at least a day or two ahead for most long-distance trains, domestic or international. Tickets with **Renfe** (☎ 902 24 02 02; ⓦ www.renfe.es), the national railways, can be purchased over the phone or online.

There's a **Renfe information and booking office** (open 7am-10pm Mon-Sat, to 9pm Sun) in Passeig de Gràcia station. You'll find some consignas (left-luggage lockers) on Via (platform) 2.

At Estació Sants, the Informació Largo Recorrido windows give information on all except suburban trains. The station has a consigna (€3/4.50 for small/big locker for 24 hours), which is open 5.30am to 11pm. It also has a tourist office, a telephone and fax office, currency-exchange booths open from 8am to 10pm daily, and ATMs.

Train timetables are posted at the main stations. Impending arrivals (arribades/ llegadas) and departures (sortides/salidas) appear on electronic boards and TV screens. Timetables for specific lines are generally available free of charge.

Eurail, InterRail, Europass and Flexipass tickets are valid on Renfe trains throughout Spain. Be aware, though, that supplements apply on some services.

Types of Train in Spain

A host of different trains coast the widegauge lines of the Spanish network. A saving of a couple of hours on a faster train can mean a big hike in the fare.

For short hops, bigger cities have a local network called cercanías. In Barcelona they are known as rodalies.

Most long-distance (largo recorrido) trains have 1st (preferente) and 2nd (turista) class. The cheapest and slowest of these are the regionales, generally all-stops jobs that go between provinces within one region (although a few travel between regions). If your train is a *regional exprés* it will make fewer stops.

All trains that do journeys of more than 400km are denominated Grandes Líneas services – really just a fancy way of saying long distance. Among these are *diurnos* and *estrellas*, the standard inter-regional trains. The latter is the night-time version of the former. These are gradually being replaced by more modern trains.

Faster, more comfortable and expensive are the Talgos (Tren Articulado Ligero Goicoechea Oriol). They make only major stops and have extras such as TVs. The Talgo Pendular is a sleeker, faster version of the same thing that maintains speed by leaning into curves.

Some Talgos and other modern trains are used for limited-stop trips between major cities. These services are known as Inter-City (and, when they're really good, Inter-City Plus!). A more expensive derivative is the classier Talgo 200, a Talgo Pendular using the standard-gauge, high-speed Tren de Alta Velocidad Española (AVE) line between Madrid and Seville on part of the journey to such southern destinations as Málaga, Cádiz and Algeciras. Another AVE line is being built between Madrid and Barcelona, which will eventually link up with the French TGV.

Other new and fast services include the Barcelona-Valencia-Alicante Euromed and Arcos trains, and the Alaris service between Madrid and Castelló.

Autoexpreso and Motoexpreso wagons are sometimes attached to long-distance services for the transport of cars and motorcycles, respectively.

A *trenhotel* is an expensive sleeping-car train. There can be up to three classes on these trains, ranging from *turista* (for those sitting or in a couchette), *preferente* (sleeping car) and *gran clase* (sleeping in sheer bloody luxury).

Catalunya Services

Three types of local trains fan out from Barcelona across Catalunya. The slowest all-stops ones are called Regionals. Making fewer stops are the Deltas, while Catalunya Exprès trains are the fastest (and about 15% dearer than the others).

Long-distance mainline trains also stop at several Catalan destinations, but fares are more expensive still. Regional trains within Catalunya depart from Estació Sants; many also stop at Catalunya, Passeig de Gràcia and a couple of other of Barcelona's stations.

Rodalies are a more reliable way to get to some destinations not too far out from Barcelona (such as Sitges). They run on a six-zone system, but in January 2002 the services were integrated into a global fare system with other forms of Barcelona's public transport (see the Getting Around chapter).

For how to get about the Catalunya region, see individual destination sections in the Excursions chapter.

Other Parts of Spain

Trains run to Barcelona from most Spanish cities. There is a mind-boggling array of fare options.

The trip from Madrid can take seven to nine hours and a basic *turista* fare for the longer trip is €31 one way. The Talgo (which is quickest) costs €42 (€56 in *preferente*). If you buy a return ticket, you get 20% off the return run (25% for a same-day return). Other examples of 2nd-class travel in *diurno/estrella* trains include:

destination	duration (hrs)	fare (€)
Granada	11-12	47
Pamplona	6-7	27-36.50
San Sebastián	8-9	31-41
Zaragoza	3½-5	18.10-37.50

Euromed & Arco A high-speed AVE train on standard Spanish track connects Barcelona with Valencia (three hours) five times daily, and thrice daily with Alicante (4¾ hours). The respective *turista/preferente* fares are €32/49.50 to Valencia and €41/63.50 to Alicante. The service is known as Euromed.

The stylish Arco train connects Portbou and Alicante. It takes about 45 minutes longer than Euromed to reach Valencia from Barcelona. *Turista/preferente* fares are €29/38 to Valencia (four times daily) and €37/49 to Alicante (once daily).

The UK

Your choices from London are limited by the options in Paris, where you must change trains (for more details, see under France later in this section). If you optimise your choice of departure from London to keep waiting times for connections to a minimum, the journey time by train to Barcelona is comparable with the bus.

The privatising of the railways in the UK has created a frustrating situation for travellers. If you wish to buy a ticket straight through to a Spanish destination you are obliged to travel with Eurostar to Paris for the initial leg, which can be an expensive business if you don't book far enough ahead. To use the ferries that connect the UK with France, you will only be able to book your trip as far as Paris, where you would then have to buy another ticket for the onward journey.

Assuming you plump for Eurostar, the cheapest adult return fare to Barcelona was around UK£199 at the time of writing. You need to book at least a month ahead for such a price. People aged under 26 pay a little less. Eurostar trains leave from Waterloo station and arrive at Gare du Nord in Paris. From there you proceed to either Gare d'Austerlitz (RER B to St Michel and change for the RER C to Austerlitz), Gare Montparnasse (Metro 4) or Gare de Lyon (RER B to Châtelet and then RER A for Gare de Lyon), depending on which connection you will make.

For bookings, contact **Rail Europe Travel Centre** (☎ 0870 584 8848; W *www.raileurope .co.uk; 179 Piccadilly, London, W1V 0BA*). For information and bookings on Spanish railways from the UK, you can approach **Prestige International UK Ltd** (☎ 020-7409 0379; W *www.spanishrail.co.uk; Berkeley Square House; Berkeley Square, London W1J 6BS*).

France

The only truly direct train to Barcelona is the *trenhotel* sleeper-only job. It leaves

Gare d'Austerlitz in Paris, at 8.32pm daily and arrives at 8.24am (stopping at Limoges, Figueres, Girona and Barcelona Sants). The standard one-way fare in a couchette is €106 (€180 return). The most expensive option is a single bed in Gran Clase at €273 one way (€464 return).

Otherwise, the cheapest and most convenient option to Barcelona is the night train from Gare d'Austerlitz (leaving at 9.56pm), changing at Latour-de-Carol (7.55am) and arriving in Barcelona Sants towards the middle of the following day. That trip costs €113.70 return in 2nd class. There is an alternative train with a change at Portbou (on the coast). Under-26s get a 25% reduction. Fares rise in July and August.

Up to three TGVs (*trains de grande vitesse* – high-speed trains) also put you on the road to Barcelona (from Paris' Gare de Lyon), with a change of train at Montpellier or Narbonne. Prices and timetables vary.

Two daily direct Talgo services connect Montpellier with Barcelona (€42.10 one way in 2nd class, 4¼ hours). A couple of slower services (with a change at Portbou) also make this run. All stop in Perpignan.

When appropriate track is eventually laid, Barcelona will be linked to the French TGV network.

From Estació Sants, eight to 11 trains daily run to Cerbère (2½ hours) and four to five to Latour-de-Carol (3½ hours). From these stations you have several onwards connections to Montpellier and Toulouse.

Other International Services

Direct overnight trains from Estació Sants also run from Zürich (13 hours) and Milan (12¾ hours), from three to seven days per week, depending on the season. These trains meet connections for numerous other cities. Adult return fares from Zürich range from Sfr240 (seated) to Sfr722 (Gran Clase single bed). From Milan the fares are €154 and €476, respectively. Prices rise a little in high season. If you get standard trains (which will require at least one change in France), you are looking at Sfr129/258 one way/return from Geneva and Sfr196/369 from Zürich.

CAR & MOTORCYCLE

To give you an idea of how many clicks you'll put behind you if travelling with your own wheels, Barcelona is 1932km from Berlin, 1555km from London, 1146km from Paris, 1300km from Lisbon, 1199km from Milan, 780km from Geneva and 690km from Madrid – quite central in its own way!

Paperwork & Preparations

Vehicles must be roadworthy, registered and insured for third party at least. The Green Card, an internationally recognised proof of insurance, is compulsory.

A European breakdown assistance policy such as the AA Five Star Service or the RAC Eurocover Motoring Assistance is a good investment.

In the UK, further information can be obtained from the **RAC** (☎ 0870 572 2722; W www.rac.co.uk) or the **AA** (☎ 0870 550 0600; W www.theaa.co.uk).

For details of driving conditions in Barcelona and renting or purchase, see Car & Motorcycle in the Getting Around chapter. See also Driving Licence & Permits in the Facts for the Visitor chapter.

Access Routes

The A-7 *autopista* is the main toll road from France (via Girona and Figueres). It skirts inland around the city before proceeding south to Valencia and Alicante. About 40km southwest of Barcelona, the A-2, also a toll road, branches westwards off the A-7 towards Zaragoza. From there it links up with the N-II dual carriageway for Madrid (no tolls). Several other shorter tollways fan out into the Catalan heartland from Barcelona.

As a rule, alternative toll-free routes are busy (if not clogged). The N-II is the most important. From the French border it follows the A-7, branches off to the coast and then drops into Barcelona, from where it heads west to Lleida and beyond. Interestingly, drivers in Catalunya are the most heavily penalised – one-third of the entire country's tollways are in this region.

Coming from the UK you can put your car on a ferry from Portsmouth to Bilbao with **P&O Ferries** (☎ 0870 242 4999; W www.poportsmouth.com) or from Plymouth or Portsmouth to Santander with **Brittany Ferries** (☎ 0870 556 1600; W www.brittanyferries.co.uk). From either destination you still have a fair drive to Barcelona.

Otherwise you can opt for a ferry to France or the Channel Tunnel car train, **Eurotunnel** (☎ 0870 535 3535; W www.eurotunnel.com). The latter runs around the clock, with up to four crossings (35 minutes) an hour between Folkestone and Calais in the high season. You pay for the vehicle only and fares vary according to the time of day and season. A standard return fare for a car and passengers is UK£237. You can book in advance by phone or online, but the service is designed to let you just roll up.

Driving in Spain

Road Rules In general, standard European road rules apply. In built-up areas the speed limit is usually 50km/h, rising to 100km/h on major roads and 120km/h on *autopistas* and *autovías* (toll and toll-free motorways).

Motorcyclists must use headlights at all times. Crash helmets are obligatory on bikes of 125cc or more.

Vehicles already on roundabouts have right of way.

The blood-alcohol limit is 0.05%. Breath tests are becoming more common and if found to be over the limit you can be judged, condemned, fined and deprived of your driving licence in 24 hours. Fines for various traffic offences range from €91 for minor offences to €602 for serious ones. Nonresident foreigners will be asked to pay up on the spot. Pleading linguistic ignorance will not help – your traffic cop will produce a list of infringements and fines in as many languages as you like. If you don't pay on the spot, or have a Spanish resident go guarantor for you, your vehicle will be impounded.

Petrol Prices vary between petrol stations *(gasolineras)* and fluctuate with oil tariffs and tax policy. At the time of research, lead free (*sin plomo; 95 octane*) was priced at an average €0.77/L. A 98-octane variant cost €0.84/L, while the 97 octane type, introduced to replace leaded super (many cars in Spain still ran on super when leaded petrol was banned in January 2002), cost €0.83/L. Diesel (or *gasóleo*) comes in at €0.67/L.

Road Assistance The head office of **Real Automóvil Club de España** *(RACE; ☎ 902 30 05 05; Calle de Eloy Gonzálo 32)* is in Madrid. Its 24-hour, countrywide emergency breakdown-assistance service is free for RACE members. Your own national motoring organisation, which like the RAC and AA may have a mutual agreement with the RACE, will generally provide you with a special emergency-assistance number for use when in Spain.

The Catalunya version of RACE is **Reial Automòbil Club de Catalunya** *(RACC; ☎ 902 30 73 07; headquarters: Map 1; Avinguda Diagonal 687)*. Its assistance number is ☎ 902 10 61 06.

Whichever numbers you use, in Catalunya you may well be assisted by the RACC. If you plan on a long stay in Barcelona, you may want to take out local insurance with the RACC, which is quite possible for foreign-registered cars.

BICYCLE

If you plan to bring your own bicycle by plane, check with the airline about any hidden costs. It will have to be disassembled and packed for the journey. Bicycle (especially mountain bike) touring is growing in popularity in Catalunya. UK-based cyclists planning to do some of this during their time in Barcelona might want to contact the **Cyclists' Touring Club** *(☎ 0870 873 0060;*

> ### Warning
>
> If you are driving a foreign-plated vehicle be aware that there have been reports of 'highway pirates' at work, especially on the highways leading to Barcelona from the French border. For more information, see the Getting Around chapter.

Ⓦ *www.ctc.org.uk; Cotterell House, 69 Meadrow, Godalming, Surrey GU7 3HS)*. It can supply information to members on cycling conditions, itineraries and cheap insurance. Membership costs UK£27 per year (UK£10 for under-26s).

HITCHING

Hitching is never entirely safe and we don't recommend it. Travellers who choose to hitch will be safer if they travel in pairs and let someone know where they plan to go.

To get out of Barcelona, start well out of the city centre. The chances of anyone stopping for you on *autopistas* are low – try the more congested national highways (such as the N-II described earlier).

BOAT
Balearic Islands

Passenger and vehicular ferries to/from the Balearic Islands, operated by Trasmediterránea, dock along both sides of the Moll de Barcelona wharf in Port Vell (Map 1). Information and tickets are available from **Trasmediterránea** *(☎ 902 45 46 45;* Ⓦ *www.trasmediterranea.es)* at its terminal building on Moll de San Beltran or in the other terminal building on Moll de Barcelona, or from travel agencies.

Scheduled summer ferry service destinations to/from Barcelona are: Palma (two catamarans/one Super Ferry per day, 3¾/seven hours); Maó (once daily, Super/standard ferry, 5¼/seven hours); Ibiza City (once or twice daily, 8½ to 10½ hours). The frequency of services drops somewhat at other times of the year.

The standard fare between Barcelona and any of the islands is €25.30 one way for a 'Butaca Turista' (seat) on both standard ferries and the Super Ferry. On high-speed boats the standard fare is €47.70, or €74.30 for a 1st-class *(preferente)* seat; transporting a small car costs €135.20. On the slower boats, beds in cabins of up to four people are also available, and you'll pay up to €145.70 per person. The cost of transporting a small car is €93.30. The 'Paquente Ahorro' is a deal for four passengers with one car, which costs €357.30/366 in sleeper accommodation on standard/ Super Ferries, or €324.20 on the high-speed boats (on which a sleeper is not necessary).

An alternative fast service to/from Alcúdia (Mallorca) and Ciutadella (Menorca) is **Turbocat** (Map 1; ☎ 902 18 18 88; W www .turbocatonline.com). Buy tickets at its desk in the Moll de Barcelona terminal or at travel agencies. The service operates from April to October (daily from mid-June to mid-September). A one-way *turista* class ticket from Ciutadella to Barcelona costs €65, and from Alcúdia to Barcelona it's €62. Depending on whether your vessel calls at Alcúdia or Ciutadella first, the trip can take from three to five hours.

Italy

The Grimaldi's **Grandi Navi Veloci** (☎ 010 58 93 31, fax 010 550 92 25; W www.grimaldi .it; Via Fieschi 17/17a, Genoa) runs a high-speed, roll-on roll-off ferry service from Genoa to Barcelona three times a week.

Departures from Genoa are at 10pm (9pm late June to mid-September) Monday, Wednesday and Friday. The journey takes 18 hours and costs anything from €54 for an economy class airline-style seat in low season to €164 for a single cabin with windows (there are also some more expensive suites). A car costs from €84 to €138 depending on size and season. Departures from Barcelona are at 10pm on Tuesday and Thursday (9pm from late June to mid-September) and 2am on Sunday.

The ferry terminal in Genoa is at Via Milano (Ponte Assereto). You can book direct over the phone, through a travel agency, at the docks (if there is space) or at its website. In Barcelona, where you can book through any travel agency, the boat docks at Moll de San Beltran (Map 1). You can also get tickets directly at both ports.

ORGANISED TOURS

If you prefer to opt for a package trip to Barcelona, perhaps including some day trips to some of the destinations beyond the capital suggested in the Excursions chapter, you'll find a host of tour operators willing to help. Approach your closest Spanish tourist office for a list of tour operators in your country. A package deal can save you a little bit of hassle – at a price. For details of tour operators in Barcelona, see the Getting Around chapter.

The UK

Cresta Holidays (☎ 0870 238 7711; W www .uk.mytravel.com), which operates with the My Travel website, offers a range of city tours, fly-drive trips and other holiday options to Spain.

Another Spain specialist is **The Individual Travellers Spain** (☎ 0870 077 3773 in the UK only; 01798-869433; W www.indiv-travellers.com; Manor Court Yard, Bignor, Pulborough RH20 1QD).

Citalia (☎ 020-8686 3638; W www .citalia.com, Marco Polo House, 3-5 Lansdowne Rd, Croydon CR9 1LL) offers a long catalogue of hotels and residences in Spain in its The Real Spain program.

Caledonia Languages Abroad (☎ 0131-621 7721, fax 621 7723; The Clockhouse, Bonnington Mill, 72 Newhaven Rd, Edinburgh EH6 5QG) organises trips to southern Spain, with both activities and language-study components.

Arblaster & Clarke (☎ 01730-89334, fax 892888; W www.arblasterandclarke.com; Clarke House, Franham Rd, West Liss, Hants GU33 6JQ) organises the occasional wine-touring holidays to the Penedès region.

Cruises Barcelona is a major port of call for cruise ships (a business that suffered enormously after September 11). Trips tend

One of the cruise ships that berth at Barcelona's seafront

MANFRED GOTTSCHALK

to take a couple of weeks and typically include either a one- or two-night stop in Barcelona. One company is **Fred. Olsen Cruise Lines** (☎ 01473-742424, fax 292345; Ⓦ www.fredolsencruises.co.uk; Fred. Olsen House, White House Rd, Ipswich, Suffolk IP1 5LL). More expensive is **Holland America Line** (☎ 020-7940 4466, fax 7940 4461; Ⓦ www.hollandamerica.com; Carnival House, 5 Gainsford St, London SE1 2NE).

The USA
In the USA, **Spanish Heritage Tours** (☎ 718-544 2752, 800-456 5050; Ⓦ www.shtours .com; 116-147 Queens Blvd, Forest Hills, NY 11375) is a reputable mainstream operator that can organise a broad array of tours, including city breaks.

Australia
You can organise tours of Spain, taking in Barcelona, through **Ibertours Travel** (☎ 03-9670 8388; Ⓦ www.ibertours.com.au; 1st floor, 84 William St, Melbourne, Victoria 3000) and **Spanish Tourism Promotions** (☎ 03-9650 7377; Ⓔ sales@spanishtravels .com .au; Level 1, 178 Collins St, Melbourne, Victoria 3000).

Getting Around

EL PRAT AIRPORT
Barcelona's airport lies 12km southwest of the city at El Prat de Llobregat. The airport building contains three terminals. Terminal A handles the bulk of international arrivals and departures by non-Spanish airlines. Terminal B handles international and domestic departures with Spanish airlines, and some overspill from Terminal A (which is to be substantially expanded from 2003). Terminal C (also being expanded) is for the Pont Aeri (Puente Aereo), the Barcelona-Madrid shuttle. A new runway is planned for 2003 and a new terminal building for 2005 – all part of Barcelona's efforts to become a regional hub.

The arrivals halls are located on the ground floor; departures are on the 1st floor. The **main tourist office** (☎ 93 478 47 04; open 9am-9pm daily) is on the ground floor of Terminal B. A smaller office operating the same hours can be found on the ground floor of Terminal A.

ATMs are scattered about all three terminals and currency-exchange facilities are available at Terminals A and B. You'll also find a *correus* (post office) at these two terminals. Newspaper stands and bookshops, a smattering of bars and restaurants and duty-free gift shops provide all the essentials for airport survival.

When you arrive inside the terminals, follow the Recollida d'Equipatges/Recogida de Equipajes (baggage claim) signs to passport control (there is usually no passport control for arrivals from Schengen countries; see Visas & Documents in the Facts for the Visitor chapter).

For flight information call ☎ 93 298 38 38 (it's an automated service, so you'll need to understand Spanish enough to choose English on the options menu).

Left Luggage
The left-luggage office *(consigna)*, open 24 hours, is on the ground floor at the end of Terminal B closest to Terminal C. It charges €3.90 per item per 24-hour period or a fraction thereof.

Lost Luggage
Each terminal has a lost-luggage office on the arrivals floor if your bags don't appear on the carousel. You can also call **Alobex** (☎ 93 401 31 29) for Iberia flights, and **Eurohandling** (☎ 93 298 33 30).

TO/FROM THE AIRPORT
Train
The airport is the terminus for Renfe's *rodalies* (*cercanías* in Castilian) train line 1 (which heads for Mataró and beyond on the northeastern edge of Barcelona). With piped classical music in the background, this is a highly civilised introduction to Barcelona! These trains stop at several stations with metro connections, including Estació Sants, Catalunya, Passeig de Gràcia, Arc de Triomf and Clot. A one-way ticket costs €2.15. Since January 2002, Renfe services around Barcelona have been integrated into the ticket system for the metro, FGC railway and buses. This means you can use ordinary metro tickets and passes (see Targetas later in this section) for *rodalies* services too. If you plan to use public transport during your stay (probable) then you should ask for one of these passes rather than a simple Renfe ticket.

Trains run every 30 minutes from 6.13am to 11.15pm daily. It takes 17 minutes to Sants and 23 minutes to Catalunya station. Departures from Sants to the airport are from 5.43am to 10.16pm; from Catalunya they're six minutes earlier.

The only drawback with the train is that it's a five-minute hike (eased by moving walkways) to/from the terminal buildings – a bit of a pain if you're heavily loaded up. The station lies between terminals A and B. You get tickets either at the booth or from the automatic machines if you have coins; you then stamp them in the turnstile slot as you pass onto the platform.

Metro
In June 2000 a plan to build a new metro line (Línia 9) was approved. It will start at the airport and cross Barcelona to the planned high-speed train (AVE) station at Sagrera and beyond. Optimists predict it will be in operation by 2004.

Bus
The **A1 Aerobús** (☎ 93 415 60 20) service runs from the airport to Plaça de Catalunya via Plaça d'Espanya every 12 minutes from 6am to midnight Monday to Friday (from 6.30am on weekends and holidays). Departures from Plaça de Catalunya are from 5.30am to 11.30pm Monday to Friday (from 6am on weekends and holidays). The trip is about 40 minutes – depending on traffic – and costs €3.30.

Cheaper suburban buses (Buses EA and its night version, the EN) leave every one hour and 40 minutes for Plaça d'Espanya and cost €1. The trip takes about an hour.

In both cases you pay on the bus (unless, on the suburban bus, you have some kind of multi-trip ticket or pass – for details see Public Transport later in this section).

Taxi
A taxi to/from the centre – about a 30-minute ride depending on traffic – costs €15 to €18. There is generally no shortage of them. Occasionally unscrupulous drivers overcharge. Fares and charges are generally posted inside the passenger side of the taxi.

Parking
The short-term car parks in front of the terminals charge €1.30 per hour for the first two hours, then €0.97 per hour. If you leave the car for eight hours or more, the daily charge becomes €9.10. From the sixth day on you pay €6.10 per day. You pay at the machines (coins or credit cards) before going to your car – once you have paid, you have 20 minutes to get your car out.

You may wish to avail yourself of the **Parking VIP service** (☎ 93 478 66 71, 93 297 13 81, fax 93 478 14 85). You drive to the terminal and a driver takes your car to a covered parking area that offers permanent

surveillance. When you return, you call ahead to have your car delivered to you at your arrival terminal. You pay for a minimum of two days (€39.03). Each extra day costs about €14.

PUBLIC TRANSPORT
The metro is the easiest way of getting around and reaches most places you're likely to visit. It is supplemented by a few train lines run by Ferrocarrils de la Generalitat de Catalunya (FGC).

The main tourist office gives out the comprehensive *Guia d'Autobusos Urbans de Barcelona*, with a metro map and all bus routes. You can call for public transport information on ☎ 010.

Four **Centres d'Atenció al Client** (customer service centres), run by the Transportes Metropolitans de Barcelona (TMB), can be found in Estació Sants *(the mainline Renfe station; open 7am-9pm daily)*, and in the metro stops of Universitat, Diagonal and Sagrada Família *(all three centres open 8am-8pm Mon-Fri)*.

The **Autoritat del Transport Metropolità** *(ATM;* ⓦ *www.atm-transmet.es)* is an umbrella organisation set up since the integration of Renfe's *rodalies* service into the unified fare system in 2001.

Tickets & Targetas
In January 2002, public transport in and around Barcelona underwent an administrative overhaul, with metro, FGC trains, *rodalies* and buses all coming under the one zoned fare regime. This is mostly of interest to the commuter belt crowd, but also affects visitors to places such as Sitges (see the Excursions chapter). Single-ride tickets on all standard transport within Zone 1 (which extends beyond the airport) cost €1.

Targetas are multiple-trip transport tickets and offer worthwhile savings. They are sold at most city-centre metro stations. Targeta T-10 (€5.60) gives you 10 rides on the metro, buses and FGC trains. Each ride is valid for 1¼ hours and permits you to make changes between metro, FGC, *rodalies* and buses. On each change you validate the ticket again – if you are within the allotted time only the one trip will be deducted from your ticket. Targeta T-DIA (€4.20) gives unlimited travel on all transport for one day. Tickets can be bought at metro and FGC stations as well as TMB Centres d'Atenció al Client.

Two-/three-/four-/five-day tickets for unlimited travel on all transport *except rodalies* cost €7.60/10.80/14/16.50. These tickets, which can be good value if you move around a lot, can be bought at metro stations, tourist offices and on the Aerobús.

If you take the Aerobús from the airport, you can get an all-in-one ticket for that bus and unlimited use of Barcelona's buses and metro for two/three/four/five days at a cost of €12/14.80/17.50/19.50.

Many other options exist, including monthly passes for unlimited use of all public transport at €36.30. The Targeta T-50/30 (for 50 trips within 30 days; €23.40) and discounted tickets/passes for pensioners, students and families are further possibilities. The prices given here are for travel in Zone 1 (which includes the airport).

Bus

Buses run along most city routes every few minutes from 5am or 6am to 10pm or 11pm. On Friday, Saturday and the day before public holidays the service runs to 2am. Many routes pass through Plaça de Catalunya and/or Plaça de la Universitat. After 11pm (or 2am), a reduced network of yellow *nitbusos* (night buses) run until 3am or 5am. Some of these run to municipalities beyond the city. All night-bus routes pass through Plaça de Catalunya and most run every 30 to 45 minutes. A series of minibus routes *(bus de barri)* weave around congested areas of the city where standard buses cannot be used.

By 2005 the entire bus fleet should be equipped to deal with disabled passengers.

Bus Turístic ✸

This bus service covers two circuits (involving 27 stops) linking virtually all the major tourist sights. Tourist offices, TMB offices and many hotels have leaflets explaining the system. Tickets, available on

the bus, cost €14 for o[ne day's] rides, or €18 for two con[secutive days. The fre-]quency of buses varies fr[om 10 to 30 min-]utes, depending on the sea[son. Runs 9am to] 7.45pm daily.

Tickets entitle you to discounts of up to €2 on admission prices to more than 20 attractions, the *tramvia blau* (see Tibidabo in the Things to See & Do chapter), funiculars and cable cars, as well as shopping discounts and a meal at Kentucky Fried Chicken and Pizza Hut (oh great!). The discounts don't have to be used on the day(s) you use the bus.

Tombbus

The T1 Tombbus (€1.30) route has been thought out for shoppers and runs regularly from Plaça de Catalunya up to Avinguda Diagonal, along which it proceeds west to Plaça de Pius XII, where it turns around. On the way you pass such shopping landmarks as El Corte Inglés (several of them), Bulevard Rosa and FNAC.

Metro

The metro has five lines, which are numbered and colour-coded, and is very user friendly. Tickets are available from machines and staffed booths at most stations. The metro runs from 5am to midnight (to 11am on lines 1 and 4) Monday to Thursday, 5am to 2am on Friday, Saturday and days preceding holidays; 6am to midnight on Sunday and holidays, and 6am to 2am on holidays immediately preceding another holiday. Line 2 has access for the disabled and a handful of stations on other lines has lifts. The city's transport plan envisages that all stations will have disabled access by about 2006.

See the colour metro map at the back of the book.

FGC Suburban Trains

Suburban trains run by the FGC include a couple of useful city lines. One heads north from Plaça de Catalunya. A branch of it will get you to Tibidabo and another within spitting distance of the Monestir de Pedralbes. Some trains along this line continue beyond

.celona to Sant Cugat del Vallès, Sabadell and Terrassa.

The other FGC line heads to Manresa from Plaça d'Espanya and is less likely to be of use (except for the trip to Montserrat – see the Excursions chapter).

These trains run from about 5am (only one or two services before 6am, though) to 11pm or midnight (depending on the line) Sunday to Thursday, and 5am to 2am on Friday and Saturday.

Rodalies/Cercanías

These Renfe-run local trains serve towns around Barcelona, as well as the airport (see earlier in this chapter). For more details see the Getting There & Away chapter.

Fines

The fine for being caught without a ticket on buses is €30 and €40 on the metro and other trains.

CAR & MOTORCYCLE

An effective one-way system makes traffic flow along fairly smoothly, but you'll often find yourself flowing the opposite way that you want to go – unless you happen to have an adept navigator with you and a map with a comprehensive street index showing the

---

The Perils of Parking

MW

As you will soon discover, parking is no easy task (except in August, when half the city departs on annual vacation). Parking in Ciutat Vella is virtually impossible and frankly not worth trying for all the stress it will cause. The narrow streets of Gràcia are almost worse. The broad boulevards of l'Eixample offer a few possibilities, but you need to watch out for a lot of things. On some streets you may not park at all. In other cases you will see parts of streets marked in red – also no go. Blue markings mean you must stick money in the meter (€1.70 per hour) and leave the ticket on the dash. Obviously you can't park in driveways and the like, and anything marked in yellow usually means you are permitted to stop for up to 30 minutes for loading (càrrega) and unloading (descàrrega) only. Many people opt to take their chances and leave cars in such zones for longer – eventually you'll get a ticket and towing is common.

As a rule, the zones marked in yellow are only problematic from 8am to 8pm Monday to Saturday. This includes most of the handy, chopped-off angles (chaflanes) at intersections in l'Eixample. Meter parking is enforced during similar hours (with a break for a couple of hours around lunchtime).

There are streets in l'Eixample where – if you can find a space – you can park without worry. If the only road markings you see are white and there are no parking restriction signs, you should be OK.

The same rules apply elsewhere in the centre. Other tricks abound though. In some roads you can only park on one side, and this is swapped around every two weeks – this should be signposted (usually a round no-parking symbol with '1-15' or '16-31', meaning the first and second fortnight of the month). If you leave your car in a legal spot for any length of time and find it has been shifted days later, it's probable that some kind of road works had to be done and your car was moved.

Parking motorbikes and scooters is obviously easier. On occasion you'll see spaces marked out especially for them. Parking on the footpaths is illegal but just about everyone seems to do it.

If you get towed, call the **Dipòsit Municipal** (car pound; ☎ 93 428 45 95). Depending on where your car was nabbed, you will be directed to one of several pounds around town. You pay €100.60 for the tow and €1.60 per hour (maximum of €16 per day). Oh, the first four hours your car is held are free!

one-way streets (as do the more expensive map guides).

For the most part, it's better to abandon your car while you're here and, instead, use Barcelona's public transport.

Car Rental

You obviously wouldn't want to rent a car to slope around Barcelona, but one could come in handy for touring the countryside. It won't pay if you only intend to make a few simple day trips.

If you haven't organised a rental car from abroad, local firms such as Julià Car and Vanguard (see later for details) are generally cheaper than the big international names. From these, a typical small car such as a Peugeot 106, Opel Corsa or Fiat Punto should cost from around €42 per day with unlimited kilometres and personal accident insurance. If you hire a car for three days or more, the price starts to come down. The same car hired for a week costs €36 per day. You then have to add the 16% IVA and fuel costs. Special low weekend rates (from Friday lunchtime or afternoon to Monday morning) are worth looking into.

A popular option is to hire a little car (class A Mercedes) with **EasyCar** *(Map 6; in the UK* ☎ *0906 333 3333 at 60p per minute; in Spain* ☎ *906 29 28 27;* ⓦ *www .easycar.com).* The car pick-up and drop-off point is at Passeig de Lluís Companys (Map 6), in the underground parking area below the boulevard – the car entrance is at the northern end near the Arc de Triomf. Its opening hours are 7am to 11pm daily. Rates depend on demand and how far in advance you book – the further the better. You can be looking at €12 per day plus a €8 preparation charge and €0.08 a kilometre over the first 100km. The vehicles are tiny and, worse, bear enormous EasyCar banners – which is a bit like screaming out 'Pick me!' – but the deal can work out quite cheaply. Another option is **Holiday Autos** *(*☎ *902 44 84 49;* ⓦ *www.holidayautos.com).*

A different approach is the **Taloncar** system *(*☎ *906 30 04 01).* You buy a booklet of 10 coupons (each worth €12.62) which you can then use for car hire. The coupons

(talones) can be organised in most travel agencies, through whom you can then arrange car hire. A small car can 'cost' two coupons per day.

Rental firms (several have branches all over town) include:

Avis (Map 2; ☎ 902 13 55 31, 93 237 56 80) Carrer de Còrsega 293-295
Europcar (Map 2; ☎ 902 10 50 30) Gran Via de les Corts Catalanes 680
Hertz (Map 2; ☎ 902 40 24 05, 93 270 03 30) Carrer d'Aragó 382-384
Julià Car (Map 4; ☎ 93 402 69 00) Carrer de València 4
National/Atesa (Map 4; ☎ 902 10 01 01, 93 323 07 01) Carrer de Muntaner 45
Vanguard (Map 3; ☎ 93 439 38 80) Carrer de Viladomat 297

Avis, Europcar, Hertz and several other big rental companies have desks at the airport, Estació Sants train station and Estació del Nord bus terminus.

Vanguard also rents out motorcycles. If you want something decent for touring outside Barcelona, you'll be looking at around €87 per day.

An alternative to standard rental is to take out a short-term lease on a new Renault. There is a pick-up point in Barcelona. For details of how this operates check Renault's Eurodrive website at ⓦ www.eurodrive .renault.com.

If you are given a car with dents or other signs of wear and tear, a couple of digital camera photos when you pick it up can work wonders on the off chance the rental outlet tries to attribute the damage to you on return of the vehicle.

Purchase

Only legal residents in Spain may buy vehicles there. One way around this is to have a friend who is a resident put the ownership papers in their name.

Car-hunters need a reasonable knowledge of Spanish to get through the paperwork and understand dealers' patter. Trawling around showrooms or looking through classifieds can turn up second-hand Seats (eg, Ibiza) and similar small cars in good condition costing €1500 to €2000. The annual cost of third-party insurance on such a car, with theft and fire cover and national breakdown assistance, comes in at between €240 and €300 (with annual reductions if you make no claims).

Vehicles of five years and older must be submitted for roadworthy checks, known as Inspección Técnica de Vehículos (ITV). If you pass, you get a sticker for one or two years. Check that this has been done when buying: the test costs about €25.

For inexpensive travel, you can purchase a second-hand 50cc motorbike for anything from €250 up to €600.

Warning

If you drive a foreign or rental car to and around Barcelona, take extra care. Groups of delinquents are known to zero in on them. On the road they get you to pull over indicating you have a problem with a tyre. While you and one of them are busy examining the 'problem', the guy's sidekick empties your car.

Theft is a growing problem at the airport, too, where there have been reports of false rental-car company employees telling customers they will park the car for them. The car (and anything the poor victim hasn't taken out) then disappears. Be aware that rental-car company employees do *not* park cars for customers.

TAXI

Some 10,500 black-and-yellow taxis ply the city streets and cost €1.10 flagfall (€1.25 on Sundays and holidays, and €2.66/3.32 if you order a taxi by phone) plus meter charges. These work out to €0.84 per kilometre (slightly more from 10pm to 6am and all day weekends and holidays). A further €2 is added for airport trips, and €0.80 for each piece of luggage bigger than 55x35x35cm. The trip from Estació Sants to Plaça de Catalunya costs about €5.

You can call a taxi on: ☎ 93 303 3033, 93 225 00 00, 93 330 03 00 or 93 322 22 22. General information is available on ☎ 010. **Radio Amic** (☎ *93 420 80 86*) has taxis adapted for wheelchair users.

A green light on the roof means the taxi is for hire (*lliure/libre* in the either Catalan/Castilian sign placed in the windscreen). With 10,500 taxis in action, you rarely have to wait long to grab one (except at times on Friday and Saturday nights). There is a taxi rank by the Monument a Colom at the bottom of La Rambla (Map 5) and another on Plaça de Catalunya (Map 6).

BICYCLE & MOPED

The moped rules in Barcelona, although plenty of people zip around on bicycles.

Bike lanes have been laid out along quite a few main roads (eg, along Gran Via de les Corts Catalanes, Avinguda Diagonal, Carrer d'Aragó, Avinguda de la Meridiana and Carrer de la Marina), and most of the town is pretty flat. Otherwise, dodging around in the traffic can be a little hairy. A bike path has also been traced out along much of the waterfront from Port Olímpic towards the Riu Besòs. There are several scenic routes mapped out for bike-riders in the Collserola parkland, around Tibidabo.

You can occasionally pick up a cycle route map at the tourist office.

Bicycles on Public Transport

You can transport your bicycle on the metro except during rush hours on Monday to Friday (ie, not between 6.30am and 9.30am or 4.30pm and 8.30pm). On weekends and holidays, and throughout July and August, there are no restrictions. You can use FGC trains to carry your bicycle at any time. Finally, you can transport your bicycle on *rodalies* from 10am to 3pm Monday to Friday and all day on weekends and holidays.

Bicycle Rental

Several outlets rent out bicycles. **Un Cotxe Menys** (Map 6; ☎ *93 268 21 05; Carrer de l'Esparteria 3*) charges €9/15 for a half/whole day. Several bike-rental places just off the Born at the bottom end of Passeig de Picasso (Map 6) charge similar prices. **BCN Bike** (Map 6; ☎ *93 268 44 89; Carrer de l'Argenteria 57bis*), on a little passage off Carrer de l'Argenteria, rents out electric scooters to groups only.

Moped Rental

For nipping about town, you could make a two-stroke contribution to the city's noise pollution by renting a small-cylinder scooter. On average it will cost you up to €42 per day (plus 16% IVA). You are not supposed to take scooters beyond the city limits. **Vanguard** *(Map 3; ☎ 93 439 38 80; Carrer de Viladomat 297)* rents them out.

WALKING

Barri Gòtic and surrounding areas are ideal for walking, but you'll probably need to use public transport to reach further-flung sights (such as La Sagrada Família, Parc Güell, the Monestir de Pedralbes, Montjuïc and Tibidabo) more efficiently.

Although drivers here are generally more considerate than in, say, Madrid, do not take it for granted that cars will stop at pedestrian crossings. In fact, play it safe and assume they won't. Drivers respect red lights although they tend to set off just before they turn green.

One of the great rules of wandering around cities is 'look up' – you never know what you might see. Unfortunately, 'look down' is in some respects a safer bet in Barcelona, especially in the centre, liberally besprinkled with dog-do.

ORGANISED TOURS
Bicycle Tours

Un Cotxe Menys *(Map 6; ☎ 93 268 21 05; Carrer de la Espartería 3)* organises bicycle tours around the old centre of town, La Barceloneta and Port Olímpic. Daytime tours take place on Saturday and Sunday, starting from the store at 10am and finishing at 12.30pm. The €20 price includes a stop for a drink in Port Vell. The night version is on Tuesday and Saturday, starting at 8.30pm and finishing at midnight. The €40 price tag includes a drink stop and a meal along the Barceloneta waterfront. If you

have a large group, it will do these tours on other days of the week, too.

The **Travel Bar** (see later for details) also organises bicycle tours of the old town.

Other Tours

The Bus Turístic (see Public Transport in this chapter) is better value than conventional tours for getting around the sights, but if you want a guided trip, try **Julià Tours** *(Map 4; ☎ 93 317 64 54; Ronda de la Universitat 5)* and **Pullmantur** *(Map 2; ☎ 93 318 02 41; Gran Via de les Corts Catalanes 645)*. Both do daily city tours by coach, plus out-of-town trips to Montserrat, Vilafranca del Penedès, the Costa Brava, Girona and Figueres. Its city tours cost €32 for a half-day, €70 to €83 for a full day.

A walking tour of the Barri Gòtic on Saturday and Sunday mornings departs from the **Oficina d'Informació de Turisme de Barcelona** *(Map 6; ☎ 906 30 12 82; Plaça de Catalunya 17; tours adult/child €7/3; English at 10am, Spanish & Catalan at noon)*.

The **Travel Bar** *(Map 6; ☎ 93 342 52 52; Carrer de la Boqueria 27)* organises daily walking and weekend bicycle tours of the old city. The former take about two hours and cost €15, while the latter take up a morning and cost €20.

La Casa Elizalde *(Map 2; ☎ 93 488 05 90; Carrer de València 302)* organises courses and all sorts of other activities across the city. Also on offer here are some Barcelona walks (which generally occupy a morning and cost €5 per person) and one-day or weekend excursions outside the city. The tours are generally aimed at locals but if you can deal with Catalan (you may find this the majority language), they can be fun and informative.

For other guided services and tailor-made options, get in touch with the Barcelona Guide Bureau *(☎ 93 310 77 78; W www .bgb.es)*.

Walking Tours

Before getting into the nitty-gritty of what there is to see and do in Barcelona, here are some thematic itineraries to get you oriented. We suggest two general themes, each divided into two connecting walks.

The first two take you around Ciutat Vella (old city), a route spanning Roman times to the 18th century. The second walk follows on where the first left off, and together they form a single circuit – too much for one day if you intend to do anything more than march past and join the dots. This is not the idea!

The second theme is devoted entirely to Modernisme. Again, the second walk takes up where the first left off.

You will notice a few overlaps between the Ciutat Vella and Modernisme circuits, so you may want to combine elements of the tours, or come up with your own. Sights preceded by an asterisk are dealt with in the Things to See & Do chapter.

Quite a few sights beyond the thematic and/or geographical scope of these tours are mentioned only in passing or not at all – you can read more about them in the Things to See & Do chapter. Conversely, several minor sites get just a quick mention here.

CIUTAT VELLA CIRCUITS

A walking tour of the medieval rabbit warren that is Old Barcelona will necessarily weave, wind and bend back on itself. If you intend to stop at sights along the way, you'll need to allow two good, long days to be able to complete both walks.

Walk 1: Barri Gòtic & La Ribera

In this walk (about 3.5km) you explore the heart of the city. This is where the Romans built their outpost, upon the core of which medieval Barcelona slowly grew – it remains the secular and religious centre of the city to this day.

Plaça de Sant Jaume This square (item #1 on map) is in the heart of Barcelona and

makes a reasonable place from which to start the walk.

The northwestern and southeastern sides of the square are lined by the *Palau de la Generalitat (#2) and *Ajuntament (#3), the seats of regional and city government, respectively. Just north of the medieval square, and possibly incorporating some of it, lay Roman Barcino's forum, opposite which stood the temple on a slight rise known as Mont Taber. Together these features formed the centre of civic and religious life. The town's two main roads crossed through the forum. From roughly north to south ran the *decumanus* (now Carrer del Bisbe Irurita), intersected by the *cardo* – the standard Roman town plan. Barcino was a military camp turned into a town – you can learn more about it in the Museu d'Història de la Ciutat.

Jewish Quarter & Around From Plaça de Sant Jaume, head west along Carrer del Call, which is the main street in medieval Barcelona's Jewish quarter (Call). Carrer de Ferran, the straight street just below it, also leading towards La Rambla, was rammed through in 1823. At No 5, the jewellery shop just past Carrer de Ramon del Call, you can see remnants of the Roman walls and southwestern gate. A block north up here you reach Carrer de Marlet. At No 1 is a Hebrew inscription in the wall, one of the few overt reminders of the area's former identity. According to the Castilian translation underneath (1820), a rabbi, Samuel Hasareri, must have lived or died here. What is truly intriguing is the apparent date of his death (AD 692).

The next junction is with Carrer dels Banys Nous, where the Jewish community was permitted to build new public baths just beyond the then city walls (before Jaume I raised new walls along La Rambla). From here the street changes name to Carrer de la Boqueria. Take the next right and follow it into Plaça de Sant Josep Oriol (a nice spot for a drink). The Gothic church in front of you is ***Santa Maria del Pi** (#4; entrance in the adjoining square). Opposite it, at No 4, stands the **Palau de Fiveller** (#5), a one-time private mansion dating to 1571.

Wend your way back east down Carrer de l'Ave Maria, dogleg left up Carrer dels Banys Nous and first right up Baixada de Santa Eulàlia (we are back in the Call). Where the street name changes to Carrer de Sant Sever, you'll see a tiny lane to your left. Head down this into a quiet, leafy, but a tad neglected square, which boasts the rather obscure **Museu del Calçat** *(#6; ☎ 93 301 45 33; Plaça de Sant Felip Neri 5; admission €2; open 11am-2pm Tues-Sun)*, or footwear museum (with everything from Egyptian sandals to dainty ladies' shoes of the 18th century). The church before you is the baroque **Església de Sant Felip Neri** (#7), completed in 1752. It adjoins the ***Palau Episcopal** (#8; or Palau del Bisbat). Follow Carrer de Montjuïc del Bisbe, surely one of the narrowest lanes in Barcelona, into Carrer del Bisbe Irurita.

The Catedral You are facing the entrance into the shady cloister of the ***Catedral** (#9). You *could* turn right and head back to Plaça de Sant Jaume, passing first the modest **Església de Sant Sever** (#10) and then the main Gothic facade of the Palau de la Generalitat.

Roman Route However, we will turn left (northwest) and head out through the old city gates (parts of the Roman originals are still extant) where Carrer del Bisbe Irurita leads into Plaça Nova. (For the record, the southwestern gates stood on Carrer del Call. To the southeast, the entrance to Barcino was on what is now Carrer de Regomir, while the northeastern exit was about where Carrer de la Llibreteria runs into Baixada de la Llibreteria.)

Proceed up Carrer dels Arcs and a short way along Avinguda del Portal de l'Àngel before hanging a left into Carrer de la Canuda. It is speculated this was part of the Roman branch road off the Via Augusta (that linked Rome to Cádiz) into Barcelona.

Rough Justice

At the junction of Baixada de Santa Eulàlia and Carrer de Sant Sever you may notice a devotional niche and a ceramic plaque quoting a passage from one of the works of the 19th-century Catalan cleric and writer Jacint Verdaguer. He talks of one of the many tortures of Santa Eulàlia, joint patron saint of Barcelona. Supposedly born in Roman Barcino before Christianity became the empire's official religion, Eulàlia was so appalled by the licentious living of her contemporaries that she became a Christian.

This apparently was not considered good form, and the locals took time off to demonstrate the extent of their disapproval. Flung into a tower in the Call, she subsequently underwent a series of highly unpleasant trials – apparently one of them was to be stuffed into a barrel (some versions say with nails hammered into it) which was rolled down the hill of what is now Baixada de Santa Eulàlia. She eventually died at the stake (no-one can agree where) and her purported remains lie buried in the crypt of the Catedral. At least that's what we think. Many experts actually identify her with a like-named saint from Mérida (Extremadura, western Spain) and there is no shortage of doubting Thomases who claim the whole story is a load of old tosh.

Proceed until you hit Plaça de la Vila de Madrid, marked by a **Roman cemetery** (#11) with a few sad looking tombs.

In Search of Guifré el Pelós Take Carrer de Bertrellans north a block to Carrer de Santa Anna. Turn right and you'll find almost immediately to your left a lane that leads into a surprisingly tranquil square backed by the unassuming **Església de Santa Anna** (#12). It dates to the 12th century, but little remains of the original Romanesque structure. The Gothic cloister is a shady haven – if you can get in.

Back on Carrer de Santa Anna, cross Avinguda del Portal de l'Àngel and continue down

WALK 1: BARRI GÒTIC & LA RIBERA

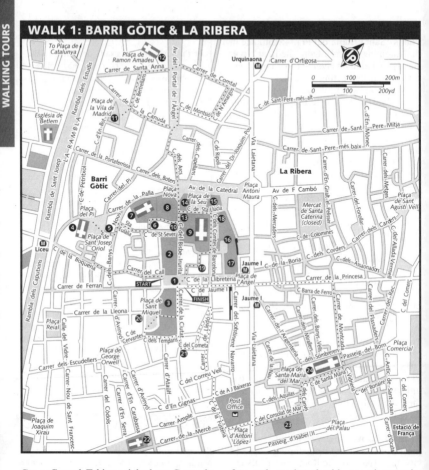

Carrer Comtal. Taking a right down Carrer de N'Amargos is interesting if only to see the plaque at No 8. It claims the palace garden walls of the first Comte (Count) of Barcelona, Guifré el Pelós (Willy the Hairy – see History in the Facts about Barcelona chapter) stood here. Carrer de N'Amargos was also the first in the city to get gas lighting.

Back to the Catedral Turn right at Carrer de Montsió, and at Avinguda del Portal de l'Àngel take a left turn and retrace your steps to Plaça Nova and the Catedral. The narrow lanes around the Catedral are traffic

free and are dotted with sometimes quite accomplished buskers.

Re-enter the Roman gates (note on your left the remnants of the aqueducts that supplied Roman Barcino with water) and take the first left. You are on Carrer de Santa Llúcia. On your right is the Romanesque *Capella de Santa Llúcia (#13; wedged onto the Catedral) dedicated to the saint of the same name. On your left is *Casa de l'Ardiaca (#14). Further ahead on your right is the main entrance to the Catedral. The building directly ahead of you is the *Casa de la Pia Almoina (#15).

Way to go (clockwise from top left): a taxi passes a modern mural in El Raval; spot a speedy route with a bicycle map; Barcelona's metro lines, Plaça de Catalunya; a bus displays the colours of Barça, the city's prestigious soccer team; popular parking spot for motorbikes in Plaça de Catalunya

BARBARA VAN ZANTEN

NEIL SETCHFIELD

MARTIN HUGHES

VITO VAMPATELLA

The rhythms of Barcelona (clockwise from top left): fiery flamenco stirs spirits at a *tablao* (flamenco show); all ages join in a performance of Catalunya's national dance each week on Plaça de la Seu; a *toreror* (bullfighter) takes his toll; passionate Barcelonins let the conversation flow on La Rambla

The lane heading southeast down the eastern flank of the Catedral, Carrer dels Comtes de Barcelona, will lead you to the complex of buildings making up the former Palau Reial Major. Turn left into the courtyard known as *Plaça del Rei (#16); access to the complex (which includes an underground tour of this sector of Roman Barcino) is through the *Museu d'Història de la Ciutat (#17) and the *Museu Frederic Marès (#18). When you're through, leave Plaça del Rei via the street you entered it from, cross over Carrer dels Comtes de Barcelona and take the next left to dogleg your way down Carrer del Paradis for a quick look at what's left of the *Temple Romà Augusti (#19), Barcino's Roman temple. This brings you back to Plaça de Sant Jaume, and this might be a jolly good moment to take a breather.

Southern Barri Gòtic From Plaça de Sant Jaume, head southeast down Carrer de la Ciutat along the only remaining Gothic facade of the Ajuntament (town hall). Turn right around the building and you end up in the rather nondescript Plaça de Sant Miquel. The one-time Roman baths here have long since been covered up. Still in one piece, however, is the charming 15th-century Casa Centelles (#20), on the corner of Baixada de Sant Miquel. You can wander into the fine Gothic-Renaissance courtyard if the gates are open, but that's as far as you'll get.

Head northeast again along Carrer dels Templaris and make a right down Carrer de la Ciutat. Where it becomes Carrer de Regomir you will notice the site of Roman Barcino's southernmost **city gate** and parts of the 3rd- and 4th-century AD city wall. To get a closer look, walk up a side passage and enter the Centre Cívic Pati Llimona (☎ 93 268 47 00). Here they stage art shows and the like and you can wander in for free from 9am to 2pm and 4.30pm to 8.30pm daily.

Just beyond the gate at No 13 is another 15th-century mansion, Casa Gualbes (#21). Just for fun, backtrack a little and turn into Carrer del Cometa and then left into Carrer de Palma. Follow this into the charming little Plaça de Sant Just, flanked by a Gothic church of the same name and a lovely spot for a rest and coffee.

From the square you can now take another street back down towards the waterfront, Carrer de Lledó. It's a rundown old lane, but once was a fine medieval residential street. Follow it (don't mind the changes of name en route) all the way down to **Carrer de la Mercè**. The baroque church of the same name, **Església de la Mercè** (#22; home to Barcelona's most celebrated patron saint), lies three blocks southwest.

La Ribera You are going to head northeast, so cross Via Laietana into La Ribera, and stroll along Carrer del Consolat de Mar past **La Llotja** (#23), the city's medieval stock exchange. The fine Gothic interior built in the 14th century is encased in a neoclassical facade. Picasso and Miró both attended art school in this building. It is now the seat of Barcelona's Chamber of Commerce but for some years renovation works have made visits by the public impossible. At the time of writing it was not known when such visits might again become an option. For information on the latest situation call ☎ 93 416 93 00.

When you see Carrer dels Canvis on your left, take this to reach Plaça de Santa Maria del Mar. The area is sprinkled with appealing little bars and places to eat, and dominated by the Gothic *Església de Santa Maria del Mar (#24). Wander along its eastern flank and around the apse you'll find yourself in *Carrer de Montcada, a fine medieval street bursting with mansions, museums, shops and a couple of choice watering holes. This is a good area to hang about and you may well want to save any further leg-stretching for another day.

If not, the remainder of our route takes you back across Barri Gòtic along Carrer de la Princesa, over Via Laietana, and along Carrer de Jaume I back to Plaça de Sant Jaume.

Walk 2: El Raval
This wander will have you in motion for about 3.3km. Beginning at **Plaça de Sant**

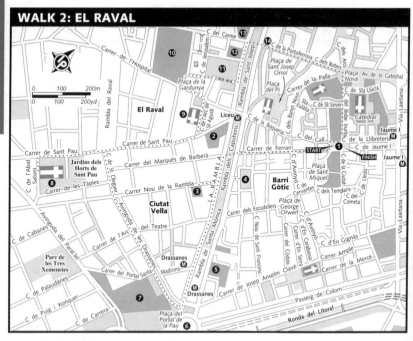

WALK 2: EL RAVAL

Jaume (item #1 on map), follow Carrer de Ferran until it spills on to La Rambla; you'll see *Gran Teatre del Liceu (#2; see the Entertainment chapter) virtually in front of you. Our objective now is to reach the waterfront.

As you wander down La Rambla you can duck to the right down Carrer Nou de la Rambla (carved through El Raval at the end of the 18th century to give quicker access to Montjuïc from the centre) to see Gaudí's *Palau Güell (#3; see Walk 3) or to the left for *Plaça Reial (#4). Further down La Rambla on the left is the *Museu de Cera (#5; wax museum) and right on the waterfront traffic circle the 19th-century *Monument a Colom (#6; known to Anglos as Columbus). Over to your right are the great Gothic shipyards, the *Drassanes (#7), which house the fine *Museu Marítim.

From here each sight requires a bit of legwork. Head west along Avinguda de les Drassanes and on to Carrer de Sant Pau. A few blocks towards Avinguda del Paral.lel is the Romanesque *Església de Sant Pau del Camp (#8). You then backtrack most of the way along Carrer de Sant Pau towards La Rambla, turning left up Carrer de l'Arc de Sant Agustí. Església de Sant Agustí (#9) is where the city's main Good Friday procession begins. At Carrer de l'Hospital head west for the *Antic Hospital de la Santa Creu (#10).

For a change of scene and a departure from the medieval side of Barcelona's life, you can wander from the hospital across Plaça de la Gardunya into the back end of the bustling *Mercat de la Boqueria (#11) before re-emerging on La Rambla. To the left (heading towards Plaça de Catalunya) are, firstly, the 18th-century *Palau de la Virreina (#12) and then, across Carrer del Carme, the baroque *Església de Betlem (#13). Cross the road to No 118 – the Llibreria & Informaciò Cultural de la Generalitat de Catalunya, housed in a former mansion, the **Casa de Comillas** (#14), which was built in 1774. It was one of many such houses of the well-to-do that went up along La Rambla during the late 18th and early 19th centuries.

Should you want to return to the centre of Barri Gòtic and the starting point of this series of walks, simply head down Carrer de la Portaferrissa – you'll emerge onto Plaça Nova near the Catedral. Follow Carrer del Bisbe Irurita southeast to return to Plaça de Sant Jaume.

MODERNISME CIRCUIT

If you wanted to see every vaguely Modernista building or facade in Barcelona, you'd probably need a week. The itineraries that follow are by no means exhaustive but include the main edifices and a sprinkling of lesser known ones. Where possible, the completion dates of buildings are given.

Walk 3: Modernista Architecture (1)

On the assumption that you are feeling methodical, are chronologically inclined and have nosed around Ciutat Vella, we'll start this 2.5km meander there too.

*Palau Güell (#1), on Carrer Nou de la Rambla in El Raval, is our starting point. It is an early job done by Gaudí (1886) for his main patron, the industrialist Eusebi Güell. Walk a few paces east on to La Rambla and turn left (north). Within a couple of blocks you pass the **Antiga Casa Figueras** (#2; 1902) at No 83, with its elaborate tilework and, virtually across the road, **Casa Quadros** (#3), lavishly decorated in oriental style with outward-jutting dragon and umbrellas (which tell you what this place once sold). Make a quick detour down Carrer de Sant Pau and peer inside the restaurant of the **Fonda Espanya** (#4; 1903, now part of Hotel España – see the Places to Stay chapter). Ramon Casas had a hand in the decoration.

*Mercat de la Boqueria (#5) is on your left as you proceed up La Rambla. It is one of several covered markets that can be considered Modernista constructions, although it was built over a long period – 1840 to 1914. Cross the boulevard and head northeast along Carrer de Santa Anna, take a right on to Avinguda del Portal de l'Àngel and then turn left into Carrer de Montsió. Here you can admire **Casa Martí** (#6) – Els Quatre Gats restaurant – which, along with being *the* hang-out for Modernista artists and other hip souls from 1897 to 1903, was in fact one of Puig i Cadafalch's very first creations (1896).

Take the first left (Passatge del Patriarca), then make a right turn down Carrer Comtal. This takes you into the busy boulevard Via Laietana. Head north a few paces and cross to the little lane called Carrer de Ramon Mas. Spare a moment to admire the **Caixa de Pensions** (#7) on Via Laietana 56. This largely neo-Gothic fantasy was headquarters to the bank of the same name from 1914 to 1917. Follow Carrer de Ramon Mas (it turns right down Carrer de Francesc de Paula into Carrer de Sant Pere més alt), to stand before Domènech i Montaner's *Palau de la Música Catalana (#8). Now backtrack to Via Laietana and cruise north along Carrer de les Jonqueres and cross Plaça d'Urquinaona. As you head up Carrer de Roger de Llúria you will pass the **Cases Cabot** (#9; 1905) at Nos 8–14, designed by Josep Vilaseca. The first doorway has fine decoration. Around the corner is Gaudí's **Casa Calvet** (#10; 1900) on Carrer de Casp 48. Inspired by the baroque, the main attraction is the staircase inside.

We continue up to Gran Via de les Corts Catalanes where, at No 654, we pass Enric Sagnier's **Casa Mulleras** (#11; 1904), the best feature of which is the gallery on the facade. Further west, Josep Vilaseca's **Casa Pia Batlló** (#12; 1906), on Rambla de Catalunya 17, is most interesting for its use of ironwork.

Cross the Gran Via and then head northwest a couple of blocks along Rambla de Catalunya, turn right into Carrer del Consell de Cent and on a block to the corner of Passeig de Gràcia. Here is *Casa Lleo Morera (#13; 1905), first of the Manzana de la Discordia buildings. The other two, *Casa Amatller (#14) and *Casa Batlló (#15), are around the corner to your left.

WALKS 3 & 4: MODERNISTA ARCHITECTURE

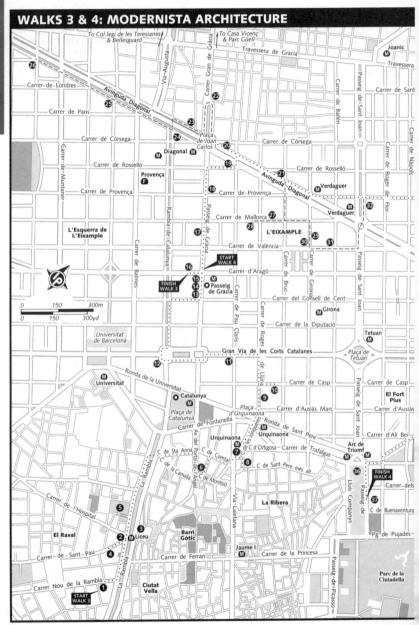

The next left into Carrer d'Aragó takes you to the ***Fundació Antoni Tàpies** (#16), originally built by Domènech i Montaner for the publishers Editorial Montaner i Simon (1885).

Especially if you choose to visit Palau Güell and the Fundació Antoni Tàpies, that will probably do you for one day. You can relax a bit at one of the several barnlike tapas bars along the lower end of Passeig de Gràcia of sip a coffee in **Café Torino** at Passeig de Gràcia 59. This is also a handy place to end the walk as you have the Passeig de Gràcia metro station to hand.

Walk 4: Modernista Architecture (2)

The core of this walk is about 5km, but you can prolong it by including some lesser buildings, or ease the pain by occasionally jumping on to the metro.

Starting from where the previous walk ends, head up Passeig de Gràcia (you will have noticed the boulevard's Modernista street lamps) from the metro stop past **Casa Enric Batlló** (#17) at No 75, another apartment building by Vilaseca. Cross at Carrer de Provença for Gaudí's masterpiece, ***La Pedrera** (#18; formerly called Casa Milà) before turning right at the next block into Carrer de Rosselló. On the corner of Carrer de Pau Claris is Puig i Cadafalch's ***Palau Quadras** (#19).

Across Avinguda Diagonal is the **Casa Comalat** (#20; 1911) by Salvador Valeri. The Gaudí influence on this Modernista late-comer is obvious. Head around the back to Carrer de Còrsega to see a lighter, more playful facade. If you can sneak in, you can admire the fine mosaics and stained glass inside. Heading east a couple of blocks down Avinguda Diagonal you reach ***Casa de les Punxes** (#21).

At this point you've probably had more than enough for one day. If you are a die-hard, another half dozen or so buildings can be seen around here and further west up the Diagonal. On the walking-tour map they are Nos 22-26: Domènech i Montaner's **Casa Fuster** (#22; 1910); Sagnier's **Església de Pompeia** (#23; 1915); Puig i Cadafalch's

Gaudí Beyond the Walk

Separate excursions should be planned for Gaudí's **Parc Güell** in the northwest of the city, **Finca Güell** (better known as the Palau Reial) and, out of town, the **Colònia Güell**. Another building well worth going to is **Casa Vicenç** (1888; Carrer de les Carolines 22; FGC Plaça Molina). Its angular appearance is enough proof that this is early Gaudí, but it is awash with colour and shape that make it stand out in any case.

Gaudí also added some touches to the **Col·legi de les Teresianes** in 1889 – the most distinctive features are the parabolic arches. It is possible to visit the school on Saturday mornings (but not during Easter, July or August), but you have to call ☎ 93 212 33 54 to arrange it. Gaudí fanatics might want to reach **Bellesguard** (Map 1), a house he built in 1909 on the site of the ancient palace of the Catalan King Martí I. It's quite a walk from the nearest FGC station, Plaça de John F Kennedy.

Many of these places are normally closed to the public, but the rule was loosened for the Gaudí year (which, alas, ended October 2002).

Casa Serra (#24; 1903); Manuel Sayrach's **Casa Sayrach** (#25; 1918); and also Puig i Cadafalch's **Casa Company** (#26; 1911).

A further cluster of minor Modernista creations lies sprinkled south of Avenida Diagonal between Carrer de Roger de Llúria and Passeig de Sant Joan. On the walking tour map they are items #27–32. However, you still have some major Modernista sights to deal with and, as it is preferable to see them, you might be better off leaving this lot for another day or forgetting about them altogether.

Should you get around to them, from Casa de les Punxes (#21) drop down Carrer del Bruc to Carrer de Mallorca. **Casa Thomas** (#27; 1898), at No 291 built by Domènech i Montaner, is your first port of call. It is one of his earlier efforts – the ceramic details are a trademark. Less than a block away, **Palau Montaner** (#28) was finished off by the same architect in 1893. Jeroni Granell's **Casa Granell** (#29; 1903), on Carrer de Girona 122, is a colourful companion. Virtually across the road at No 113 is Domènech i Montaner's **Casa Lamadrid** (#30; 1902). **Casa Llopis i Bofill** (#31; 1902), on Carrer de València 339, is an interesting block of flats by Antoni Gallissà – the facade is particularly striking. Puig i Cadafalch's **Casa Macaya** (#32; 1901), on Passeig de Sant Joan 108, has a wonderful courtyard, if you can manage to get a look inside.

However, let's assume you don't want to run around here yet. You have reached ***Casa de les Punxes** (#21), and those who don't want to head straight for a footbath will probably have their hearts set on Gaudí's ***La Sagrada Família** (#33). To save on toe power you could jump on the metro at Verdaguer station and travel one stop on line 5.

Another stop on line 5 takes you to the ***Hospital de la Santa Creu i de Sant Pau** (#34). Or you could walk up along Avinguda de Gaudí, which sports some fine Modernista street lamps.

Even if you are not interested in bullfighting, you might want to cast your eye briefly over the ***Plaça de Braus Monumental** (#35; 1915), five blocks or one metro stop southeast of La Sagrada Família (metro Monumental), on the corner of Gran Via de les Corts Catalanes and Carrer de la Marina. It was built by Ignasi Mas and is the larger of the city's two bullfighting rings. The other, Les Arenes, on Plaça d'Espanya, was built around the same time but is no longer in use. Both edifices play with Islamic themes, but you could swear that Mas had a dash of Dalí's blood in his veins – the arena is topped by ceramic-clad eggs!

From the Plaça de Braus Monumental, walk two blocks southeast to Carrer de Ribes, where you swing south towards the ***Arc de Triomf** (#36), built by Vilaseca for the Universal Exhibition in 1888. Heading southeast again along Passeig de Lluís Companys towards the Parc de la Ciutadella you pass on your left the **Palau de Justicia** (#37; 1915), a rather austere, modern building done largely by Sagnier.

At Passeig de Pujades you swing right and then left into Passeig de Picasso. On your left is Domènech i Montaner's ***Castell dels Tres Dragons** (#38), now the Museu de Zoología.

Things to See & Do

Barcelona offers a rich palette of sights with something to interest everyone: from the remains of Roman Barcino to the early opus of Picasso; from a grand medieval seafaring museum to one of Europe's most astounding aquariums; from the monuments of the Modernistas to the modern art of Miró.

Museum and art gallery opening hours vary considerably, but as a rule of thumb you should be OK between about 10am and 6pm in most places (many shut for lunch from around 2pm to 4pm, though). Most museums and galleries close all day Monday and from 2pm Sunday. Each year there is talk of night-time opening in some museums during the summer – check with the tourist office for the latest details.

Explanations tend to be in Catalan, although English gets a fairly good run – sometimes better than Castilian!

Tickets & Discounts

Admission prices vary, but €2 to €7 covers the range of most. Students generally pay a little over half this, as do senior citizens (aged 65 and over) with appropriate ID and children aged under 12.

Possession of a Bus Turístic ticket (see under Public Transport in the Getting Around chapter) entitles you to discounts to some museums.

The Ruta del Modernisme ticket (see the boxed text later in this chapter) entitles you to discounted admission to several key Modernista sights. It is good value.

Articket gives you admission to six important art galleries for €15. The galleries included are the Museu Nacional d'Art de Catalunya, the Museu d'Art Contemporani de Barcelona (Macba), the Fundació Antoni Tàpies, the Cultura Contemporània de Barcelona (CCCB), the Fundació Joan Miró and La Pedrera.

You can pick up the ticket through **Tel-Entrada** (☎ *902 10 12 12*; ⓦ *www.telentrada .com*), at the tourist office located on Plaça

Highlights

- Behold the inspired magic of Gaudí's unfinished masterpiece, La Sagrada Família
- Take courage and 'run the fire' during the madness of the Festa de la Mercè in September
- Savour fine seafood in one of Barcelona's quality restaurants
- Board a full-size replica of Don Juan's galley in the swash-buckling Museu Marítim
- Ferret out the many hidden bars secreted away throughout Ciutat Vella
- Ride the city's only surviving tram up to Tibidabo and feast on the views
- Sip a summer's evening flute of *cava* on the weird roof of La Pedrera
- Go underground at the Museu d'Història de la Ciutat to discover Barcelona's Roman origins
- Take a stroll down La Rambla – any time of the day or night
- Indulge in a drink or three at a summertime terrace on Gràcia's Plaça del Sol

de Catalunya or at selected branches of Caixa Catalunya bank.

If you intend to get around Barcelona fast and want to visit multiple museums in the blink of an eye, the Barcelona Card might come in handy. It costs €16.25/19.25/22.25 (a little less for children aged four to 12) for 24/48/72 hours. You get free transport and up to 50% off admission prices to many museums and other sights, as well as minor discounts on purchases at a limited number of shops, restaurants and bars. The card is available at the main tourist office, where you should have a look at the pamphlet first to see whether the discounted sights are what you were hoping to see.

Heritage Havens

Barcelona counts five Unesco World Heritage Sites: Palau Güell, Parc Güell, La Pedrera (Casa Milà), Palau de la Música, and Hospital de la Santa Creu i de Sant Pau. All are Modernista sites, the first three by Gaudí and the others by Domènech i Montaner.

LA RAMBLA (MAP 6)

Spain's most famous street, although clearly the preserve of visitors, is still a worthy place to first take the city's pulse. Flanked by narrow traffic lanes, the middle of La Rambla is a broad, tree-lined pedestrian boulevard, crowded every day until the wee hours with a cross-section of Barcelona's varied populace and out-of-towners.

Dotted with cafés, restaurants, kiosks and newsstands that sport reams of international newspapers and pornography, and enlivened by buskers, pavement artists, mimes and living statues, La Rambla rarely allows a dull moment.

La Rambla gets its name from a seasonal stream (*raml* in Arabic) that once ran here. It was outside the city walls until the 14th century, and built up with monastic buildings and, subsequently, mansions of the well-to-do from the 16th to the early 19th centuries. Unofficially, it's divided into five sections – this explains why, to many people, the boulevard also goes by the name of Las Ramblas – but street numbers are in a single sequence starting at the bottom (waterside) end. The following follows La Rambla south from Plaça de Catalunya.

Rambla de Canaletes

Near the northern end of La Rambla is a turn-of-the-century **drinking fountain**, the water of which supposedly emerges from what were once known as the springs of Canaletes. It used to be said of people who lived in Barcelona that they 'drank the waters of Les Canaletes'. Nowadays they say that anyone who drinks from the fountain will return to Barcelona, which is not such a bad prospect. A block to the east at the end of this first stretch of La Rambla along Carrer de la Canuda, is Plaça de la Vila de Madrid, with a sunken garden where some **Roman tombs** have been exposed (see also the Walking Tours chapter).

Rambla dels Estudis

This second stretch, from below Carrer de la Canuda to Carrer de la Portaferrissa, is also called Rambla dels Ocells (birds) because of its twittering bird market.

Just before Carrer del Carme, the **Església de Betlem** was constructed in baroque style for the Jesuits in the late 17th and early 18th centuries to replace an earlier church destroyed by fire in 1671. Fire was a bit of a theme for this site: the church was once considered the most splendid of Barcelona's few baroque offerings, but leftist arsonists torched it in 1936.

Rambla de Sant Josep

This section, from Carrer de la Portaferrissa to Plaça de la Boqueria, is lined with verdant **flower stalls**, which give it the alternative name Rambla de les Flors (flowers).

The **Palau de la Virreina** (*La Rambla de Sant Josep 99*) is a grand 18th-century rococo mansion housing an arts/entertainment information and ticket office run by the Ajuntament (town hall).

Continuing towards the waterfront, you are confronted by the bustling sound, smell and taste-fest of the **Mercat de la Boqueria**. It is possibly La Rambla's most interesting building, not so much for its Modernista-influenced design as for the action of the food market.

Barcelona seems to take pride in being a pleasure centre and in the **Museu de l'Eròtica** (☎ *93 318 98 65, fax 93 301 08 96; La Rambla de Sant Josep 96; admission €7; open 11am-midnight daily*) you can observe how people have been enjoying themselves since ancient times – lots of Karma Sutra and flickering porn flicks from the 1920s.

Plaça de la Boqueria, where four side streets meet just north of Liceu metro station, presents the opportunity to walk all over a Miró – the colourful **Mosaïc de Miró** in the pavement, with one tile signed by the artist.

THINGS TO SEE & DO

Rambla dels Caputxins

Also called Rambla del Centre, this stretch of La Rambla runs from Plaça de la Boqueria to Carrer dels Escudellers. The latter street is named after the potters' guild, founded in the 13th century, whose members lived and worked here (their raw materials came principally from Sicily). On the western side of La Rambla is the side facade of the **Gran Teatre del Liceu**, Barcelona's famous 19th-century opera house, which was reopened in late 1999 after being gutted by fire in 1994. The Liceu launched such Catalan stars as Josep (aka José) Carreras and Montserrat Caballé. It is possible to get onto a guided tour of the theatre that are held from 9.45am to 11am daily. Call ☎ 93 485 99 00 or enquire at the theatre's box office to reserve yourself a place.

Further south on the eastern side of Rambla dels Caputxins, is the entrance to the palm-shaded Plaça Reial (see the Barri Gòtic section for details). Below this point La Rambla gets seedier, with a few strip clubs and peep shows.

Rambla de Santa Mònica

The final stretch of La Rambla widens out to approach the Columbus monument (Monument a Colom; see following) overlooking Port Vell. The road is named after the Convento de Santa Mònica that once stood on the western flank of the street and has since been converted into an art gallery and cultural centre, the **Centre d'Art Santa Mònica** (Map 6; ☎ 93 316 28 10; La Rambla de Santa Mònica 7).

On the eastern side of Rambla de Santa Mònica, at the end of narrow Passatge de la Banca, is the **Museu de Cera** (wax museum; ☎ 93 317 26 49; Passatge de la Banca 7; adult/child under 12 yrs €6.65/3.75; open 10am-1.30pm & 4pm-7.30pm Mon-Fri, 11am-2pm & 4.30pm-8.30pm Sat-Sun & holidays). Inside are about 300 wax figures, ranging from tableaux of a Gitano (gypsy) cave, a bullring medical room and a hall of horror, to statues of Cleopatra, Franco and even Yasser Arafat. Also in the roll call are several good and great Catalans, such as writer Ramon Llull.

Monument a Colom (Map 5)

The goings on around the bottom of La Rambla and the harbour beyond it, are supervised by the tall Columbus monument (lift €1.80; open 9am-8.30pm daily June-24 Sept, 10am-2pm & 3.30pm-7.30pm Mon-Fri, 10am-7.30pm Sat-Sun & holidays Apr-May, 10am-1.30pm & 3.30pm-6.30pm Mon-Fri, 10am-6.30pm Sat-Sun & holidays 25 Sept-Mar), built for the Universal Exhibition in 1888. It was in Barcelona that Columbus gave the delighted Catholic Monarchs a report of his first discoveries in the Americas, but that's about the extent of his involvement with the place. Or is it? It was popularly believed in the 19th century that Columbus was one of Barcelona's most illustrious sons, although it is commonly accepted that he was born and raised in Genoa (that town's senior officials attended the inauguration of the monument). Then, in 1998, a Catalan historian announced he had evidence to prove Columbus was in fact a Catalan, which would put the mockers on claims that a little cottage preserved in downtown Genoa is his birthplace. At any rate, Columbus died penniless and forgotten in 1506 in Valladolid, central Spain.

Museu Marítim (Map 5)

West of the Monument a Colom, on Avinguda de les Drassanes, stand the Reials Drassanes (royal shipyards), a rare work of nonreligious monumental Gothic architecture that now houses the Museu Marítim (☎ 93 342 99 20; Avinguda de les Drassanes; adult/student & senior €5.40/2.70; open 10am-7pm daily) – a fascinating tribute to the seafaring exploits that shaped much of Barcelona's history. Pick up the multilingual headsets with your tickets.

The shipyards were, in their heyday, among the greatest in Europe. Begun in the 13th century and completed by 1378, the buildings demonstrate that the Catalan Gothic penchant for broad, stout construction had useful applications. Look at the ceilings and you feel you are looking at the upturned hulls of so many galleys. The long arched (the highest arches reach 13m) bays once sloped off as slipways directly into the water – which lapped the seaward side of the Drassanes until at least the end of the 18th century.

By then, shipbuilding had ceased and the buildings were being used for artillery production and as a training ground, ammunition dump and barracks. Only in 1935 was the site handed over to the Ajuntament for conversion into a maritime museum. This happened in 1941 after civil war had returned the site to the role of arms factory. Only from 1987 were the shipyards restored to their medieval glory and the museum completely revamped.

In the first room you are confronted by seven *mascarons* (the figureheads that adorned the prow of sailing ships). Sailors hoped these figures would help steer their vessels clear of unwanted nastiness. The following room contains modern murals illustrating medieval Catalan expansion in the Mediterranean. Stairs lead up to a small floor dedicated to temporary exhibits.

From these first rooms you enter the main bays of the shipyards, dominated by a full-size replica (made in the 1970s) of Don John (Juan) of Austria's flagship, which he took into battle against the Turks off Lepanto (Italy) in 1571. The result of this, the last great sea struggle between fleets of galleys (under sail or otherwise), was a famous (if ultimately fruitless) victory for the Christians. This part of the museum is full of vessels (some real but mostly models) of all types and epochs, from coastal fishing skips to giants of the steam age. You can wander through life-sized dioramas on board a sailing ship, read captains' logs and watch videos (in Catalan) on different aspects of sailing history.

Best of all, head for Àmbit (area) 12, pick up the audio phones and follow the red lights. This wonderful little tour takes you amidships of Don Juan's galley, where audiovisuals help you to imagine the ghastly life of the slaves, prisoners and volunteers (!) who at full steam could haul this vessel along at nine knots. They remained chained to their seats, four to an oar, at all times. Here they worked, drank lots (fresh water was stored below decks, where the infirmary

was also located), ate, slept and went to the loo. It seems unlikely they greatly enjoyed their maritime adventures. The tour takes you on to a dockside scene in Havana at the time when Barcelona's merchants were doing a brisk business in late-19th-century Cuba; you also board an ocean steam liner and join Narcís Monturiol i Estarriol on his underwater experiments. For more details, see the boxed text 'Taking a Dive'.

Many of the explanations are in Catalan only, but scattered about the various sections are sheets in several languages explaining key points. The headsets (see above) are a useful tool.

BARRI GÒTIC (MAP 6)

The 'Gothic quarter' is the nucleus of old Barcelona. The medieval city was elevated on the Roman core, which in succeeding centuries slowly spread north, south and west. Barri Gòtic is a warren of narrow, winding streets and unexpected little squares, and now home to a dense concentration of budget hotels, bars, cafés and restaurants. Few of its great buildings date from after the early 15th century – the decline Barcelona went into at that time curtailed grand projects for several centuries.

Barri Gòtic stretches from La Rambla in the west to Via Laietana in the east, and roughly from Carrer de la Portaferrissa in the north to Carrer de la Mercè in the south. Carrer de Jaume I and Carrer de Ferran (the latter, which was named after King Fernando VII, was sliced through the city in 1823) form a kind of halfway line: these streets and those to their north tend to be airier and dotted with chic little shops; those to their south become darker and a little seedier – albeit still full of perfectly respectable places to eat, drink, shop and stay. Work to rejuvenate the area continues. Pickpockets work Barri Gòtic so keep an eye out.

Plaça de Sant Jaume

In the 2000 or so years since the Romans settled here, the area around this square (often remodelled) has been the focus of Barcelona's civic life. Facing each other across it are the Palau de la Generalitat (seat

Taking a Dive

Would the real Captain Nemo please stand up? Narcis Monturiol i Estarriol (1819–85) was a curious character with, from all appearances, a generous heart. His interests were wide-ranging. As an editor of publications defending workers' and women's rights he ran into trouble with the authorities and their censor's scissors. He also followed closely attempts to set up some (rather pitiful in retrospect) utopian societies in the Americas.

His optimism reached its high point in a rather different field – scientific invention. The bee in his bonnet was the submarine. By the beginning of the 19th century, several attempts had been made to take vessels below the sea, some of them successful. But these projects did not attract funds and generally ended where they had started, on the drawing board.

In 1856 Monturiol got to work on his first wooden, fish-shaped sub, the *Ictíneo*. It was about 6m long – a cramped little beast – but it worked. The screws were driven by the crew's muscle power and a shortage of air made the dives fairly brief affairs, but Monturiol made more than 50 dives in the couple of years after he launched the sub in 1859.

He became an overnight celebrity but got no money from the navy. Undeterred, Monturiol sank himself further into debt by designing *Ictíneo II*. This time he really did come up with a first. Seventeen metres long, its screws were steam driven and Monturiol had worked out a system for renewing the oxygen inside the vessel. Nothing like it had been built before. It trialled in 1864 but again attracted no money, either from the navy or from private industry. Everyone had something nice to say about it, but Monturiol had spent a huge sum of money. In 1868, his creditors lost patience and had it broken up for scrap, a blow from which Monturiol never really recovered.

of Catalunya's government) on the northern side and the Ajuntament to the south. Both have fine Gothic interiors which, unhappily, the public can only enter at limited times.

Palau de la Generalitat Founded in the early 15th century to house Catalunya's parliament, the palace was extended over the centuries as its importance (and bureaucracy) grew. It is open to the public only on 23 April, the Día de Sant Jordi (St George, Catalunya's patron saint), and also on 24 September (Festes de la Mercè).

At any time, however, you can admire the original Gothic main entrance on Carrer del Bisbe Irurita (designed by medieval architect Marc Saffont). Of lesser interest are the facades around the back on Carrer de Sant Sever and on Carrer de Sant Honorat, but at least they too preserve something of the feeling of the building's ancient roots. The modern main entrance on Plaça de Sant Jaume is a late Renaissance job with neoclassical leanings – nothing to write home about. If you wander by in the evening, squint up through the windows into the Saló (Hall) de Sant Jordi and you will get some idea of the sumptuousness of the interior.

If you *do* get inside, you're in for a treat. Normally you will have to enter from the rear (Carrer de Sant Sever). The first rooms you pass through are characterised by low vaulted ceilings. From here you pass upstairs to the raised courtyard known as the **Pati dels Tarongers**, a modest Gothic orangery. The 16th-century Sala Daurada i de Sessions, one of the rooms leading off the patio, is a splendid meeting hall lit up by huge chandeliers. Still more imposing is the Renaissance Saló de Sant Jordi, whose murals were added this century – many an occasion of pomp and circumstance takes place here. Finally, you descend the staircase of the Gothic Pati Central to leave by what was, in the beginning, the building's main entrance.

Ajuntament Facing the Palau de la Generalitat across the square, and otherwise known as the Casa de la Ciutat, the Ajuntament *(town hall; admission free; open 10am-2pm Sat & Sun)* has been the seat of city power for centuries. The Consell de Cent, from medieval times the ruling council of the city, first sat here in the 14th century, but the building has lamentably undergone many changes since the days of Barcelona's Gothic-era splendour.

Only the original, now disused, entrance on Carrer de la Ciutat retains its Gothic ornament. The main 19th-century neoclassical facade on the square is a charmless riposte to the Palau de la Generalitat and the remaining sides of the building are recent and utterly depressing.

Inside, however, it is quite a different story. You enter a courtyard and will probably be directed to the right (pick up a brochure on the way) to the **Escala d'Honor**, a majestic staircase that leads you up to the Gothic gallery.

From here you enter the **Saló de Cent**, the hall in which the town council once held its plenary sessions. The broad vaulting is pure Catalan Gothic and the wooden *artesonado* ceiling demonstrates fine work. In fact, however, much of what you see is comparatively recent. The building was badly damaged in a bombardment in 1842 and has been repaired and tampered with repeatedly. The wooden neo-Gothic seating was added at the beginning of the 20th century,

as was the grand alabaster *retablo* (retable, or altarpiece) at the back. To the right you enter the small **Saló de la Reina Regente**, built in 1860, where the Ajuntament now sits. To the left of the Saló de Cent you reach the **Saló de les Croniques** – the murals here recount Catalan exploits in Greece and the Near East in Catalunya's merchant empire-building days.

As you head down the other set of stairs to the courtyard, you may notice several statues of women – the least recognisable as such is Joan Miró's *Dona*!

Around the west of the building into Plaça se Sant Miquel brings you face to face with a monstrosity – a mid-rise Franco-era block of city office buildings. The Ajuntament decided in 2001 to chop the top four floors off this horror and remodel the square. That latter decision reopened an old debate – should the Roman baths buried beneath the asphalt be brought to the light of day? The answer will likely be no.

Catedral & Around

Approached from the broad Avinguda de la Catedral, Barcelona's central place of worship *(☎ 93 310 25 80; open 8am-1.30pm & 4pm-7.30pm Mon-Fri, 8am-1.30pm & 5pm-7.30pm Sat & Sun)* presents a magnificent image. The richly decorated main (northwestern) facade, laced with gargoyles and all the stone intricacies you would expect of northern European Gothic, sets it quite apart from the other churches in Barcelona. The facade was actually added in 1870, although it is based on a 1408 design. The rest of the building was built between 1298 to 1460. The remaining facades are sparse in decoration, and the octagonal, flat-roofed towers are a clear reminder that, even here, Catalan Gothic architectural principles prevailed.

The interior is a broad, soaring space divided into a central nave and two aisles by lines of elegant, slim pillars. The cathedral was one of the few churches in Barcelona spared by the anarchists in the civil war, so its ornamentation, never over-lavish, is intact.

In the first chapel on the right from the northwestern entrance, the main Crucifixion figure above the altar is the **Sant Crist de Lepant**. It is said Don Juan's flagship bore it into battle at Lepanto and that the figure acquired its odd stance by dodging an incoming cannon ball. Further along this same wall, past the southwestern transept, are the wooden **coffins** of Count Ramon Berenguer I and his wife Almodis, founders of the 11th-century Romanesque predecessor of the present cathedral.

Smack in the middle of the central nave is the late-14th-century **coro**, or choir stall (€0.90).

A broad staircase before the main altar leads you to the **crypt**. It contains the tomb of Santa Eulàlia, one of Barcelona's two patron saints. The carving on the alabaster sarcophagus, executed by Pisan artisans, recounts some of her tortures and, along the top strip, the removal of her body to its present resting place.

You can visit the cathedral's **roof** and tower by an *ascensor* (lift), which rises every half hour from 10.30am to 12.30pm and 4.30pm to 6pm Monday to Saturday, from the Capella de les Animes del Purgatori near

---

Measure for Measure

Have a close look at the external wall of the Romanesque Capella de Santa Llúcia. At about waist level you can make out the inscription '*A 2 Canas lo Pou*'. The *cana* was a unit of measurement (eight palms or 1.55m) once in common use by tailors. Apparently a well *(pou)* was situated about 3m from where you stand. If you inspect the corner of the same building, you'll notice two vertical grooves etched into the stone – they measure two *canas*. The story goes that if, after having bought some material, you discovered you had been cheated by the tailor, you could search for the local gendarmes who in turn would have the good salesman accompany them to this spot to verify whether the *cana* he was using gave the full measure. Of course, the tailor may have kept an instrument with a proper *cana* hidden away for just an occasion.

---

the northeastern transept. Tickets cost €1.35 (buy them at the choir stall).

From the southwestern transept, exit to the lovely **cloister**, with its trees, fountains and flock of 13 geese (who supposedly represent the age of Santa Eulàlia at the time of her martyrdom). They make fine watchdogs! One of the cloister chapels commemorates 930 priests, monks and nuns martyred in the civil war.

Along the northern flank of the cloister you can enter the **Sala Capitular** *(chapter house; admission €1)*. Although bathed in rich reds of carpet and cosseted by fine timber seating, the few artworks gathered here are of minor interest. Among them figure a *Pietat* by Bartolomeo Bermejo. A couple of doors down in the northwestern corner of the cloister is the **Capella de Santa Llúcia**, one of the few bits of Romanesque Barcelona still intact. Walk out the door on to Carrer de Santa Llúcia and turn around to look at the exterior – you can see that, although incorporated into the Catedral, it is in fact a separate building.

Turn on your heels and you are facing the 16th-century **Casa de l'Ardiaca** *(archdeacon's house; open 9am-9pm Mon-Fri, 9am-2pm Sat)*, which now serves as an archive. You may wander into the supremely serene courtyard, cooled by trees and a fountain. Climb the stairs to the next level, from where you can look down into the courtyard and across to the Catedral. Inside the building itself you can see parts of the **Roman wall**.

Across Carrer del Bisbe Irurita is the 17th-century **Palau Episcopal** or Palau del Bisbat (bishop's palace). Virtually nothing remains of the original 13th-century structure. The Roman city's northwestern gate stood here and you can see the lower segments of the Roman towers that stood on either side of the gate at the base of the Palau Episcopal and Casa de l'Ardiaca. In fact, the lower part of the entire northwestern wall of the Casa de l'Ardiaca is of Roman origin – you can also make out part of the first arch of the one-time Roman aqueducts, which supplied the ancient town with water.

[Continued on page 116]

HOLIDAYS & FESTIVALS

Although the Barcelonins may have a reputation with other Spaniards for working hard and taking things all rather seriously, they love an excuse to take a break and celebrate a long list of special days throughout the year. Some holidays are more staid than others, while the key *festes*, such as the Mercè in September, are a kaleidoscope of entertainment, parades and partying.

PUBLIC HOLIDAYS

As in the rest of Spain, in Barcelona there are 14 official holidays per year – some observed nationwide, some locally. When a holiday falls close to a weekend, people like to make a *pont/puente* (bridge) – meaning they take the intervening day off too. On the odd occasion when a couple of holidays fall close, they make an *acueducto* (aqueduct)! Offices, banks and many shops close on holidays. Restaurants, bars and the like soldier on, as do most museums and other attractions.

National Holidays

The major public holiday in Barcelona is the Divendres Sant/Viernes Santo, celebrated at Easter.

Divendres Sant/Viernes Santo Occurring on Good Friday (March/April), it's not, in general, celebrated with the verve it is accorded further south in Spain, you get a taste of it with the Procesión del Padre Jesús del Gran Poder (Processions of Father Jesus of the Great Power) and of the Virgen de la Macarena from the Església de Sant Agustí in El Raval in the early afternoon. It starts at 5pm and ends in front of the Catedral three hours later.

Accompanying the huge image of the Virgin that is the centrepiece of the march (which then proceeds up La Rambla and on to Plaça de Catalunya) are solemn bands, members of various religious fraternities *(cofradías)* dressed in robes and *capilotes* (tall conical hoods).

Most striking perhaps are the barefoot women penitents dressed in black and dragging heavy crosses and chains around their ankles. The more emotional bystanders shed a tear while the volubile may be heard to shout to the Virgin: *Guapa, guapa, guapa!* (Beautiful!).

Other National Holidays The other six national holidays are:

Any Nou/Año Nuevo (New Year's Day) 1 January. There are plenty of parties in the discos and bars on New Year's Eve (Cap d'Any/Noche Vieja) – expect to pay higher than usual prices. As the clock strikes midnight you are expected to eat a grape for each chime.

Dia del Treball/Fiesta del Trabajo (Labour Day) 1 May. In this one-time anarchist stronghold where nowadays the Socialists always win the municipal elections, Labour Day once attracted big demonstrations. That is all but a memory now – you'll probably hardly notice it's a holiday except for all the closed offices, banks and shops.

Inset: A *gegant's* (giant's) sculptured head, worn during the Festes de la Mercè.

Photo by: Damien Simonis

111

L'Assumpció/La Asunción (Feast of the Assumption) 15 August. This is the country's main Marian holiday, although in Barcelona it does not attract so much attention.

Festa de la Hispanitat/Día de la Hispanidad (Spanish National Day) 12 October. The day off work is appreciated, but predictably no special celebrations mark this national day.

La Immaculada Concepció/La Inmaculada Concepción (Feast of the Immaculate Conception) 8 December

Nadal/Navidad (Christmas) 25 December. This is a family time. Many celebrate with a big midday meal, although some prefer to to have the meal on Christmas Eve *(nit de Nadal/nochebuena)*.

One of the oddest things about Christmas is the nativity scenes that families traditionally set up at home (a giant one goes up in Plaça de Sant Jaume too). The cribs themselves are common throughout the Catholic world, and particularly in the Mediterranean. What makes these ones different is the presence, along with the baby Jesus, Mary, Joseph and the Three Kings, of a chap who has dropped his pants and is doing number twos. The Catalans proudly claim the *caganer* (the crapper) as their own but if, indeed, he is a Catalan invention, he has wide appeal – similar figures can be seen in the family cribs as far away as the Canary Islands.

Local Holidays

In addition to these national holidays, the Generalitat and Ajuntament add the following holidays during the year. The city's *festa major* or Big Party is the Festes de la Mercè.

Festes de la Mercè This four-day period of intense festivities begins on 24 Septeber, shortly after the official close of summer and acts as a final burst of prewinter madness all over Barcelona, although the bulk of the activities take place in the centre of town. Nostra Senyora de la Mercè (whose image lies in the church of the same name on Plaça de la Mercè) was elevated to co-patron of the city after she single-handedly beat off a plague of locusts in 1637!

In 1714, as Barcelona faced defeat in the War of the Spanish Succession, light-headed town elders at one point appointed Our Lady commander-in-chief of the city's defences (an eloquent expression of hopelessness if ever there was one).

There's a swimming race across the harbour, a fun run, an outstanding series of free concerts organised under the auspices of BAM (Barcelona Acció Musical; see Festivals following), and a bewildering program of cultural events all over town and in many of the museums and galleries. There's also all the predictable stuff that usually accompanies a major Catalan festa: *castellers* (human castle builders), *sardanes* (traditional folk dancing), parades of *gegants* and *capgrossos* (giants and big heads) and a huge *correfoc* (fire race). The latter is a pyromaniac's dream. It's held on the last night (a Sunday), and crowds hurl themselves through the streets before fire-spurting demons (not to mention children armed with high-calibre fire-crackers) who have been released from the Porta de l'Infern (Gate of Hell), located before the Catedral.

Barcelona's colourful festivals (clockwise from top left): *castellers* (human pyramid builders) at the Festes de la Mercè in Barri Gòtic; decorations for the Festes del Cel (Festival of the Sky); choir girls at the Easter Monday procession

The Festes de la Mercè (Barcelona's major celebration) brings out the wild and the wonderful (clockwise from top left): a parade of *bèsties de foc* (beasts of fire) and *dimonis* (demons); *gegants* (giants); and *capgrossos* (big heads)

The fire race can be dangerous and you are advised to wear old cotton clothes (long sleeves and trousers) and a hood to cover up your head, earplugs and running shoes if you intend to participate in all the madness. The heat can be intense, but an old habit of tipping water from balconies above over participants has been banned – apparently mixing water with gun powder can have unpredictable consequences.

Other Local Holidays These are:

Epifanía (Epiphany) or El Dia dels Reis/Día de los Reyes Magos (Three Kings' Day) 6 January. This is a day when children traditionally receive presents (generally they get little or nothing at Christmas). See also the Cavalcada dels Reis later.

Dilluns de Pasqua Florida (Easter Monday) March/April – One of the most remarkable aspects of this day is the choking traffic around Barcelona as locals stream back after what for most is the first little holiday of the year.

Dilluns de Pasqua Granda May/June – the day after Pentecost Sunday

Dia de Sant Joan/Día de San Juan Bautista (Feast of St John the Baptist) 24 June. The night before this day the people of Barcelona hit the streets or hold parties at home for an evening to celebrate the Berbena de Sant Joan, which involves drinking, dancing and fireworks. The latter can be seen in districts all over town (and indeed across Catalunya), for which reason the evening is also known as La Nit del Foc, or Fire Night.
The traditional pastry to eat on this summer solstice is a kind of dense candied cake known as *coca de Sant Joan*.

Diada Nacional de Catalunya 11 September. Catalunya's national day commemorates Barcelona's surrender to the Spaniards at the end of the War of the Spanish Succession in 1714. It is a relatively sober occasion, when small independence groups demand the predictable without anyone paying too much attention.

El Dia de Sant Esteve 26 December. The local equivalent of Boxing Day, it is a family occasion, much like Christmas Day, with festive lunches.

FESTIVALS

Barcelona is perhaps not as addicted to partying as some more southerly Spanish cities, but it puts in a fair effort with some wild occasions dotting the calendar in between the official holidays. Several *barris* celebrate their own *festes majors*. See also Public Holidays above, as some of the official holidays are themselves cause for much merry-making. For details of arts and music festivals, see the following section.

Carnestoltes/Carnaval (Carnival)

Celebrated in February or March, this festival involves several days of fancy-dress parades and merrymaking, usually ending on the Tuesday 47 days before Easter Sunday. For about 10 days there are parades and dancing, and parties in the discos and clubs. It is not as riotous as the Canary Islands version of Carnaval, but busy enough to keep most punters happy. Indeed, the 2002 edition was the most festive and multitudinous on record. As it does elsewhere in Spain, the Carnaval culminates in the odd and inexplicable *Enterrament de la Sardina* (Burial of the Fish), often on Montjuïc. The whole affair makes a dramatic way to celebrate the end of winter.

Down in Sitges, just south of the city, a much wilder version of the festivities takes place. The gay community stages gaudy parades and party-goers keep the bars and clubs heaving to all hours for several days running.

Festa Major de Gràcia

Apart from the Festes de la Mercè, this local festival, which happens around 15 August, is one of the biggest in Barcelona. More than a dozen streets in Gràcia are decorated by their inhabitants according to a certain theme as part of a competition for the most imaginative street of the year. Locals set up tables and benches to enjoy local feasts, but people from all over the city pour in to participate. In squares (particularly Plaça del Sol) and intersections all over the *barri*, bands compete for attention. Snack stands abound and there are numerous bars open onto the streets to sell rivers of drink. Local residents who hope to get any sleep in this week tend to stay with friends or leave town!

Other festivals These include:

Cavalcada dels Reis 5 January. The day preceding Epiphany (a public holiday) sees the Three Kings 'arrive' in Barcelona at Moll de la Fusta in Port Vell and then parade up into town (the route tends to change). As the Kings parade around with floats, they hurl sweets to the kids in the crowd.

Festes dels Tres Tombs 17 January. A key part of the district festival of Sant Antoni Abat, the *festa* of the Three Circuits involves a parade of horsemen and carriages around Ronda de Sant Antoni to Plaça de Catalunya, down La Rambla and back up Carrer Nou de la Rambla. Sant Antoni Abat (St Anthony the Abbot) is the patron saint of domestic and carriage animals. The *festa* has been celebrated since the mid-19th century.

Festes de Santa Eulàlia February. Coinciding with Carnaval (see earlier), this is the feast of Barcelona's first patron saint. The Ajuntament organises all sorts of cultural events, from concerts through to performances by *castellers* and the appearance of *mulasses* (dragons) in the main parade.

Dia de Sant Jordi 23 April. This is the day of Catalunya's patron saint (St George) and also the Day of the Book – men give women a rose, women give men a book; publishers launch new titles, while La Rambla and Plaça de Sant Jaume are filled with book and flower stalls.

L'Ou com Balla May/June. A curious tradition with several centuries of history, the 'Dancing Egg' is an empty shell that bobs on top of the flower-festooned fountain in the cloister of the Catedral. This spectacle is Barcelona's way of celebrating Corpus Christi (the Thursday after the eighth Sunday after Easter Sunday). Other dancing eggs can be seen on the same day in the courtyard of the Casa de l'Ardiaca and various other fountains in Barri Gòtic.

Dia per l'Alliberament Lesbià i Gai Around 28 June. This is a gay and lesbian festival and parade that takes place on the Saturday nearest this date. The boisterous parade kicks off in the evening from Plaça de l'Universitat.

Festa Major de Sants Around August 24. The district of Sants launches its own version of decorated mayhem, hard on Gràcia's heels. Although the festival has neither the history nor the grandeur of the Gràcia festival, locals have, in recent years, injected an increasing amount of life into it and here you'll experience the true flavour of the barri.

Festa Major de la Barceloneta September/October. Barcelona's partiers have a short wait until the next opportunity for merry-making comes along. Although on a small scale, La Barceloneta's gig involves plenty of dancing and drinking (especially down on the beach).

Arts & Music Festivals

Barcelona plays host to several arts-oriented festivals in the course of the year. Among the more important are:

Sonar June. Sonar is Barcelona's celebration of electronic music. It is claimed to be Europe's biggest such event and you can get into the latest house, hip-hop, trip-hop, eurobeat and anything else they have come up with in the meantime. The organisers like to mix in a few surprises, such as the Pet Shop Boys in 2002. Locations change each year so watch for announcements in the local press.

Festival del Grec Late June to August. Many theatres shut down for summer but into the breach steps this eclectic program of theatre, dance and music. Performances are held all over the city, not just at the amphitheatre on Montjuïc (Map 7) from which the festival takes its name. Programs and tickets are available from the Palau de la Virreina on La Rambla (see under Tourist Offices) and at a temporary booth set up on Avinguda del Portal del Àngel (off Plaça de Catalunya).

BAM Around 24 September. All the great free music put on for the Festes de la Mercè (see Local Holidays earlier) is organised as Barcelona Acció Musical. Most of the performances take place on squares in the centre of town and/or on the waterfront.

Festival Internacional de Jazz de Barcelona Around November. For a week the big venues (from the Auditori down) across town host a plethora of international jazz acts. At the same time, a more home-spun jazz fest takes place for about a month in bars across the old city. The dates for this Festival de Jazz de Ciutat Vella can spill over into October or December. Many of the performances are free.

[Continued from page 110]

Across Plaça Nova from the Catedral your eye may be caught by what seem child-like scribblings on the façade of the Col.legi de Arquitectes (Architectural College). It is, in fact, a giant contribution by Picasso done in 1962.

Casa de la Pia Almoina The Roman walls continued across present-day Plaça de la Seu into what subsequently became the Casa de la Pia Almoina. In the 11th century the city's main centre of charity was located here, although the much-crumbled remains of the present building date to the 15th century. It houses the **Museu Diocesà** *(Diocesan Museum;* ☎ *93 315 22 13; Avinguda de la Catedral 4; admission €1.90; open 10am-2pm & 5pm-8pm Tues-Sat, 11am-2pm Sun),* where you can see a sparse collection of medieval religious art. Otherwise there's little there, unless a temporary exposition is on, in which case you may pay more to enter.

Temple Romà d'Augusti Opposite the southeastern end of the Catedral, narrow Carrer del Paradis leads towards Plaça de Sant Jaume. Inside No 10 are four columns of Barcelona's main Roman temple, dedicated to Caesar Augustus and built to worship his imperial highness in the 1st century AD. You are now standing on the highest point of Roman Barcino – Mont Taber. Though it is generally said that this mound is 15m high, a plaque outside No 10 insists it is 16.9m. You can visit (free) anytime the door is open. This tends to be in the morning only, from around 10am to 2pm, although there is no timetable and you may have to take pot luck.

Plaça del Rei & Around

Plaça del Rei, to the southeast of the Catedral, is the courtyard of what was the Palau Reial Major, the palace of the counts of Barcelona and monarchs of Aragón. It's surrounded by tall, centuries-old buildings, most of which are now open to visitors as the Museu d'Història de la Ciutat (the city's history museum).

Museu d'Història de la Ciutat You enter this museum *(*☎ *93 225 47 00; Carrer del Veguer; admission €3.50, free 4pm-8pm 1st Sat of month; open 10am-2pm & 4pm-8pm Tues-Sat, 10am-2pm Sun),* one of the most intriguing in Barcelona, at **Casa Padellàs** and is well worth a visit.

When you enter Casa Padellàs, built for a 15th-century noble family, you find yourself in a courtyard typical of Barcelona's Gothic mansions, with an external staircase up to the 1st floor.

Buy your tickets inside on the ground floor, then pass through a few small rooms housing a handful of ancient artefacts from Roman and pre-Roman days. The informative video presentation (28 minutes) was not working at the time of writing but watch out in case the museum reinstates it. You get an elevator down to a remarkable piece of Barcelona – a whole stretch of the excavated Roman town. The elevator is cute. Instead of the floor number it has the year 1996. You get out at Year 12 (presumably 12 BC) in...Barcino.

As you wander around the ruins you can inspect part of the *cardo* or main crossroad, and remains of a defensive tower, shops, houses (a few with floor mosaics intact), public baths and storage areas for wine and *garum* (a kind of fish sauce that was a staple throughout the Roman empire). The walk takes you right under the Catedral so you can see what little remains of its Romanesque and Visigothic predecessors (the latter consists of a baptismal font).

Once you are through, you will emerge at a hall and ticket office set up on the northern side of Plaça del Rei. To your right is the **Saló del Tinell**, the banqueting hall of the royal palace and a fine example of Catalan Gothic (built 1359–70). Its broad arches and bare walls give a sense of solidity and solemnity that would have made an appropriate setting for Fernando and Isabel to hear Columbus' first reports of the New World. The hall is sometimes used for temporary exhibitions, which may mean an extra charge for admission. It also may mean that your peaceful contemplation of its architectural majesty is somewhat obstructed.

As you back out of the saló you end up in the **Capella Reial de Santa Àgata**, the palace chapel, also built in the 14th century. Outside, a spindly bell tower rises from the northeastern side of Plaça del Rei. Inside all is bare except for the 15th-century altarpiece and the magnificent *techumbre* (decorated timber ceiling). The altarpiece is considered to be one of Jaume Huguet's finest surviving works. The stained glass is a recent addition.

Head into Plaça del Rei down the fanshaped stairs and bear left to the entrance to the multi-tiered **Mirador del Rei Martí** (lookout tower of King Martin), built in 1555. It is part of the museum and leads you to the gallery above the square. You can also climb to the top of the tower, which dominates Plaça del Rei and rewards you with excellent views over the city.

It's possible to join guided evening tours for €6. Since most of the explanations in the museum are in Catalan and/or Castilian (and very occasionally in English), it is worth asking for the pamphlet in your language to give you some clues as to what you will be looking at.

Palau del Lloctinent The southwestern side of Plaça del Rei is taken up by this palace *(admission free)*, built in the 1550s as the residence of the Spanish viceroy of Catalunya. It is worth wandering in (from Carrer dels Comtes de Barcelona) and upstairs – the building is somewhat rundown but boasts a fine wooden ceiling and pleasing courtyard.

Until 1993 it housed the Arxiu de la Corona d'Aragón, a unique collection documenting the history of the kingdom prior to unity under Fernando and Isabel. When you walk back outside, have a look at the walls of the Catedral. See all the grooves cut into the stone? It appears the viceroy's soldiers who were housed here used the church walls to sharpen their weapons.

Museu Frederic Marès A short way off, this museum *(☎ 93 310 58 00; Plaça de Sant Iu 5-6; admission €3, free Wed afternoons & 1st Sun of month; open 10am-7pm Tues-Sat,* *10am-3pm Sun & holidays)* is housed in yet another building of the Palau Reial Major. Frederic Marès i Deulovol (1893–1991) was a rich sculptor, traveller and obsessive collector. He specialised in medieval Spanish sculpture, huge quantities of which are displayed on the ground and 1st floors – including some lovely polychrome wooden sculptures of the Crucifixion and the Virgin.

The top two floors hold a mind-boggling array of knick-knacks, from toy soldiers and cribs to scissors and 19th-century playing cards, from early still cameras to pipes, from fine ceramics to a room that once served as Marès' study and library, now crammed with his sculpture.

Roman Walls

From Plaça del Rei it's worth a little detour northeast to see the two best surviving stretches of Barcelona's Roman walls. One is on the southwestern side of Plaça Ramon de Berenguer el Gran, with the Capella Reial de Santa Àgata atop them. The other is a little further south, by the northern end of Carrer del Sotstinent Navarro. They date from the 3rd and 4th centuries AD, when the Romans rebuilt their walls after the first attacks by Germanic tribes from the north.

Plaça de Sant Josep Oriol & Around

This small plaza, not far off La Rambla, is the prettiest in Barri Gòtic. Its bars and cafés attract buskers and artists and make it a lively place to hang out for a while. It is surrounded by quaint little streets, many of them dotted with other appealing cafés, restaurants and shops.

Looming large over the plaza itself is the **Església de Santa Maria del Pi** *(open 8.30am-1pm & 4.30pm-9pm Mon-Sat, 9am-2pm & 5pm-9pm Sun & holidays)*, a Gothic church built in the 14th to 16th centuries. The beautiful rose window above its entrance on Plaça del Pi is claimed by some to be the world's biggest. The interior of the church was gutted by fire in 1936 and most of the stained glass is modern. The third chapel on the left is dedicated to Sant Josep Oriol, with a map showing spots in the church where he worked numerous miracles. According to the legend, a 10th-century fisherman discovered an image of the Virgin Mary in a pine tree (*pi*) he was intent on cutting down to build a boat. Struck by the vision, he instead built a little chapel, later to be succeeded by this Gothic church. A pine still grows in the square.

The area between Carrer dels Banys Nous (to the east of the església) and Plaça de Sant Jaume is known locally as the **Call**, Barcelona's former Jewish quarter and centre of learning from at least the 11th century, until anti-Semitism saw Jews expelled in the late 15th century (see also the Walking Tours chapter). Even before the expulsion, Jews were not exactly privileged citizens. As in many medieval centres, they were obliged to wear a special identifying mark on their garments and had trouble getting permission to expand their ghetto as the Call's population increased.

Plaça Reial & Around

Just south of Carrer de Ferran, near its La Rambla end, is Plaça Reial, a large, traffic-free plaza whose 19th-century neoclassical facades hide numerous eateries, bars, nightspots and budget places to stay. The lampposts by the central fountain are Antoni Gaudí's first known works.

Residents here have a rough time of it, with noise a virtual constant as punters crowd in and out of restaurants, bars and *discotecas* (clubs) at all hours. Downright dangerous until the 1980s, the square retains a restless atmosphere, where unsuspecting tourists, respectable citizens, ragged buskers, down-and-outs and sharp witted pickpockets come face to face. Don't be put off, but watch your bags and pockets.

This southern half of Barri Gòtic is imbued with the memory of Picasso, who lived as a teenager with his family in Carrer de la Mercè, had his first studio in Carrer de la Plata (now a rather cheesy restaurant) and was a regular visitor to a brothel at Carrer d'Avinyó 27, to the west of the plaça. That experience may have inspired his 1907 painting *Les Demoiselles d'Avignon*.

EL RAVAL

West of La Rambla, the Ciutat Vella spreads to Ronda de Sant Antoni, Ronda de Sant Pau and Avinguda del Paral.lel, which together trace the line of Barcelona's 14th-century walls. Known as El Raval, from an Arabic word that denoted the one-time suburban sprawl *extra muros*, the area contains what was one of the city's most dispiriting slums, the seedy red-light zone of Barri Xinès, at its south.

For centuries it has been home to whores, louche lads and, at times, a bohemian collection of interlopers. In the 1920s and '30s especially, it was a popular playground with Barcelonins of many classes, busy at night with the activity in taverns, *cafés concerts*, cabarets and brothels. In the harsh light of day, the tawdriness and poverty is more evident, hardly surprising given the concentration of people living in often less-than-ideal circumstances. Carrer Nou de la Rambla, where Picasso lived for a while, was particularly lively. By the 1960s many of the brothels and bars had shut down, but there was still plenty of activity there, especially when the American fleet came to town. In later years, drug abuse became an increasing problem and small-time dealing still takes place in some the area's seedier back streets.

Past and present lend Barri Xinès a certain fascination, but this is not the place to bring your Rolex. It's not overly dangerous but, among the mixed bag of whores (of all ages and gender types) and pimps, drug abusers and a picaresque assortment of local low life, the percentage of dodgy characters with a keen eye for more prosperous pockets is high.

Recent waves of immigration have changed the makeup of El Raval, which has become the main centre for the city's Pakistani population. North Africans, mainly Moroccans, have also arrived in force, although around here they often tend to be young delinquents.

There is a reason for the delinquents to be here. While it is true a poorer migrant class is moving in, slowly supplanting the old working-class Catalans, the place is also getting more attention from a new wave of Bohemians. New bars and restaurants are opening up, attracting to the district 'adventurous' young people, some of whom are choosing to live here.

El Raval has not been completely abandoned by the town fathers. A broad new boulevard, La Rambla del Raval, was opened up at the dawn of the new millennium and slum housing is being pulled down. Plans to build a big hotel complex just off the new *rambla* have not met with universal approval, but at least the city appears to be making a bit of an effort to breathe life into the district.

Església de Sant Pau del Camp (Map 5)

Back in the 9th century, when monks founded the monastery of Sant Pau del Camp (St Paul in the Fields), it was a good walk from the city gates amid fields and gardens. Today you see only the church and cloister *(cloister open 5pm-8pm Mon & Wed-Sat, closed public holidays)* erected in the 12th century. Sadly neglected amid the worst squalor El Raval has to offer, it is one of the best of Barcelona's few Romanesque remnants. The doorway to the church bears some rare Visigothic decoration, predating the Muslim invasion of Spain.

Antic Hospital de la Santa Creu (Map 6)

Almost directly north from the Església de Sant Pau del Camp stands what was, in the 15th century, the city's main hospital. The Antic Hospital de la Santa Creu today houses the Biblioteca de Catalunya (the National Library of Catalunya) and the Institut d'Estudis Catalans. The library is the single most complete collection of documents (estimated at around three million) tracing the region's long history. In its medieval heyday, the hospital was deemed one of Europe's best, where the sick got (for the times) comparatively good care and abandoned children and lunatics were also taken in – presumably they were housed in separate wards. Parts of what you see today were added in the 16th and 17th centuries. The

hospital, construction of which began in 1401 during the reign of Martí, lies on what was the main entrance to the city from the road to Madrid.

As you enter the main courtyard, you can't help being reminded you are in El Raval. Dilapidated, it serves as a kind of park to all and sundry – round old ladies gossiping and walking their little dogs, the occasional drunk taking a snooze, outmoded young punks having a snack. Earnest students and academics from other parts of town head for the **library** *(open 9am-8pm Mon-Fri, 9am-2pm Sat)*. Inside you can admire fine Catalan Gothic vaulting in the ceiling. The **chapel** *(☎ 93 442 71 71; Carrer de l'Hospital 56; open noon-2pm & 4pm-8pm Tues-Sat, 11am-2pm Sun)* of the former hospital is worth poking your nose into as well. It is often used for temporary exhibitions.

Palau Güell (Map 6)

A few steps off La Rambla, the Palau Güell *(☎ 93 317 39 74; Carrer Nou de la Rambla 3-5; adult/student €3/1.50, half-price with Ruta del Modernisme ticket; open 10am-6.15pm Mon-Sat)* is one of the few Modernista buildings in Ciutat Vella. Gaudí built it in the late 1880s for his most important patron, the industrialist Eusebi Güell. It was intended as a guest wing and social annexe to Güell's main mansion on La Rambla. It lacks some of Gaudí's later playfulness but is still a characteristic riot of styles (Gothic, Islamic, Art Nouveau) and materials. After the civil war, the police occupied it and tortured political prisoners in the basement.

Visitors will be taken on a compulsory guided tour of the place, which is a compendium of Gaudí's earlier architectural ideas. When you enter the building, turn around to face the inside of the main entrance – it is a parabolic arch, the predominant form throughout the building, and characteristic of other Gaudí constructions.

You will first be taken downstairs to the low-vaulted brick stables. Even the solid upwards-fanning pillars are of slim brick – at the time considered by more conventional designers an ignoble material best

THINGS TO SEE & DO

hidden from view. *Au contraire*, said Gaudí and the Modernistas – just look at the great works of Islamic and Mudéjar architecture spread across Spain, all in unclad brick.

From the ground floor you are led up dark-grey marble stairs to the next floor, whose main feature are backlit mirrors posing as windows to increase the impression of space. Up another floor and you reach the main hall and its annexes. The hall is like a four-sided empty parabolic pyramid – each wall an arch stretching up three floors and coming together to form a dome that reaches the ceiling. The chapel that once filled one of the walls was partly destroyed in the civil war.

The adjoining rooms boast varying themes on *artesonado* ceilings – finely carved wood, drawing on a long tradition with its roots in Islamic design. The liberal use of wrought iron in decoration, for example in the one-time gas lamps and ceiling ornamentation, is another reaffirmation of the value of 'ignoble' materials.

The whole effect, while a masterful insight into Modernista ideas and in particular those of Gaudí, is a little gloomy until you emerge onto the flat roof to be confronted by a riot of tiled colour and fanciful design in the building's chimney pots.

Tours of the Palau Güell usually start on the hour. See also the boxed text 'Ruta del Modernisme' later in this chapter.

Picasso – who, incidently, hated Gaudí's work – began his Blue Period in 1902 in a studio across the street at Carrer Nou de la Rambla 10.

Museu d'Art Contemporani de Barcelona (Macba) & Around (Map 6)

One event that gave the northern half of El Raval a great fillip was the opening, in 1995, of the vast white Macba (☎ 93 412 08 10; *Plaça dels Àngels 1; admission €5.11, €2.55 on nonholiday Wed; open 11am-7.30pm Mon & Wed-Fri, 10am-8pm Sat, 10am-3pm Sun & holidays*).

The ground and 1st floors are given over to exhibitions from the gallery's own collections, which count more than 1600 pieces,

only a portion of which is ever on show. They tend to change things here a lot, so it is difficult to give clear hints on what or whom you might see. Works start with artists such as Antoni Tàpies, Joan Brossa, Paul Klee and Alexander Calder. Artists such as Miquel Barceló and Ferran García Sevilla, protagonists of neoexpressionism who emerged in the 1980s, also generally get a run. Other contemporary Catalan artists whose work you may well come across include Susana Solano, Juan Muñoz and Carlos Pazos, but on the whole the collection offers a broadly international outlook.

The gallery also presents temporary exhibitions and boasts a good art bookshop.

Behind the museum you will find the **Centre de Cultura Contemporània de Barcelona** (CCCB; Map 4; ☎ 93 306 41 00; *Carrer de Montalegre 5*), a complex of auditoriums and exhibition and conference halls opened in 1994 in what had been an 18th-century hospice. The big courtyard, with a vast glass wall on one side, is spectacular. With 4500 sq metres of exposition space in four display areas, the centre hosts a constantly changing program of exhibitions, some of which have 'the city' as their core theme. Often staged in conjunction with other European museums and galleries, the exhibitions range broadly from architectural studies to photo exhibits. For instance, a major exposition during 2002 was dedicated to the Moroccan city of Fez. The centre also organises all sorts of other activities, from folk music performances to art lectures.

A relative newcomer to the exposition scene here is the renovated **Convent dels Àngels** (Map 6; ☎ 93 301 77 75; *Plaça dels Àngels*), which occasionally plays host to anything from art and photo displays to minor fashion shows.

LA RIBERA (MAP 6)

Another area of Ciutat Vella is La Ribera, which is northeast of Barri Gòtic, from which it's divided by noisy Via Laietana, driven through this part of the city in 1907. La Ribera, whose name refers to the waterfront that once lay much further inland than today and was the main commercial dockland of medieval Barcelona, preserves a network of intriguing, narrow streets. These streets are peppered with some major sights, good bars and restaurants, and the area lacks the seedy character of some parts of Barri Gòtic.

Palau de la Música Catalana

This concert hall (☎ 93 295 72 00; Carrer de Sant Pere més alt 11; admission €5 by guided tour; 50-minute tours every half hour 10am-3.30pm daily) is one of the high points of Modernista architecture. It's not exactly a symphony, more a series of crescendos in tile, brick, sculptured stone and stained glass. Built between 1905 and 1908 by Lluís Domènech i Montaner for the Orfeo Català musical society, with the help of some of the best Catalan artisans of the time, it was conceived as a temple for the Catalan Renaixença (Renaissance). The palace was built in the cloister of the former Convent de Sant Francesc, and since 1990 it has undergone several changes, the latest of which will see a new subterranean auditorium opening in 2003–04, along with a new annex, whose facade on Carrer de Sant Pere més alt will feature a grand sculpted tree visible from Via Laietana. The original Modernista creation did not meet with universal approval in its day. The doyen of Catalan literature, Josep Pla, did not hesitate to condemn the structure as quite simply 'horrible', but few share his sentiments today.

You can see some of its splendours, such as the main facade with its mosaics, floral capitals and the sculpture cluster representing Catalan popular music from the outside, and you can glimpse lovely tiled pillars inside the ticket office entrance on Carrer de Sant Francesc de Paula. Best, however, is the richly colourful auditorium upstairs, with its ceiling of blue and gold stained glass and, above a bust of Beethoven, a towering sculpture of Wagner's Valkyries (Wagner was top of the Renaissance charts).

Carrer de Montcada

Possibly an early example of deliberate town planning, this medieval high street was driven down towards the sea from the road that in the 12th century led north from the city walls. It would, in time, become the best address in town for the city's merchant class, and the bulk of the great mansions that remain intact today date back (albeit often tampered with later) to the 14th century. This area was the commercial heartland of medieval Barcelona.

Mercat de Santa Caterina The big produce market a block northwest of Carrer de Montcada was knocked down in 1999 but is being rebuilt. The process has taken longer than expected because archaeologists needed to time to inspect what was found *beneath* the market – the site of what was once a sprawling Dominican convent.

Capella d'En Marcús On the little square of the same name that caps the top (northwestern) end of Carrer de Montcada lies the often unnoticed chapel of this 12th-century alms house. Erected on land that at the time lay beyond the city walls, the complex was a halfway house for poor wayfarers and also served as a small hospital. Construction was financed as a private work of charity by a wealthy businessman, Bernat Marcús. Although its original Romanesque elements are recognisable, the tiny chapel has been much meddled with over the centuries.

Museu Picasso Barcelona's most visited museum, the Museu Picasso (☎ 93 319 63 10; W www.museupicasso.bcn.es; Carrer de Montcada 15-23; adult/child under 15 yrs €4.80/ free, free 1st Sun of month; open 10am-8pm Tues-Sat & holidays, 10am-3pm Sun) occupies four of the many fine medieval stone mansions on Carrer de Montcada. It is worth wandering in just to admire the courtyard and internal staircase of the first of these buildings, but few people do so without subsequently devoting a couple of hours to the collection.

Although Picasso never visited Spain during the Franco years, he always had a soft spot for Catalunya, and in 1962 agreed to the idea of his old Barcelona friend and secretary Jaume Sabartés that a Picasso museum be founded here. Sabartés' collection was combined with works already owned by the city. Later, Picasso himself made large donations (including many early works and a bequest of graphics) to the museum, and in 1981 his widow, Jacqueline Roque, contributed 141 ceramics.

The collection's look is bound to change as an enormous amount of renovation is being carried out and is not due to finish before late 2003. It is strongest on Picasso's earliest years, up until 1904, but there is enough material from subsequent periods to give you a deep impression of the man's versatility and genius. Above all, you feel that Picasso is always one step ahead of himself, let alone anyone else, in his search for new forms of expression.

The collection starts, naturally enough, at the beginning, with sketches, oils and doodling from Picasso's earliest years in Málaga and La Coruña – most of it done around 1893–95. Some of his self-portraits and the portraits of his father, which date from 1896, are evidence enough of his precocious talent. *Retrato de la Tía Pepa* (Portrait of Aunt Pepa), done in Málaga in 1897, is a key painting. In Rooms 4 and 5 are a couple of his most important art school period efforts. The enormous *Ciència i Caritat* (Science and Charity) is proof to anyone that, had he wanted to, Picasso would have made a fine mainstream artist.

On the 2nd floor you are in a pivotal year of the master's life – 1900. By now he is gaining confidence and abandoning the strictures of academic painting. This was the year of his first exhibition in Els Quatre Gats and his first trip to Paris. The lines are fluid and alive, and soon he embarks on his first conscious thematic adventure, the Blue Period (Room 12). From this point he distanced himself increasingly from simply depicting scenes of life in Barcelona or Paris, from the streets to the cabarets, to interpreting them more symbolically. The blue-tinted glasses through which he regards the world lend to many of his paintings in this period a melancholy air. His nocturnal view of *Terrats de Barcelona* (The Rooftops of

Barcelona) and *El Foll* (The Madman) are both a little cold and cheerless. Just one portrait from the Pink (or Rose) Period is on show (Room 12).

From here on the collection is less comprehensive. There is a modest selection of Cubist paintings (Room 14) and some of his loopier ceramics (Room 15).

More significant is the section from Rooms 16 to 19. From 1954 to 1962, Picasso was obsessed by the idea of researching and 'rediscovering' the greats, in particular Velázquez. In 1957 he executed a series of renditions of the latter's masterpiece, *Las Meninas* (which hangs in El Prado, Madrid). It is as though Picasso has looked at the original Velázquez painting through a prism reflecting all the styles he had worked through until then. The series includes studies of single characters from the original work through to depictions of the work as a whole. Room 18 contains eight appealing treatments of *Pichones* (pigeons).

There are additional charges for special exhibitions.

Museu Tèxtil i d'Indumentària This Textile & Costume Museum (☎ 93 310 45 16; Carrer de Montcada 12-14; admission €3.50 with adjacent Museu Barbier-Mueller d'Art Precolombí, both museums free 1st Sun of month; open 10am-6pm Tues-Sat, 10am-3pm Sun & holidays) occupies the 13th-century Palau dels Marquesos de Lió, and part of the Palau Nadal next door (both buildings underwent repeated alterations into the 18th century). Its 4000 items range from 4th-century Coptic textiles to 20th-century local embroidery, but best is the big collection of clothing from the 16th century to the 1930s. The items in the museum were collected over a period of more than 100 years. The old courtyard is graced with an agreeable café.

Museu Barbier-Mueller d'Art Precolombí Occupying the rest of the Palau Nadal, this museum (admission as per Museu Tèxtil i d'Indumentària) holds part of one of the most prestigious collections of South American pre-Colombian art in the world.

The artefacts from these 'primitive' cultures come from the treasure-trove of the Swiss businessman Josef Mueller (who died in 1977) and his son-in-law Jean-Paul Barbier, who directs the Musée Barbier-Mueller in Geneva, Switzerland.

All the rooms have been blacked out, with only the artefacts on display eerily lit up in the gloom. The first room you enter is given over to South American gold jewellery. From then on you pass through a series of rooms containing ceramics, jewellery, statues, textiles and other objects. Explanations are provided in several languages including English.

Other Sights Along Carrer de Montcada Several other mansions on this street are now commercial art galleries where you're welcome to browse (they often stage exhibitions). The biggest is the **Galeria Maeght** (No 25) in the 16th-century Palau dels Cervelló. For more tips on art galleries, turn to the Shopping chapter. If you can get a peek into the baroque courtyard of the originally medieval **Palau de Dalmases** (No 20) – now a hideously expensive place to sip wine (see the Entertainment chapter) – do so as it is one of the finest on the strip.

Passeig del Born

Carrer de Montcada opens, at its western end, into **Passeig del Born**, a plaza where jousting tournaments took place in the Middle Ages and which was Barcelona's main square from the 13th to 18th centuries. They used to say *roda el món i torna al Born* (go around the world and return to the Born), and the merchants and shipowners who lived and dealt around here no doubt saw the area as the navel of their world. Since the mid-1990s it has become the most popular part of the old city, with bars and restaurants multiplying and house prices soaring at a dizzying rate.

The former **Mercat del Born**, a late 19th century produce market built of iron and glass and disused now for decades, has been set aside as the future site of Barcelona's provincial library, but all could change. Excavation on the site in 2002 unearthed great chunks of one of the areas of the city flattened to make way for the much hated Ciutadella (see later in this chapter). Historians have found intact streets and the remains of houses dating as far back as the 15th century and in late March it was decided that the excavated site had to be preserved. If the library project cannot be adapted to protect the finds, it has been mooted that it could be relocated to the nearby and underutilised Estació de França train station.

Església de Santa Maria del Mar

At the end of Passeig del Born stands one of Barcelona's finest Catalan Gothic churches, Santa Maria del Mar (open 9am-1.30pm & 4.30pm-8pm daily). Built in the 14th century, Santa Maria was lacking in superfluous decoration even before anarchists gutted it in 1909 and 1936. This only serves to highlight its fine proportions, purity of line and sense of space. The apse features a beautiful slim arcade and some of the 15th- to 18th-century stained glass is particularly fetching.

Keep an eye out for music recitals here – the acoustics aren't the best, but the church makes a wonderful setting for the baroque and classical concerts staged here.

Museu de la Xocolata (Map 6)

In this Museum of Chocolate (☎ 93 268 78 78; Plaça de Pons i Clerch; admission €3.60; open 10am-7pm Mon & Wed-Sat, 10am-3pm Sun & holidays) you can trace the origins of this fundamental foodstuff, its arrival in Europe and the many myths and images that surround it. In among the informative stuff (with panels in various languages), are extraordinary models in chocolate of buildings such as La Pedrera and La Sagrada Família, along with characters such as Winnie the Pooh! It's enough to have you making for the nearest sweets store but you don't have to, because here they sell chocolate in all sorts of forms, from liquid to solid.

PARC DE LA CIUTADELLA (MAP 5)

East of La Ribera and north of La Barceloneta, Parc de la Ciutadella (open

8am-8pm daily Oct-Mar, to 9pm Apr-Sept) is perfect if you just need a bit of space and greenery, but also has a couple of more specific attractions.

After the War of the Spanish Succession, Felipe V built a huge fort (La Ciutadella) to keep watch over Barcelona. It became a much loathed symbol of everything Catalans hated about Madrid and was later used as a political prison. Only in 1869 did the central government allow its demolition (you can see a diorama of the fortress in the Museu Militar on Montjuïc). The site was turned into a park and used as the main site for the Universal Exhibition of 1888.

The single most impressive thing in the park is the monumental **Cascada** (waterfall) near the Passeig de Pujades entrance, created in 1875–81 by Josep Fontsère with the help of the young Gaudí. It's a dramatic combination of classical statuary, rugged rocks, greenery and thundering water. Nearby, you can hire little rowboats to paddle about the small lake – a potential diversion for recalcitrant kids.

Museu Nacional d'Art Modern de Catalunya

In the southeast of the park, next door to the **Parlament de Catalunya**, where the regional parliament meets, this art gallery *(☎ 93 319 57 28; admission €3, half-price with Ruta del Modernisme ticket; open 10am-7pm Tues-Sat, 10am-2.30pm Sun & holidays)* is housed in the fort's former arsenal. By the time you read this, it is possible (although dates were not yet fixed) that the collection will have been put into storage. The museum buildings are to be handed over to the parliament and the collection is destined to be transferred to the Museu Nacional d'Art de Catalunya in Montjuïc between 2003 and 2004.

The collection consists of Catalan art from the mid-19th century to the mid-20th century. Most of the paintings are of comparatively little interest, spanning the periods of Catalan Realisme, Anecdotisme, Modernisme (Ramon Casas and Santiago Rusiñol are each represented by about a dozen paintings, among the most interesting

being Casas' depiction of himself and Pere Romeu on a tandem bicycle. Romeu was the director of Els Quatre Gats, the tavern in Barcelona where Modernista artists and hangers on hung out) and into Noucentisme.

Among the Noucentistas' work on display, perhaps that of Joaquim Sunyer is the most striking. Three fairly minor works by Dalí have managed to find their way in here as well.

More attention-grabbing are the many items of Modernista interior and, in the case of iron grills created by Gaudí for the Casa Vicenç, exterior design. They include doors, furniture, lampshades and so on.

Zoo

The southern end of the park is occupied by a large Parc Zoològic *(zoo; ☎ 93 225 67 80; adult/child €10/6.50; open 10am-7.30pm daily Apr-Sept, to 5pm Oct-Mar)*, which is best known for its albino gorilla Floquet de Neu (Snowflake, or Copito de Nieve in Castilian), who was orphaned by poachers in Guinea (Africa) in the 1960s (see the boxed text 'Little White Wonder'). Floquet is claimed to be the only albino gorilla in the world and is something of a symbol for the zoo.

Around the Park

Along the Passeig de Picasso (Map 6) side of the park are several buildings constructed for, or just before, the Universal Exhibition. The one at the top end is the most interesting. Known as the **Castell dels Tres Dragons**, it is a product of the imagination of Domènech i Montaner, who put the castle trimmings on a pioneering steel frame. The coats of arms are all invented and the whole building exudes a rather playful air. It was used as a café-restaurant during the exhibition. Now it houses the **Museu de Zoologia** *(Map 6; ☎ 93 319 68 95; admission €3; open 10am-2pm Tues-Sun, to 6.30pm Thur)*. If you like stuffed animals, model elephants and the inevitable skeletons of huge ex-living things, this rather fusty institution is the place for you.

To the south is **L'Hivernacle**, one of two arboretums, a mini botanical garden with a

Little White Wonder

When a group of Guineans stumbled across a trembling white baby gorilla in the jungle in 1963 they thought they'd contact a white man, Jordi Sabater. Sabater, a naturalist working in what was then Spanish-controlled Guinea, could hardly believe his eyes. Or his ears when the Guineans named a price of 20,000 ptas (a substantial sum in those days) in exchange for their prize. The baby gorilla had been orphaned by hunters and Sabater struck a deal. He would look after the little white animal and, if it survived, would buy it. And so it was. Offered a million dollars to transfer it to Canada, he opted for his home town of Barcelona, where Snowflake arrived in November 1996. In his early 40s, he is getting on (gorillas tend not to live longer than 50 years) but his zoo guardians are confident that, in their care, he will have a long innings.

pleasant café in its midst. Next is the **Museu de Geologia**. Most people would have to have rocks in their heads to spend too much time in here, but then again, budding geologists may well want to examine the stones, minerals and fossils on display. Admission times and price are as for the Museu de Zoologia. Further along from the museum is L'Umbracle, another arboretum.

Northwest of the park, Passeig de Lluís Companys is the imposing Modernista **Arc de Triomf** (Map 6; metro Arc de Triomf), designed by Josep Vilaseca as an entrance to the Universal Exhibition, with unusual, almost Islamic-style brickwork. Just what the triumph was is a trifle hard to guess. It is difficult to put yourself back into the clothes and feelings of Barcelonins in the late 1880s. The exhibition was an (at times farcical and certainly very expensive) attempt to put this middle-ranking and much-ignored city on the world map. The wheels of industry were turning (albeit not at the pace of great European centres further north) and the loss of Cuba, (see History in the Facts about Barcelona chapter), which

would have a devastating impact on Barcelona's trade and manufacturing, was 10 years off. The town fathers were obviously feeling in good spirits, even if no particular 'victory' offered itself as cause for erecting triumphal arches!

Màgic BCN

This 40-minute special effects 'ride' (Map 5; ☎ 93 300 29 93; Passeig de Lluís Companys 10-12; adult/child under 12 yrs €5.40/3.90; operates 6pm & 7pm daily, also noon, 1pm & 5pm Sat & Sun) gives you the impression of travelling by train through scenes and countryside all over the world. It's quite clever and will doubtless appeal to the kiddies.

PORT VELL (MAP 5)

Barcelona's old port at the bottom of La Rambla, once such an eyesore that it caused public protests, has been transformed beyond recognition since the 1980s. Instead of the sight of warehouses, railyards and dumps, you are confronted by chic shopping, harbourside munching, movies-on-the-sea, discos and Irish pubs, parking for yachts and a huge aquarium. All these elements and more have left the 'old port' looking brand spanking new.

For a view of the harbour from the water, you can take a **golondrina** excursion boat (☎ 93 442 31 06; trips adult/child aged 11-18 yrs/child aged 4-11 yrs €8.10/5.90/3.60) from Moll de les Drassanes in front of the Monument a Colom. The 1½-hour trip takes you out to sea and as far north as the Platja de Marbella before returning. The number of departures depends largely on season and demand. You can get a 35-minute excursion just as far as the breakwater (€3.30/1.70 for adults/children). Breakwater trips normally go at least hourly in the daytime, Port Olímpic trips at least three times daily.

Northeast from the golondrina quay stretches the palm-lined promenade Moll de la Fusta. Moored here is the **Pailebot de Santa Eulàlia** (Map 5; adult/child €2.40/1.20, free with Museu Marítim ticket; open 11am-7.30pm), a 1918 sailboat restored by the Museu Marítim.

THINGS TO SEE & DO

At the centre of the redeveloped harbour is the **Moll d'Espanya**, a former wharf linked to Moll de la Fusta by a wave-shaped footbridge, the **Rambla de Mar**, which rotates to let boats enter the marina behind it.

Orsom *(Map 5; ☎ 93 225 82 60;* |W| *www .barcelona-orsom.com)* has a catamaran that leaves from Maremàgnum and sails around to Port Olímpic and back in about 1½ hours. The boat can take up to 100 passengers and costs €9/7/4.20 for adults/children aged 11 to 18/children aged four to 10.

Rising up at the end of Moll d'Espanya is the glossy Maremàgnum shopping and eating complex, but the major attraction is **L'Aquàrium** *(☎ 93 221 74 74; adult/child €11/7; open 9.30am-9pm Sept-June, to 11pm July-Aug)* behind it – an ultra-modern aquarium that opened in 1995. It's claimed to be Europe's biggest and to have the world's best Mediterranean collection. It is divided into 21 tanks, of which the 80m-long shark tunnel is a highlight. All up, some 8000 fish (including 11 sharks) have taken up residence here. Admission is steep. Beyond L'Aquàrium is the Imax Port Vell big-screen cinema.

The **cable car** *(telefèric or funicular aereo; operates 10.45am-5.30pm Oct-Mar, to 7pm Apr-Sept)* strung across the harbour to Montjuïc provides another view of the city. You can get tickets at Miramar (Montjuïc) and the Torre de Sant Sebastià (in La Barceloneta). A one-way/return ticket from Sant Sebastià to Miramar costs €7.21/8.41. A return to the middle Jaume I tower costs €7.21, or you can just take the lift up for €3.61. Alternatively you could pay a lot more to head up and eat in the Torre d'Alta Mar restaurant (see the Places to Eat chapter)!

LA BARCELONETA & PORT OLÍMPIC

It used to be said that Barcelona had 'turned its back on the sea', but an ambitious Olympics-inspired redevelopment program has returned to life a long stretch of coast northeast of Port Vell.

La Barceloneta is a mid-18th century sailors' and fishermen's quarter laid out by the French engineer Prosper Verboom to replace housing destroyed to make way for the building of La Ciutadella. The narrow grid system of streets was quite an innovation in its time, although the dreary five and six-storey apartment blocks that make up the area today are hardly enticing. By the 19th century it was a pretty squalid spot, especially in hard times (read the first few chapters of Eduardo Mendoza's *City of Marvels* to get an idea of what it must have been like). La Barceloneta is still known for its seafood restaurants, of which several good ones survive (see the Places to Eat chapter), although many disappeared in the coastal redevelopment programs that came with the Olympics.

Museu d'Història de Catalunya (Map 5)

The Palau de Mar building facing the harbour once served as warehouses, but was transformed in the 1990s into something quite different. Below the seaward arcades is a string of good restaurants. Inside is the museum *(Museum of Catalonian History; ☎ 93 225 47 00; Plaça de Pau Vila 3; admission €3; open 10am-7pm Tues-Sat, to 8pm Wed, 10am-2.30pm Sun & holidays)*.

The permanent display covers the 2nd and 3rd floors, taking you, as the bumph says, on a 'voyage through history' from the Stone Age through to the early 1980s. (A committee was formed in 2002 to work on its extension to 2000.) The museum is a busy hodgepodge of dioramas, artefacts, videos, models, documents and interactive bits. It is an entertaining and informative (although a little uneven) exploration of 2000 years of Catalan history. See how the Romans lived, listen to Arab poetry from the time of the Muslim occupation of the city, peer into the dwelling of a Dark Ages family in the Pyrenees, mount a knight's horse and try to lift a suit of armour, or perhaps descend into an air-raid shelter from the civil war.

The labelling is in Catalan, but you can ask for a brochure (returnable) with some explanations in your own language (quite a few tongues are catered for). Several changes are planned for the museum in the

Buffalo Barna

Back in December 1889, a curious crowd moved into what was vacant ground on the block bounded by Carrer de Muntaner, Còrsega, Rosselló and Aribau in L'Eixample.

Sioux, Cheyennes and Arapahos, accompanied by Mexican bandits and cowboys, who had arrived in Barcelona by steamship from Marseilles, erected tents and tepees. Buffalo Bill had arrived in town with his Wild West Show, bringing 184 people, 159 horses and 20 buffaloes.

William Frederick Cody (1846–1917), explorer, guide and tracker for General Custer, had quite a record. An expert shot, he had been a sheriff, member of the Pony Express, was obsessed by buffalo hunting and was reputedly a Freemason. He came to Europe to try to make a buck out of his Exhibition of American Indian and Frontier Life.

Barcelona had recently put itself on the map with the Universal Exhibition of 1888, so it seemed only natural to pay a visit. The show stayed there for five weeks, but not everything went according to plan. In between displays of Indian attacks on wagon trains and cowboys whooping it up, torrential rains forced numerous cancellations, a tepee was destroyed by fire and a 'flu epidemic killed one of the showmasters and left several Indians under the weather.

When Bill and his circus headed off for Naples, two of his crew were left behind in the Hospital de la Santa Creu. One of them is reputed to have died here and ended up buried on Montjuïc, but nobody knows for certain. Cody & Co never returned to Spain. Bill's boast that, with 30,000 American Indians, he could expel the Spanish army from Cuba probably didn't go down well. (The US Navy took care of the problem 10 years later in any case.)

coming years, including proper labelling in Castilian and English.

Beaches & Port Olímpic

Barcelona's fishing fleet ties up along the Moll del Rellotge, south of the museum. On La Barceloneta's seaward side are Platja de Sant Sebastià and Platja de la Barceloneta, the first of Barcelona's **beaches** *(Map 1)*, once dirty and unused, but now cleaned up and popular on summer weekends. **Passeig Marítim**, a 1.25km promenade from La Barceloneta to Port Olímpic – through an area formerly full of railway sidings and warehouses – makes for a pleasant stroll if you manage to dodge the rollerbladers.

Port Olímpic *(Map 1)* was built for the 1992 Olympic sailing events and is now a classy marina surrounded by bars and restaurants. An eye-catcher on the approach from La Barceloneta is the giant copper *Peix* (Fish) sculpture by Frank Gehry. The area behind Port Olímpic – dominated by Barcelona's two tallest skyscrapers, the luxury Hotel Arts Barcelona and Torre Mapfre office block – is the Vila Olímpica, which

was the living quarters for the Olympic participants, now mostly sold off as expensive apartments.

To the northeast, more beaches stretch towards the Riu Besòs (which marks the city's northeastern boundary). The initial (southernmost) stretch of Platja de Mar Bella is a nudist strip, although punters not wishing to reveal all seem to mingle comfortably enough with the in-the-altogether crowd. All these beaches are kept clean and the water is perfectly decent.

Behind Platja de Nova Mar Bella, further to the northeast, and beyond to the Besòs rise the serried skeletal hulks of what will be the hotels, conference centres and pricey apartments of the Front Marítim, Barcelona's future luxury residential district.

L'EIXAMPLE

L'Eixample (el Ensanche in Castilian, meaning the Enlargement), stretching one to 1.5km north, east and west of Plaça de Catalunya, was the city's 19th-century answer to overcrowding in the confines of the medieval city.

Work on L'Eixample began in 1869 to a design by the architect Ildefons Cerdà, who specified a grid of wide streets with plazas formed by their chamfered (cut-off) corners. Cerdà also planned numerous green spaces but these didn't survive the intense demand for L'Eixample real estate.

L'Eixample has been inhabited from the start by the city's middle classes, many of whom still think it's the best thing about Barcelona. Along its grid of straight streets are the majority of the city's most expensive shops and hotels, a range of eateries and several nightspots. The main sightseeing objective is Modernista architecture, the best of which – apart from La Sagrada Família – is clustered on or near L'Eixample's main avenue, Passeig de Gràcia.

Manzana de la Discordia (Map 2)

The so-called 'Apple (read Block) of Discord' on the western side of Passeig de Gràcia, between Carrer del Consell de Cent and Carrer d'Aragó, gets its name from three houses remodelled in highly contrasting manner between 1898 and 1906 by three of the leading Modernista architects.

On the corner of Carrer del Consell de Cent is **Casa Lleó Morera** (*Passeig de Gràcia 35*), Domènech i Montaner's contribution, with Art Nouveau carving outside and a bright, tiled lobby in which floral motifs predominate. You can no longer visit the 1st floor, which is quite giddy with swirling sculptures, rich mosaics and also whimsical decoration.

Casa Amatller (*Passeig de Gràcia 41*), by Puig i Cadafalch, combines Gothic window frames with a stepped gable borrowed (deliberately) from urban architecture of the Netherlands. The pillared entrance hall and the staircase lit by stained glass are like the inside of some romantic castle. You can wander around the ground floor and pick up a Ruta del Modernisme ticket here – see the boxed text on this value ticket later in this chapter.

Casa Batlló (*Passeig de Gràcia 43*), next door, is one of Barcelona's gems and Gaudí at his hallucinogenic best. The facade, sprinkled with bits of blue, mauve and green tile and studded with wave-shaped window frames and balconies, rises to an uneven blue tiled roof with a solitary tower. Locals know it variously as the *casa dels ossos* (house of bones) or *casa del drac* (house of the dragon). It's easy enough to see why. The balconies look like the bony jaws of some strange beast and the roof represents Sant Jordi (St George) and the dragon, and if you stare long enough at the building, it seems almost to be a living being. You might fluke your way into the foyer (but not beyond) if the main entrance is open. In the course of 2002 only, on the occasion of the city's Gaudí celebrations, the foyer and main floor were opened up to visitors (*admission €10; open 9am-2pm*).

While here, you may want to pop into the **Museu del Parfum** (*Map 2; ☎ 93 216 01 46; Passeig de Gràcia 39; admission free; open 10.30am-1.30pm & 5pm-8pm Mon-Fri, 11am-1.30pm Sat*), in the Regia store. It contains everything from ancient scent receptacles to classic Eau de Cologne bottles.

Fundació Antoni Tàpies (Map 2)

Around the corner from Manzana de la Discordia, the Fundació Antoni Tàpies (*☎ 93 487 03 15; Carrer d'Aragó 255; adult/student €4.20/2.10; open 10am-8pm Tues-Sun*) is both a pioneering Modernista building

How Do You Like The Apples?

Despite the Catalanisation of most Barcelona names in recent decades, the Manzana de la Discordia has kept its Spanish name to preserve a pun on *manzana*, which means both 'block' and 'apple'. According to Greek mythology, the original Apple of Discord was tossed onto Mt Olympus by Eris (Discord), with orders that it be given to the most beautiful goddess, sparking jealousies that helped start the Trojan War. The pun won't transfer into Catalan, whose word for block is *illa*, and for apple *poma*.

MARTIN HUGHES

MARTIN HUGHES

JENNY JONES

DAMIEN SIMONIS

cenes from Montjuïc (clockwise from top left): a cable car offers a bird's-eye view of the city; one of
an Miró's creations on the roof of the Fundació Joan Miró, a gallery dedicated to his work; the palm-
ned boulevard of Passeig de Colom; patterns in the lawns of Castell de Montjuïc

Muse over modern art (top to bottom): the palatial Museu d'Art Contemporani de Barcelona (Macba); a Picasso mural that decorates the facade of the Col.legi de Arquitectes; ramble over Joan Miró's mosaic in Plaça de la Boqueria on La Rambla

Ruta del Modernisme Ticket

Modernisme enthusiasts should consider picking up a Ruta del Modernisme ticket at the Casa Amatller. For the Gaudí year of 2002, the entire programme on offer was modified and renamed the Ruta de Gaudí. It is probable that afterwards it will revert to the old Ruta del Modernisme.

In its old form, you bought a ticket (€7.50) with guidebook and map. The ticket gave you discounted entry (usually 30%) to the following sights: Palau Güell, Palau de la Música, La Pedrera, La Sagrada Família, Fundació Antoni Tàpies, Casa-Museu Gaudí (in Parc Güell), Museu de Zoologia and the Museu Nacional d'Art Modern. Of the buildings comprising the Manzana de la Discordia, all in private hands, you can normally only enter the foyer of Casa Amatller to pick up this ticket. You can also join a guided 'tour' of the facades of the Manzana de la Discordia.

The Gaudí ticket gave discounted admission to some additional sights including: Col.legi de les Teresianes, crypt of the Colònia Güell, Finca Güell, Casa Batlló, Casa Vicenç, Torre Bellesguard and Casa Calvet.

For more information on the Ruta de Gaudí or the reinstated Ruta del Modernisme call ☎ 93 488 01 39. Casa Amatller opens 10am to 7pm daily (to 2pm on Sunday).

(completed in 1885) and the major collection of a leading 20th-century Catalan artist.

The building, designed by Domènech i Montaner for the publishing house Editorial Montaner i Simón, combines a brick-covered iron frame with Islamic-inspired decoration. Tàpies saw fit to crown the building with the meanderings of his own mind – to some it looks like a pile of coiled barbed wire, to others...well.

Antoni Tàpies, whose experimental art has often carried political messages – he opposed Francoism in the 1960s and '70s – launched the Fundació in 1984 to promote contemporary art, donating a large part of his own work. The core collection spans the whole arc of Tàpies' creation, and also includes some contributions from other contemporary artists. The Fundació houses an important research library devoted principally to Tàpies, but again embracing a wider range of contemporary art.

Tàpies' work does not appeal to everyone. He frequently uses all sorts of three-dimensional materials – everything from scrap wood to sand and rocks in his grand canvases that to many will look like meaningless blobs and splotches. Those who do like him may also be a little frustrated here, as frequently a fairly limited selection of his works is on show. Throughout most of the year much exposition space is devoted to temporary displays of other contemporary artists' work.

La Pedrera (Map 2)

Back on Passeig de Gràcia is another Gaudí masterpiece, built between 1905 and 1910 as a combined apartment and office block. Formally called the Casa Milà after the businessman who commissioned it, it's better known as La Pedrera *(The Quarry; ☎ 93 484 59 95; Carrer de Provença 261-265; admission €6; open 10am-8pm daily)* because of its uneven grey stone facade, which ripples around the corner of Carrer de Provença. The wave effect is emphasised by elaborate wrought-iron balconies.

The Fundació Caixa Catalunya has opened the top floor flat, attic and roof to visitors, organising it as the Espai Gaudí (Gaudí Space). The roof is the most extraordinary element, with its giant chimney pots looking like multicoloured medieval knights. Gaudí wanted to put a tall statue of the Virgin up here too: when the Milà family said no, fearing it might make the building a target for anarchists, Gaudí resigned from the project in disgust. One floor below the roof, where you can appreciate Gaudí's taste for McDonald's M-style parabolic arches (if McDonald's had existed in those days, would he have come up with something else?), is a modest museum dedicated to his work. You can see models and videos dealing with each of his buildings.

Downstairs on the next floor you can inspect the apartment (El Pis de la Pedrera). It is fascinating to wander around this elegantly furnished home, done up in the style a well-to-do family might have enjoyed in the early 20th century. The sensuous curves and unexpected touches in everything from light fittings to bedsteads, from door handles to the balconies can hardly fail to induce a heartfelt desire to move in at once. The lower floors of the building often host temporary expositions.

From July to September, La Pedrera opens on Friday and Saturday evenings (9pm to midnight). The roof is lit up in an eerie fashion and, while you are taking in the night views of Barcelona, you also get to sip a flute of *cava* and listen to live music in the background (€9).

Palau Quadras & Casa de les Punxes (Map 2)

Within a few blocks north and east of La Pedrera are two of Puig i Cadafalch's major buildings. The nearer is the Palau del Baró de Quadras (☎ 93 263 13 49; *Avinguda Diagonal 373; open 10am-2pm Tues-Sun*), created between 1902 and 1904 with detailed neo-Gothic carvings on the facade and fine stained glass. Until 2001 it housed the **Museu de la Música**, an international collection of instruments including one of the most important collections of guitars in the world, as well as a series of organs dating as far back as the 16th century. At the time of writing the collection had been removed in preparation for its transfer to l'Auditori (see the Entertainment chapter), where the display is supposed to be ready for viewing by mid-2004.

Further east and on the other side of Avinguda Diagonal, the Casa Terrades is better known as the **Casa de les Punxes** (*House of the Spikes; Avinguda Diagonal 420*) because of its pointed turrets. This apartment block of 1903–05 looks like a castle in a fairy tale.

La Sagrada Família (Map 2)

If you only have time for one sightseeing outing in Barcelona, this should probably be it. La Sagrada Família (☎ 93 207 30 31; *Carrer de Mallorca 401; adult/student €6/4, €7 combined with Casa-Museu Gaudí in Parc Güell; open 9am-8pm daily Apr-Aug, 9am-7pm Mar & Sept-Oct, 9am-6pm Nov-Feb*) inspires awe by its sheer verticality and, in the true manner of the great medieval cathedrals it emulates, it's still not half built after more than 100 years. If it's ever finished, the topmost tower will be more than half as high again as those that are standing today.

The Temple Expiatori de la Sagrada Família (Expiatory Temple of the Holy Family), in the east of L'Eixample, was the project to which Antoni Gaudí dedicated the latter part of his life.

The admission charge (which more than 1.5 million people a year pay to get in) includes a good museum in the crypt. What you're visiting is a building site, but the completed sections and the museum can be explored at leisure. Up to four times daily, 50-minute guided tours are offered at €3 per person. The entrance is by the southwestern facade fronting Carrer de Sardenya and Plaça de la Sagrada Família. Inside is a bookstall where you should invest €3 in the *Official Guide* if you want a detailed account of the church's sculpture and its symbolism. Audioguides (€3) are also available. Once inside, you can spend a further €1.50 per ride on lifts that take you up inside one of the towers located on each side of this remarkable church.

To get your bearings, you need to realise that this facade, and the opposite one facing Plaça de Gaudí, each with four sky-scraping towers, are at the *sides* of the church. The main facade, as yet unbuilt, will be at the southeastern end, on Carrer de Mallorca.

Nativity Facade This, the northeastern facade, is the building's artistic pinnacle, mostly done under Gaudí's personal supervision and much of it with his own hands. You can climb high up inside some of the four towers by a combination of lifts (when they're working) and narrow spiral staircases – a vertiginous experience. The towers are destined to hold tubular bells capable of playing complicated music at great volume. Their upper parts are decorated with mosaics spelling out *'Sanctus, Sanctus, Sanctus, Hosanna in Excelsis, Amen, Alleluia'*. Asked why he lavished so much care on the tops of the spires, which no-one would see from close up, Gaudí answered: 'The angels will see them.'

Beneath the towers is a tall, three-part portal on the theme of Christ's birth and childhood. It seems to lean outwards as you stand beneath looking up. Gaudí used real people and animals as models for many of the sculptures.

The three sections of the portal represent, from left to right, Hope, Charity and Faith. Among the forest of sculpture on the Charity portal, you can make out, low down, the manger surrounded by an ox, an ass, the shepherds and kings, with angel musicians above. Directly above the blue stained-glass window is the Archangel Gabriel's Annunciation to Mary. At the top is a green cypress tree, symbolic refuge in a storm for the white doves of peace dotted over it.

Lower sculptures on the Hope portal show the flight into Egypt and the massacre of the innocents, with Jesus and Joseph in their carpenters' workshop just above. Sculpture on the Faith portal includes, in the centre of the lower group, the child Jesus explaining the Scriptures to the priests.

Interior The semicircular apse wall at the northwestern end of the church was the first part to be finished (in 1894). The interior of the church remains a building site but progress is being made. The nave has now largely been roofed over and a forest of extraordinary angled pillars is in place. The image of the tree is in no way fortuitous, for Gaudí's plan envisaged such an effect. As the pillars soar towards the ceiling, they

THINGS TO SEE & DO

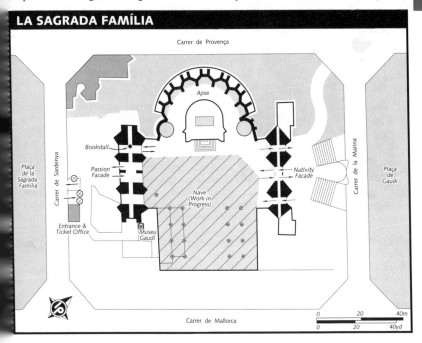

LA SAGRADA FAMÍLIA

Carrer de Provença

Apse

Bookstall

Carrer de Sardenya

Plaça de la Sagrada Família

Passion Facade

Nave (Work in Progress)

Nativity Facade

Carrer de la Marina

Plaça de Gaudí

Entrance & Ticket Office

Museu Gaudí

Carrer de Mallorca

0   20   40m
0   20   40yd

Gaudí – God's Architect

The idea for La Sagrada Família came from a rich publisher, Josep Marià Bocabella i Verdaguer, the man behind the emergence of an arch-conservative society dedicated to Sant Josep (St Joseph). The society came together, in part, as a response to calls from Pope Pius IX for a renewal of the Catholic faith, which he saw threatened in a Europe flooded with ideas of liberalism, democracy, modernity and other such iniquitous nonsense.

The Pope had concrete cause for concern: Garibaldi's victories in Italy had left the Vatican virtually bereft of secular power. Liberalism in Spain seemed equally pernicious.

Among the Pope's exhortations was a renewal of devotion to Jesus, Mary and Joseph, the Holy Family, or *La Sagrada Família*. And so Bocabella had an inspired idea. What decadent, liberal Barcelona needed was a great church raised to the Holy Family, where contrite citizens could expiate their sins. The society raised the cash and the first stone of a neo-Gothic structure was laid in 1882. The original architect soon quit, and into the breech stepped Antoni Gaudí in 1884.

He was given a free hand. He conceived a structure that drew on Gothic roots, and embellished it with his own very particular spin.

Gaudí, born into an artisan family in Reus, southern Catalunya, and trained as a metalsmith, was already a successful architect. Up to 1910 he worked on numerous buildings in Barcelona and elsewhere – beyond Catalunya he left three monuments, one each in Comillas (Cantabria), Astorga and León. After abandoning the more-or-less finished La Pedrera on Passeig de Gràcia for the Milà family, he began to narrow his efforts.

True, he continued to work for Eusebi Güell, his chief patron and wealthy industrialist, on two ambitious projects that never reached completion: the Parc Güell and Colònia Güell (see those sections later in this chapter for more on both – the crypt of the church in the latter provides many clues as to how Gaudí aimed to approach technical challenges in his masterwork). Funds for both projects had petered out by 1916, though, by which time his only interest seemed to be La Sagrada Família.

A conservative and moderate Catalanist, Gaudí became increasingly religious and came to view his great church project, into which he poured all the architectural and design knowledge he had accumulated, as a sacred mission. As Bocabella's Josephine society and

MW
Gaudí devoted everything to the Sagrada Família church – a project that was to be his last.

sprout a web of supporting branches that creates the effect of a forest canopy. Tribunes built above the aisles will be able to hold a choir of 1500!

The main Glory Facade will, like the northeastern and southwestern facades, be

crowned by four tall towers – the total of 12 representing the Twelve Apostles. Further decoration will make the whole building a microcosmic symbol of the Christian church, with Christ represented by the massive 170m central tower above the transept

Gaudí – God's Architect

Barcelona's wealthy tired of the project and having to cough up money for what seemed a bottomless pit, Gaudí resigned himself, with suitably religious stoicism, to a long struggle. He invested everything he had into it, and ran craft workshops on site to nurture a skilled workforce to carry out the kind of decoration he wanted. He was probably deep in thought about how to proceed next when he was run over by a tram on the corner of Gran Via de les Corts Catalanes and Carrer de Bailèn in 1926. He was so ragged and poor that, at first, no one recognised him. He died three days later and the whole city turned out for his funeral.

As he worked on La Sagrada Família, Gaudí evolved steadily grander and more original ideas for it. He stuck to the basic Gothic cross-shaped ground plan with an apse, but eventually devised a temple 95m long and 60m wide, able to seat 13,000 people, with a central tower 170m high and another 17 of 100m or more. With his characteristic dislike for straight lines (there were none in nature, he said), Gaudí gave his towers swelling outlines inspired by the weird peaks of the holy mountain Montserrat outside Barcelona, and encrusted them with a tangle of sculpture that seems an outgrowth of the stone.

At Gaudí's death only the crypt, the apse walls, one portal and one tower had been finished. Three more towers were added by 1930 – completing the northeastern (Nativity) facade – but in 1936 anarchists burned and smashed everything they could in the church, including the workshops, plans and models.

Work restarted in 1952 using restored models and photographs of drawings, with only limited guidance on how Gaudí had thought of solving the huge technical problems of the building. Between 1954 and 1976 the southwestern (Passion) facade, with four more towers, was completed, with only some decorative detail work outstanding. The nave, which was started in 1978, is coming along nicely.

Constant controversy has dogged the building program. Some say the quality of the new work and its materials – concrete instead of stone – are inferior to the earlier parts; others claim that, in the absence of detailed plans, the shell should have been left as it was as a monument to Gaudí; yet others simply oppose all the expenditure (although the funding is private). The present chief architect, Jordi Bonet, and his supporters, aside from their desire to see Gaudí's mighty vision made real, argue that their task is a sacred one – this is a church intended to atone for sin and appeal for God's mercy on Catalunya. The way things are going, it might be finished by 2041 – a truly medieval construction timetable.

Gaudí's own story is far from over. The rector of La Sagrada Família, Lluís Bonet Armengol (the architect's brother), is promoting Gaudí's beatification. In March 2000 the Vatican decided to proceed with the examination of the case for canonising him. Even before becoming a saint, Gaudí has started attracting pilgrims, as devotees come to pray at his tomb in the crypt of La Sagrada Família. Says Bonet Armengol, Gaudí's contemporaries 'knew he was God's architect'.

Barcelona declared 2002 the Year of Gaudí to mark the 150th anniversary of Gaudí's birth (and no doubt in the hope of generating a little more tourist revenue). One wonders whether the man himself would approve.

and the five remaining planned towers will symbolise the Virgin Mary and the four Evangelists.

Passion Facade This southwestern facade, on the theme of Christ's last days and death, has been constructed since the 1950s with, like the Nativity Facade, four needling towers and a large, sculpture-bedecked portal. The sculptor, Josep Subirachs, has not attempted to imitate Gaudí's work but has produced strong images of his own. The sculptures, on three levels, are in an S-shaped sequence starting with the Last Supper at bottom left and ending with Christ's burial at top right.

Museu Gaudí Open the same times as the church, the museum includes interesting material on Gaudí's life and other work, as well as models, photos and other material on La Sagrada Família. You can see a good example of his plumb-line models that showed him the stresses and strains he could get away with in construction. At the far end is the simple crypt in which the genius is buried.

Hospital de la Santa Creu i de Sant Pau (Map 1)

The hospital is Domènech i Montaner's Modernista masterpiece – a huge construction that today still serves as one of the city's most important hospitals. The architect wanted to create a unique environment that would hopefully cheer up the patients. The whole complex, made up of 48 pavilions, is lavishly decorated and no pavilion is the same as another.

Among the many artists who contributed statuary, ceramics and artwork was the prolific Eusebi Arnau. You can wander around the grounds at any time, and it is well worth the stroll up Avinguda de Gaudí from La Sagrada Família.

Museu del Còmic i la Il.lustració (Map 1)

The Comics and Illustration Museum (☎ 93 348 15 13; Carrer de Santa Carolina 25; admission €3; open 10am-2pm & 5pm-8pm Mon-Sat) is devoted to the history of comic strips in Spain. Starting from the very earliest caricatures of the 19th century, the display concentrates on all forms of comic in Spain. The collection also includes some strips from the USA, France and other countries that are published in Spain.

Museu Taurino (Map 1)

Housed in the Plaça de Braus Monumental bullring, this bullfighting museum (Gran Via de les Corts Catalanes; adult/child €4/3; open 11am-2pm & 4pm-8pm daily Apr-early Oct, on fight days open 10.30am-1pm only) displays bulls' heads, old posters, trajes de luces (bullfighters' gear) and other memorabilia. You also get to wander around the ring and corrals.

Museu Egipci (Map 2)

This private collection (☎ 93 488 01 88; Carrer de València 284; adult/child €5.50/4.50; open 10am-8pm Mon-Sat, 10am-2pm Sun), with some 500 objects on display, is spread out over an airy seven-floor exhibition space. The hotel magnate, Jordi Clos, behind it continues to acquire material and his museum is divided into different thematic areas (the pharaoh, religion, daily life etc). In the basement floor is an exhibition area and library, in which various volumes (including some original editions of works by Carter, the Egyptologist who led the Tutankhamen excavations) are on display. Lovers of cheese may go in for the night-time visit, in which you are regaled with a show commentated by an Egyptologist (admission €11.42; open 9.30pm-11pm Fri) or a dramatised account of the last days of Cleopatra (admission €11.42; open 9.30pm-11pm Sat).

Fundación Francisco Godia (Map 2)

This private collection (☎ 93 272 31 80; Carrer de València 284; adult/student €4.50/2.10; open 10am-8pm Wed-Mon), next door to the Museu Egipci, contains an intriguing mix of medieval art, ceramics and also modern paintings.

GRÀCIA (MAP 2)

Once a separate village north of L'Eixample, and then in the 19th century an industrial district famous for its republican and liberal ideas, Gràcia was incorporated into the city of Barcelona in 1897. In the 1960s and '70s it became fashionable among radical and bohemian types, and even today retains some of that flavour – plenty of hip local luminaries make sure they get around the bars and cafés of Gràcia.

The district's interest lies in the atmosphere of its narrow streets (don't even think about trying to park a car here!), small plazas and the bars and restaurants on them. An evening or night-time wander is the best way to savour these. Diagonal and Fontana are the nearest metro stations to central Gràcia.

The liveliest plazas are **Plaça del Sol**, **Plaça de Rius i Taulet** with its clock tower (thus also known as Plaça del Rellotge – a popular meeting point), and the clean **Plaça de la Virreina** with the 17th-century Església de Sant Josep. The local council at one point looked set to get rid of the trees, but thankfully the neighbours took up arms and put a stop to such nonsense. Gràcia isn't exactly going to win any green awards as it is! On **Plaça de Rovira i Trias** you can sit on a bench next to a statue of Antoni Rovira, Ildefons Cerdà's rival in the competition to design L'Eixample in the late 19th century. Rovira's design has been laid out in the pavement so you can see what you think of it.

Three blocks east of Plaça de Rius i Taulet you can shop for groceries in a big covered market. West of Gràcia's main street, Carrer Gran de Gràcia, is an early Gaudí house, the turreted, vaguely *Mudéjar* **Casa Vicenç** *(Carrer de les Carolines 22)*.

PARC GÜELL (MAP 1)

North of Gràcia and about 4km from Plaça de Catalunya, Parc Güell *(admission free; open 9am-9pm daily June-Sept, 9am-8pm Apr-May & Oct, 9am-7pm Mar & Nov, 9am-6pm Dec-Feb)* is where Gaudí turned his hand to landscape gardening. It's a strange, enchanting place where his passion for natural forms really took flight – to the point where the artificial almost seems more natural than the natural.

Parc Güell originated in 1900 when Count Eusebi Güell bought a tree-covered hillside (then outside Barcelona) and hired Gaudí to create a miniature garden city of houses for the wealthy, in landscaped grounds. The project was a commercial flop and was abandoned in 1914 – but not before Gaudí had created 3km of roads and walks, steps and a plaza in his inimitable manner, plus the two gatehouses. In 1922 the city bought the estate for use as a public park.

The simplest way to get to Parc Güell is to take the metro to Lesseps, then walk 10 to 15 minutes: follow the signs northeast along Travessera de Dalt, then left up Carrer de Larrard, which brings you out almost at the park's two Hansel-and-Gretel-style gatehouses on Carrer d'Olot.

The park is extremely popular, and its quaint nooks and crannies are irresistible to photographers – who on busy days have a lot of trouble trying to keep out of each other's pictures.

The steps up from the entrance, guarded by a mosaic dragon/lizard, lead to the **Sala Hipóstila**, a forest of 84 stone columns (some of them leaning), intended as a market. To the left from here curves a gallery whose twisted stonework columns and roof give the effect of a cloister beneath tree roots – a motif repeated in several places in the park. On top of the Sala Hipóstila is a broad open space whose centrepiece is the **Banc de Trencadís**, a tiled bench curving sinuously around its perimeter.

The spired house to the right is the **Casa-Museu Gaudí** *(☎ 93 219 38 11; admission €3; open 10am-8pm Mon-Sat, 10am-2pm Sun May-Sept, 10am-7pm Mon-Sat, 10am-2pm Sun Mar-Apr & Oct, 10am-6pm Mon-Sat, 10am-2pm Sun Nov-Feb)*, where Gaudí lived for most of his last 20 years (1906–26). It contains furniture by him and other memorabilia.

Much of the park is still wooded but full of pathways. The best views are from the cross-topped **Turó del Calvari** in the southwestern corner.

TIBIDABO

Tibidabo (542m) is the highest hill in the wooded range that forms the backdrop to Barcelona. It's a good place for some fresh air (it's often a few degrees cooler than the city) and, if the air's clear, it has views over the city and inland as far as Montserrat. Tibidabo gets its name from the devil, who, trying to tempt Christ, took him to a high place and said, in the Latin version: *'Haec omnia tibi dabo si cadens adoraberis me.'* ('All this I will give you if you will fall down and worship me.')

Getting There & Away

First, get an FGC train to Avinguda de Tibidabo from Catalunya station on Plaça de Catalunya – a 10-minute ride for €1. Outside Avinguda de Tibidabo station, hop on the *tramvia blau*, Barcelona's last surviving tram, which runs up between fancy turn-of-the century mansions to Plaça del Doctor Andreu (€1.40/2.70 one way/ return) – it has been doing so since 1901. The tram runs daily in summer, and on Saturday, Sunday and holidays the rest of the year, every 15 or 30 minutes from 9am to 9.30pm April to September (10am to 6pm the rest of the year). On days and times when the tram does not operate a bus (€1) serves the route (7.45am to 9pm Monday to Friday, and 6pm to 10pm Saturday, Sunday and holidays).

From Plaça del Doctor Andreu, the Tibidabo funicular railway climbs through the woods to Plaça de Tibidabo at the top of the hill (€2/3, one way/return), every 15 to 30 minutes (7.15am to 9.45pm daily April to September; 10.45am to 7.15pm Saturday, Sunday and holidays the rest of the year). If you're feeling active, you can walk up or down through the woods instead. The funicular only operates when the Parc d'Atraccions is open.

The cheaper alternative is bus No T2, the 'Tibibús', from Plaça de Catalunya to Plaça de Tibidabo (€1.90). This runs on Saturday, Sunday and holidays year-round, every 30 minutes from 10.30am. From late June to early September it runs Monday to Friday too, every hour from 10.30am. The last bus down leaves Tibidabo 30 minutes after the Parc d'Atraccions closes. You can also buy a ticket that includes the bus and entry to the Parc d'Atraccions (€17).

Temple del Sagrat Cor

The church (*Church of the Sacred Heart; open 8am-7pm daily*), looming above the top funicular station, is meant to be Barcelona's answer to Paris' Sacré Coeur. It's certainly equally visible, and even more vilified by aesthetes (perhaps with good reason). It's actually two churches, one on top of the other. The top one is surmounted by a giant Christ and has a lift to take you to the roof (€1.50; 10am to 2pm and 3pm to 7pm).

Parc d'Atraccions

The reason most Barcelonins come up to Tibidabo (☎ *93 211 79 42; usually open noon-late daily summer, about noon-7pm Sat, Sun & holidays only winter*) is for some thrills (but hopefully no spills) in this funfair, close to the top funicular station. Admission costs €7 for six rides, or €17 with access to all rides – including seven minutes in Hotel Krueger, an *hospedaje* of horrors inhabited by actors playing out their Dracula, Hannibal Lecter and other fantasies. The funfair's opening times change with the season, so check with a tourist office before you go.

Torre de Collserola

The 288m-high Torre de Collserola telecommunications tower (☎ *93 406 93 54; adult/child €4.40/3.10; open 11am-6pm Wed-Sun*) was built in 1990–92. The external glass lift to the visitors' observation area, 115m up, is as hair-raising as anything at the Parc d'Atraccions. From the top they say you can see for 70km on a clear day. The ride up costs €4.

To get there, take the same transport as for Tibidabo to Plaça de Tibidabo, then walk about 600m west along the Camí de Vallvidrera al Tibidabo.

Museu de la Ciència (Map 1)

This museum (☎ *93 212 60 50; Carrer de Teodor Roviralta 55; admission €3; open 10am-8pm Tues-Sun*) is one of those interactive science museums where you get to twiddle knobs and press buttons and so discover how the world around you works. There is also a planetarium here. In the coming years, the museum space will grow and in it a small sample of tropical jungle will be planted. This could be a good place to bring young kids, but it's awkwardly placed near the Ronda de Dalt. Bus No 60 stops close by. Otherwise you can get an FGC train to Plaça de John F Kennedy and walk uphill.

PEDRALBES (MAP 1)

This is a wealthy residential area north of Zona Universitària.

Palau Reial de Pedralbes

Across Avinguda Diagonal from the main campus of the Universitat de Barcelona, is the entrance to the verdant **Parc del Palau Reial** *(open daily)*. In the park is the Palau Reial de Pedralbes, an early-20th-century building that belonged to the family of Eusebi Güell (Gaudí's patron) until they handed it over to the city in 1926 to serve as a royal residence – among its guests have been King Alfonso XIII, the president of Catalunya and General Franco.

Today the palace houses two museums *(☎ 93 280 16 21; admission €3.50 both museums; open 10am-6pm Tues-Sat, 10am-3pm Sun & holidays)*. The **Museu de Ceràmica** has a good collection of Spanish ceramics from the 13th to 19th centuries, including work by Picasso and Miró. Spain inherited from the Muslims, and then further refined, a strong tradition in ceramics – here you can compare some exquisite work (tiles, porcelain tableware and the like) from some of the greatest centres of pottery production across Spain, including Talavera de la Reina in Castilla, Manises and Paterna in Valencia, and Teruel in Aragón. Upstairs is a display of fanciful modern ceramics from the 20th century – here they have ceased to be a tool with aesthetic value and are purely decorative.

Across the corridor, the **Museu de les Arts Decoratives** brings together an eclectic assortment of furnishings, ornaments, and knick-knacks dating as far back as the Romanesque period (early Middle Ages). The plush and somewhat stuffy elegance of Empire and Isabelline-style divans can be neatly compared with some of the more tasteless ideas to emerge on the subject of seating in the 1970s. New space for temporary exhibitions has been opened up in the former stables, which are entered directly from the gardens.

Over by Avinguda de Pedralbes are the Gaudí-designed stables and porter's lodge for the **Finca Güell**, as the Güell estate here was called. They were done in the mid-1880s, when Gaudí was strongly impressed by Islamic architecture. They can't be visited, although there is nothing to stop you admiring Gaudí's wrought-iron dragon gate from the outside.

Museu-Monestir de Pedralbes

This peaceful old convent, which is now a museum of monastic life also housing part of the Thyssen-Bornemisza art collection *(☎ 93 203 92 82; admission €4.80, or €3.50 for the monastery alone or €3 for the Thyssen-Bornemisza collection alone; open 10am-2pm Tues-Sun)* stands at the top of Avinguda de Pedralbes, about a 10-minute walk from Finca Güell. You can take the suburban FGC train from Catalunya station to Reina Elisenda (the end of the line) and then either walk (about 10 minutes) or pick up one of the buses running along Passeig de la Reina Elisenda de Montcada (such as Nos 22, 64 & 75).

The convent, founded in 1326, still houses a community of nuns who inhabit separate closed quarters. The museum entrance is on Plaça del Monestir, a divinely quiet corner of Barcelona.

The architectural highlight is the large, elegant, three-storey cloister, a jewel of Catalan Gothic, built in the early 14th century. You will be gently persuaded to head around it to your right, and the first chapel you come across is the Capella de Sant Miquel, whose murals were done in 1346 by Ferrer Bassá, one of Catalunya's earliest documented painters.

As you head around the cloister, you can peer into a restored refectory, a kitchen, stables, stores and a reconstruction of the old infirmary – all giving a good idea of convent life. Perhaps the hardest thing to imagine is spending your days in the cells on the ground and 1st floors. Here the devout nuns would spend much of their days in prayer and devotional reading.

The **Col.lecció Thyssen-Bornemisza** (entry from the ground floor), quartered in the (painstakingly restored) one-time dormitories of the nuns and the Saló Principal, is part of a wide-ranging art collection acquired by Spain in 1993. Most of it went to the Museo Thyssen-Bornemisza in Madrid; what's here is mainly religious work by European masters including Canaletto, Titian, Tintoretto, Rubens, Zurbarán and Velázquez. Around 70 paintings and eight sculptures are on display. Together with the Madrid collection, they represent an extraordinarily eclectic approach to art procurement (if you get a chance to go to Madrid, the collection there, virtually across the road from El Prado, is a must). The sculptures and about a quarter of the paintings were produced by mostly anonymous medieval Italian artists. Next come around 20 pieces belonging to the early Renaissance period in Germany (including Cranach the Elder), accompanied by another group by northern Italian artists stretching into the 16th century. The collection is capped by about a dozen late-baroque works.

CAMP NOU (MAP 1)

Among Barcelona's most visited museums – hard on the heels of the Museu Picasso – comes the **Museu del Futbol Club Barcelona** (☎ 93 496 36 08; adult/child €3.80/2.80; open 10am-6.30pm Mon-Sat, 10am-2pm Sun & holidays, closed Mon Oct-Mar; metro Collblanc), at the club's giant Camp Nou (sometimes also known as Nou Camp) stadium. Barça is one of Europe's top football clubs and its museum is a hit with football fans the world over.

Camp Nou, built in 1957 and enlarged for the 1982 World Cup, is one of the world's biggest stadiums, holding 120,000 people, and the club has a world record membership of 110,000. Soccer fans who can't get to a game (see the Entertainment chapter for details) should find the museum (on the Carrer d'Aristides Maillol side of the stadium) worthwhile. The best bits are the photo section, the goal videos, and the views out over the stadium. Among the quirkier paraphernalia are old sports board games, a 19th-century leather football, the life-size diorama of old-time dressing rooms, posters and magazines from way back and the futbolín (table soccer) collection.

MONTJUÏC

Montjuïc, the hill overlooking the city centre from the southwest, is home to some fine art galleries and leisure attractions, soothing parks and the main group of 1992 Olympic sites.

The name Montjuïc (Jewish Mountain) indicates there was possibly once a Jewish settlement, or at least a Jewish cemetery, here. Before Montjuïc was turned into parks in the 1890s, its woodlands had provided food-growing and breathing space for the people of the cramped Ciutat Vella. Montjuïc also has a darker history: its fort was used by the Madrid government to bombard the city after political disturbances in 1842, and as a political prison up to the Franco era. The first main burst of building on Montjuïc came in the 1920s when it was chosen as the stage for Barcelona's 1929 World Exhibition. The Estadi Olímpic, the Poble Espanyol and some museums all date from this time. Montjuïc got a face-lift and more buildings for the 1992 Olympics.

Abundant roads and paths, with occasional escalators, plus buses and even a chair lift allow you to visit Montjuïc's sights in any order you choose. The six main attractions are the Poble Espanyol, CaixaForum, the Museu Nacional d'Art de Catalunya, the Estadi Olímpic, the Fundació Joan Miró and the views from the fort. Visiting them all would make for an extremely full day.

Getting There & Away

You *could* walk from Ciutat Vella (the foot of La Rambla is 700m from the eastern end of Montjuïc). Local bus No 50 make its way up here from the other side of town along Gran Via de les Corts Catalanes via Plaça de l'Universitat and Plaça d'Espanya. Bus No 61 runs six times a day, Monday to Friday, along Avinguda del Paral.lel to Montjuïc via Plaça d'Espanya. The Bus Turístic (see the Getting Around chapter) also makes several stops on Montjuïc.

In some respects, unfortunately, the most reliable way to get to where you want to go on Montjuïc is one of those silly little road trains. The Tren Turístic operates daily from

Big Plans

The Ajuntament (city hall) has big plans for Montjuïc. Apart from converting the old fun park into part of an expanded botanical gardens, work is being done all over the mountain to revitalise other gardens and paths that had long fallen into disrepair. Road traffic will be limited, a monorail may be installed in the highest parts of the mount and a single ticket to all its attractions introduced. A tourist bus would be laid on to transport visitors between all the sights.

late June to at least mid-September and during Easter. Otherwise it sometimes operates on weekends – ask at the tourist office. It leaves Plaça d'Espanya every half hour from 11am to 8.30pm and stops at all the museums and other points of interest. An all-day ticket costs €3/2.40 for adults/children (get on and off as often as you like). A single ride costs €1.80/1.45.

Another way of saving your legs is the funicular railway from the Paral.lel metro station to Estació Parc Montjuïc. This goes from 11am to 10pm daily from mid-June to mid-September, 10.45am to 8pm during the Christmas and Easter holiday periods, 10.45am to 8pm on Saturday, Sunday and holidays only during the rest of the year. Tickets cost €1.70/2.25 one way/return.

From Estació Parc Montjuïc, the Telefèric (cable car) de Montjuïc will carry you yet higher, to an upper entrance of the now closed Parc d'Atraccions (Mirador stop) and then the Castell (Castle) de Montjuïc (Castell stop). The chair lift operates from 11.15am to 9pm daily from mid-June to mid-September, 11am to 7.15pm from mid-September to early November and the Easter and Christmas periods, 11am to 7.15pm on Saturday, Sunday and holidays only during the rest of the year. Tickets cost €3.20/4.50 one way/return.

A further option is the *funicular aereo* the cable car that runs between Miramar and Torre de Sant Sebastià (La Barceloneta). See Port Vell earlier in this chapter.

Around Plaça d'Espanya (Map 4)

The approach to Montjuïc from Plaça d'Espanya gives you the full benefit of the landscaping on the hill's northern side and allows Montjuïc to unfold before you from the bottom up. On Plaça d'Espanya's northern side is the big **Plaça de Braus Les Arenes** bullring, built in 1900 but no longer used for bullfights. The Beatles played here in 1966. Behind the bullring is the **Parc Joan Miró**, created in the 1980s – worth a quick detour for Miró's giant, highly phallic sculpture *Dona i Ocell* (Woman and Bird) in the western corner. Actually, locals know the park (which apart from Miró is a fairly sad affair) as the Parc de l'Escorxador (abattoir park), as that's what once stood here – not surprising given the proximity to the bullring.

Just south of Estació Sants is the rather odd **Parc d'Espanya Industrial**. Looked at in the most favourable light possible, it is supposed to be an inventive public space, full of metallic towers and other ingenious things. It is actually a dispiriting cement structure and about the only useful thing about it is the sports centre.

Fountains (Map 7)

Avinguda de la Reina Maria Cristina, lined with modern exhibition and congress halls, leads from Plaça d'Espanya towards Montjuïc. On the hill ahead of you is the Palau Nacional de Montjuïc, and stretching up a series of terraces below it are Montjuïc's fountains, starting with the biggest, La Font Màgica. This comes alive with a music and light show on summer evenings – a unique performance in which the water at times looks like seething fireworks or a mystical cauldron of colour. Depending on the music chosen, it can be quite moving. And it's free! On the last evening of the Festes de la Mercè in September there's a particularly spectacular display that includes fireworks. The regular show lasts about 15 minutes and takes place every half hour from 9.30pm to 11.30pm, Thursday to Sunday, from June to September. During the rest of the year it happens only from 7pm to 9pm on Friday and Saturday.

Pavelló Mies van der Rohe (Map 7)

Just to the west of the Font Màgica is a strange building. In 1929 Ludwig Mies van der Rohe erected the Pavelló Alemany *(German Pavilion; ☎ 93 423 40 16; adult/child under 18 yrs €3/free; open 10am-8pm)* for the World Exhibition. Now known by the name of its architect, it was actually removed after the show. Decades later, a society was formed to rebuild what was in hindsight considered a gem. Reconstructed in the 1980s, it is a curious structure of interlocking planes – walls of marble or glass, ponds of water, ceilings and just plain nothing. This is Mies van der Rohe's temple to the new urban environment but, at the time, its importance as a key work in the trajectory of one of the world's most important modern architects was lost. Opinion is divided as to whether it should have been rebuilt, but most modern architecture buffs will love it.

CaixaForum (Map 7)

This art expo space *(☎ 902 22 30 40; Avinguda del Marquès de Comillas 6-8; admission free; open 10am-8pm Tues-Sun)* is the latest cultural addition to the Montjuïc area and hosts part of the Caixa bank's extensive collection of modern art from around the globe. It is housed in a completely renovated former factory, the Fàbrica Casaramona, itself an outstanding Modernista structure designed by Puig i Cadafalch. From 1940 to 1993 it housed the First Squadron of the police cavalry unit – 120 horses in all. Now it houses selected items of the 800-strong collection, rotated on view every month or two, while some space is set aside for external temporary exhibitions. The permanent collection contains, among others, works by Antoni Tàpies, Miquel Barceló and a stone circle by Richard Long. In the courtyard where the police horses used to drink is a steel tree designed by the Japanese architect Arata Isozaki.

Museu Nacional d'Art de Catalunya (Map 7)

The Palau Nacional, built in the 1920s for the World Exhibition, houses the Museu Nacional d'Art de Catalunya *(☎ 93 622 03 60; admission €4.80, free 1st Thur of month; open 10am-7pm Tues, Wed, Fri & Sat, to 9pm Thur, 10am-2.30pm Sun & holidays)*. The building itself is quite overwhelming and, although designed by Catalan architects, is interpreted by some as an expression of central Castilian dominance over all Spain, including Catalunya (the World Exhibition was held in 1929, under the dictatorship of Miguel Primo de Rivera).

The museum's two main permanent expositions cover Romanesque and Gothic art. The former is by far the most interesting, and one of the most important concentrations of early medieval art in the world. It consists of frescoes, woodcarvings and painted altar frontals (low-relief wooden panels that were the forerunners of the elaborate altarpieces adorning later churches) transferred from country churches across northern Catalunya early in the 20th century. The insides of several churches have been re-created and the frescoes – in some cases fragmentary, in others extraordinarily complete and alive with colour – have been placed as they were when *in situ*. The Gothic collection includes some art from outside Catalunya and is less extensive. Most of the explanations are in Catalan only, but you can pick up a catalogue-style booklet that at least gives you an idea of what you are looking at.

The first thing you see as you enter the Romanesque section is a remake of the apse of the church of Sant Pere de la Seu d'Urgell, dominated by a beautiful fresco from the early 12th century. In this first hall (Àmbit I) there are coins from the early days of the Comtes de Barcelona, capitals from columns used in Muslim monuments and some finely decorated altar frontals.

In Àmbit III, the frescoes from the church of Sant Pere d'Àger are particularly striking (item No 31). The depiction of Christ on wood from the church of Sant Martí de Tost (No 47 in Àmbit IV) is in a near-perfect state of preservation – the vividness of the colours can only make you wonder what some of the more faded, grander frescos must once have looked like.

Another good piece is No 49, an altar frontal depicting Christ and the Apostles.

One of the star attractions is the fresco of Mary and the Christ Child from the apse of the church of Santa Maria de Taüll (No 102 in Àmbit VII). In Àmbit X, have a look at No 116, an altar frontal in which the martyrdom of several saints figures among the main themes – here you can see the medieval mind at work, depicting holy individuals who apparently contemplate their own slow deaths with supreme indifference – whether boiling in water, having nails slammed into the head, being sliced up by sword or, a personal favourite, being sawn in half from head to toe!

Moving right along, the Gothic art section reveals clearly the development of painting – from two-dimensional and disembodied didactic painting to a more impassioned, human depiction of religious figures and events. In these halls you can see Catalan Gothic painting (look out especially for the work of Bernat Martorell in Àmbit XI and Jaume Huguet in Àmbit XII), and that of other Spanish and Mediterranean regions. If the saintly suffering theme appeals to you, look out for the depiction of the martyrdom of Santa Llúcia and Sant Vicenç in Àmbit III.

Following the Gothic collection is a substantially smaller group of minor European works spanning the 16th and 18th centuries. It is planned to move the contents of the Museu Nacional d'Art Modern de Catalunya (see earlier in this chapter) here by the end of 2004.

Poble Espanyol (Map 7)

This 'Spanish Village' (☎ 93 508 63 00; Avinguda del Marquès de Comillas; adult/student & senior/child under 12 yrs €7/4.40/3.60; open 9am-8pm Mon, 9am-2am Tues-Thur, 9am-4am Fri & Sat, 9am-midnight Sun), in the northwest of Montjuïc is about a 10-minutes' walk from Plaça d'Espanya. It's both a cheesy souvenir-hunters' haunt and an intriguing scrapbook of Spanish architecture. Built for the Spanish crafts section of the 1929 exhibition, it's composed of plazas and streets lined with surprisingly

good copies of characteristic buildings from all the country's regions.

You enter from beneath a towered medieval gate from Ávila. Inside, to the right, is an information office with free maps. Straight ahead from the gate is a Plaza Mayor, or town square, surrounded with mainly Castilian and Aragonese buildings. Elsewhere you'll find an Andalucían barrio, a Basque street, Galician and Catalan quarters and even – at the eastern end – a Dominican monastery. The buildings house dozens of moderately priced to expensive restaurants, cafés, bars, craft shops and workshops, and a few souvenir stores.

At night, the restaurants, bars and discos become a lively corner of Barcelona's nightlife. If you want more information or a guided tour, call the village.

Museu Etnològic & Museu - d'Arqueologia (Map 7)

Down the hill east of the Museu Nacional d'Art, these museums are worth a visit if their subjects interest you, although neither is very excitingly presented and most of the explanatory material is in Catalan.

The **Museu Etnològic** (Ethnological Museum; ☎ 93 424 68 07; Passeig de Santa Madrona; admission €3; open 10am-2pm Wed & Fri-Sun, to 7pm Tues & Thur) organises extensive temporary exhibitions on a range of cultures from other continents.

The **Museu d'Arqueologia** (Archaeological Museum; ☎ 93 423 56 01; Passeig de Santa Madrona 39-41; admission €2.40; open 9.30am-7pm Tues-Sat, 10am-2.30pm Sun) covers Catalunya and related cultures elsewhere in Spain. Items range from copies of pre-Neanderthal skulls to lovely Carthaginian necklaces and jewel-studded Visigothic crosses. There's good material on the Balearic Islands (rooms X to XIII) and Empúries (Emporion), the Greek and Roman city on the Costa Brava (rooms XIV and parts of XVII). The Roman finds upstairs were mostly dug up in Barcelona.

Anella Olímpica (Map 7)

The 'Olympic Ring' is the group of sports installations where the main events of the

1992 Olympics were held, on the ridge just above the Museu Nacional d'Art de Catalunya. Westernmost is the **Institut Nacional d'Educació Física de Catalunya** (INEFC), a kind of sports university, designed by Ricard Bofill. Past a circular arena, the Plaça d'Europa, with the **Torre Calatrava** communications tower (apparently inoperative) behind it, is the **Piscines Bernat Picornell** building, where the swimming events were held (now open to the general public – see Swimming & Gym under Activities later in this chapter). Next comes a pleasant little park, the Jardí d'Aclimatació.

Estadi Olímpic (Map 7)

You enter the main stadium of the Olympic Games *(admission free; open 10am-6pm daily, to 8pm May-Sept)* from the northern end. If you saw some of the Olympics on TV, the 65,000-capacity stadium may seem surprisingly small.

So may the Olympic flame-holder rising at the northern end, into which a long-range archer spectacularly deposited a flaming arrow in the opening ceremony. (Well, nearly. The archer actually missed, but the clever organisers had foreseen this possibility. The flame-holder was alive with gas, so the arrow only had to pass within 2m of it to set the thing on fire. A gleeful Barcelona TV crew was waiting on the other side for just such a 'failure'.)

The stadium was opened in 1929 but completely restored for 1992. At its southern end (enter from outside) is the **Galería Olímpica** *(☎ 906 30 17 75; admission €1.75; open only to groups by prior arrangement)*, which has an exhibition, including videos, on the 1992 games. You will need to be quite a fan of all things Olympian to get anything out of this. Favourite items are the models of the standard daily diet of cyclists and gymnasts – there's something intriguing about looking at a plate of plastic pasta. Or you can behold the splendours of an athlete's bed made up with duvet and pillow cases sporting Barcelona's Olympic mascot, Cobi. Speaking of which, a whole display is dedicated to Cobi.

West of the stadium is the **Palau Sant Jordi**, a 17,000-capacity indoor sports, concert and exhibition hall opened in 1990 and designed by Isozaki.

Jardí Botànic (Map 7)

South across the road from the Estadi, this botanical garden *(☎ 93 426 49 35; Carrer del Doctor Font i Quer; admission €3; open 10am-5pm Apr-June & Sept-Oct, 10am-3pm Nov-Mar & July-Aug)* was created atop what was an old municipal dump. The theme is 'Mediterranean' fauna and the collection includes some 2000 species thriving in areas with a climate similar to that of the Med, including the Eastern Mediterranean, Spain (including the Balearic and Canary Islands), North Africa, Australia, California, Chile and South Africa.

Cementiri del Sud-Oest (Map 7)

On the hill south of the Anella Olímpica you can see the top of a huge cemetery, the Cementiri del Sud-Oest or Cementiri Nou, which extends down the southern side of the hill. Opened in 1883, it's an odd combination of elaborate architect-designed tombs for rich families and small niches for the rest. It includes the graves of numerous Catalan artists and politicians.

Fundació Joan Miró (Map 7)

Barcelona's gallery for one of the greatest Catalan artists of the 20th century, Joan Miró *(☎ 93 443 94 70; admission €7.20; open 10am-7pm Tues-Sat, to 8pm summer, 10am-9.30pm Thur, 10am-2.30pm Sun & holidays)* is 400m downhill east of the Estadi Olímpic. Miró established the foundation in 1971. Its light-filled buildings were designed by his close friend and architect Josep Lluís Sert, who also built Miró's Mallorca studios.

This, the greatest single collection of the artist's work, comprises around 300 of his paintings, 153 sculptures, some textiles and more than 7000 drawings spanning his entire life, of which only a part is ever on display. The exhibits tend to concentrate on Miró's more settled last 20 years, but there are some important exceptions. The ground floor Sala (room) Joan Prats shows the younger Miró moving away, under surrealist influence, from his *relative* realism (for instance his 1917 painting of the *Ermita de Sant Joan d'Horta*), then starting to work towards his own recognisable style. This section includes the 1939–44 Barcelona series of tortured lithographs – which was Miró's comment on the Spanish Civil War.

The Sala Pilar Juncosa (named after his wife), upstairs, also displays works from the 1930s and '40s. After this room, the bulk of what you see is from his latter years – mostly paintings, but some sculpture (especially some playful items on the outdoor terrace). While some of the paintings are classics of the style for which he is best known, with an almost childlike delight in primary colours, in the 1970s he opted for an exploration of more muted greens, browns and black.

Another interesting section is devoted to the 'Miró Papers', which include many preparatory drawings and sketches, some on bits of newspaper or cigarette packets. *A Joan Miró* is a collection of work by other contemporary artists, donated in tribute to Miró. The Fundació has a contemporary-art library open to the public, a good specialist art bookshop and a café. It also stages exhibitions and recitals of contemporary art and music.

Castell de Montjuïc & Around (Map 7)

The southeast of Montjuïc is dominated by the Castell ('castle' or 'fort'). Near the bottom of the ruined remains of what was the Parc d'Atraccions (amusement park) are the Estació Parc Montjuïc funicular/telefèric station and the ornamental **Jardins de Mossèn Cinto Verdaguer**. The one-time amusement park is destined to become part of a larger botanical garden.

From the **Jardins del Mirador** opposite the Mirador telefèric station there are fine views over the port of Barcelona.

The Castell de Montjuïc dates, in its present form, from the late 17th and 18th centuries. For most of its existence it has been used to watch over the city and as a political prison and killing ground. Anarchists were

executed here around the turn of the century, fascists during the civil war and Republicans after it – most notoriously Lluís Companys in 1940. The army finally handed it over to the city in 1960. The castle is surrounded by a network of ditches and walls, and today houses the **Museu Militar** (☎ 93 329 86 13; *admission €2.40; open 9.30am-5pm Tues-Fri, 9.30am-8pm Sat-Sun*). You enter an artillery-lined courtyard, off which rooms are filled with a ragbag of weapons old and new, as well as uniforms, yellowing maps and so on. Stairs lead down to another series of halls lined with more of the same, along with castle models, a couple of portraits of General Franco and even an equestrian statue of him. In 2002 a handful of flags and other memorabilia from the Republican side in the civil war were added to the collection – a highly symbolic move.

In Room 18 are some tombstones, some dating to the 11th century, from the one-time Jewish cemetery on Montjuïc. Best of all are the excellent views from the castle area of the port and city below. You can eat amid the artillery at the museum café.

Towards the foot of this part of Montjuïc, above the thundering traffic of the main road to Tarragona, the **Jardins de Mossèn Costa i Llobera** (*admission free; open 10am-sunset*) have a good collection of both tropical and desert plants – including a veritable forest of cacti.

THE OUTSKIRTS
Jardins del Laberint d'Horta

Laid out in the twilight years of the 18th century by Antoni Desvalls, Marquès d'Alfarras i de Llupià, this carefully manicured park (☎ 93 424 38 09; *Carrer dels Germans Desvalls; admission €2, free Wed & Sun; open 10am-sunset daily*) remained a private family idyll until the 1970s, when it was opened to the public. Many a fine party and theatrical performance was held here over the years, but now it serves as a kind of museum-park. The gardens take their name from a maze in their centre, but other paths take you past a pleasant artificial lake *(estany)*, waterfalls, a neoclassical pavilion and a false cemetery. The latter is inspired by 19th-century romanticism, often characterised by an obsession with a swooning, anaemic vision of death.

To get to the gardens you can take the metro to Montbau (Line 3); from there you still have about a 15-minute walk east along the Ronda de Dalt freeway to the gardens.

Colònia Güell

Apart from La Sagrada Família, the last grand project Gaudí would turn his hand to was the creation of a kind of Utopian workers' complex outside Barcelona at Santa Coloma de Cervelló. His main role was to erect the colony's church – workers' housing and the local cooperative were in the hands of other architects. He first thought about it in 1898, but work on the church's crypt started in 1908. It proceeded for eight years, at which point interest in the whole idea fizzled. The crypt today still serves as a working church (☎ 93 640 29 36). At the time of writing you could only get a look in 10am to 1.30pm Sunday and holidays.

This structure is an important part of Gaudí's oeuvre, little visited by tourists and yet a key to understanding what the master had in mind for his magnum opus, La Sagrada Família. The mostly brick-clad columns that support the ribbed vaults in the ceiling are inclined in much the way you might expect trees in a forest to lean at all angles (reminiscent also of Parc Güell, which Gaudí was working on at much the same time). Gaudí had worked out the angles in such a way that their load would be transmitted from the ceiling to the earth without the help of extra buttressing. Similar thinking lay behind his plans for La Sagrada Família, whose Gothic-inspired structure would tower above anything ever done in the Middle Ages but not require so much as one buttress to hold it all up.

Down to the wavy design of the pews, Gaudí's hand is visible (you can see an example of the seating in the Museu Nacional d'Art Modern de Catalunya in the Parc de la Ciutadella too). The primary colours in the curvaceous plant-shaped stained-glass windows are another reminder of the era in which the crypt was built.

The easiest way to get there is to take an FGC train (the S3, €1) from Plaça d'Espanya and get off at Molí Nou station, the last stop (train No S33 leaves roughly hourly, usually at a quarter past the hour, for Santa Coloma station, one further on). When you reach the Molí Nou station, exit by the underpass and turn right (north) up the BV-2002 road towards Santa Coloma de Cervelló. It's a 15-minute walk (the first five minutes on this traffic-choked road will be equivalent to your year's air pollution intake). You will then walk alongside the walls of a light industrial complex called Recinto Colonia Güell, at the corner of which you turn left – follow this road as it veers to the right and you enter the small settlement – some of the houses and shops are unmistakable leftovers of the Modernistas' planned workers' village. Keep straight uphill to reach the crypt.

Alternatively, you could get off the train one stop earlier at Sant Boi de Llobregat and catch the L76 bus right to Santa Coloma, but this will end up taking longer.

Sant Cugat del Vallès

When the marauding Muslims tramped through the one-time Roman encampment turned Visigothic monastery of Sant Cugat del Vallès in the 8th century, they razed the lot to the ground. These things happen, so after the Christians got back in the saddle, work on a new monastic complex (☎ 93 590 29 74; Plaça Octavià; adult/child €2.40/1.20; open 10am-1.30pm & 3pm-6.30pm Tues-Sun June-Sept, 10am-1.30pm & 3pm-5.30pm Tues-Sun Oct-May) was stoically begun. What you see today is a combination of Romanesque and Gothic buildings. The lower floor of the cloister is a fine demonstration of Romanesque and the principal reason for making the effort to come here (Sant Cugat may have been a favourite summer getaway for Barcelonins at the turn of the 19th century, but those days are now long gone). The Gothic church and upper storey of the cloister also repay some quiet contemplation.

To get here, take the FGC train from Catalunya station (lines S1, S2, S5 or S55)

Architectural surprises (clockwise from top left): a wedge-shaped building in Barri Gòtic; Gaudí's whimsical chimney pots at Palau Güell; Casa Milà, better known as La Pedrera (The Quarry), another of Antoni Gaudí's masterpieces

The Casa de les Punxes (House of Spikes), L'Eixample (top left); Fundació Antoni Tàpies, a Modernista building by Domènech i Montaner (top right); another Gothic treasure in Barcelona's stylish streets (bottom right); rows of red candles in a 13th-century cathedral in Barri Gòtic (bottom left)

MARTIN HUGHES

DAMIEN SIMONIS

JONATHAN CHESTER

PAUL KENNEDY

to Sant Cugat del Vallès (€1.50, 25 minutes). If you go on the second or fourth Sunday of the month, you may catch a *clàssic tren*, a vintage electric job from the 1920s that will take you up to the sounds of live jazz or classical music. Tickets are the same price as for normal trains. For more information call **FGC** (☎ 93 205 15 15).

From the Sant Cugat train station you could wait for a local circle-line bus, but the walk is hardly taxing. Head left out of the station along Avinguda d'Alfonso Sala Conde de Egara and turn right down Carrer de Ruis i Taulet, followed by a left into Carrer de Santiago Rusiñol, which leads to the monastery.

ACTIVITIES
For information on where you can practise sports in Barcelona, try the **Servei d'Informació Esportiva** (Map 7; ☎ 93 402 30 00; Avinguda de l'Estadi 30-40, Montjuïc; open 8am-2pm & 4pm-6pm Mon-Thur), located in the same complex as the Piscines Bernat Picornell on Montjuïc.

Skiing
In the ski season, several bus companies put on services departing from Ronda de l'Universitat 5 and Estació d'Autobusos de Sants to various ski resorts in the Catalan Pyrenees and Andorra. You can get day and weekend return tickets including lift pass and the price can range from around €30 for a day to €104 for a weekend with hotel room included.

Swimming & Gym
Admission to the Olympic pool, the **Piscines Bernat Picornell** (Map 7; ☎ 93 423 40 41; Avinguda de l'Estadi 30-40, Montjuïc; open 7am-midnight Mon-Fri, to 9pm Sat, 7.30am-4pm Sun) costs €7.96, including use of the good gym inside. Access to the outdoor pool (open 10am-6pm Mon-Sat, to 2.30pm Sun Oct-May, 9am-9pm Mon-Sat, to 8pm Sun June-Sept) alone costs €4.20 in summer *only*. If you are about for any length of time and want regular access to the pool, gym and other facilities, think about taking out membership. You need to have a local bank

account, as the monthly charge is made by direct debit *(domiciliació bancària)*. You pay €23.44 to join and the same each month.

The nearby open-air **Piscina Municipal de Montjuïc** (open 10am-6pm Sat & Sun July-Aug), used for diving and water polo during the 1992 Olympic Games, has a rather forlorn air about it. It costs €3.60.

Another pool option for lap swimmers are the **Banys Sant Sebastiá** (Map 1; ☎ 93 221 00 10; main – indoor – pool open 7am-10.30pm Mon-Sat, 8am-5pm Sun), down by La Barceloneta beach. Admission costs €6.75, which includes use of the gym. You can also become a member under conditions similar to those outlined for Piscines Bernat Picorell. Several other private and municipal pools are scattered about the city.

Tennis
About the most pleasant and relatively convenient tennis option is the **Tennis Municipal Pompeia** (Map 7; ☎ 93 423 97 47; Avinguda del Marquès de Comillas 29-41, Montjuïc). Court hire costs €9.72 an hour.

COURSES
The youth information service, **CIAJ** (Centre d'Informació i Assessorament per a Joves; Map 6; ☎ 93 402 78 00; Carrer de Ferran 32, Barri Gòtic; open 10am-2pm & 4pm-8pm Mon-Fri), has information on the various courses available throughout the city.

Language Courses
Some of the best-value Spanish-language courses are offered by the **Universitat de Barcelona**, which runs intensive courses (40-hours tuition over periods ranging from two weeks to a month; €301) year-round. Longer Spanish courses, and courses in Catalan, are also available.

For more information ask at the university's **Informació** office (Map 4; Gran Via de les Corts Catalanes 585; open 9am-2pm Mon-Fri). Otherwise try (for Spanish) its **Instituto de Estudios Hispánicos** (☎ 93 403 55 19, fax 93 403 54 33), or (for Catalan) its **Servei de Llengua Catalana** (☎ 93 403 54 77, fax 93 403 54 84) – both in the same building as the information office.

THINGS TO SEE & DO

The **Escola Oficial d'Idiomes de Barcelona** *(Map 6; ☎ 93 324 93 30, fax 93 934 93 51; Avinguda de les Drassanes; metro Drassanes)* offers economical 80-hour summer Spanish courses, as well as longer part-time courses in Spanish and Catalan. Because of the demand for Spanish, there is no guarantee of a place. Generally there is no problem with Catalan.

Across Catalunya, more than 220 schools teach Catalan. Pick up a list at the **Llibreria & Informaciò Cultural de la Generalitat de Catalunya** *(Map 6; ☎ 93 302 64 62; Rambla dels Estudis 118)*.

International House *(Map 6; ☎ 93 268 45 11, fax 93 268 02 39; Carrer de Trafalgar 14)* has intensive courses from around €320 per week. It can also organise accommodation.

Advertisements for language courses and private tuition are posted at the university, the **Come In bookshop** *(Map 2; Carrer de Provença 203)* and the **British Council** *(Map 3; Carrer d'Amigó 83)*.

Other Courses

Check out course lists at CIAJ. These examples and many other courses are really aimed at people hanging around for a while. In most cases reasonable Spanish, if not Catalan, will be required.

La Cafetera de l'Esbart Català de Dansaires (Map 6; ☎ 93 303 10 01) Passatge del Crèdit 8. This group organises courses in Catalan dance for anyone from beginners to advanced, and is of special interest to professionals. Usually the sessions are held on Monday.

Centre Cívic Drassanes (Map 6; ☎ 93 441 22 80) Carrer Nou de la Rambla 43. This civic centre puts on all sorts of courses and workshops ranging from didgeridoo to Windows 98.

Barcelona Centre d'Imatge (☎ 93 311 92 73) Carrer de Pons i Gallarza 25, Sant Andreu; metro Sant Andreu. It offers various levels offered in photography.

Àrea Espai de Dansa i Creació (Map 1; ☎ 93 210 78 50) Carrer d'Alegre de Dalt 55 bis, Gràcia. This is one of the best spots in town to learn contemporary dance – some English is spoken.

Places to Stay

Barcelona attracts more tourists with every passing year, so it's getting squeezy. The peak (high season) periods are Setmana Santa (Easter week), summer (especially July and August), during the Festes de la Mercè (second half of September), Christmas and New Year. Finding a room around these times can be a real pain. Local tourism authorities happily claim an average year-round room-occupation rate of 80%. With a little searching you'll usually find something, but you will need patience. Arrive in the morning for the best results – checkout time is generally midday.

Seasons, Reservations & Prices

Prices can vary with the season. Some places have separate price structures for the high season *(temporada alta)*, mid-season *(temporada media)* and the low season *(temporada baja)*, all usually displayed on a notice in reception or close by. (Hoteliers are not bound by these displayed prices. They are free to charge less, which they quite often do, or more, which happens fairly rarely.)

The bad news is that popularity pushes up prices. New hotels (largely the four-star 'blah' variety) continue to go up and, although the events of September 11 put a brake on things for six months, Barcelona remains a favoured destination. This means that, while the prices in this guide were correct at the time of research, there is every chance they may have risen by the time you read this. Always check prices before committing yourself. Many smaller places will insist you pay in advance each day.

You can find out about accommodation by calling the tourist office at Plaça de Catalunya on ☎ 93 304 32 32 or at W www .barcelona-on-line.es.

Taxes

Virtually all accommodation prices are subject to IVA, the Spanish version of value-added tax, which is 7%. This is often included in the quoted price at cheaper places, but less often at more expensive ones. To check, ask: *'¿Está incluido el IVA?'* ('Is IVA included?'). In some cases you will only be charged IVA if you ask for a receipt.

PLACES TO STAY – BUDGET
Camping

A series of vast but well-equipped camping grounds lie virtually side by side to the southwest of Barcelona on the coastal C-31 road, the Autovía de Castelldefels. All are reachable by bus No L95 from the corner of Ronda de la Universitat and Rambla de Catalunya. All are inconvenient if you want late nights in Barcelona, because the only way back late at night is by taxi. They include (with prices for a car, a tent and two adults) the following.

El Toro Bravo *(☎ 93 637 34 62; Carretera C-31, Km 11, Viladecans; sites €19.80; open year-round)* is a tad shabby but is a handy option and offers a fair amount of shade, a pool and a supermarket.

Filipinas *(☎ 93 658 28 95; Carretera C-31, Km 12, Viladecans; sites €20.88; open year-round)* has similar facilities but is a slightly more pleasant stop.

La Ballena Alegre *(☎/fax 93 658 05 04; Carretera C-31, Km 12.4, Viladecans; sites €19.26; open Mar-Nov)*, just a little further on, is vast and offers all sorts of amenities.

Camping Masnou *(☎ 93 555 15 03; Camí Fabra 33, El Masnou; sites €19.30; open year-round)* is 11km northeast of the city, and 200m from El Masnou train station (which is reached by suburban *rodalies/cercanías* trains from Catalunya station on Plaça de Catalunya).

Youth & Backpacker Hostels

Barcelona has several Hostelling International (HI) hostels and non-HI hostels, of which a selection appears below. All require you to rent sheets (around €2) if you don't have any and some lock their gates in the early hours so aren't suitable if you plan to party on late. Except at the Kabul, which doesn't take bookings, it's advisable to call ahead in summer. Most have washing machines. Prices provided here are for a dorm bed.

Youth Hostel Kabul (Map 6; ☎ 93 318 51 90, fax 93 301 40 34; Plaça Reial 17; €18, plus €10 key deposit), a non-HI hostel, gets mixed reports. It's a rough-and-ready place but does have, as its leaflets say, a 'great party atmosphere' and there's no curfew. Safes are available for your valuables. There's room for 130 people in 10-person bare bunk rooms.

Alberg Mare de Déu de Montserrat (Map 1; ☎ 93 210 51 51, fax 93 210 07 98; Passeig de la Mare de Déu del Coll 41-51; under 26 yrs or ISIC card-holders/others up to €18.03/22.24 depending on the season) is the biggest and most comfortable hostel. Rates include breakfast. This 223-place hostel is 4km north of the centre, a 10-minute walk from Vallcarca metro or a 20-minute ride from Plaça de Catalunya on bus Nos 25, 28 and N4 (night bus), which stop almost outside the gate. The main building is a former private mansion with a *Mudéjar*-style lobby. Most rooms sleep six. A hostel card is needed. The hostel is in HI's International Booking Network (IBN), which enables you to book through about 200 other HI hostels and booking centres around the world. You can also book through the central booking service of Catalunya's official youth hostels organisation, the **Xarxa d'Albergs de Catalunya** (☎ 93 483 83 63, fax 93 483 83 50).

Alberg Center Rambles (Map 6; ☎ 93 412 40 69, fax 93 317 17 04; Carrer de l'Hospital 63; under 26 yrs or ISIC card-holders/others up to €15.03/19.23 including breakfast) is a brand-new HI hostel right in the thick of things. Beds are in single-sex dorms of four to 10 people. The place is open 24 hours and is secure. Safes are available.

Ideal Youth Hostel (Map 6; ☎ 93 342 61 77, fax 93 411 38 48; Carrer de l'Unió 12; €15) is an odd arrival on the hostel circuit, located just off La Rambla. Described by one reader as 'funky', it is OK, although

staff are not always helpful. All rooms have shower and loo.

Alberg Hostel Itaca (Map 6; ☎ 93 301 97 51; w www.itacahostel.com; Carrer de Ripoll 21; €15) is a bright new hostel option with room for 35 people in spacious dorms (for six, eight and 12 people). Breakfast costs €2 and you can make use of the upstairs kitchen. It has a double room with private bathroom for €36.

Alberg Juvenil Palau (Map 6; ☎ 93 412 50 80; Carrer del Palau 6; €13) in Barri Gòtic has a friendly atmosphere and just 40 places in single-sex bunk rooms. The rates also include breakfast.

Alberg Pere Tarrès (Map 3; ☎ 93 410 23 09, fax 93 419 62 68; Carrer de Numància 149; B&B under 25 yrs or ISIC card-holders/others €15.93/20.43), 1km north of Estació Sants, has 92 places in dorms of four to eight bunks. The gates are shut from 11am to 3pm and 11pm to 8.30am (they're opened briefly to let guests in at 2am, though).

Hostales, Pensiones & Hotels

Barcelona is a favourite with travellers so rooms in any price range are at a premium. Try to get into town early and start calling around or walking – the good thing about many budget places is that they don't take bookings, so it's first in best dressed. You are unlikely to find anything for much less than about €20/35 (singles/doubles). At such prices you are generally looking at rooms without bathroom (sometimes you get a shower and sometimes just a basin). In such cases, the bathroom is in the corridor. For a room with a bathroom you are looking at anything from €26/45 to €40/75. A lot depends on the size and condition of the room, and whether or not your room has a balcony or some sort of view.

La Rambla Several options line La Rambla. Many are rather basic affairs and it's a noisy location.

Pensión Noya (Map 6; ☎ 93 301 48 31; Rambla de Canaletes 133; singles/doubles €20/40), at the top of La Rambla, above Restaurante Nuria, has 15 smallish but clean rooms (the shower and loo rooms are in the corridor). The front rooms overlooking La Rambla can be noisy.

Hotel Cuatro Naciones *(Map 6; ☎ 93 317 36 24, fax 93 302 69 85;* Ⓦ *www.h4n.com; La Rambla 40; singles/doubles €48.15/74.90 including breakfast)* has adequate rooms. It was built in 1849 and was once – a long time ago – Barcelona's top hotel. Buffalo Bill preferred it to a wagon when he was in town, back in 1889.

Barri Gòtic This central, atmospheric area has many of the better budget places. A few of those listed below are not, strictly speaking, in the Barri Gòtic but within a couple of minutes' walk of it.

Hostal Campi *(Map 6; ☎ 93 301 35 45, fax 93 301 41 33;* ⓔ *Hcampi@terra.es; Carrer de la Canuda 4; singles/doubles without bathroom €19/37, doubles with shower & toilet €44)* is an excellent deal. The best rooms at this friendly place, if you can afford them, are the doubles. They are extremely roomy and bright.

Hostal Lausanne *(Map 6; ☎ 93 302 11 39; Avinguda del Portal de l'Àngel 24; singles/ doubles without bathroom €25/50; doubles with bathroom €60)* is a friendly, helpful place with good security. The doubles without bathroom are clean. Getting a single seems impossible.

Hostal Fontanella *(Map 6; ☎/fax 93 317 59 43; Via Laietana 71; singles/doubles without bathroom €26/41, with bathroom €32/ 65)* is a friendly, immaculate place, with 10 (in some cases smallish) rooms.

Hostal Galerias Maldà *(Map 6; ☎ 93 317 30 02; Carrer del Pi 5; singles/doubles €12/ 24)*, upstairs in the arcade, is a rambling family house with 21 rooms, some of them really big. It's one of the cheapest places in town, and has one great single set in a kind of tower. It doesn't take bookings.

Hostal-Residencia Rembrandt *(Map 6; ☎/fax 93 318 10 11; Carrer de la Portaferrissa 23; singles/doubles without bathroom €25/ 42, doubles with bathroom from €48)* is a popular choice with good clean rooms.

Pensión Bienestar *(Map 6; ☎ 93 318 72 83; Carrer d'En Quintana 3; singles/doubles without bathroom €22/33)* is a quiet cheapy in a back-street. The rooms are nothing special but they are perfectly acceptable for the money. The beds, though, are a little past their prime.

Pensión Fernando *(Map 6; ☎ 93 301 79 93; Carrer de Ferran; postal address Carrer de l'Arc del Remedio 4; singles/doubles without bathroom €21/40, doubles with bathroom €54)* has single beds in dorms (which start at four beds). Otherwise, there are doubles and triples as well. You can catch some rays on the roof.

Hotel Call *(Map 6; ☎ 93 302 11 23, fax 93 301 34 86; Carrer de l'Arc de Sant Ramon del Call 4; singles/doubles €37/50)* is an OK deal, smack in the heart of the old Jewish quarter. The rooms here are comfortable and some were refurbished in 2002. All have bathroom and phone. Some, however, are terribly small.

Hotel Rey Don Jaime I *(Map 6; ☎/fax 93 310 62 08; Carrer de Jaume I 11; singles/ doubles with shower & toilet €31/58)* is not a bad deal in the upper budget range if you can get a quiet room – the street noise can be a bit much in the front.

Pension Villanueva *(Map 6; ☎ 93 301 50 84; Plaça Reial 2; doubles €25-50)* is the place to head if you want a nice double on the square. The lowest prices are for basic rooms, and the most expensive rate is for the best rooms – spacious doubles with own bathroom and looking onto the square. There are no singles.

Hotel Roma Reial *(Map 6; ☎ 93 302 03 66, fax 93 301 18 39; Plaça Reial 11; singles /doubles in high season €50/65)* has decent rooms, all with bathroom.

Hotel Comercio *(Map 6; ☎ 93 318 74 20, fax 93 318 73 74; Carrer dels Escudellers 15; singles/doubles €45/75)* is not a bad little upper-budget-range hotel run by the same people who own Hotel Roma Reial. The rooms have all the usual amenities and you can't get much closer to the action in the depths of Barri Gòtic.

Hotel Barcelona House *(Map 6; ☎ 93 301 82 95, fax 93 412 41 29; Carrer dels Escudellers 19; singles €27-38.80, doubles €55-76)* has quite a range of rooms that, although a mite pricey in some cases, are quite good.

A couple of the more expensive older-style doubles are nice.

Hostal Levante *(Map 6; ☎ 93 317 95 65; Baixada de Sant Miquel 2; singles/doubles without bathroom €27/46, doubles with bathroom €52)*, off Plaça de Sant Miquel, is a large, bright hostal with rooms of all shapes and sizes. The cheaper rates are for smallish singles. Try for a double with a balcony. The owners have some apartments nearby, too, which can work out well for groups of four or more – just ask at the reception.

Casa Huéspedes Mari-Luz *(Map 6; ☎ 93 317 34 63; Carrer del Palau 4; 4-share room €16 per person, doubles €40)* is another fine budget option. The bright, sunny rooms with wooden beams in the ceiling are well kept and the management chirpy. The place has a genuinely social atmosphere. You have the option of sleeping in a room for four or more people, or taking a double room.

Hostal El Cantón *(Map 6; ☎ 93 317 30 19; Carrer Nou de Sant Francesc 40; singles/doubles without bathroom €18/31, with bathroom €20/43)*, moving a little further towards the waterfront, is another good budget bet. Some of its rooms are spacious with sparkling new bathrooms, fan, fridge and balcony.

Hostal Nilo *(Map 6; ☎ 93 317 90 44; e march@retemail.es; Carrer de Josep Anselm Clavé 7; singles/doubles without bathroom €18/30, doubles with bathroom €36)* is not as good as Hostal El Cantón, but is handy for the waterfront. The rooms, though, are perfectly acceptable.

El Raval On the fringe of Barri Xinès, **Hotel Peninsular** *(Map 6; ☎ 93 302 31 38, fax 93 412 36 99; Carrer de Sant Pau 34; singles/doubles without bathroom €22/45, with bathroom €45/65)* is a bit of an oasis. Once part of a convent, it has a plant-draped atrium extending the full height and most of the length of the hotel. The 80 rooms are clean and (mostly) spacious but otherwise nothing particularly special. A continental breakfast is included and the good news (in a sense) is that it doesn't take bookings.

Hostal Gat Raval *(Map 6; ☎ 93 481 66 70, fax 93 342 66 97; w www.gataccommodation.com; Carrer de Joaquín Costa 44; singles/doubles without bathroom €39.60/52.45, doubles with bathroom €71.70)* has opted for a sickening pea-green colour scheme for its young new hostal on the 2nd floor. Rooms are pleasant, secure and each behind a green door. The place has safes.

Hostal Residencia Opera *(Map 6; ☎ 93 318 82 01; Carrer de Sant Pau 20; rooms with bathroom €31/50)* is a bit tatty, but it's worth trying if other places are full and is perfectly comfortable.

Hostal La Terrassa *(Map 6; ☎ 93 302 51 74, fax 93 301 21 88; Carrer de la Junta del Comerç 11; singles without bathroom €18, doubles with bathroom €34)* is a big hostal with basic rooms that are OK for what you pay. You can sun yourself in the patio out the back.

L'Eixample A few cheapies are spread strategically across this upmarket part of the city north of Plaça de Catalunya.

Hostal Australia *(Map 4; ☎ 93 317 41 77; Ronda de l'Universitat 11; singles/doubles €23/39, doubles with bathroom €48)* is a charming and tiny family establishment up on the 4th floor. The owners lived in Australia for many years. With only five rooms and a faithful clientele, the hostal has the luxury of working almost exclusively with phone bookings.

Hostal Central *(Map 4; ☎ 93 302 24 20; e hostalcentral@wanadoo.es; Ronda de l'Universitat 11; singles/doubles without bathroom €33/39, with bathroom €48/60)* spreads out over several completely renovated flats in the same building. Some of the larger rooms have charming enclosed terraces looking onto the admittedly noisy street. Mosaic and parquet floors and some nice decorative touches make it an attractive option for you to consider.

Hostal Goya *(Map 5; ☎ 93 302 25 65, fax 93 412 04 35; e goya@cconline.es; Carrer de Pau Claris 74; singles without bathroom €27-32.10, doubles without bathroom €44.94-73.30, doubles with bathroom €54.57-88.28)* has 12 nice, good-sized rooms, some with

mid-range prices. Rooms on the unrenovated floor are cheaper.

Hostal Oliva *(Map 2; ☎ 93 488 01 62, fax 93 488 17 89; Passeig de Gràcia 32; singles without bathroom €24, doubles without/with bathroom €45/52)* is worth checking out just for the quaint old lift, which you will want to take up to the 4th floor. The rooms are basically well kept, but some of those that don't have a bathroom have little room for anything but the bed.

Hostal Neutral *(Map 2; ☎ 93 487 63 90, fax 93 487 68 48; Rambla de Catalunya 42; doubles without/with bathroom €39/45)* is a slightly ageing but reliable option in a leafy location. It has a couple of little singles without bathroom but they are generally occupied. The doubles without loo do have a shower.

Pensión Aribau *(Map 4; ☎ 93 453 11 06; Carrer d'Aribau 37; singles/doubles €28/42, doubles with bathroom €48.50)* offers very reasonable rooms. The singles might only have a basin but do come with a TV, while the doubles have a shower, loo, TV and even a fridge.

Near Estació Sants Handily placed for the train station, **Hostal Sans** *(Map 1; ☎ 93 331 37 00, fax 93 331 37 04; Carrer de Antoni de Capmany 82; singles/doubles without bathroom €18/28, with bathroom €22/34)* is a reliable if somewhat unexciting modern option.

Hostal Sofia *(Map 4; ☎ 93 419 50 40, fax 93 430 69 43; Avinguda de Roma 1-3; singles/doubles without bathroom €20.50/36, with bathroom €36/48.80)* is just across the square in front of the Sants station and rather more expensive. It has 12 sparkling-clean rooms.

Gràcia If you want to stay out of the tourist heart of Barcelona and mix with more of a local crowd, you might want to try staying up in Gràcia. You have a handful of choices available here.

Hostal San Medín *(Map 2; ☎ 93 217 30 68, fax 93 415 44 10; ⓔ info@sanmedin.com; Carrer Gran de Gràcia 125; singles/doubles without bathroom €28/48, with bathroom*

€30/60)* is a simple place with spartan but clean rooms. It is better than it appears from the outside.

Pensión Norma *(Map 2; ☎ 93 237 44 78; Carrer Gran de Gràcia 87; singles/doubles without bathroom €27/42, doubles with en suite €48)* is another good one further down the road.

PLACES TO STAY – MID-RANGE

There are not too many choices at this price range. Most of the rooms come with private bathrooms. Prices start at around €60/75 for singles/doubles.

La Rambla

Hotel Oriente *(Map 6; ☎ 93 302 25 58, fax 93 412 38 19; La Rambla 45; singles/doubles €84.20/122.70)* is known for its Modernista design and has a fine sky-lit restaurant and other public rooms, but staff can be off-hand. The bedrooms are slightly past their prime but still comfortable, with tiled floors and bathrooms, safes and TV.

Barri Gòtic

Hotel Nouvel *(Map 6; ☎ 93 301 82 74, fax 93 301 83 70; Carrer de Santa Anna 18-20; singles/doubles €89.90/158.40 including breakfast)* has some elegant Modernista touches and good air-con rooms with satellite TV.

Hotel Jardí *(Map 6; ☎ 93 301 59 00; Plaça de Sant Josep Oriol 1; singles/doubles €60/75)* has doubles with a balcony over the lovely square. The hotel has been refurbished and is a gem.

Hotel Racó del Pi *(Map 6; ☎ 93 342 61 90, fax 93 342 61 91; ⓦ www.hotelh10racodel pi.com; Carrer del Pi 7; singles/doubles €110/160 including breakfast)*, although part of a chain, has been stylishly carved out of a pleasant Barri Gòtic building. The 37 comfortable rooms have all you would expect and the location is terrific.

Hotel Suizo *(Map 6; ☎ 93 310 61 08, fax 93 315 04 61; ⓦ www.gargallo-hotels.com; Plaça de l'Àngel 12; singles/doubles €115.60/148.75)* looks old on the outside, but is modern within and has a restaurant. The unspectacular rooms are comfortable, and a fine breakfast is included.

PLACES TO STAY

El Raval

Hotel España (Map 6; ☎ 93 318 17 58, fax 93 317 11 34; Carrer de Sant Pau 9-11; singles/doubles €59/83 including breakfast) is famous for its two marvellous dining rooms designed by the Modernista architect Lluís Domènech i Montaner. One has big sea-life murals by Ramon Casas; the other has floral tiling and a wood-beamed roof. It has 60-plus simple but comfortable rooms.

Hotel Principal (Map 6; ☎ 93 318 89 70, fax 93 412 08 19; w www.hotelprincipal.es; Carrer de la Junta del Comerç 8; singles/doubles from €64/82), not as interesting as the España, but a quite reasonable option, has functional rooms with TV, air-con and safe. Renovated doubles cost €106. It also runs **Hotel Joventut**, virtually next door, at the same rates.

Hostal Mare Nostrum (Map 6; ☎ 93 318 53 40, fax 93 412 30 69; Carrer de Sant Pau 2; doubles without/with bathroom €61.24/93) is a good clean option although with something of the atmosphere of a cheaper hostal than a lower mid-level hotel. Rooms are attractive and come with TV, air-con and heating.

Hotel Mesón de Castilla (Map 4; ☎ 93 318 21 82, fax 93 412 40 20; w www.husa.es; Carrer de Valldonzella 5; singles/doubles €92/118 including breakfast) has some lovely Modernista touches – stained glass and murals in its public rooms, and Gaudíesque window mouldings. There are 56 good, quaintly decorated rooms. There's easy parking too.

Hotel San Agustín (Map 6; ☎ 93 318 16 58, fax 93 317 29 28; w www.hotelsa.com; Plaça de Sant Agustí 3; singles/doubles €96/128.40 including breakfast) has a little more character, if only because of its location on a quiet square. Rooms all have air-con, heating and satellite TV.

Hotel Lleó (Map 4; ☎ 93 318 13 12, fax 93 412 26 57; w www.hotel-lleo.es; Carrer de Pelai 22; singles/doubles €107/139), right at the top end of this *barri* and a brief stroll away from both La Rambla and Plaça de Catalunya, is a fine mid- to high-cost place with comfortable rooms, wheelchair access and a bar.

Hotel Banys Orientals (Map 6; ☎ 93 268 84 60; w www.hotelbanysorientals.com; Carrer de l'Argenteria 37; singles/doubles €85/90), which opened in mid-2002, shares its entrance with the very agreeable Senyor Parellada restaurant (see the Places to Eat chapter) a few steps away from the Església de Santa Maria del Mar. All rooms are for doubles, with a clean, modern feel, parquet floors and gleaming new bathrooms. All look onto the street or back lanes.

L'Eixample

Hotel Gran Via (Map 2; ☎ 93 318 19 00, fax 93 318 99 97; w www.nnhotels.es; Gran Via de les Corts Catalanes 642; singles/doubles €70.60/107) is a fine choice for a bit of old-fashioned style. It has 53 good-sized rooms and a big, elegant lounge opening onto a roof terrace.

Hotel AB Viladomat (Map 4; ☎ 93 229 65 65, fax 93 229 65 66; w www.abhoteles.com; Carrer de Viladomat 197; singles/doubles €115/125) is a modern and recent addition to the area. Rooms with parquet floors and crisp decor have all the mod cons. The buffet breakfast costs €10.50.

PLACES TO STAY – TOP END

Rates in Barcelona's top hotels start at the reasonable and reach for the sky. If you get lucky and turn up when business people aren't in town, you can get some good offers, as much as 50% off the prices quoted below, which are all high-season maximums. Single prices are almost always for single occupancy of a double room.

La Rambla, El Raval & Barri Gòtic

Le Meridien (Map 6; ☎ 93 318 62 00, fax 93 301 77 76; w www.meridienbarcelona.com; Rambla dels Estudis 111; singles/doubles €321/353) is an elegant establishment, and the top hotel on La Rambla. Its top-floor presidential suite is where the likes of Madonna and Julio Iglesias stay.

Hotel Inglaterra (Map 4; ☎ 93 487 39 39, fax 93 505 11 09; w www.hotel-inglaterra.com; Carrer de Pelai 14, El Raval; singles/doubles €171.20/208.65), with its classic facade, is a rather minimalist effort inside, with Japanese decoration in the comfortable but smallish rooms. The price comes down quite a bit in quieter periods and there is a solarium on the 6th floor.

Hotel Colón (Map 6; ☎ 93 301 14 04, fax 93 317 29 15; w www.hotelcolon.es; Avinguda de la Catedral 7, Barri Gòtic; singles/doubles €160.50/230) is a better choice (if you can afford it) for its location facing the cathedral. It has 146 comfortable and elegant rooms. The top rooms with a terrace are marvellous.

L'Eixample

Hotel Balmes (Map 2; ☎ 93 451 19 14, fax 93 451 00 49; w www.derbyhotels.es; Carrer de Mallorca 216; singles/doubles €115.60/181.90) is a good, modern hotel with white bricks much in evidence in the interior. The average-sized rooms with air-con, nice tiled bathrooms and satellite TV are comparatively good value. There's garage parking, a coffee shop, a garden with bar and swimming pool, and a restaurant.

Hotel Regente (Map 2; ☎ 93 487 59 89, fax 93 487 32 27; w www.hcchotels.com; Rambla de Catalunya 76; singles/doubles €197.95/240.75) is also a reasonable deal. The rooms, which have a nice feel, come with air-con and satellite TV, and feature wood panelling.

St Moritz Hotel (Map 2; ☎ 93 412 15 00, fax 93 412 12 36; w www.hcchotels.com; Carrer de la Diputació 262 bis; singles/doubles €173.35/193.67) is another upmarket hotel with 92 rooms. It has a restaurant and a pleasant terrace bar.

Hotel Majèstic (Map 2; ☎ 93 488 17 17, fax 93 488 18 80; w www.hotelmajestic.es; Passeig de Gràcia 68; singles/doubles up to €246/310.30) is a sprawling, comfortable place with a nice line in modern art on the walls and a rooftop swimming pool. The 300-plus rooms all have air-con and satellite TV. The hotel also boasts one of the city's finest restaurants (see the Places to Eat chapter).

Comtes de Barcelona (aka Condes de Barcelona Hotel; Map 2; ☎ 93 467 47 80, fax 93 467 47 85; Passeig de Gràcia 73-75;

singles/doubles from €192.60/208.65) is one of Barcelona's best hotels. It has two separate buildings facing each other across Carrer de Mallorca. The older one occupies the Casa Enric Batlló, built in the 1890s but now stylishly modernised. The air-con, soundproofed rooms have marble bathrooms.

Hotel Ritz (Map 2; ☎ 93 318 52 00, fax 93 318 01 48; w www.ritzbcn.com; Gran Via de les Corts Catalanes 668; singles/doubles €359.50/385.20) is the top choice for old-fashioned elegance, luxury, individuality and first-class service. The Ritz has been going since 1919. Some suites have a bedroom, salon and tiled step-down 'Roman bath'. These suites can cost you anything up to €1150.

Hotel Avenida Palace (Map 5; ☎ 93 301 96 00, fax 93 318 12 34; w www.avenidapalace.com; Gran Via de les Corts Catalanes 605; singles/doubles €218/272) is a less-expensive choice for old-style elegance. Broad sweeping stairways lead you up to fine rooms.

Hotel Ducs de Bergara (Map 5; ☎ 93 301 51 51, fax 93 317 34 42; w www.hoteles-catalonia.es; Carrer de Bergara 11; singles/doubles €211.85/244) is an elegant place worth considering if you can afford it. The building is a fine Modernista piece with an 18th-century artesonado ceiling and some nice Art Deco touches. Oh, and there's a pool too.

Hotel Claris (Map 2; ☎ 93 487 62 62, fax 93 215 79 70; w www.derbyhotels.es; Carrer de Pau Claris 150; doubles €353, suites up to €482) is one of the classiest addresses in town. It houses a permanent collection of Egyptian art and the rooftop restaurant is divine. Room decor varies greatly: Some rooms are strikingly modern, while others cede to more classic tastes in luxury.

Port Vell

Grand Marina Hotel (Map 1; ☎ 93 603 90 00, fax 93 603 90 90; w www.grandmarinahotel.com; Moll de Barcelona s/n; rooms €347-567, suites €642-1500) is one of the city's two prestigious waterfront hotels. Housed in the almost-complete World Trade Center, most rooms face either the city or an internal courtyard. Some of the side rooms, the best, offer views of the city and the sea.

Port Olímpic

Hotel Arts Barcelona *(Map 1; ☎ 93 221 10 00, fax 93 221 10 70; ⓦ ritzcarlton.com; Carrer de la Marina 19-21; singles/doubles €331/428)*, in one of the two sky-high towers that dominate Port Olímpic, provides Barcelona's most fashionable, if rather impersonal, lodgings. It has over 450 rooms with unbeatable views. Deutsche Bank, the hotel's owner, is considering building a neighbouring tower hotel.

LONG-TERM RENTALS

The **Universitat de Barcelona** *(Map 4; ☎ 93 402 11 00; Gran Via de les Corts Catalanes 585)*; **CIAJ** *(Map 6; ☎ 93 402 78 00; Carrer de Ferran 32)*; and the **British Council** *(Map 3; ☎ 93 241 99 77; Carrer d'Amigó 83)* have notice boards with ads for flat shares. You can also try **International House** *(Map 6; ☎ 93 268 45 11, fax 93 268 02 39; Carrer de Trafalgar 14)*. Young people and students should also check out options at **Punt d'Informació Juvenil** *(Map 4; ☎ 93 483 83 84; Carrer de Calàbria 147)*.

The English-language monthly *Barcelona Metropolitan* (see Newspapers & Magazines in the Facts for the Visitor chapter) is free and carries rental classifieds.

Otherwise, get a hold of *Anuntis*, the weekly classifieds paper. The last few pages of the *Suplement Immobiliària* (real estate supplement) carry ads for shared accommodation under the rubrique *lloguer/hostes i vivendes a compartir*. These ads tend to be in Castilian rather than Catalan. Rooms can come as cheap as €200 per month, but for something halfway decent, and not too far from the centre, you're looking at around €250 to €300, sometimes more. To this, you also need to add bills (gas, electricity, water, phone and *comunidad* – building maintenance charges).

Places to Eat

Barcelona is humming at the table, so much so that even those known food snobs, the French, are full of praise: in 2002 a Gallic food guide, *Le Guide des Gourmands*, voted Barcelona as Europe's eating capital.

Alongside great classics of local cuisine (both cheap and expensive), a veritable army of all sorts of imaginative restaurants has flourished over the past few years. You can barely walk down a street in the old town without noticing some new arrival. Seafood dishes are a strong card, but meat dishes from the interior also abound. You can knock back a cheap but filling set lunch or splurge on fine, dress-up dining. And the designer, international wave of cooking is now well implanted in Barcelona. Locals have developed a growing appetite for foreign flavours, so choices on that front are multiplying too.

FOOD

Food terminology in this chapter is given in Catalan/Castilian or Catalan alone, except in the few cases where the Castilian term is used in both languages. The idea is to reflect what you are most likely to see and hear in the streets of Barcelona, and not to descend into the murky depths of linguistic polemics.

When to Eat

You may not arrive in Barcelona with jetlag, but your tummy will soon think it has abandoned all known time zones.

Breakfast *(esmorzar/desayuno)* is generally a no-nonsense affair, taken at a bar on the way to work. Lunchtime *(dinar/ comida)* is basically from 2pm to 4pm and is the main meal of the day. No local would contemplate chomping into dinner *(sopar/cena)* before 9pm. That said, although restaurants tend to stay open until 1am or so, most kitchens close by 11.30pm.

Don't panic! If your gastric juices simply can't hold out until then, you can easily

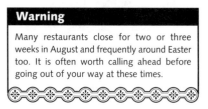

Warning

Many restaurants close for two or three weeks in August and frequently around Easter too. It is often worth calling ahead before going out of your way at these times.

track down bar snacks or fast food (local- and international-style) outside these times. And, anxious to ring up every tourist dollar possible, plenty of restaurants here cater for northern European intestinal habits – although you often pay for this with mediocre food and the almost exclusive company of other tourists.

Where to Eat

Many bars and some cafés offer some form of solid sustenance. This can range from *entrepans/bocadillos* (filled rolls) and *tapes*/tapas (bar snacks) through to more substantive *raciones* (basically a bigger version of a tapa), and full meals in *menjadors/comedores* (sit-down restaurants) out the back. *Cerveseries/cervezerías* (beer bars), *tavernes/tabernas* (taverns), *tasques/ tascas* (snack bars) and *cellers/bodegas* (cellars) are just some of the kinds of establishment in this category.

For a full meal, you are most likely to end up in a *restaurant/restaurante*, but other names will pop out at you. A *marisquería* specialises in seafood, while a *mesón* (a 'big table') might indicate (but not always!) a more modest eatery.

What to Eat

Breakfast A coffee with some sort of pastry *(pasta)* is the typical breakfast. You may get a croissant or some cream-filled number (such as a *canya*). Some people prefer a savoury start – you could go for a *bikini* – a toasted ham and cheese. A Spanish *tostada* is simply buttered toast (you might order something to go with it). The Catalan

Curros amb xocolata – the Catalan's chocolaty way to start the day!

version, a *torrada*, is usually more of an open toasted sandwich with something on it besides butter (depending on what you ask for).

Although not terribly common in Barcelona, some people go for an all-Spanish favourite, *xurros amb xocolata/churros con chocolate*, a lightly deep-fried stick of plain pastry immersed in thick, gooey hot chocolate. You'll find a few such places around town and they are great hangover material.

Lunch & Dinner Many straightforward Spanish dishes are available here as elsewhere in the country. The travellers' friend is the *menú del día*, a set-price meal usually comprising three courses, with a drink thrown in. This is often only available for lunch and can range from around €6 at budget places to €25 at posh establishments. A *plat combinat/plato combinado* is a simpler version still – a one-course meal consisting of basic nutrients – the 'meat-and-three-veg' style of cooking. You'll see pictures of this stuff everywhere. It's filling and cheap but has little to recommend it in culinary terms.

You'll pay more for your meals if you order à la carte, but the food will be better. The menu *(la carta)* begins with starters such as *amanides/ensaladas* (salads), *sopes/sopas* (soups) and *entremesos/entremeses* (hors d'oeuvres). The latter can range from a mound of potato salad with olives, asparagus, anchovies and a selection of cold meats – almost a meal in itself – to simpler cold meats, slices of cheese and olives.

The hungry Catalan, after a starter, will order a first then second course. The latter may come under headings such as: *pollastre/pollo* (chicken); *carn/carne* (meat); *mariscos* (seafood); *peix/pescado* (fish); *arròs/arroz* (rice); *ous/huevos* (eggs); and *verdures/verduras* (vegetables). Red meat may be subdivided into *porc/cerdo* (pork), *vedella/ternera* (beef) and *anyell/cordero* (lamb). Be aware that second courses frequently do not come with vegetables: You order a side dish of vegetables or salad. Often the first course is designed to take care of this side of your diet, though.

Postres (desserts) have a lower profile; *gelats/helados* (ice cream), fruit and flans are often the only choices in cheaper places. Sugar addicts should look out for local specialities, such as *crema Catalana*, where possible.

Catalan Cuisine Basques may well disagree, but Catalunya has a reputation for producing some of Spain's finest cuisine. Catalunya is geographically diverse and enjoys a variety of fresh, high-quality seafood (although, due to high demand, much seafood is now crated in from other parts of Spain and Europe), meat, poultry, game, fruit and vegetables. These can come in unusual and delicious combinations: meat and seafood (a genre known as *mar i muntanya* – 'sea and mountain'), poultry and fruit, fish and nuts. Quality Catalan food tends to require a greater fiscal effort.

The essence of Catalan food lies in its sauces for meat and fish. There are five main types: *sofregit* (fried onion, tomato and

Head to la Barceloneta for a taste of Barcelona's best seafood.

In Your Face

In late winter and early spring the Catalans indulge in an odd and rather messy local version of the BBQ, *calçotades*. *Calçots* are a kind of spring onion that ripens at this time of year. After grilling, you wrench the burnt exterior off, dip in *romesco* sauce and eat. Part of the fun is rubbing the black ash into your neighbour's face! As a rule, whether in private or in restaurants (with courtyard!), the fun is followed by a serious bout of meat-eating – and all is washed down with red wine.

garlic); *samfaina* or *chanfaina* (*sofregit* plus red pepper and aubergine or courgette); *picada* (based on ground almonds, usually with garlic, parsley, pine or hazel nuts, and sometimes breadcrumbs); *allioli* (pounded garlic with olive oil, often with egg yolk added to make more of a mayonnaise); and *romesco* (an almond, tomato, olive oil, garlic and vinegar sauce, also used as a salad dressing).

Catalans find it hard to understand why other people put butter on bread when *pa amb tomàquet* – bread sliced, then rubbed with tomato, olive oil, garlic and salt – is so easy.

Some typical dishes are listed in the Language chapter at the end of the book.

Other good things to look out for include *oca* (goose) and *canalons* (Catalan cannelloni). Wild mushrooms are a Catalan passion – people disappear into the forests in autumn to pick them. There are many, many types of *bolets*; with the large succulent *rovellons* being a favourite.

DRINKS
Nonalcoholic

In Barcelona, the tap water *(aigua de l'aixeta/agua del grifo)* is not at all tempting and most people drink *aigua/agua mineral* (bottled water). It comes in innumerable brands, either *amb/con gas* (fizzy) or *sense/sin gas* (still). A 1.5L bottle of still mineral water costs around €0.60 in a supermarket, but out and about you may be charged as much as €1.40.

Coffee In Spain, coffee is strong and slightly bitter. A *cafè amb llet/café con leche* (generally drunk at breakfast only) is about 50% coffee, 50% hot milk. Ask for *grande* or *doble* if you want a large cup, *en got/en vaso* if you want a smaller shot in a glass, or *sombra* if you want lots of milk. A *café solo* is an espresso (short black); *cafè tallat/café cortado* is an espresso with a little milk. For iced coffee, ask for *cafè amb gel/café con hielo*; you'll get a glass of ice and a hot cup of coffee, to be poured over the ice. If you can't deal with caffeine ask for a *descaféinat/descaféinado*. You usually have the choice of *de maquina* or *de sobre*. On taste the former beats the latter, which are little pouches of instant decaf that you pour into a cup of hot milk – blah!

Tea As in the rest of Spain, Barcelonins prefer coffee, but increasingly it is possible to get hold of many different styles of tea and *infusión de hierbas* (herbal concoctions). Locals tend to drink tea black. If you want milk, ask for it to come separately *(a parte)* to avoid ending up with a cup of tea-flavoured watery milk.

Soft Drinks *Suc de taronja/zumo de naranja* (orange juice) is the main freshly

International Cuisine

Barcelona offers a rapidly growing array of foreign restaurants. In case you want a break from the local stuff, a few interesting addresses are sprinkled in among the recommendations below. They include:

Betawi (p164); Bunga Raya (p165); Dionisos (p166); El Japonés (p168); El Paraguayo (p164); Gades (p165); Habana Vieja (p165); Hard Rock Café (p165); Kashmir Restaurant Tandoori (p160); Kohenoor (p166); La Carassa (p164); Maoz (p160); Margarita Blue (p164); Restaurant Kasbah (p161); Ristorante Il Mercante di Venezia (p164); Sannin (p162); Shunka (p164); Sushi-Ya (p160); Swan (p165); Thai Gardens (p165); The Bagel Shop (p160 & p162); and Yamadory (p169).

PLACES TO EAT

squeezed juice available. To make sure you are getting the real thing, ask for the juice to be *natural*, otherwise you risk getting a puny bottle of runny concentrate.

Refrescos (soft drinks) include the usual international brands, local brands such as Kas, and *granissat/granizado* (iced fruit crush).

A *batut/batido* is a flavoured-milk drink or milk shake. *Orxata/horchata* is a Valencian drink of Islamic origin. Made from the juice of *chufa* (tiger nuts), sugar and water, it is sweet and tastes like soya milk with a hint of cinnamon. A naughtier version is called a *cubanito* and involves sticking in a blob of chocolate ice-cream.

Alcoholic

Wine *Vi/vino* (wine) accompanies almost every meal. Spanish wine is robust because of the sunny climate. It comes *blanc/blanco* (white), *negre/tinto* (red) or *rosat/rosado* (rosé) in all price ranges. A €5 bottle of wine, bought from a supermarket or wine merchant, will be quite drinkable. The same money in a restaurant will get you virtually nothing. Cheap *vi de taula/vino de mesa* (table wine) can sell for less than €2 a litre, but wines at that price can be rather rank.

Catalunya's whites are better than its reds and the area is best known for *cava*, the fine local bubbly (see the Excursions chapter for more on Catalunya's main wine and *cava* region and how to identify quality wines).

You can order wine by the glass *(copa)* in bars and restaurants. At lunch or dinner it is common to order a *vi/vino de la casa* (house wine) – usually by the litre or half litre.

Beer The most common way to order *cervesa/cerveza* (beer) is to ask for a *canya*, which is a small draught beer *(cervesa/ cerveza de barril)*. A larger beer (about 300mL) is sometimes called a *tubo* (which comes in a straight glass). A pint is a *gerra/jarra*. If you just ask for a *cerveza* you may get bottled beer, which is more expensive. A small bottle of beer is called a *flascó/botellín*. The local brew is Estrella Damm (of which there are several variants, including the potent and flavoursome Voll Dam), while San Miguel, made in western Catalunya's Lleida area, is also widely drunk. The Damm company produces about 15% of all Spain's beer, as does San Miguel.

A *clara* is a shandy – a beer with a hefty dash of lemonade (7-Up).

Other Drinks *Sangría* is a wine and fruit punch, sometimes laced with brandy. It's refreshing going down but can leave you with a sore head. You'll see jugs of it on tables in some restaurants. A local speciality is *sangría de cava*, a champagne-based mix that does less damage to your neurones and also goes by the name of *tisana*.

There is no shortage of imported and Spanish-produced top-shelf stuff – *coñac* (brandy) is popular.

PLACES TO EAT – BUDGET

One traveller's budget restaurant may be another's splurge, so these categories are a little arbitrary. Those hoping to satisfy their hunger for around €6 to €10 could try the following places (in a few cases you can opt to spend a little more – say up to around €12 to €15 – and broaden your range of choices). A couple of the following recommendations are budget options only if you choose the set lunch.

Remember that, although most places recommended for tapas are placed in the budget category, if you eat a lot of tapas – which can cost €1 to €2.50 – by the time you're on your fourth or fifth (and the accompanying drinks) you'll be on the way to a more expensive meal than you might have bargained on!

JS

Fruity sangría will leave you feeling refreshed
after a day in the sun

Lighting Up

The politically correct campaigns aimed at pushing smokers and their fumes to the outer limits of acceptable society in some countries have had little impact on Barcelona or the rest of Spain. Some restaurants have no-smoking areas but, in general, it is not a consideration that's given much weight. If you are sensitive to this you should keep your eyes peeled for the tell-tale smoke signals around you before deciding on a seat.

Barri Gòtic

This area is peppered with good eateries, some of them excellent value.

Pastry Shops & Coffee Bars Tempting pastry and/or chocolate shops, often combined with coffee bars, abound.

Cafè de l'Òpera (Map 6; ☎ 93 317 75 85; La Rambla 74), opposite the Liceu opera house, is La Rambla's most interesting café. Founded in 1876 and operating as a café since at least 1929, it is pleasant for an early evening tipple or coffee and croissants.

There's a special concentration of places along Carrer and Baixada de la Llibreteria, northeast off Plaça de Sant Jaume in Barri Gòtic. Among the least-resistible pastry/chocolate places are **Santa Clara** (Map 6; Carrer de la Llibreteria 21) and **La Colmena** (Map 6; Cnr Baixada de la Llibreteria & Plaça de l'Àngel).

One place with particularly good coffee in this area is **Bon Mercat** (Map 6; Cnr Baixada de la Llibreteria & Carrer de la Freneria).

Xocolateria La Xicra (Map 6; Plaça de Sant Josep Oriol 2) has great cakes, various coffees, teas and *xocolata* (hot chocolate; €1) so thick it's listed on the menu under desserts. Nearby, two other good places to sit down for a coffee and croissant are **Granja La Pallaresa** (Map 6; Carrer de Petritxol 11) and **Croissanterie del Pi** (Map 6; Carrer del Pi 14).

Salterio (Map 6; Carrer de Sant Domènec del Call 4), just off Carrer de Ferran, is a great little place to sip a wide variety of teas

and herbal infusions in a hushed and unhurried atmosphere.

Restaurants Enter the grand arcade past the big camel and head upstairs to **Bar Jardi** (Map 6; Carrer de la Portaferrissa 17), an unexpected location for sandwiches and lunchtime snacks. Once through the market you reach a cafeteria-style place with a wonderful little garden out back where you sit to munch on your *bocadillo*.

Bar Els Hispanos (Map 6; ☎ 93 302 50 31; Carrer Sagristans 3; meals €15-20; open Mon-Sat) is one of those timeless old places where you can sidle up to the bar for tapas and a *ración* or two or head on out the back to sit at a bench for more of the same. Knock it back with *sangría*.

Santamonica (Map 6; ☎ 93 301 13 64; Plaça Reial 12; set menu €10) is a romantically lit haven on the corner of this frenetic square. The set menu offers limited options but you can also go à la carte and choose from some vegetarian options.

La Verónica (Map 6; ☎ 93 412 11 22; Carrer d'Avinyó 20; meals €15; open Tues-Sun) shines out like a beacon around here, its red decor and bright white lighting being hard to miss. Inside it serves reasonable pizzas at affordable prices in an atmosphere that could be described as fashionably camp.

Venus Delicatessen (Map 6; ☎ 93 301 15 85; Carrer d'Avinyó 25; open noon-midnight Mon-Sat), close to La Verónica, is less in your face and serves a tempting range of rather small dishes. The little marble-top tables for two form the perfect base for a fat slice of cheesecake.

Bodega La Palma (Map 6; ☎ 93 315 06 56; Carrer de la Palma de Sant Just 7, off Carrer del Cometa; meals €10-15; open Mon-Fri, & Sun evening) is a wonderful century-old tavern, with low timber-beam ceiling, dingy lighting and ageless wine barrels piled up by the entrance. Dig into plates of cheese, hams and sausage meats over a beer or two.

Bar Celta (Map 6; ☎ 93 315 00 06; Carrer de la Mercè 16; full meals around €15; open Mon-Sat) is a bright, straightforward bar-cum-restaurant. Specialists in *pulpo* (octopus), it does a good job as even the most

PLACES TO EAT

demanding of Gallegos gives this spot the thumbs up. Sit at the bar, order a bottle of Ribeiro and the traditional Gallego *tazas* (little white cups) to drink it with and proceed to tuck into *raciones*. It is one of several such places, mostly run by immigrants from northwestern Spain, along and just off this street.

Vegetarian Cuisine The popular **Self-Naturista** *(Map 6; ☎ 93 318 26 84; Carrer de Santa Anna 13; menú €6.50, mains under €8)* is a self-service vegetarian restaurant.

La Cereria *(Map 6; ☎ 93 301 85 10; Baixada de Sant Miquel 3-5; open 9am-10pm)*, a cross between a café of a century gone by and a hippy hang-out, is a cooperative that offers some tasty vegetarian cooking, great desserts and low prices. The fruit shakes are good too.

International Cuisine At **Maoz** *(Map 6; Carrer de Ferran 13; felafels €3)* they pack a lot of goodness into a tiny space. You can stuff yourself with a filling Israeli-style felafel, helping yourself to the fillings.

The Bagel Shop *(Map 6; ☎ 93 302 41 61; Carrer de la Canuda 25; Sun breakfast €4.50)*, just off La Rambla, is where you should look for a lox and cream-cheese bagel.

Sushi-Ya *(Map 6; ☎ 93 412 72 49; Carrer d'En Quintana 4; sushi set meals €6)* is a simple place for cheap Japanese food. The sushi set meal is hard to argue with in terms of price, and you can take food away. Or six pieces of maki sushi cost €2.80 to €3.60. Don't expect top Japanese cuisine, but it makes an affordable change.

El Raval

Elisabets *(Map 6; ☎ 93 317 58 26; Carrer de Elisabets 2-4; set lunch €7; open Mon-Fri, & Sat lunch)* in the lean 1950s was a small office. Then it became the unassuming eatery it is today. The walls are lined with old radio sets and the lunch menu varies daily. Try the *ragú de jabalí* (wild boar stew) and finish with *mel i mató* (honey and soft cheese) for dessert.

Restaurante Pollo Rico *(Map 6; Carrer de Sant Pau 31)* specialises in cheap grub. You can pick up mains of chicken, meat and various other options from around €4.50 to €9. Skip the paella, though.

Bar Kasparo *(Map 6; ☎ 93 302 20 72; Plaça de Vicenç Martorell 4; meals €10-15)* is a relaxed Australian-run place where you can get great mixed salads and other healthy light food – perfect in summer on this quiet, pedestrianised square.

Buenas Migas *(Map 6; ☎ 93 412 16 86; Plaça del Bonsuccés 6)* is a charming hole in the wall where you can pick up a decent focaccia, as well as pizza slices and other pleasant snacks.

Ra *(Map 6; ☎ 93 301 41 63; Plaça de la Gardunya; menú del día €15; open Mon-Sat)*, which looks a beach bar that got lost and ended up in the car park, offers a vaguely vegetarian menu, with a couple of meat options thrown in. The food is OK but unexceptional. The atmosphere is decidedly groovy. You can get fruit shakes here and breakfast, too.

Pla dels Angels *(Map 6; ☎ 93 329 40 47; Carrer de Ferlandina 23; meals €14)* proposes nicely priced inventive Med cooking, with pasta dishes (such as *gnocchi con salsa à la moussaka*!).

Tresss I No Res *(Map 4; ☎ 93 441 30 16; Carrer de la Cera 53; full pizza €10.80; open Mon-Sat)* is a popular, unassuming spot on the edge of El Raval. Rock up for lunchtime pizza or pasta (€6). You can eat the former, thick and with all sorts of original toppings, by the slice (€1.35).

Vegetarian Cuisine A surprisingly expansive vegetarian restaurant, **Biocenter** *(Map 6; ☎ 93 301 45 83; Carrer del Pintor Fortuny 25; open 1pm-5pm Mon-Sat)* hosts lunch only. You can opt for the *menú del día* (€7.50) or a *combinat* (€5.50), a huge plate onto which is heaped your choice of hot food and you then add as much salad as you can.

International Cuisine Tasty curries and biryanis can be found at **Kashmir Restaurant Tandoori** *(Map 6; Carrer de Sant Pau 39)* for around €5 to €6. It is one of a growing number of curry houses around here, that

The Temple del Sagrat Cor (Church of the Sacred Heart) on Tibidabo overshadows an amusement park (top) and the city (bottom right); a statue at La Sagrada Família appears to be waiting for the work to finally finish

PASCALE BEROUJON

JESSE MECHLING

DAMIEN SIMONIS

DALE BUCKTON

DAMIEN SIMONIS

PASCALE BEROUJON

Tile style: fine examples of mosaics, a feature of Gaudí's work, can be found at the back of the Nativity Facade, La Sagrada Família (top left) and in Parc Güell (top right and bottom)

reflects a growing wave of mainly Pakistani immigration into El Raval.

Sant Antoni & Poble Sec

Horchatería Sirvent *(Map 4; ☎ 93 441 27 20; Carrer del Parlament 56, Sant Antoni; open Mon-Sat)*, the haven of *orxata* in Barcelona, serves up the best you'll try without catching the Euromed train down to this drink's spiritual home, Valencia. You can get it by the glass or take it away by the bottle. This place also sells ice cream, *granissat* and *turrón* (nougat).

Restaurant Kasbah *(Map 7; ☎ 93 329 83 84; Carrer de Vila i Vilà 82, Poble Sec; open Tues-Sun; meals €12-15)* features Moroccan and other North African dishes. A variety of *tajines* (a spicy stew) cost €7 each, or you can try the limited French menu. The mint tea is exceptionally good.

La Ribera

El Xampanyet *(Map 6; Carrer de Montcada 22)*, the city's best known *cava* bar, is a small, cosy place with tiled walls, good tapas and *cava* by the glass.

Restaurant L'Econòmic *(Map 6; Plaça de Sant Agustí Vell 13; meals €8-20)* is a popular local hang-out that offers a straightforward set lunch and a more expensive version for gourmet palates.

Glüh *(Map 6; ☎ 93 310 68 90; Carrer de Verdaguer i Callís 6; meals €15; open Tues-Sun)* has some interesting offerings such as ostrich in a green pepper sauce, but some dishes are a little precious. Upstairs is cute and cosy but not for very tall people!

Hivernacle *(Map 6; ☎ 93 295 40 17; Passeig de Picasso)* is a pleasant café/restaurant set amid the trees of this arboretum in the Parc de la Ciutadella. Sit in the hothouse or outside facing the street. It sometimes stages a little live music here and the food is OK.

Restaurante Estrella *(Map 6; ☎ 93 310 27 68; Carrer de Ocata 6; set lunch menu €8; evening meals €25; open Tues-Sat, & Mon lunch)* is an unprepossessing but pleasantly arranged locale where local public servants pile in for a good-value set lunch. In the evening it's more of a gourmet story.

Vegetarian Cuisine Modern **Comme-Bio** *(aka La Botiga; Map 6; ☎ 93 319 89 68; Via Laietana 28 • Map 5; Gran Via de les Corts Catalanes 603; lunchtime buffet €7.97)* will appeal to most vegetarians. It's a chemical- and additive-free vegetarian restaurant and wholefood shop. Go for the all-you-can-eat buffet at lunchtime or try à la carte dishes, including spinach-and-Roquefort crepes and pizzas.

L'Eixample

Tapas, Snacks & Coffee For excellent coffee, try **Cafè Torino** *(Map 2; ☎ 93 487 75 71; Passeig de Gràcia 59)*, on the corner of Carrer de València. It's a neat and friendly place, popular with a mildly chic, young clientele. At lunchtime you can munch on a *ciabatta* or focaccia.

You'll find a number of glossy but informal tapas places near the bottom end of Passeig de Gràcia. **Quasi Queviures** *(aka Qu Qu; Map 2; ☎ 93 317 45 12; Passeig de Gràcia 24)* is one and has a big choice including sausages and hams, pâtés and smoked fish. Most tapas cost over €2.50, but the portions are decent.

Restaurants Open until dawn, **Bar Estudiantil** *(Map 4; Plaça de la Universitat; open till late)* has economical *plats combinats*, hamburgers and sandwiches. This place is filled with an odd crowd of students, bums and, on early weekend mornings, bleary-eyed clubbers.

L'Hostal de Rita *(Map 2; ☎ 93 487 23 76; Carrer d'Aragó 279; menú del día €7-8, meals €10-15)*, a block east of Passeig de Gràcia, is an excellent mid-range restaurant. Expect to queue.

Restaurant Madrid Barcelona *(Map 2; ☎ 93 215 70 27; Carrer d'Aragó 282; meals €15)* is owned by the same people and serves homey Catalan cooking. It is so popular that staff set up odd little cardboard stools outside for waiting customers.

Centro Asturiano *(Map 2; ☎ 93 215 30 10; Passeig de Gràcia 78; menú del día €8; open for lunch Mon-Sat)* is a great little club tucked away up on the 1st floor. It opens its doors to the lunchtime rabble for the solid *menú del día*. The interior patio is a nice spot to eat.

FrescCo *(Map 2; ☎ 93 301 68 37; Carrer de València 263; lunch/dinner buffet €6.90/ 8.80)*, half a block east of Passeig de Gràcia, packs them in with its all-you-can-eat buffet of salads, soups, pizza, pasta, fruit, ice cream and drinks. It is part of a chain.

La Barceloneta
Can Paixano *(Map 6; ☎ 93 310 08 39; Carrer de la Reina Cristina 7)* is tucked away amid the bright tacky lights of cheap electronics stores. At this fine old champagne bar munch on *bocadillos* while sipping elegant little glasses of bubbly rosé.

Gràcia
Sol Soler *(Map 2; ☎ 93 217 44 40; Plaça del Sol 21-22)* is a pleasant little corner of this busy square. Gather around the tiny marble-top tables for a drink and some enticing and inventive snacks. Choose the latter at the bar. It still serves food at midnight.

International Cuisine For some reason, Gràcia has become the epicentre of Lebanese and other Middle Eastern places, often good value for money. The Greeks are also here, with a few concentrated on or near Carrer del Torrent de l'Olla.

Sannin *(Map 1; ☎ 93 285 00 51; Carrer de l'Encarnació 44)* is a good down-to-earth Lebanese place. A full meal of old favourites such as shawarma, hummus, tabbouleh, dessert and drinks need not cost much more than €15.

The Bagel Shop *(Map 2; ☎ 93 217 61 01; Plaça de Rius i Taulet 8; open Wed-Mon)* has opened a branch here after the success of its eatery in Barri Gòtic (see earlier).

Sarrià
Bar Tomàs *(Map 1; ☎ 93 203 10 77; Carrer Major de Sarrià 49; FGC Sarrià; open Thur-Tues)* is the best place in Barcelona for *patatas bravas* (potato bits dripping with a slightly spicy tomato sauce mixed with mayonnaise). The place itself is, otherwise, an unassuming bar – it does other tapas as well.

Restaurant Chains
There are a few local restaurant chains where you can get a quick, decent snack or meal with minimum effort. A few of the branches are listed below.

Bocatta *(Map 6; Carrer de Santa Anna 11 • Map 6; Plaça de Sant Jaume • Map 6; Cnr Carrer de Comtal & Carrer de N'Amargos • Map 2; Rambla de Catalunya, north of Carrer de Valencia; most branches open 8am-midnight)* sells hot and cold baguettes with a big range of fillings, costing up to €5.

Pans & Company *(Map 6; La Rambla 123 • Map 6; Carrer de Ferran 14 • Map 6; Carrer dels Arcs • Map 4; Ronda de la Universitat 7 • Map 5; Rambla de Catalunya 13 • Map 2; Passeig de Gràcia 39 • Map 2; Carrer de Provença 278)* provides much the same fare for similar prices to Bocatta.

Self-Catering
Mercat de la Boqueria *(Map 6; La Rambla; open 8am-8pm Mon-Sat)* has great fresh food of all types. You will also find a couple of bar-restaurants here where you can eat surprisingly well and cheaply of the fresh products that surround you.

Mercat de Santa Caterina *(Map 6; La Ribera)*, another good shopping choice, has been temporarily shifted to Passeig de Lluís Companys.

In Gràcia there's a big covered **food market** *(Map 2)* just off Travessera de Gràcia. Or you can try the nearby **Mercat de la Llibertat** *(Map 2; Plaça de la Llibertat)*.

Champion *(Map 6; La Rambla dels Estudis 113)*, near the northern end of La Rambla, is a convenient central supermarket. In the heart of Barri Gòtic, **Superservis** *(Map 6; Carrer d'Avinyó 13)* is handy.

PLACES TO EAT – MID-RANGE
Opening your purse wider will improve your options greatly. At these places expect to pay from €15 to around €35 for a full meal.

La Rambla & Barri Gòtic
Café Zurich *(Map 6; ☎ 93 317 91 53; Carrer de Pelai 39)*, right on Plaça de Catalunya near La Rambla, has been resuscitated after

Dying for a Tapa or Two?

Barcelona's cooking traditions do not really include the *tapa*, that delicious little bar snack that can come in the form of anything from a little pile of olives to a Basque-style *canapé*. The basic idea comes from deeper into Spain, in Castilla and Andalucía, where in most bars you would traditionally get a *tapa* (little saucer) with a salty appetiser or two to accompany your drink (and encourage you to drink more, naturally). In the Basque country, an altogether different tradition arose, with gourmet toppings on little slices of baguette the norm (these are basically *canapés*, what Spaniards elsewhere would refer to as *montaditos*). In some eateries you will be confronted with an array of food options at the bar. You ask for a few *tapas* or *raciones*, which are larger serves (three or four *raciones* generally make a full meal for the average being).

Apart from the touristy places along La Rambla and the barn-like options along the lower end of Passeig de Gràcia (some of the latter have been mentioned in this chapter for the record), where can you get good *tapas* in Barcelona? The following selection includes a couple of Basque places, some grand Barcelona institutions, some more expensive gourmet options and a couple of *cava* bars where the bubbly is used to wash down snacks: Bar La Esquinica (p167); Bar Celta (p159); Bodega La Palma (p159); Cal Pep (p167); Can Paixano (p162); Centre Cultural Euskal Etxea (p164); Cerveseria Catalana (p165); El Xampanyet (p161); Estrella de Plata (p167); Irati (p163); Luz de Gas Port Vell (p166); and Vaso de Oro (p166).

years of closure. It is an old-style café, great for the morning paper, but a little more expensive than the average such place.

Irati *(Map 6; ☎ 93 302 30 84; Carrer del Cardenal Cassañas 17; full meals €35; open Tues-Sat, & Sun lunch)* is a Basque favourite. If you don't want the expense of the sit-down meal, just munch away on tapas at the bar over a glass of beer or six (but watch how your debts mount!).

Les Quinze Nits *(Map 6; ☎ 93 317 30 75; Plaça Reial 6; meals around €15-20)* is a stylish, bistro-like restaurant, on the borderline between smart and casual, with a long menu of solid Catalan and Spanish dishes. It's a little formulaic but pleasant nonetheless. You almost always have to queue.

Los Caracoles *(Map 6; ☎ 93 302 31 85; Carrer dels Escudellers 14; meals €25-35; open daily)* started life as a tavern in the 19th century and is one of Barcelona's best-known restaurants – although it's now frequented by tourists rather than by the celebrities whose photos adorn the walls. It's still good and lively, and offers a big choice of seafood, fish, rice and meat. Try the snails or, of course, the grilled chicken you'll see on the spits before you enter.

El Gran Café *(Map 6; ☎ 93 318 79 86; Carrer d'Avinyó 9; à la carte mains €7-18; open Mon-Sat, closed holidays)* has classy Modernista decor and serves good Catalan/French food.

Restaurant Pitarra *(Map 6; ☎ 93 301 16 47; Carrer d'Avinyó 56; mains around €25-30; open Mon-Sat)* serves up quality Catalan food. The old house is named after a late-19th-century playwright, Serafí Pitarra.

Mastroqué *(Map 6; ☎ 93 301 79 42; Carrer de Còdols 29; meals €23; open Tues-Fri, Sat & Mon evenings)* is in a cavernous locale, with typical Catalan slender roof beams and low lighting. You choose from a menu of about 20 small dishes (four or five recommended for two people), which can range from *foie gras* to beef *carpaccio* sprinkled with Manchego cheese.

Cometacinc *(Map 6; ☎ 93 310 15 58; Carrer del Cometa 5; meals €25; open dinner only Wed-Mon)* explores all sorts of culinary nooks and crannies, from tempting salads to Thai chicken in almonds and curry. Take a little white wooden seat at one of the candle-lit tables on two levels.

Vegetarian Cuisine A couple of doors down from Irati, **Juicy Jones** *(Map 6; ☎ 93 302 43 30; Carrer del Cardenal Cassañas 7; veggie set menu €7; open Mon-Sat)* is a

PLACES TO EAT

psychedelic eatery with a vegetarian set menu, or you can just sip the pleasant juices (around €2.25).

International Cuisine Tasty Indonesian food is offered at **Betawi** *(Map 6; ☎ 93 412 62 64; Carrer Montsió 6; mains €7-10; open Tues-Sat & Mon evening)* in a soothingly lit environment. This is where to come and get your *nasi goreng* hit.

Shunka *(Map 6; ☎ 93 412 49 91; Carrer Sagristans 5; meals €25; open Tues-Sun)* is a good spot for Japanese food. As you enter you pass the bar behind which the cooks are at work. You can eat there or proceed around to the tables. The many Japanese customers are a good sign!

Ristorante Il Mercante di Venezia *(Map 6; ☎ 93 317 18 28; Carrer de Josep Anselm Clavé 11; meals €18-20; open Tues-Sun)* offers reasonable Italian dishes (with a northern leaning) and a limited list of Italian wines. When they're on the ball the food is convincing.

Margarita Blue *(Map 6; ☎ 93 317 71 76; Carrer de Josep Anselm Clavé 6; meals €12-20)* does imaginative versions of Mexican food and doubles as a bar.

El Paraguayo *(Map 6; ☎ 93 302 14 41; Carrer del Parc 1; meals €15; open Tues-Sun)*, just off Carrer de Josep Anselm Clavé, is a great place to eat succulent slabs of meat bigger than your head. Try the *entraña*; the word means 'entrails' but the meal is in fact a juicy slice of prime beef folded over onto itself and accompanied by a herb sauce. The *dulce de leche* (a South American version of caramel) desserts are to die for.

El Raval

Urban revival is bringing new life into El Raval, one of the poorest quarters of old Barcelona. Several tempting places have popped up, attracting a hip, young clientele.

Rita Blue *(Map 6; ☎ 93 412 34 38; Plaça de St Agustí 3; meals €18-20; open Mon-Fri, & dinner Sat & Sun)* is a pleasant designer restaurant with a whiff of New York in the air, but be prepared to wait at the bar. The food is a tempting mix of Mediterranean dishes with a hint of the exotic. For instance,

you could order Mexican *fajitas* here with tandoori chicken.

Lupino *(Map 6; ☎ 93 412 36 97; Carrer del Carme 33; meals about €20)* has a self-styled designer 'restaurant lounge' – proceed down the long hall to eat outside on Plaça de Gardunya. Try a first course of *tempùra de verdures* (vegetable tempura) followed by *couscous al xai* (lamb). You can also hang around in the bar for post-prandial drinks.

Restaurant El Cafétí *(Map 6; ☎ 93 329 24 19; Passatge de Bernardí, off Carrer de l'Hospital 99; meals €25; open Tues-Sat, & Sun lunch)* is well hidden down a narrow passage off the street. This diminutive and cosy little eatery is one of those happy surprise packets. Even London's mayor 'Red' Ken Livingstone liked it! Try a succulent serve of chicken grilled in cream of *cava*.

Poble Sec

Restaurant Elche *(Map 7; ☎ 93 441 30 89; Carrer de Vila i Vilà 71; meals around €20)* does some of Barcelona's best paella and good *fideuá* (similar to paella, but made with vermicelli noodles). Several varieties are on offer, all of them good.

La Ribera

Pla de la Garsa *(Map 6; ☎ 93 315 24 13; Carrer dels Assaonadors 13; lunch menú €20-25; open Tues-Sun)* is an old-style Catalan restaurant decorated with attractive tiles, lamps and paintings.

Senyor Parellada *(Map 6; ☎ 93 310 50 94; Carrer de l'Argenteria 37; meals €20-25; open Mon-Sat)* concentrates on Catalan/French dishes, served in a charming atmosphere. Try the *carpaccio de salmó* (thin strips of garnished uncooked salmon).

La Carassa *(Map 6; ☎ 93 310 33 06; Carrer de Brosoli 1; open Mon-Sat)* has the best fondue in town. It's a cosy, intimate place, but so popular that there are often two shifts, one at 9pm and another at 11pm. If you get in for the first, they'll boot you out at 11pm to make way for the next round.

Centre Cultural Euskal Etxea *(Map 6; ☎ 93 310 21 85; Placeta de Montcada 1; meals €12-20; open Tues-Sat, & Sun lunch)* is a fine San Sebastián–style bar where you can wash down the scrummy tapas with glasses of the tangy Basque white wine, *txacoli*.

Little Italy *(Map 6;* ☎ *93 319 79 73; Carrer del Rec 30; set lunch €10.50, meals €18-20; open Mon-Sat)* offers a stylish mix of Mediterranean dishes, some of them (mostly the first courses) vaguely Italian.

L'Ou Com Balla *(Map 6;* ☎ *93 310 53 78; Carrer dels Banys Vells 20; meals €30; open dinner only)* presents a sometimes exquisite choice of local, sort-of-Moroccan and more-or-less French dishes in an inviting space with low lighting and well-chosen ambient music. If it's full you'll be sent across the road to **El Pebre Blau** *(Map 6;* ☎ *93 319 13 08; Carrer dels Banys Vells 21)*, which has the same menu; the setting is less personal and the queues shorter.

Coses de Menjar *(Map 6;* ☎ *93 310 60 01; Pla de Palau 7; meals €30; open Mon-Sat)* means 'things to eat'. A curious place with weird and wonderful floor tiles, a wall lined with bottles (the wine list goes on for pages) and otherwise the vague feeling of being in somebody's drawing room. Soft music and lighting accompanies imaginative cooking. The *lluç amb formatge* (cod prepared in cheese) melts in the mouth and the *delirium tremens de xocolata* dessert speaks for itself.

Vegetarian Cuisine For inventive vegetarian cuisine or free-range meat at mid-range prices, try **La Flauta Mágica** *(Map 6;* ☎ *93 268 46 94; Carrer dels Banys Vells 18; meals €20; open Wed-Mon)* in a pastel-coloured salon. How about *rice 'n' curry del país de la eternal sonrisa* (from the land of the eternal smile)?

International Cuisine You can get a mix of Malaysian and Indonesian food at **Bunga Raya** *(Map 6;* ☎ *93 319 31 69; Carrer dels Assaonadors 7; meals €15-20; open Tues-Sun)*.

Gades *(Map 6;* ☎ *93 310 44 55; Carrer de l'Esparteria 10; open Mon-Sat)* is a smart address for fondue, of which they do nearly a dozen varieties for around €10.

Habana Vieja *(Map 6;* ☎ *93 268 25 04; Carrer dels Banys Vells 2; meals €25; open Mon-Sat)* is the spot to seek out *ropa vieja* and other Cuban classics.

L'Eixample

Restaurant de l'Escola de Restauració i Hostalatge *(Map 4;* ☎ *93 453 29 03; Carrer de Muntaner 70-72)* is where many cooks learn their trade – and in general they appear to be learning it rather well. Meals are modestly priced and the menu varies regularly.

Cerveseria Catalana *(Map 2;* ☎ *93 216 03 68; Carrer de Mallorca 236; light meals €15-20)* provides a spectacular cornucopia of tapas and *montaditos*. You can sit at the bar or in the restaurant at the back. The variety of hot tapas, mouthwatering salads and other snacks makes it a popular spot.

El Racó d'en Baltà *(Map 2;* ☎ *93`453 10 44; Carrer d'Aribau 125; meals €20; open Mon-Sat)* spreads out over three floors and it has a cool bar next door where diners will be offered a complimentary *chupito* (shot) after their meal. Food offerings include hearty meat mains and dreamy desserts.

Gargantúa i Pantagruel *(Map 4;* ☎ *93 453 20 20; Carrer d'Aragó 214; meals €25)* is warm and inviting and serves Catalan country cooking – you can sit and watch your meat being grilled.

International Cuisine If you want American portions of American-style food, the **Hard Rock Café** *(Map 6;* ☎ *93 270 23 05; Plaça de Catalunya 21; meals €15-20)* may well be the place for you. It has a branch in every major city. Buy the T-shirt next door.

Swan *(Map 2;* ☎ *93 488 09 77; Carrer de la Diputació 269; meals €15-20)* offers some of the better-quality Chinese food in Barcelona (the city has plenty of the cheap and cheerful variety).

Thai Gardens *(Map 2;* ☎ *93 487 98 98; Carrer de la Diputació 273; meals around €25-30; open Mon-Sat)* is practically next door to Swan. You can pop in for a limited set-lunch menu or try the more extensive evening spread.

Gràcia

La Singular *(Map 2;* ☎ *93 237 50 98; Carrer de Franciso Giner 50; meals €15-18; open Thur-Tues)* does fantastic salads (with salmon, tuna or pâté) as mains. You can also munch on a selection of tapas.

Cal Juanito (Map 2; ☎ 93 213 30 43; Carrer de Ramon i Cajal 3; meals €25; open Tues-Sat, & Sun lunch) is a classic of Catalan cuisine – try the *botifarra amb mongetes* (pork sausage with fried white beans). It's a delightful place with tiled decor, wooden rafters and walls covered in plates signed by all the great and good who have munched here over the decades.

International Cuisine Pleasing and spacious **Dionisos** (Map 2; ☎ 93 237 34 17; Carrer del Torrent de l'Olla 144; meals €22) is a Greek place where starters include old faves such as *taramasalata* and *tzatziki*. Washed down with a crisp Santorini white, it makes for a nice eastern Mediterranean change.

Tibidabo
Plaça del Doctor Andreu, at the foot of the Tibidabo funicular, is a charming place to halt on your way to or from Tibidabo, if only for the views.

Mirablau Terrazza (Map 1), an open-air café by the *tramvia blau* stop, affords the best views. There's a couple of more expensive restaurants across the street, which are the only alternative.

Port Vell & La Barceloneta
In the Maremàgnum complex on the Moll d'Espanya you can eat close to the water's edge at a handful of fairly slapdash spots. The attraction is location rather than high-quality food.

Vaso de Oro (Map 5; ☎ 93 319 30 98; Carrer de Balboa 6; meals around €12-20; open 11am-midnight) has been serving up tapas to a faithful crowd of locals for what seems like forever. The narrow crowded bar is food chaos and the bar staff, with their slightly maritime-looking uniforms, put on quite a show.

Restaurant Set (7) Portes (Map 6; ☎ 93 319 30 33; Passeig d'Isabel II 14; paella up to €15) is a classic, founded in 1836. The old-world atmosphere is reinforced by the decor of wood panelling, tiles, mirrors and plaques naming some of the famous – such as Orson Welles – who have eaten here. Paella is the speciality.

La Barceloneta is lined with seafood restaurants. **Puda Can Manel** (Map 5; ☎ 93 221 50 13; Passeig de Joan de Borbó 60-61; meals around €25; open Tues-Sun) is one of the best along this strip. The paella is fine but the *crema Catalana* for dessert is not so hot.

Luz de Gas Port Vell (Map 5; ☎ 93 209 77 11; meals €20; open noon-3am May-Oct) combines tapas, tipples and a view of tall ships. To sit on the top deck of this boat is to let go of the day's cares. You can hang about and just use it as a bar. On shore they play some good music.

Port Olímpic
The harbour here is lined on two sides by dozens of **restaurants** and **tapas bars** (Map 1), which are extremely popular in spring and summer. They are not cheap and mostly rely on the frenetic portside activity for atmosphere. It would be unfair to recommend any one place here. The food is generally average and the touting waiters can be a pain.

Agua (Map 1; ☎ 93 225 12 72; Passeig Marítim de la Barceloneta 30; meals €30) is a classy alternative. You enter by what looks vaguely like an elevator shaft on the waterfront and wander downstairs into a brightly lit dining area at beach level. By day you almost feel you are *on* the beach. Food is bright and tasty, with some original options such as *pastel d'escalivada*, a light pie version of the Catalan starter.

Sants
Shellfish (Map 4; ☎ 93 431 90 59; Carrer Riego 27; full meals around €18; open Tues-Sat, & Sun lunch) is an interesting fast fresh-food idea. You wander in, choose from the seafood on display as though at a fish market, and you are allotted a table. Then you head around and ask for your wine, water and plates, as though in a self-service canteen and wait for them to cook your food and call out your table number.

International Cuisine For Indian food, try **Kohenoor** (Map 4; ☎ 93 422 99 03; Carrer Riego 31; meals around €15; open Tues-Sun). There's bright lights and too much pink but prices are reasonable and the cooking isn't bad. The Indian punters are a good sign.

Nou Barris

Bar La Esquinica (☎ 93 358 25 19; Passeig de Fabra i Puig 296; meals €20; open Tues-Sun; metro Virrei Amat) is not in a part of town you would normally make any effort to get to, but the wonderful Aragonese tapas bar-restaurant is worth making the trip. Since the Aragonese diminutive often ends in 'ico', everything on the menu is a 'little' something.

PLACES TO EAT – TOP END

Although Barcelona is not to be compared with the likes of London, it is possible to part company with more serious sums of money. Dining at the following restaurants will see your wallet lightened by anything from €30 up. In some cases, if you choose carefully, you might bring the bill down just a tad.

Barri Gòtic

Els Quatre Gats (Map 6; ☎ 93 302 41 40; Carrer de Montsió 3 bis; mains around €11-26; open Mon-Sat, & Sun evening), once a turn-of-the-20th-century artists' lair (see the boxed text 'The Coolest Cats in Town') is now an expensive restaurant with somewhat dismissive service. It has been restored to its original appearance and displays reproductions of some of its former customers' portraits, painted by other former customers. Just have a drink if you only want to sample the atmosphere. Otherwise head out to the grand rear dining area, a gorgeous setting for a meal.

Restaurant Agut d'Avignon (Map 6; ☎ 93 302 60 34; Carrer del la Trinitat 3; meals €30-35), discreetly hidden away in a little dead-end lane, has the feel of a timeless old Catalan country home, with ceramics and paintings for decor. It specialises in Catalan classics such as *oca amb peres* (goose prepared with pears).

El Raval

Casa Leopoldo (Map 6; ☎ 93 441 30 14; Carrer de Sant Rafael 24; meals €50 including wine) was long well hidden in the slum alleys of El Raval, much favoured by local politicians and other important personages. Since the Rambla del Raval was crashed through this down-at-heel part of town, it has become easier to find! You can eat well à la carte or choose a special set menu for €36. Several rambling dining areas, sporting magnificent tiled walls and timber-beam ceilings, make this a fine option. The seafood menu is extensive and the wine list is strong.

Ca L'Isidre (Map 5; ☎ 93 441 11 39; Carrer de les Flors 12; meals €45; open Mon-Sat) is another one of those old-world gems lurking in the unappealing back streets of El Raval. The cuisine is standard Catalan fare and well done. The place is frequently full, though.

La Ribera

Cal Pep (Map 6; ☎ 93 310 79 61; Plaça de les Olles 8; full meals from €30; open Tues-Fri, & Mon dinner, closed holidays) is a fave on the Barcelona foodie circuit. People queue to gobble up gourmet tapas.

Estrella de Plata (Map 6; ☎ 93 319 60 07; Pla del Palau 9; tapas from €5; open Tues-Sat), not far from Cal Pep, is if anything a further cut above the rest in the classy tapas stakes.

Hofmann (Map 6; ☎ 93 319 58 89; Carrer de l'Argenteria 74; meals €40-50; open Mon-Fri) is tucked away upstairs in the plant-filled annexe to one of the city's renowned cuisine schools. Some of the nation's great chefs learned the trade here and you will not be disappointed with the present students' efforts. An imaginative and constantly changing menu keeps chefs and diners on their toes.

Espai Sucre (Map 6; ☎ 93 268 16 30; Carrer de la Princesa 53; meals €30; open dinner only Tues-Sat) is a singular minimalist temple of Barcelona haute cuisine. Here the cooks specialise in sweets (hence the name, Sugar Space), and you can choose from one of two set menus, either of which will have you in a delirium of sugar and spice. A few savoury dishes are also on offer, just to take the edge off all that sugar.

PLACES TO EAT

The Coolest Cats in Town

Modernisme has survived in the imagination as a wholly architectural and design phenomenon. In its time, however, it was a much broader, albeit in some respects effete, artistic 'movement'. On canvas, Ramon Casas and Santiago Rusiñol were the leading lights, although neither could pretend to greatness. Casas was something of a well-lined dandy. He and Rusiñol had both spent time in Parisian artistic circles, as had many other hopefuls and hangers-on. Among their pals were Miguel Utrillo, another painter, and Pere Romeu. The latter was an intriguing character who had dropped painting in favour of shadow puppetry. His hobbies ranged from swimming to cycling, from cabaret to sports cars.

From 1892 until 1899 Rusiñol, who thought he had developed new, symbolic ways of expression through his art, organised *festes modernistes* down in what was destined to become the eternal playground of Sitges. Somehow, these eccentric little get-togethers of artists, musicians, writers and partygoers seemed a little insubstantial and so, in 1897, it was decided to establish a permanent base.

Casas had the dosh, so he bought an early Modernista house (Josep Puig i Cadafalch's first creation) on Carrer de Montsió and entrusted its management to Romeu. It became a restaurant, bar and meeting place for the luminaries of Barcelona Modernisme, and came to be known as Els Quatre Gats (the Four Cats). In Catalan the expression also means 'a handful of people'. That handful consisted of Casas, Rusiñol, Romeu and Utrillo, who proceeded to organise all sorts of cultural get-togethers, from art exhibitions to concerts by such emerging composers as Isaac Albéniz and Enric Granados. The young - Picasso, in whom the Cats saw great potential, had his first exhibition here in 1900.

Of course Pere Romeu put on puppet shows, as often as not for children. A couple of anti-establishment magazines also emerged, and one of them, *Pèl & Ploma* (Paper & Pen), published an article on Picasso in 1901.

It was fun while it lasted, but it didn't last terribly long. By 1903 Els Quatre Gats had closed. The building was later taken over by a rather conservative art circle and underwent several metamorphoses before ending up as what it is today, a somewhat pricey restaurant feasting on its brief but much-glamorised past.

Abac (Map 6; ☎ 93 319 66 00; Carrer del Rec 79-89; meals €55-60; open Tues-Sat, & Mon evening) is rated by local gourmands one of the city's best restaurants. Great attention is paid to detail in this haven of classic cooking. The decor is minimalist, the service impeccable.

L'Eixample

You could easily miss **Tragaluz** (Map 2; ☎ 93 487 01 96; Passatge de la Concepció 5; meals with wine around €35) – but don't. It serves inventive Mediterranean cuisine (with an Italian leaning) and mouthwatering desserts – what about the *tarta de manzana con helado de dulce de leche* (apple pie with caramel ice cream!)? Directly across the road is **El Japonés** (open to midnight), the restaurant's Japanese branch.

At **Principal** (Map 2; ☎ 93 272 08 45; Carrer de Provença 286-288; meals €45) the Tragaluz group of restaurants has outdone itself with nouvelle eating in designer surrounds. You definitely want to be well dressed to get in here for the at times rather microscopic servings of admittedly fine delicacies. There is a garden out the back and the restaurant is frequently fully booked.

Drolma (Map 2; ☎ 93 496 77 10; Passeig de Gràcia 68; meals €65-80; open Mon-Sat) at Hotel Majèstic is a star in the Barcelonin culinary firmament – and a costly one. In a luxurious setting you will be served classic Catalan cuisine of the highest quality.

La Dama (Map 2; ☎ 93 202 06 86; Avinguda Diagonal 423; meals €40-50), at home in Modernista Casa Sayrach, is a luxury establishment with a leaning towards

Catalan-French cuisine. The wine list is very impressive.

International Cuisine Barcelona's first Japanese restaurant, **Yamadory** *(Map 4; ☎ 93 453 92 64; Carrer d'Aribau 68; meals €30-40; open Mon-Sat)*, is still one of its best.

Gràcia
Botafumeiro *(Map 2; ☎ 93 218 42 30; Carrer Gran de Gràcia 81; meals around €70)* is reputedly the place where shellfish is about as good as it gets in all Barcelona. It would want to be at these prices.

    Restaurant Roig Robí *(Map 2; ☎ 93 218 92 22; Carrer de Seneca 20; full meals €40-45)* is one of the city's more highly regarded top-end spots. Grab a quiet table by the windows or, in summer, in the little internal courtyard. The *mandonguilles de lluç amb bolets i sipia* (salt cod meatballs with mushrooms and cuttlefish) are delicious.

Sarrià
Via Veneto *(Map 3; ☎ 93 200 72 44; Carrer de Ganduxer 10; meals from €50; open Mon-Fri, & Sat evening)* is a real classic of the Barcelona high-cuisine scene. A meal here is a dress occasion that has occupied the number-one position (or close) in the city's high society for many a long year. Catalan dishes predominate, the service is impeccable and the desserts and post-prandial cheeses are impressive.

Tibidabo & Horta
La Balsa *(Map 1; ☎ 93 211 50 48; Carrer de la Infanta Isabel 4; full meals around €50; open Tues-Sat, Mon evening only)* is in a beautiful spot, and has a timber ceiling and scented gardens surrounding the open-terrace dining area, making it one of the city's top dining experiences. The menu changes frequently and is a mix of traditional Catalan and carefully off-centre inventiveness. In August it lets the plebs in for an all-you-can-eat buffet at €25. The food is not of so high a quality then, but the experience remains delightful.

    Gaig *(☎ 93 429 10 17; Passeig de Maragall 402; metro Horta; meals €45-50; open Tues-*

Sat & Sun lunch), with its charming interior garden in the back dining room, is a classic of Franco-Catalan cuisine in Barcelona. Carlos Gaig's motto is 'more than three elements in a dish is excessive'.

La Barceloneta
Merendero de la Mari *(Map 5; ☎ 93 221 31 41; Plaça Pau Vila 1; full meals €35; open Mon-Sat, & Sun lunch)* is probably the best of the restaurants lining the waterfront in the shadow of the Palau de Mar. The *fideua* is cooked to just the right point and the *salteado de gambitas* (sautéed shrimps) are delicious.

    Can Solé *(Map 5; ☎ 93 221 50 12; Carrer de Sant Carles 4; full meals €35; open Tues-Sat, & Sun lunch)* is the place to head for a real treat (and splurge). The food is superb, the desserts are to die for and the service is little short of amazing – when you're halfway through your fish, staff come and remove it and discreetly strip away all the bones for you.

    Restaurant Barceloneta *(Map 5; ☎ 93 221 21 11; L'Escar 22, Moll dels Pescadors; meals €50)* is a place where a booking is essential here and you should aim for a table on the balcony, from where you can contemplate the expensive yachts bobbing up and down. The paella is well prepared as are the fish dishes, but you are paying for the privilege.

    Torre d'Alta Mar *(Map 1; ☎ 93 221 00 07; Torre de Sant Sebastiá; meals €50-60; open Mon-Sat)* is an extraordinary addition to the high-class dining scene in Barcelona. Head up to the top of the Torre de Sant Sebastiá and instead of taking the cable car take a seat for fine seafood (and a few meat alternatives) and remarkable views across the city and out to sea.

El Poblenou
Restaurant Els Pescadors *(Map 1; ☎ 93 225 20 18; Plaça de Prim 1; full meals €35)* is on a small square still surrounded by local fishermen's houses. This fine place with a mainly seafood menu is excellent. Diners are attracted from far and wide to this otherwise fairly grubby, post-industrial part of town.

Entertainment

To get an idea of what's on, grab *Guía del Ocio* (€0.90), the city's weekly entertainment rag. It is not as complete as it could be but it is a good starting point.

For a better take on what's hip and what's not in bars and *discotecas* (clubs), you need to dig up the freebie magazines and booklets that are distributed around some of the cooler bars. They include *Micro* and *Go Mag*, both better than *Guía del Ocio* for getting a grip on the club and music scene.

BARS

You could write a book solely on Barcelona's bars (but it might not be good for your health), which run the gamut from wood-panelled wine cellars to bright waterfront places and trendy haunts sporting gimmicky modern designs. Each is a different scene. Some bars are very local, some are full of foreigners, some are favoured by students, others by the well-dressed middle classes. Some play great music, others are places for a quiet chat.

You can pay anything up to €3 for a bottle of beer (for the same quantity, draught costs less) – a lot depends on where and at what time you buy it. Mixed drinks start at about €3.50 but frequently cost €5 to €6.

Most bars are at their liveliest from around 11pm and close between 2am (Sunday to Thursday) and 3am (Friday and Saturday). A handful of places keep their doors open as late as 5am.

Barri Gòtic

Bar del Pi *(Map 6; Plaça de Sant Josep Oriol)*, a characterful little bar, has a mixed local clientele. You can sip an early evening aperitif outside on one of Barri Gòtic's nicest plazas.

Travel Bar *(Map 6; ☎ 93 342 52 52, fax 93 481 75 74; Carrer de la Boquería 27; open to 1am)* is a good place to meet up with other travellers and shoot the breeze.

Bar Roca *(Map 6; Carrer d'En Roca 14)* is a curiously dingy dive. Wander in and you'll

probably find yourself in the company of no more than a dozen or so punters, tippling or smoking spliffs and generally being laid back. Closing time is flexible.

Segunda Acto *(Map 6; Carrer d'En Roca 18)* is just a few doors down from Bar Roca and falls into the same category.

del Paradis *(Map 6; Carrer del Paradis; open to around 3am Wed-Sat)* is a reggae hideaway just off Plaça de Sant Jaume.

Glaciar *(Map 6; ☎ 93 302 11 63; Plaça Reial 3)* is a classic old bar that is popular with a young crowd of foreigners and locals in the evening.

Bar Malpaso *(Map 6; Carrer d'En Rauric 20)* fills at night with a young, casual crowd and plays great Latin and African music, although frequently the DJs indulge in only one musical theme or another – it takes a while to get into gear.

Schilling *(Map 6; ☎ 93 317 67 87; Carrer de Ferran 23; open 10am-2am)* is a much classier, low-lit place with a varied, gay-friendly clientele. Getting a table isn't always easy.

Al Limón Negro *(Map 6; Carrer dels Escudellers Blancs 3)* has decor that keeps changing, but it remains a favoured laid-back place for a few tipples until well into the night.

Shanghai *(Map 6; Carrer de N'Aglá 9)*, a few yards closer to the waterfront, is a humming but cosy place for a beer and a chat – you can actually hear yourself talk and you can get to the bar with little trouble.

Thiossan *(Map 6; Carrer del Vidre 3)* is a cool Senegalese haunt where you can get a bite to eat or just sit in mellow contentment listening to the African rhythms and allowing soothing ales to do their work.

Zoo *(Map 6; ☎ 93 302 77 28; Carrer dels Escudellers 33)* is a busy little watering hole. It caters to foreigners' desires for *sangría* but the place gets quite a few locals in too. Out the back is an interesting little restaurant, should hunger overtake your thirst.

Dot *(Map 6; ☎ 93 302 70 26; Carrer Nou de Sant Francesc 7; open to about 3am Sun-Thur,* *later Fri-Sat)* is one of the hippest hang-outs in this part of town. Each night the musical theme changes, from space funk on Friday and drum 'n' bass on Saturday to easy listening on Sunday.

Síncopa *(Map 6; Cnr Carrer d'Avinyó & Carrer de Milans)* is a place for lovers of self-conscious grunge. A short saunter brings you to nearby Plaça de George Orwell, which is surrounded by little bars, at their best when the summer terraces are in action.

Parnasse *(Map 6; ☎ 93 310 12 47; Carrer d'En Gignàs 21)* is tucked away in the backstreets near the main post office. You can drink anything here, from malt whisky to Screaming Orgasms.

El Raval

Long neglected, El Raval is getting attention from city planners and a new wave of tipplers. There are vague signs that what happened in the Born area is beginning to happen here – new bars and dance places are opening up breaches along the long, slummy alleys. Alongside them some great old harbour-style bars still thrive – dark, wood-panelled and bare except for the odd mirror and vast arrays of bottles behind the bar. What has changed is the clientele – the rough lads and seamen have been replaced by a young and somewhat grunge set. You won't see any *pijos* (rich kids) from the *Zona Alta* down here!

Boadas *(Map 6; ☎ 93 318 95 92; Carrer dels Tallers 1)*, off La Rambla, appears to be in a time warp. To pass by this place you'd hardly think of pushing open the door. Do it. Inside is one of the city's oldest and best cocktail bars. The bow-tied waiters have been serving up their poison since 1933. Joan Miró, among others, used to have a tipple in here.

L'Ovella Negra *(The Black Sheep; Map 6; ☎ 93 317 10 87; Carrer de les Sitges 5)* is a rather different story. It's a noisy, fun, barn-like tavern popular with a young set and has pool and *futbolín* (table football). It attracts a big foreign crowd.

Bar Marsella *(Map 6; Carrer de Sant Pau 65)* is one not to miss. It opened its doors in 1820 and still specialises in its *absenta*

(absinthe), a beverage hard to find because of its supposed narcotic qualities. Your glass of absinthe comes with a lump of sugar, a fork and a little bottle of mineral water. Hold the sugar on the fork, over your glass, and drip the water onto the sugar so that it dissolves into the absinthe, which turns yellow. The result should be a warm glow in you and a mellow atmosphere in the bar; however, at weekends the place is so crammed that mellow is not the word that springs to mind.

The Quiet Man *(Map 6; ☎ 93 412 12 19; Carrer del Marquès de Barberà 11)*, near Bar Marsella, is a relaxed Irish pub where you can occasionally hear live music.

Casa Almirall *(Map 6; Carrer de Joaquím Costa 33)* has been going since the 1860s. It's dark and intriguing, with Modernista decor and a mixed clientele. This is a busy little corner of Barcelona.

Granja de Gavà *(Map 6; Carrer de Joaquím Costa 37)* has an outsized statue of a big lady with a banana. In the building that houses this one-time bodega (wine cellar), now a relaxed little bar, the Barcelona writer Terenci Moix was born in 1942.

Benidorm *(Map 6; Carrer de Joaquím Costa 39)* is something of a throwback to the 1970s. A lone mirror ball brings flashes of light to the red walls of what could almost be someone's lounge. A good mix of music attracts foreigners and local journalism students.

Imprevist *(Map 4; ☎ 93 342 58 59; Carrer de Ferlandina 34)* is a recent addition to the area's crowd of drinking establishments. Not only can you sit down for a tipple, you can have some cake too. It's all very funky.

Café Que Pone Muebles Navarro *(Map 6; Carrer de la Riera Alta 4-6; open to around midnight Tues-Sun)* is an art-gallery-cum-lounge-cum-bar where you can get great cheesecake. It attracts an arty, studenty, hip kinda crowd. The name translates as 'Café Where The Sign Says Navarro Furniture'.

Salsitas *(Map 6; ☎ 93 318 08 40; Carrer Nou de la Rambla 22)* is one of a new brand of places gaining popularity in Barcelona – it's a restaurant, bar and club rolled into one. You'll need to book ahead if you want to eat as this cavernous place is always packed to the gills. Otherwise, later at night, just join the queue.

Milk House Café *(Map 6; Carrer Nou de la Rambla 24; open 10pm-3am daily)* is just down the road from Salsitas. You enter an ill-lit, predominantly red tube of a building. Immediately on your right is a bar and there's another deep at the other end. It's popular with a mixed clientele with a gay leaning.

Bar Pastís *(Map 6; ☎ 93 318 79 80; Carrer de Santa Mònica 4)* is a tiny old bar with a French cabaret theme (with lots of Piaf in the background). It's been going, on and off, since the end of WWII. Tuesday is live tango night – you'll need to be in here before 9pm to have a hope of sitting, getting near the bar or anything much else. On some other nights there are live acts here, usually performing French classics.

London Bar *(Map 6; ☎ 93 318 52 61; Carrer Nou de la Rambla 36; open to 5am Tues-Sun)* is your best bet if you still need a drink at 2.30am, when all or most of the other places have shut their doors. It occasionally stages off-the-wall music acts; a bottled beer costs about €3. Open since 1909, the bar started as a hang-out for circus hands and in later years was frequented by the likes of Picasso, Miró and Hemingway.

Kentucky *(Map 6; Carrer de l'Arc del Teatre; open until 5am Mon-Sat)* attracts all sorts of local types who mix with stray foreigners at its long American-style bar. For years it was a key haunt of visiting US Navy boys, but they don't come to town any more.

Bar Aurora *(Map 5; ☎ 93 442 30 44; Carrer de l'Aurora 7; admission €3; open 6am-3am)* is the place to head if you still haven't had enough or you are just emerging from the clubs and need a little more fuel or a slow landing. It starts getting punters in at 6am at weekends. One hour later it is heaving – you can barely move or breathe for all the people, drink and smoke. Punters on all speeds try to chat and dance amid the elbows.

La Ribera

Palau de Dalmases – Espai Barroc *(Map 6; ☎ 93 310 06 73; Carrer de Montcada 20; open 8pm-2am Tues-Sat, 6pm-10pm Sun)* has a baroque magnificence that is matched

by film-director Peter Greenaway–style luxury inside. You almost feel you should don a powdered wig to sip on your cocktails here, and on Thursday night you'll have live classical music or a few opera snippets playing in the background (from 11pm). The snag is the price – a glass of no-name wine costs about €6!

El Nus *(Map 6; Carrer dels Mirallers 5)* is a small, dim, chic bar in the narrow old streets near Església de Santa Maria del Mar, done out with pictures of its maharishi-lookalike owner. It's good for a quiet post-prandial drink.

Along and near Passeig del Born, which links Església de Santa Maria del Mar and the former Mercat de Born, you'll find stacks of bars. Since the early 1990s, when you could find little more than a couple of sad old bars for sad old punters, the place has been completely transformed. Worth a try are **El Copetín** *(Map 6; Passeig del Born 19)* for cocktails and **Miramelindo** *(Map 6; Passeig del Born 15)*, a spacious tavern.

La Tinaja *(Map 6; Carrer de l'Esparteria 9; open 5pm-2am daily)* was once a warehouse. Sitting at a small table by candlelight beneath the brick vaults, sipping on wine and indulging in a few snacks, is a pleasurable way to pass an evening.

Mudanzas *(Map 6; Carrer de la Vidrieria 15)* has been around for a lot longer. It's a popular little bar and you can often hear live music here. Around the corner, shady Plaça de les Olles is a charming little square in summer when the terraces are in operation.

La Vinya del Senyor *(Map 6; Plaça de Santa Maria del Mar)* is a nearby wine bar in a class of its own. Come here to taste a selection of wines and *cavas* (the Catalan version of champagne), accompanied by simple snacks.

Va de Vi *(Map 6; ☎ 93 319 29 00; Carrer dels Banys Vells 16; open 6pm-2am)* provides a wonderful Gothic setting – all heavy stone arches – in which to taste a broad selection of Spanish wines. You can also order nibbles.

Abaixadors 10 *(Map 6; Carrer dels Abaixadors 10; admission up to €8; open Wed-Sun)* is difficult to classify. You climb upstairs to a place divided up into several spaces – a low-lit theatre-bar where you can hear good music until about 3.30am, and another brighter bar with a restaurant attached. Once upon a time this was one of Barcelona's more intimate dance locales. The main drawback is the admission charge, which includes a drink.

Borneo (Map 6; ☎ 93 268 23 89; Carrer del Rec 49) is a busy bar with two levels and wide windows onto the street. If you are heading north off Passeig del Born, you would probably never think to trudge up Carrer del Rec to this place. Do it.

Gimlet (Map 6; ☎ 93 310 10 27; Carrer del Rec 24), across the road from Borneo and a few doors up, does some mean cocktails for about €5.

Suborn (Map 6; ☎ 93 310 11 10; Carrer de la Ribera 18; open to at least 2.30am Tues-Sun), near Parc de la Ciutadella, is several things to several people. After dabbling in original cuisine in the earlier part of the evening, the place gradually turns into a groovy little bar where you can dance to whatever the guest DJ is spinning.

La Barceloneta, Beaches & Port Olímpic

The Fastnet (Map 5; ☎ 93 295 30 05; Passeig de Joan de Borbó 22, La Barceloneta) has a clear nautical bent, from the naval charts on the ceiling to the ads for yacht hands by the bar. The place is perfectly designed for a late-afternoon drink, as it catches the last rays of the setting sun.

All the beaches have at least one little *chiringuito*, a covered beach bar where you can get drinks, ice creams and occasionally even snacks. They generally stay open until about 8pm. A particularly hip one, known as **DJ Zone** (Map 1), although it has no sign, is located at the southern end of Platja de Mar Bella.

The Port Olímpic yacht harbour is lined with bars and clubs, all with tables out front in the open air; some have good music inside too. The area is touristy and the bars brassy, with a reputation in many cases of being unsophisticated pick-up joints.

L'Eixample

La Bodegueta (Map 2; Rambla de Catalunya 100) is a classic wine cellar. Bottles and barrels line the walls and wooden stools surround the marble tables.

Michael Collins Pub (Map 2; ☎ 93 459 19 64; Plaça de la Sagrada Família 4; open noon-3am daily) is one of the city's best loved Irish pubs, a favourite with locals and expats alike.

Gràcia

Café del Sol (Map 2; ☎ 93 415 56 63; Plaça del Sol 16) is a lively bar on one of Gràcia's liveliest squares. It has tapas and tables outside and attracts a vaguely bohemian crowd.

Café Salambó (Map 2; Carrer de Torrijos 51) is a gentle designer haunt that imitates a village bar, with benches at low tables. It has an upper level with pool tables and food is available too.

Café la Virreina (Map 2; ☎ 93 237 98 80; Plaça de la Virreina), a block north of the Carrer de Torrijos and Carrer de la Perla intersection, is a relaxed place with a mixed-ages crowd, 1970s rock music, cheap hot *bocadillos* (filled rolls) and tables outside on the leafy square.

Buda (Map 2; Carrer del Torrent de l'Olla 134) puts on a reasonable mix of mainstream music but not so loudly that you can't talk. A couple of split-level floors reach back from the bar.

Check out Carrer de Mozart and the parallel Carrer de Francisco Giner, where about a dozen bars of widely varying nature compete for your attention.

Gusto (Map 2; Carrer de Francisco Giner 24; open 10pm-3am Wed-Sat) has spotlighted modern artworks hanging in an atmosphere otherwise dominated by the colour red and the smell of dope. It attracts a mostly young-20s crowd who sip mixed drinks while listening to 1980s music – clearly an anthropological exercise for the young nostalgics.

Sabor Cubano (Map 2; ☎ 93 217 35 41; Carrer de Francisco Giner 32; open 10pm-2.30am), ruled since 1992 by the charismatic Havana-born Angelito, is a simple den of *ron y son* (rum and sound). A mixed crowd of Cubans and fans of the Caribbean island come to drink *mojitos*, a rum-based drink, and shake their stuff down.

Bar Musical Zimbabwe (*Map 2; ☎ 679 56 62 77; Carrer de Mozart 13; open 8pm-2.30am*) sounded like a nice name to the couple from Equatorial Guinea who run this hang-out. Chill to the reggae, afro and funky rhythms over a cool beer or cocktail, or head around the back for a game of pool.

Maria (*Map 2; Carrer Maria 5; open to 2am mid-week, to 3am weekends*) has been a local pleaser for the past 20-odd years – even the music hasn't changed. Those longing for the days of rock 'n' roll crowd into this animated, dark bar, listen to the old hits and knock back beers.

Alfa (*Map 2; ☎ 93 415 18 24; Carrer Gran de Gràcia 36; open until 4am*) is a stalwart last resort for the inhabitants of Gràcia. It is divided into two parts: a sit-down bar as you enter and a no-frills dance area straight after, where the decibels are higher.

Western Gràcia/Avinguda Diagonal

The area around Carrer de Marià Cubí gets busy with locals at the weekend. It's a little on the *pijo* (posh) side, but can be fun all the

---

Castles in the Air

It's difficult to know how to classify making human castles, but to many a Catalan, the *castellers* (castle builders) are as serious in their sport as any footballer.

The 'building' of *castells* (castles) is particularly popular in central and southern Catalunya. *Colles* (teams) from various parts of Catalunya compete in the summer and you are most likely to see *castellers* in town festivals. The amateur sport began in the 1880s and although Barcelona's home teams are not among the best, it is always fun to watch. When teams from other towns come to compete, it can be quite exciting.

Without going into the complexities, the teams aim to erect human 'castles' of up to 10 storeys. These usually involve levels of three to five people standing on each others' shoulders. A crowd of team-mates and supporters forms a supporting scrum around the thickset lads at the base. To successfully complete the castle, a young (light!) child called the *anxaneta* must reach the top and signal with his/her hand. Sometimes the castle then falls in a heap (if it has not already done so) but successful completion also implies bringing the levels back down to earth in orderly fashion.

Home and away teams sometimes converge on Plaça de Catalunya, Plaça de Sant Jaume and other city squares for friendly competitions during the various festivals. Ask the tourist office for more details. Beyond Barcelona, competition events can be seen in many towns, including Vilafranca del Penedès and Tarragona.

JS

same. And it's not likely to be filled with tourists. Don't bother earlier in the week, as the area tends to be dead. The street is lined with bars of various types and should keep you well occupied for a night.

Mas i Mas *(Map 3; ☎ 93 209 45 02; Carrer de Marià Cubí 199)* is one of the area's best-known drinking spots.

Universal *(Map 3; ☎ 93 201 35 96; Carrer de Marià Cubí 182; open to 4.30am Mon-Sat)* is another must around here. It sometimes has live music.

El Poblenou

Here's another part of town that the flood of foreigners doesn't reach – Carrer de Zamora (metro Marina or Bogatell) is the place to head for.

Megataverna Ovella Negra *(Map 1; ☎ 93 309 59 38; Carrer de Zamora 78; open to 3am Thur-Sun)* is perfect if you prefer your bars to be barn-like. There's a handful of other drinking spots nearby.

Tibidabo

On Thursday to Saturday nights the long winding road down from Plaça del Doctor Andreu is lined with cars. This is one of the heartlands of so-called Pijolandia, where the young, well-off sophisticates come to tipple and dance.

Mirablau *(Map 1; ☎ 93 418 58 79; Plaça del Doctor Andreu; open to about 5am)* is a bar upstairs, from where you have unbeatable views across the entire city. Downstairs, get down to a little disco dancing. In summer, punters often spill out on to the small terrace.

Merbeyé *(Map 1; ☎ 93 417 92 79; Plaça del Doctor Andreu; open 11pm-3am)* is a more tranquil cocktail bar opposite Mirablau. It plays a good selection of mainstream music, past and present.

LIVE MUSIC

There's a good choice most nights of the week. Many venues double as bars and/or clubs. Starting time is rarely before 10pm and more often around midnight. Admission charges range from nothing to €20; the higher prices often include a drink.

Jazz fans are in for a treat in November, when the city's annual jazz festival is staged in bars across the city.

To see big-name acts, either Spanish or from abroad, you will probably pay more. They often perform at venues such as Palau Sant Jordi (capacity 17,000) on Montjuïc or the Teatre Mercat de les Flors, located at the foot of Montjuïc.

Barri Gòtic

Barcelona Pipa Club *(Map 6; ☎ 93 302 47 32; Plaça Reial 3; open to 2am or 3am)* generally has jazz from around midnight from Thursday to Saturday. It resembles someone's flat inside, with all sorts of little interconnecting rooms and knick-knacks – notably the pipes after which the place is named. You buzz at the door and head two floors up.

Harlem Jazz Club *(Map 6; ☎ 93 310 07 55; Carrer de la Comtessa de Sobradiel 8; admission up to €8; performances usually 11pm-2am Tues-Sun)* is a stalwart stop on the Barcelona jazz circuit, although there are sometimes other acts (including some rock and Latin music).

Jamboree *(Map 6; ☎ 93 301 75 64; Plaça Reial 17; admission up to €9)* offers a full program of varied jazz, blues and funk most nights, although it is sometimes closed on Sunday. The place becomes a club after the live stuff ends.

Sala Tarantos *(Map 6; ☎ 93 318 30 67; Plaça Reial 17; admission around €10)*, next door to Jamboree, sometimes puts on reasonable flamenco – most often on Friday and Saturday at midnight.

Sidecar *(Map 6; ☎ 93 302 15 86; Carrer de Heures 4-6; admission up to €8; open to around 3am)*, just off Plaça Reial, presents pop and rock bands of various denominations several nights a week, usually starting at 11pm. Upstairs is an open-plan bar looking onto the square. Head downstairs for the dance area, a red-tinged dungeon.

El Raval

Jazz Sí Club *(Map 4; ☎ 93 329 00 20; Carrer de Requesens 2; open 9pm-11pm)* could not be more hidden away. This tiny, crumpled little place with the air of a neighbourhood social centre occasionally attracts some good jazz and, given its hours, is a mellow way to start the evening.

La Ribera

El Foro (Map 6; ☎ 93 310 10 20; Carrer de la Princesa 53; admission varies; usually open from 11pm Wed-Sun) has jazz, tango and other music sessions. This place, with a restaurant and bar upstairs and a club downstairs, attracts a broad range of acts as well as punters.

L'Hivernacle (Map 6; ☎ 93 413 24 00; Passeige de Picasso), apart from being a charming café in the midst of the greenery of this arboretum in Parc de la Ciutadella, also puts on frequent jazz sessions.

Little Italy (Map 6; ☎ 93 319 79 73; Carrer del Rec 30; open Mon-Sat) is better known as an eatery but offers live jazz from 10pm on Wednesday and Thursday night.

Poble Sec

Club Apolo (Map 5; ☎ 93 441 40 01; Carrer Nou de la Rambla 113; big-name bands €9) is the place for world music – chiefly African, Latin and Spanish – from 10.30pm several nights a week. Big-name bands are followed by live salsa or, on Friday and Saturday, the DJ team Nitsaclub.

Gràcia

Teatreneu (Map 2; ☎ 93 284 77 33; Carrer de Terol 26) occasionally stages concerts, ranging from techno to acid jazz. Check if anything is on the program. Otherwise, you can just wander into their pleasant bar (☎ 93 284 48 96).

The first two places listed below are within a few blocks of Avinguda Diagonal; the nearest train stations are Diagonal (metro), Hospital Clínic (metro) and Gràcia (FGC).

La Boîte (Map 3; ☎ 93 319 17 89; Avinguda Diagonal 477; admission €6-12) is one of the classic live-music haunts of Barcelona and offers jazz, rhythm and blues, and swing, with the occasional jam session several nights a week at midnight. Later on the place becomes a club.

Luz de Gas (Map 2; ☎ 93 209 77 11; Carrer de Muntaner 246; admission up to €20) has live soul, country, salsa, rock, jazz or pop most nights at midnight or 1am.

Bikini (Map 3; ☎ 93 322 00 05; Carrer de Déu i Mata 105; admission €11-20; open midnight-5am Tues-Sat) is a multi-hall dance space that frequently stages quality acts ranging from funk guitar to rock.

The Sutton Club (Map 2; ☎ 93 414 42 17; Carrer de Tuset 13) puts on regular concerts in what was once one of the city's grand old dance halls. About 1400 people can squeeze in here. Admission depends on the group playing.

Cova del Drac (Map 3; ☎ 93 200 70 32; Carrer de Vallmajor 33; admission free; open Tues-Sun), also known as Jazzroom, is a good spot for jazz sessions most nights of the week. Admission is free but drinks can be expensive. A taxi is the best way to get here.

El Clot

Savannah (Map 1; ☎ 93 231 38 77; Carrer de la Muntanya 16; metro Clot; admission up to €10; open to midnight Sun, to 3am Tues-Thur, to 5am Fri & Sat) is one of the city's big clubs that allows rock bands on stage a few nights a week, often starting at around 10.30pm.

DISCOTECAS

Barcelona's clubs (or discotecas to locals) come alive from about 2am until 5am or 6am, and are best on Thursday, Friday and Saturday night.

As anywhere else, it is a constantly changing scene, but the city is also littered with some old favourites. Different parts of town offer a widely varying flavour. Down in the labyrinth of the old town lurks a surprising variety of spots, ranging from plush former old-time dance halls to grungy subterranean dance venues that fill to bursting. They attract a broad range of inner-city folk, tourists and the occasional curious Barcelonins from other parts of town. Up in Gràcia is a handful of places of similar ilk.

Along the waterfront it's completely another ball game. The Maremàgnum complex hosts a series of blaring discos with

OLIVER STREWE

GUY MOBERLY

PASCALE BEROUJON

OLIVER STREWE

GUY MOBERLY

The aromas of Barcelona (clockwise from top left): the pick of the crop at Mercat de la Boqueria; some *rovellons* (mushrooms) at a street stall; tapas for all tastes; paella, which gets its name from the pan used for cooking over an open wood fire; candy for kids

Just sit back and enjoy (clockwise from top left): *sangría* and sunshine on Plaça Reial; whip up a dessert storm and indulge in a caramel flan; sniff out fresh bread at a bakery; wash down Spanish delicacies with a glass of *vi* (wine); hot chicks at Los Caracoles Restaurant, Ciutat Vella

MARTIN MOOS

OLIVER STREWE

OLIVER STREWE

NEIL SETCHFIELD

OLIVER STREWE

go-go girls and strobe lighting. This place fills up with a mix of foreigners attracted by the bright lights and local youngsters. Further north at Port Olímpic a sunscorched crowd of visiting yacht folk mixes it up with tourists and a sprinkling of locals.

Class, they will tell you, is reserved for L'Eixample and the Zona Alta (literally the 'High Zone', the area up towards Tibidabo). A sprinkling of well-known clubs is spread out over these parts of town. As a rule of thumb they attract a beautiful crowd, although that is in the eye of the beholder. There is no reason not to cross over from one reality to be part of another, but it is amazing how many locals don't!

A new trend in Barcelona is the restaurant-club. You come to dine (say around 9pm or 10pm), and from about midnight on the tables are cleared away and you go into club mode. No taxis, no endless discussions in the street along the lines of, 'OK, where to now?'. It's catching on.

Some of the well-known clubs stage live music before converting into clubs (see Live Music earlier in this chapter). Cover charges range from nothing to as much as €12. It depends partly on how busy the place is and whether the bouncers like your look (dress smartly to be sure of admission). If you go early, you'll often pay less. In almost all cases the admission price includes your first drink. After that you're on your own – a beer can easily cost €5.

La Rambla & Barri Gòtic

Panams (Map 6; ☎ 93 302 20 09; La Rambla 27; open midnight-5.30am) can only be described as bizarre. It's basically a dance dive but a fun one. You have two options: go downstairs for the live sex show or upstairs for the dancing. A dance floor spreads away from the bar with no concessions to luxury but the music is consistently good and rocky. This is not for club sophisticates.

Jamboree (Map 6; see Live Music earlier) becomes a crowded dance scene from around 1.30am, after the live stuff finishes. It has two spaces – one for Latin rhythms, the other for rock.

Karma (Map 6; ☎ 93 302 56 80; Plaça Reial 10; admission usually €8; open around midnight-5am Tues-Sun) is a young, student-type basement place with good music. Admission covers a drink. It can get so packed you can barely move – thank God for the air-conditioning!

El Raval

Enfants (Map 6; ☎ 93 412 00 48; Carrer Guàrdia 3; admission €7; open 11pm-4am Thur-Sat) is a longtime Raval dance dive. The main open dance floor is flanked by a couple of others to either side, one with bar (drinks cost around €7). The music is fairly light House. Early in 2002 the Muzakclub DJ team moved in.

Moog (Map 6; ☎ 93 318 59 66; Carrer de l'Arc del Teatre 3; admission €6; open to about 6am Fri & Sat), a fun club, plays Latin and dance hits from as far back as the 1970s upstairs; downstairs it has strobe lights and techno music.

La Paloma (Map 4; ☎ 93 301 68 97; Carrer del Tigre 27; admission €6; open to about 6am) has the Bongo Lounge DJ team on Thursday and Friday nights from about 2.30am (drinks around €8). This is one of the city's last functioning old-time dance halls, but on these nights a strange metamorphosis takes place as the big band gives way to DJs spinning techno. It is a remarkable place from another age.

La Ribera

Luz de Luna (Map 6; ☎ 93 310 75 42; Carrer del Comerç 21; open to about 4am/6am midweek/weekends) is a sassy salsa place, where early in the week you can sip on piña coladas and other South American mixes and dance on the luridly decorated dance floor. Midweek, it fills up from around 2am.

Magic (Map 6; ☎ 93 310 72 67; Passeig de Picasso 40; open 11pm-5am Wed-Sun) is a more straightforward dance place. It sometimes gets live acts but it's basically a club playing a mixture of rock, dance favourites and Spanish pop.

República (Map 6; ☎ 93 300 40 17; Estació França; admission €12) is the latest reincarnation of a Barcelona classic, the former Fellini, in the basement of Estació França. All sorts of theme nights take place in the various dance spaces here, with DJs from all over the country and abroad.

Port Vell

A bevy of bars and clubs in the Maremàgnum complex stay open until the wee hours. In July and August the place is particularly popular.

Boîte Nayandei (Map 5; ☎ 93 225 80 10; Maremàgnum complex; open to 5am nightly) is one of the places to watch for – it's a huge strobe-lit place on the top floor of the Maremàgnum complex.

Other possibilities range from Irish pubs to salsa spots such as **Mojito Bar** (Map 5; ☎ 93 225 80 14; open to 5am nightly). You can get salsa lessons here every evening. In the heat of the summer all these places throw open all doors to let in whatever breeze might come in off the harbour.

Beaches & Port Olímpic

Baja Beach Club (Map 1; ☎ 93 225 91 00; Passeig Marítim; open to 5am Thur-Sun), right on the beach, is the most interesting of the clubs here, although it loosely falls into the meat-market category.

L'Eixample

Row (Map 2; ☎ 93 205 80 70; Carrer del Rosselló 208; open 11.30pm-5am Thur-Sat), in a big 1980s designer bar, is one of the city's club hits. Row's DJ team, with plenty of foreign guests, mixes up a set of vanguard House Thursday to Saturday – it is a favourite with Barcelona's clubbers.

Satanassa (Map 4; ☎ 93 451 00 52; Carrer d'Aribau 27; admission free; open 11pm-4am) is an 'antidesign' haunt of androgynous people (with a notable gay leaning), with gaudy erotic murals.

Velvet (Map 2; ☎ 93 217 67 14; Carrer de Balmes 161) is a smallish, designer bar and club inspired by the film Blue Velvet, which plays 1960s music. It is busy with a fairly straight crowd.

La Fira (Map 2; Carrer de Provença 171; admission €8; open 11pm-5am) is a designer bar with a difference. You wander in past distorting mirrors and ancient fairground attractions from Germany. Put in coins and listen to hens squawk. Speaking of squawking, the music swings wildly from 1990s hits to Spanish pop classics. The place attracts a young and beautiful crowd.

Sala Cibeles (Map 2; ☎ 93 457 38 77; Carrer de Còrsega 363; open midnight-5.30am) was long the area's dance-hall magnet for old-time shakers. That's all changed and late into the night it booms to the latest sounds in club music. Theme nights alternate. Mond Club stages indie music on Friday.

Fuse (Map 2; ☎ 93 481 31 74; Carrer de Roger de Llúria 40) is one of Barcelona's most popular dance havens. The DJs spin an eclectic mix of House and related rhythms, and at weekends you may find yourself emerging on the streets at 10am! It is also in the vanguard of the restaurant-club trend in Barcelona. Eat, drink and dance till you drop, all in the same place!

Razzmatazz (Map 2; ☎ 93 320 82 00; Carrer dels Almogàvers 122; open 1am-6am Fri & Sat) is the latest reincarnation of what has long been one of Barcelona's key clubs. The place is huge and divided into several parts. The Razz Club drums up indie, techno and pop-rock whereas The Loft is all about electronic dance music.

Gràcia & Around Avinguda Diagonal

KGB (Map 1; ☎ 93 210 59 06; Carrer de Ca l'Alegre de Dalt 55; open 1am-6am Fri & Sat) maintains a hard-rock warehouse-type scene and is for tireless all-nighters.

Otto Zutz (Map 2; ☎ 93 238 07 22; Carrer de Lincoln 15; admission €12), west of Via Augusta, is for beautiful people (the bouncers will decide how beautiful you are) and those who favour wearing black.

Luz de Gas (Map 2; ☎ 93 209 77 11; Carrer de Muntaner 246; admission up to €15) converts to heaving club once any live acts have given up the stage (see Live Music earlier in this chapter). The music is a good mix of rock and mainstream dance tunes. Indeed it is very much a mainstream club with a fairly heavy air of the pick-up culture.

Lolita *(Map 3; ☎ 93 272 09 10; Plaça de Joan Llongueras; admission €12; open midnight-6am Fri & Sat)* is devoted to electronic dance music with DJs from both Barcelona and beyond.

Vlad *(Map 3; Plaça de Joan Llongueras; open 7.30pm-3am Sun-Wed)*, right next door to Lolita, serves up yet more electro stuff in a chilled environment on those evenings of the week when most good people are tucked up in bed. That partly explains the more moderate opening hours.

Up & Down *(Map 3; ☎ 93 205 51 94; Carrer de Numància 179; open Tues-Sat)* is another option. There's not much point in arriving before 1am at this club. The upstairs half is for an older clientele while bright young solvent Barcelonins head downstairs and try to score with one another.

Bikini *(Map 3; ☎ 93 322 00 05; Carrer de Déu i Mata 105; admission €11-20; open midnight-5am Tues-Sat)*, with dance spaces devoted to Latin, funk, House and dance pop, is frequently a stage for live acts earlier in the night (see Live Music earlier).

Tibidabo

Atlàntic Club *(Map 1; ☎ 93 418 52 94; Avinguda del Tibidabo 50; admission €8; open 10pm-5am Thur-Sat)* is a startling mansion with many storeys, turned into club. From the cool terrace outside you enjoy views as far as Montjuïc. Dance inside to a broad mix of oldies, Spanish and foreign pop and some vaguely Housey numbers – the mixed music attracts a mixed crowd.

Rosebud *(Map 1; ☎ 93 418 88 85; Carrer d'Adriá Margarit 27; open 9am-5am)*, inspired in name only by the film *Citizen Kane* is an assault on the senses with blaring music, flashing lights and go-go dancers to keep punters in rhythm. From Tibidabo, it looks like an enormous glass enclosure.

Montjuïc & Poble Sec

Torres de Ávila *(Map 7; ☎ 93 424 93 09; Poble Espanyol; admission €7; open 11pm-5am Thur-Sat)* is the most original of several lively bars at the Poble Espanyol. It's inside the tall entrance towers themselves. Created by designer Javier Mariscal (responsible for the Olympics mascot Cobi in 1992), it has several levels and all sorts of surreal touches, including an egg-shaped room and glass lifts that you fear will shoot you through the roof.

Terrrazza *(Map 7; ☎ 93 423 12 85; Avinguda del Marquès de Comillas; open Fri & Sat)* is the place to head to when Torres de Ávila starts dying down. It is one of the most popular summertime dance spots in town. It's out the back of the Poble Espanyol. During winter it goes indoors and becomes **Discothèque**.

Club Apolo *(Map 5; ☎ 93 441 40 01; Carrer Nou de la Rambla 113, Poble Sec; admission up to €12)* plays a range of ethnic, funk, House, soul, and rhythm and blues from 1.30am on. Nitsaclub is the Friday and Saturday DJ team.

El Clot & Beyond

Savannah *(Map 1; ☎ 93 231 38 77; Carrer de la Muntanya 16; metro Clot; admission up to €10; open to midnight Sun, 3am Tues-Thur, 5am Fri & Sat)* plays good dance music and is one of the city's big clubs. See also Live Music earlier in this chapter.

Fish *(Passeig de Sant Andreu s/n; admission €10; open midnight-6am Fri & Sat)*, in the Heron City mall complex, is quite simply the city's most enormous club, with space for 4000 heaving bods.

GAY & LESBIAN VENUES
Barri Gòtic & El Raval

Antinous *(Map 6; ☎ 93 301 90 70; Carrer de Josep Anselm Clavé 6, Barri Gòtic)* is a gay bookshop and café.

Bar La Concha *(Map 6; Carrer de la Guàrdia 14; open to 3am)* is in El Raval. If it were a theme bar, the theme would be the actress from Castilla–La Mancha, Sara Montiel. The place is covered in more than 250 photos of her, which seem to be the big attraction for a largely gay and transvestite crowd. The music ranges from *paso dobles* (the Spanish quickstep) to modern Spanish hits.

L'Eixample

Three good gay bars, located virtually next door to each other, are at the core of what has come to be known as the 'Gaixample'. These are:

Punto BCN *(Map 4; ☎ 93 453 61 23; Carrer de Muntaner 63-65)* is a relaxed place to meet a 30-something plus crowd.

Dietrich *(Map 4; Carrer del Consell de Cent 255; open to about 3am)*, a big, friendly place around the corner from Punto BCN, is more of a theatre-café, often with very camp entertainment.

Átame *(Map 4; Carrer del Consell de Cent 257)* is perhaps a tad more self-conscious.

Gràcia

Café de la Calle *(Map 2; Carrer de Vic 11)* is a cosy meeting place for lesbians and gays.

Bahía *(Map 2; Carrer de Seneca 12; open to about 2.30am)* is a good lesbian bar.

Member's *(Map 2; ☎ 93 237 12 04; Carrer de Seneca 3)*, which is nearby, is another. Both Member's and Bahía, though, are open to all comers.

La Rosa *(Map 3; ☎ 93 414 61 66; Passatge de Brusi 39)* is more exclusively lesbian.

Discotecas

The two top gay clubs are **Metro** *(Map 4; ☎ 93 323 52 27; Carrer de Sepúlveda 185)*, near Plaça de la Universitat, and **Martin's** *(Map 2; ☎ 93 218 71 67; Passeig de Gràcia 130)*. Metro attracts some lesbians and heteros as well as gay men. It's packed for its regular Monday-night cabarets and other shows are staged during the week. Martin's is for gay men only. Both open from midnight to 5am and have dark rooms.

Arena *(Map 4; ☎ 93 487 83 42; Carrer de Balmes 32; open midnight-5am)* is popular with a young, cruisy gay crowd. It has a dark room.

Arena Clasic *(Map 4; ☎ 93 487 83 42; Carrer de la Diputació 233)*, just around the corner from Arena, is a little more sedate.

Arena VIP & Dandy *(Map 4; Gran Via de les Corts Catalanes 593; open midnight-dawn)* are more mixed, mainstream locales with a gay flavour. They share the same building but have different entrances.

Salvation *(Map 5; ☎ 93 318 06 86; Ronda de Sant Pere 19-21; open Fri & Sat)* is another good *discoteca* that doesn't get started until

around about 3am. Lots of magazine-model barmen keep you well lubricated as you switch from the House dance floor to the rock hits section.

CLASSICAL MUSIC & OPERA

Guía del Ocio has ample listings, but the monthly *Informatiu Musical* leaflet has the best coverage of classical music (as well as other genres). You can pick it up at tourist offices and the **Palau de la Virreina** *(Map 6; ☎ 93 301 77 75; La Rambla de Sant Josep 99)*, which also sells tickets for many events. You will see from the leaflet that recitals take place all over the city and beyond, and venues include theatres, museums and monasteries.

The easiest way to get hold of tickets for most of the venues listed and for other theatres throughout the city is through the **Caixa de Catalunya's Tel-Entrada service** *(☎ 902 10 12 12; W www.telentrada.com)* or **ServiCaixa** *(☎ 902 33 22 11; W www.servicaixa.com)*. There's also a ticket office on the ground floor of the Corte Inglés on Plaça de Catalunya and at the FNAC store on the same square.

To get half price on some tickets, you can buy them personally at the Caixa de Catalunya desk in the **tourist office** *(Map 6)* on Plaça de Catalunya. To qualify, you must purchase the tickets in person no more than three hours before the start of the show you wish to see. The system is known as Tiquet-3. In the *Guía del Ocio*, shows for which you can get such tickets are marked with an asterisk.

Gran Teatre del Liceu *(Map 6; ☎ 93 485 99 13; W www.liceubarcelona.com; La Rambla 51-59)*, Barcelona's grand old opera house, reopened in September 1999, more than five years after being destroyed by fire, as one of the most technologically advanced theatres in the world. Apart from opera, you can see performances by world-class dance companies or attend classical-music concerts and recitals. Tickets can cost anything from €5 for a cheap seat behind a pillar to €50 for a well-positioned night at the opera. You will need to book well in advance for the big shows.

ENTERTAINMENT

Palau de la Música Catalana *(Map 6; ☎ 93 295 72 00; Carrer de Sant Pere més alt 11)*, in La Ribera, is Barcelona's chief venue for classical and choral music. It has a busy and wide-ranging program. Attending a concert here is also a fine way to see the gorgeous interior of this Modernista building. You could easily find yourself paying from €5 to €90 for the more prestigious international performances.

L'Auditori *(Map 1; ☎ 93 247 93 00; Carrer de Lepant 150)* swung into action in the late 1990s. Barcelona's impressive (if rather bland compared with the Palau) new home for serious music lovers, L'Auditori puts on plenty of orchestral, chamber, religious and other music throughout the year. You can often hear fine performances (Catalan Jordi Savall's baroque music, for instance) for around €8 to €42.

Palau Sant Jordi *(Map 7; Montjuïc)* is occasionally used for bigger concerts.

Teatre Mercat de les Flors *(Map 7; ☎ 93 426 18 75; Carrer de Lleida 59)*, at the foot of Montjuïc, is an important venue for music, dance and drama.

Palau Robert *(Map 2; ☎ 93 238 40 00; Passeig de Gràcia 107)* hosts concerts once a month in the gardens.

CINEMAS

A ticket usually costs around €5.25 to €5.60 but most cinemas have a weekly *día del espectador* (viewer's day), often Monday or Wednesday, when they charge around €4.

Foreign films, shown with subtitles and original soundtrack rather than dubbed, are marked 'v.o.' *(versión original)* in movie listings. Cinemas to check for these include the following:

Casablanca (Map 2; ☎ 93 218 43 45) Passeig de Gràcia 115
Maldà (Map 6; ☎ 93 317 85 29) Carrer del Pi 5
Renoir Floridablanca (Map 4) Carrer de Floridablanca 135
Renoir-Les Corts (Map 3; ☎ 93 490 55 10) Carrer de Eugeni d'Ors 12
Verdi (Map 2; ☎ 93 238 79 90) Carrer de Verdi 32
Verdi Park (Map 2; ☎ 93 238 79 90) Carrer de Torrijos 49

Yelmo Cineplex Icària (Map 1; ☎ 93 221 75 85) Carrer de Salvador Espriu 61

Filmoteca *(Map 3; ☎ 93 410 75 90; Avinguda de Sarrià 31-33)* specialises in film seasons that concentrate on particular directors, styles and eras of film.

Méliès Cinemes *(Map 4; ☎ 93 451 00 51; Carrer de Villarroel 102)* shows old classics in the original language.

THEATRE

Theatre is nearly all in Catalan or Spanish *(Guía del Ocio* specifies which). For all that's happening in theatre head for the arts information office in **Palau de la Virreina** *(Map 6; ☎ 93 301 77 75; La Rambla de Sant Josep 99)*. Look for the many leaflets and the monthly listings guide *Teatre BCN*.

Keep your eyes peeled for any of the eccentric (if not downright crazed) performances of Barcelona's La Fura dels Baus theatre group. It has won worldwide acclaim for its brand of startling, often acrobatic, theatre in which the audience is frequently dragged into the chaos.

Teatre Lliure de Gràcia *(Map 2; ☎ 93 218 92 51; Carrer de Montseny 47)* in Gràcia is dedicated to theatre in Catalan – if you're into the language you can see anything from the classics to the latest avant-garde productions. Actors play on a stage located in the middle of the theatre, surrounded by the audience.

Teatre Lliure – Espai Lliure *(Map 7; ☎ 93 228 97 47; Plaça de Margarida Xirgu 1)* opened up in the former Palau de l'Agricultura building on Montjuïc (opposite the Museu d'Arqueologia) in 2001. A restaurant on the premises makes a night out here easier. Like its sister theatre in Gràcia, it puts on a broad range of pieces in Catalan.

Artenbrut *(Map 2; ☎ 93 457 97 05; Carrer del Perill 9-11)* concentrates more on new and rising directors. Performances are usually in Catalan and occasionally in Castilian.

Teatre Malic *(Map 6; ☎ 93 310 70 35; Carrer de la Fusina 3)* is a relatively small spot that offers a packed program including music, alternative theatre and a mix of better-known local talent and emerging genius.

Teatre Nou Tantarantana (Map 5; ☎ 93 441 70 22; Carrer de les Flors 22), apart from staging all sorts of contemporary theatre, also puts on kids' shows, including pantomime, puppets and so on. These shows start at 6pm.

Teatre Nacional de Catalunya (Map 1; ☎ 93 306 57 07; Plaça de les Arts 1; metro Glòries) was originally destined to become the home of Catalan theatre. Ricard Bofill's ultra-neoclassical theatre opened its doors in 1997. So far it has put on a mixed bag of (not always exciting) theatre but it is worth keeping an eye on the program.

Teatre Victòria (Map 5; ☎ 93 443 29 29; Avinguda del Paral.lel 67-69) often stages ballet and contemporary dance but otherwise is used by well-known companies such as Tricicle. This trio of comic mimes has been doing the rounds with their version of 'intelligent humour' for 20 years. The good thing about these guys is that anyone can enjoy the fun because language is not an issue.

Teatre Principal (Map 6; ☎ 93 301 47 50; La Rambla 27) opened again in 1998 after a long absence and tends to stage a hotchpotch of theatre and musicals.

Teatre Romea (Map 6; ☎ 93 317 71 89; Carrer de l'Hospital 51) puts on a range of interesting plays, generally classics, in both Catalan and Castilian. In 2002, the offerings included modern renditions of *Macbeth* and *Woyzeck*.

Teatre Llantiol (Map 5; ☎ 93 329 90 09; Carrer de la Rierreta 7) is a curious little place on a dark alley in El Raval. It stages all sorts of stuff, from concerts and ballads to magic shows. This unlikely backstreet happens to be the home of a nest of artists' studios.

DANCE
Sardana

The *sardana*, Catalunya's national dance, is danced every week – except sometimes in August – on **Plaça de la Seu** in front of the cathedral at 6.30pm on Saturday and at noon on Sunday. These are not shows for tourists but feature ordinary Catalans doing something they enjoy. The dancers join hands to form ever-widening circles, placing their bags or coats in the centre. The dance is intricate but, in true Catalan style, hardly flamboyant. The steps and the accompanying brass and reed music are rather sedate; at times jolly, at times melancholy, rising to occasional crescendos, then quietening down again. It's a bit of an acquired taste. For more details see the boxed text 'A Slow Number' in the Facts about Barcelona chapter.

Flamenco

Although quite a few important flamenco artists grew up in the *gitano barrios* (Gypsy districts) of Barcelona, seeing good performances of this essentially Andalucian dance and music here is not so easy. A few tacky *tablaos*, where punters see flamenco while eating dinner, are scattered about. On occasion class acts perform here, but you need to be in the know; otherwise, it's rather second class and touristy.

El Tablao de Carmen (Map 7; ☎ 93 325 68 95; Carrer dels Arcs 9) is in the Poble Espanyol, while **Tablao Cordobés** (Map 6; ☎ 93 317 66 53) is at La Rambla 35. Make sure you book ahead.

Sala Tarantos (Map 6; ☎ 93 318 30 67; Plaça Reial 17) is another place to look out for (see Live Music earlier in this chapter for more details).

CASINO

Gran Casino de Barcelona (Map 1; ☎ 93 225 78 78; Carrer de la Marina 19-21; open 1pm-5am daily), in Port Olímpic, is the place for you if you feel either lucky or unfairly endowed in the fiscal department. Apart from the usual one-armed bandits and more sophisticated games, there are restaurants, bars and a club.

SPECTATOR SPORTS
Football

Barcelona Football Club has not only one of Europe's best teams, Barça, but also one of its best stadiums – the 120,000-capacity **Camp Nou** (Map 1; metro Collblanc), near Zona Universitària in the west of the city. Games are quite an occasion as long as the opposition is good enough to fire up the home team. Tickets for national league

The Boots of Barça

In 1895, a group of English residents kicked off a local football tournament in Barcelona. This odd activity, imported from Perfidious Albion, caught on. The first local club to be formed was Palamós (still in 2nd division) in 1898. On 29 November of the following year, FC Barcelona came into being.

Competition didn't really get going until the following year when three more groups formed. These were L'Hispània, l'Irish and the Societat Espanyola de Futbol (which kept changing its name but always retained the 'Espanyol' bit). Interestingly, the latter was the only one to permit only Spanish players. The bulk of FC Barcelona's players were English, German and Swiss, with only a few token Catalans. Some would mutter that things haven't changed much today! L'Hispània was mostly Scottish and there are no prizes for guessing who filled the ranks of l'Irish.

In November 1900, the dozen or so teams that then existed formed a league, with four of them (including FC Barcelona) in the first division. The Copa Macaya, Catalunya's first championship, which was fought out the following month, saw the Scots of L'Hispània take the honours. Thus began Catalan football.

In the meantime, football was spreading across the rest of Spain. In 1902 the first national championships, the Campeonato de Copa de España (later known as the Copa del Rey, Spain's equivalent of the British FA Cup) were staged. Barcelona went under to Biscaia 2-1.

By 1910, FC Barcelona was the premier club in a rapidly growing local league. The red and blue colours were already well known and the first signs of professionalism in the game emerged – paid transfers of players were recorded and Espanyol's management charged spectators. Barça had 560 members (about 110,000 today), who were all mighty chuffed at the team's victory at that year's national championship.

Antagonism between Catalan FC Barcelona and Castilian Spanish Espanyol (not to mention from Madrid's premier team, Real Madrid) was often cause for violent contests before the civil war – FC Barcelona fans will tell you it was a constant struggle against dodgy decisions in the national league. After Franco's victory in 1939, things didn't get any easier, but massive migration in the 1950s and '60s brought new players and supporters – it was one way for newcomers to integrate into local society. The team was for its supporters a potent Catalan symbol during the Franco years and remains so today.

Barça remains one of Spain's great teams – one of only three (along with Real Madrid and Athletic de Bilbao) never to have been relegated to the second division. Since the league got fully under way in 1928, Barça has emerged champion 16 times, second only to arch rivals Real Madrid (with 29 victories). Between them the two have virtually monopolised the game – only seven other teams have managed to come out on top (three of them only once or twice) in more than 60 years of the competition.

Outside the first division championship, Barcelona has emerged as the top cup-winning team in Spain. The side has grabbed 24 Copas del Rey (Real Madrid has won 17), four UEFA Cups (Real Madrid has taken two) and four Cup Winner's Cups (Real Madrid has yet to lay its hands on this trophy). The European Champions League has been more of a struggle. Barcelona took it in 1998, but lags well behind Real Madrid's record eight trophies.

The 2001-2002 season was disappointing for fans used to victory; Barça failed to win any of the national competitions.

games are available at the stadium and through the ServiCaixa ticketing service and cost from €18 to €90, depending on the seat and match. For more information call ☎ 93 496 36 00. Tickets go on sale on the Monday before the match. During the week the box office at the stadium opens from 9am to 1.30pm and 3.30pm to 6pm. It opens again on Saturday morning and in the afternoon until the game starts. If the match is on Sunday, it opens Saturday morning only and then on Sunday as well until the match starts. Usually tickets are *not* available for matches with Real Madrid, the club's arch rivals.

The city's other club, Espanyol, based at the **Estadi Olímpic** *(Map 7; Montjuïc)*, traditionally plays a quiet second fiddle (in the top division) to Barça, although they can shape up the star side every now and then.

Bullfights

Death in the Afternoon is not a favourite Catalan theme, but there are some fights on Sunday afternoon in spring and summer at the **Plaça de Braus Monumental** *(Map 1; ☎ 93 245 58 02; Cnr Gran Via de les Corts Catalanes & Carrer de la Marina; metro Monumental)*. The 'fun' usually starts at 6pm. Tickets are available at the arena from 10.30am to 2pm and 6pm to 7pm Wednesday to Saturday, from 10am on Sunday, or by phoning ☎ 902 33 22 11. Prices range from €15 to €75, the latter is for the front row in the shade – any closer and you'd be fighting the bulls yourself.

See Treatment of Animals in the Facts about Barcelona chapter for information on organisations that oppose bullfighting.

Toro, Toro, Toro For many, bullfighting is a sickening affair; others view it as a noble battle. Whichever way you look at it, there is little doubt about the cruelty of it or about the risks that *toreros* (bullfighters) run. The *corrida* (bullfight) is a spectacle with a long history – even the Romans enjoyed a good bullfight.

The *corrida* is about many things – death, bravery, performance. It is certainly bloody and cruel and there is nothing worse than to

see a matador and his sidekicks mess up the kill. *La lidia*, as the art of bullfighting is also known, took off in an organised fashion in Spain in the mid-18th century. In the 1830s, Pedro Romero, the greatest *torero* of the time was, at the age of 77, appointed director of the Escuela de Tauromaquia de Sevilla, the country's first bullfighters' college. It was around this time, too, that breeders succeeded in creating the first reliable breeds of *toro bravo* (fighting bull).

The Fight As a rule, six bulls and three matadors are on the day's card. If any are considered not up to scratch they are booed off (the president will display a green handkerchief) and replacements brought on. Each fight takes about 15 to 20 minutes.

Traditionally, young men have aspired to the ring in the hope of fame and fortune, much like boxers. Most attain neither. Only champion matadors make good money, and some make a loss as the matador must rent or buy his outfit and equipment, pay for the right to fight a bull and pay his *cuadrilla* (team).

You will notice the team is made up of quite a few people. Firstly, there are several *peones*, junior bullfighters under the orders of the main *torero*, who is the matador. The *peones* come out to distract the bull with great capes, manoeuvre him into the desired position and so on.

Then come the *picadores*, mounted on horseback. Charged by the bull, which tries to eviscerate the (nowadays) heavily padded and blind-folded horse, the *picador* shoves his lance into the withers of the bull. The *peones* then return to the scene to measure their courage against the (it is hoped) charging bull.

The *picador* is followed by the *banderilleros*. Two *banderilleros* will each successively race towards the charging bull and attempt to plunge a pair of colourfully decorated *banderillas* (short prods that have harpoon-style ends) into the bull – again aiming for the withers.

The dress of the *matador* could be that of a flamenco dancer. At its most extravagant, the *traje de luces* (suit of lights) can be an extraordinary display of bright, spangly colour. Most of the *toreros*, with the exception of the *picadors* and sometimes the matadors, wear the black *montera* (the Mickey Mouse–ears hat). The *torero's* standard weapons are the *estoque* or *espada* (sword) and the heavy silk and percale *capa* (cape). You will notice, however, that the *matador* uses a different cape with the sword – a smaller piece of cloth held with a bar of wood called the *muleta* and used for a number of different passes, or *faenas*.

How well he is doing can be judged by the cries from the crowd. The various moves must be carried out in certain parts of the stadium, which is divided into three parts: the *medios* (centre), *tercios* (an intermediate, chalked-off ring) and *tablas* (the outer ring).

When the bull seems tired and unlikely to give a lot more, the matador chooses his moment for the kill. Placing himself head-on he aims to sink the sword cleanly into the animal's neck *(estocada)* for an instant kill. It's easier said than done.

The sad carcass is dragged out by a team of drayhorses and the sand is raked in preparation for the next bull. The meat ends up in the butcher's.

Marathon

Thousands of eager runners converge on Barcelona every March to participate in the city's marathon. For the past couple of years the 42km course has been exactly the same, starting and finishing at the foot of the Palau Nacional d'Art de Catalunya (Map 7) in Montjuïc.

Formula One

Since 1991 the dashing knights in shining motorised armour have come to the Montmeló track, about a 30-minute drive north of Barcelona, every April to burn rubber. A seat for the Grand Prix race at the **Circuit de Catalunya** (☎ 93 571 97 71; W *www.circuitcat.com*) can cost anything from €179 to €314 depending largely on how far in advance you purchase your ticket. You can get a regular *rodalies* train to Montmeló (€1.10, 30 minutes) but will still need to find a local taxi (about €6 to €8) to reach the track itself.

Shopping

Although not quite in the same league as Paris or Milan, Barcelona is certainly among Europe's cities of style. It is a natural magnet for the fashion-conscious and there is no shortage of design outlets for even the most tireless consumer.

Everything from books to jewels, *haute couture* (local and international), designer furniture, *cava* and condoms is on offer. Several markets animate squares around the centre of town.

Most of the mainstream stores can be found on a shopping 'axis' that looks something like the hands of a clock set at a quarter to five. From the waterfront it leads up La Rambla through Plaça de Catalunya and on up Passeig de Gràcia (Maps 1 and 2). At Avinguda Diagonal you turn left.

From here as far as Plaça de la Reina Maria Cristina (especially the final stretch from Plaça de Francesc Macià) the Diagonal is jammed with places where you can empty your bank account. The T1 Tombbus service has been laid on for the ardent shopper (see the Getting Around chapter) and eventually a tram may run the length of Avinguda Diagonal, too.

The best shopping areas in central Barcelona are Passeig de Gràcia and the streets to its southwest, including the Bulevard Rosa arcade (Map 2) just north of Carrer d'Aragó, and Barri Gòtic streets such as Carrer de la Portaferrissa, Carrer de la Boqueria, Carrer del Call, Carrer de la Llibreteria and Carrer de Ferran, and around Plaça de Sant Josep Oriol (all Map 6).

Department-store bargain-hunters should note that the winter sales officially start on or around 10 January and their summer equivalents on or around 5 July.

The big department stores (such as El Corte Inglés) and shopping complexes (such as El Triangle) tend to open from 9am or 10am through to 9pm or 10pm at night, Monday to Saturday. Smaller shops often close for a few hours at lunchtime (around 2pm to 4pm).

ANTIQUES

If you can't break away from the old town, Carrer dels Banys Nous in Barri Gòtic (Map 6) is lined with antique shops and is a good area to start. The side streets in the immediate area, including Carrer de la Palla, also hide a bevy of antique shops. While you're wandering along Carrer de la Palla, glance up at No 21 – it was once the Hospital de Sant Saver – founded back in 1462. There are alternatives. Bulevard dels Antiquaris, Passeig de Gràcia 55 (Map 2; part of the Bulevard Rosa arcade complex) is jammed with more than 70 antiques shops, most of a general nature (furnishings, paintings, decorative items) with a few specialists: **Brahuer** (jewellery), **Dalmau** (wooden picture frames), **Govary's** (porcelain dolls) and **Victory** (crystal).

ART

You could start hunting for art in several places. Along Carrer de Montcada (Map 6) are several commercial galleries, the biggest being **Galeria Maeght** *(Carrer de Montcada 25)*. Others include the **Galeria Surrealista**, next to the Museu Picasso, the Sala Montcada of the **Fundació La Caixa** *(Carrer de Montcada 16)*, **Galeria Beaskoa** next door and **Galeria Montcada** (jammed in next to the Palau de Dalmases). In Barri Gòtic you'll find several galleries in Carrer de Petritxol.

Predictably enough, the presence of the Museu d'Arte Contemporani de Barcelona in El Raval is turning the surrounding area into an artsy zone. You'll find a half dozen small galleries and designer stores on Carrer del Doctor Dou, Carrer d'Elisabets and Carrer dels Àngels (all Map 6).

The classiest concentration of galleries – about a dozen of them – is on the short stretch of Carrer del Consell de Cent between Rambla de Catalunya and Carrer de Balmes (Map 2). A particularly interesting place is **Galeria Victor Saavedra** *(Map 2; ☎ 93 238 51 61; Carrer d'Enric Granados 97)*.

Saavedra, himself an artist, has been promoting all sorts of artists from around Europe since the late 1980s.

The *Guía del Ocio* (see the Entertainment chapter) carries a limited list of art galleries.

ART PRINTS & POSTERS

For many, a big Miró print or a Picasso poster would make the perfect gift. The **Fundació Joan Miró** *(Map 7)*, **Museu Picasso** *(Map 6)* and **Museu d'Art Contemporàni de Barcelona** *(Macba; Map 6)* are all well stocked. The souvenir shops in the **Oficina d'Informació de Turisme de Barcelona** *(Map 6; Plaça de Catalunya 17)*, and **Palau de la Virreina** *(Map 6; La Rambla de Sant Josep 99)* also carry limited offerings.

For high-quality postcards of Barcelona, prints and the like investigate **Estamperia d'Art** *(Map 6; ☎ 93 318 68 30; Plaça del Pi 1)*.

BARÇA

For some, football is the meaning of life. If you fall into that category your idea of shopping heaven may well be **La Botiga del Barça** *(Map 1; Carrer de Arístides Maillol s/n)*, near the team's Museu del Futbol at the Camp Nou stadium and its **branch** *(☎ 93 225 80 45)* in the Maremàgnum complex (Map 5). There you can get shirts, keyrings, footballs, the works – anything you could think of featuring the famous red and blue colours.

BOOKS

There is no shortage of decent bookshops in Barcelona, but the local product is pricey, largely due to high printing costs in Spain.

La Rambla

Llibreria & Informaciò Cultural de la Generalitat de Catalunya (Map 6; ☎ 93 302 64 62) Rambla dels Estudis 118. This is a good first stop for books and pamphlets on all things Catalan, although a lot of it is highly specialised and technical.

Llibreria de la Virreina (Map 6; ☎ 93 301 77 75) Palau de la Virreina, La Rambla de Sant Josep 99. Here you'll find an assortment of art/architecture and art history books, many with at least some relevance to Barcelona.

Barri Gòtic & El Raval

Antinous (Map 6; ☎ 93 301 90 70) Carrer Josep Anselm Clavé 6. This is a good gay bookshop and café.

Cómplices (Map 6; ☎ 93 412 72 83) Carrer de Cervantes 2. It has gay and lesbian books.

Documenta (Map 6; ☎ 93 317 25 27) Carrer del Cardenal Casañas 4. Documenta has novels in English and French, and maps.

Próleg (Map 6; ☎ 93 319 24 25) Carrer de la Daguería 13. Próleg is a women's bookshop.

Quera (Map 6; ☎ 93 318 07 43) Carrer de Petritxol 2. It's a specialist in maps and guides, including for walking and trekking.

L'Eixample

Alibri (Map 4; ☎ 93 317 05 78) Carrer de Balmes 26. This is one of the city's best general bookstores, with a wealth of material and foreign language books too.

Altaïr (Map 4; ☎ 93 342 71 71) Gran Via de les Corts Catalanes 616. Altaïr is a great travel bookshop with maps, guides and travel literature.

Casa del Libro (Map 2; ☎ 93 272 34 80) Passeig de Gràcia 62. With branches elsewhere in Spain, the 'Home of the Book' is a well-stocked general bookshop.

Come In (Map 2; ☎ 93 453 12 04) Carrer de Provença 203. It is a specialist in English-language teaching books; there are also plenty of novels and books on Spain, in English and French.

The English Bookshop (Map 4; ☎ 93 425 44 66) Carrer de Entença 63. A good range of literature, teaching material and children's books can be found here.

Laie (Map 2; ☎ 93 518 17 39) Carrer de Pau Claris 85. Laie has novels and books on architecture, art and film in English, French, Spanish and Catalan. It has a great café where you can examine your latest purchases.

CANDLES

Even if you're not interested in all the mounds of wax, you may want to pop in to **Cereria Subirà** *(Map 6; ☎ 93 315 26 06; Baixada de la Llibreteria 7)* just to say you have been in the oldest shop in Barcelona. It started trading in 1761.

CERAMICS

A couple of interesting ceramics and pottery shops owned by the same people are hidden north of the Catedral. **Ceràmiques i Terrisses Cadí** *(Map 6; ☎ 93 317 73 85; Carrer*

SHOPPING

de les Magdalenes 23) has a diverse range of plates, jugs and so on. The owners will either be here or in the twin store (simply called Ceramica) across the road.

CLOTHING & FABRICS

If you're after international fashion, Avinguda Diagonal (Maps 2 and 3) is the place to look. Shops along here include **Calvin Klein** *(Map 2; No 484)*, **Giorgio Armani** *(Map 2; No 490; • Map 3; No 620)*, **Gianni Versace** *(Map 3; No 606)* and **Gucci** *(Map 2; No 415)*. **Jean Pierre Bua** *(Map 3; No 469)* hosts designers ranging from Jean Paul Gaultier through to Helmut Lang.

Max Mara *(Map 2; ☎ 93 488 17 77; Passeig de Gràcia 23)* has several branches around town.

Loewe *(Map 3; ☎ 93 216 04 00; Avinguda Diagonal 570)* is one of Spain's leading and oldest fashion stores, founded in 1846. There's another branch, which opened in 1943, in the Modernista Casa Lleo Morera (Map 2; Passeig de Gràcia).

Try **Ortiga** *(Map 3; Carrer de Bori i Fontestà 10)* if you're looking for prêt-a-porter evening dresses.

Adolfo Domínguez *(Map 2; Passeig de Gràcia 32)* is a star name in Spanish fashion and **Gonzalo Comella** *(Cnr Passeig de Gràcia & Carrer de Casp)* is known for men's clothing.

Zara *(Map 3; l'Illa del Diagonal shopping complex – see Department Stores later in this chapter; Avinguda Diagonal 584 • Map 3; Passeig de Gràcia 16 • Map 6; Hostal Lausanne, Avinguda del Portal de l'Àngel 24)* is one of the country's most successful outlets for women's fashion.

Antonio Miró *(Map 2; Carrer del Consell de Cent 349)* concentrates on light, natural fibres to produce smart, unpretentious men's and women's fashion – jackets are a strong point.

Jeanne Weiss *(Map 6; ☎ 93 301 04 12; Carrer d'En Rauric 8)* has some nice lines in African printed fabrics, cushions and shirts.

Obach *(Map 6; ☎ 93 318 40 94; Carrer del Call 2)* has, since 1924, been purveying hats in the heart of the Call.

Loft Avignon *(Map 6; ☎ 93 301 24 20; Carrer d'Avinyó 22)* is one of several hip

Unfriendly Rivalry

Being more flouncing than usual marked Barcelona's and Madrid's respective fashion shows in the early months of 2002. Conscious that in neighbouring countries the big international fashion spectacles are associated with one town (Paris, London, Milan), the Spanish government has adopted a plan to meld the two shows into one. The only problem is that Spain's eternal rivals are in no mood to cede to one another.

The Gaudí catwalk in Barcelona kicked off first and was a big local hit. Madrid's Cibeles show came shortly after and also went well, but was marked by continuing polemics over which side should cave in to the other. Seeing that neither of the two can accept relegation, the city of Valencia piped up and suggested itself as the perfect neutral alternative to the squabbling cities for future galas. Needless to say, that proposal won few plaudits from the main contenders and the dream of a united show remains, for the moment at least, a dead letter.

young fashion stores that have sprouted along this once sombre Barri Gòtic street.

In El Raval along Carrer de la Riera Baixa, a string of clothing stores has appeared in the past couple of years. The kind of clothes, from pseudo military through to grunge, reflects the still gritty nature of this part of the old town.

CONDOMS

La Condoneria *(Map 6; ☎ 93 302 77 21; Plaça de Sant Josep Oriol 3)* is a handy spot where you can purchase your KY gel, condoms of every colour and shape you could dream of (and some that might never have occurred to you), and a range of novelties.

CRAFTS

For an overview of high-quality Catalan crafts *(artesania)*, pop into the **Centre Català d'Artesania** *(Map 2; ☎ 93 467 46 60; Passeig de Gràcia 55)*. It is dedicated to promoting and maintaining Catalan craft traditions.

Natura Selection (Map 2; ☎ 93 488 19 72; Carrer del Consell de Cent 304) has a big stock of ethnic bags (leather and cloth), jewellery, pots, drums, candles, carvings, glass, baskets, tablecloths, rugs and more.

Casa Miranda (Map 6; ☎ 93 301 83 29; Carrer de Banys Nous 15) offers you woven baskets of all shapes and sizes.

Galeria Àfrica Negra (Map 6; ☎ 93 319 16 31; Carrer dels Banys Vells 5), unsurprisingly, specialises in a wide range of crafts from all over Africa.

DEPARTMENT STORES

The single best department store is **El Corte Inglés** (Map 5; ☎ 93 306 38 00; Plaça de Catalunya), with smaller offshoots spread about the surrounding area. It has another important branch northwest of town on Plaça de la Reina Maria Cristina and a third on Avinguda Diagonal (both on Map 3).

FNAC (Map 3; Avinguda Diagonal 549), the French-owned store specialising in CDs, tapes, videos and books, is worth exploring for these items. The shop is part of a huge shopping mall – l'Illa del Diagonal – considered one of the city's more interesting architectural developments since the Olympic Games.

A more central shopping centre, **El Triangle** (Map 5; Plaça de Catalunya) houses a branch of FNAC and a collection of other stores, including **Habitat**.

If you like shopping emporia, the **Centre Comercial de les Glòries** (Map 1), by the massive roundabout and metro stop of the same name, could be for you. It counts 250,000 sq metres of space in the grounds of the former Hispano Olivetti factory, and is also home to a range of bars and eateries to take your mind off shopping for a while.

Hypermarket lovers in Barcelona were given the ultimate treat in 2001 with the opening of Heron City, an enormous complex of shops, cinemas, bars, restaurants and other diversions. It's located well out of the centre of town at Passeig de Andreu Nin, just off Avinguda de la Meridiana about 4km north of Plaça de les Glòries Catalanes (metro Fabra i Puig). Yes, mall mentality has arrived.

DESIGN

Vinçon (Map 2; ☎ 93 215 60 50; Passeig de Gràcia 96) has the slickest designs in furniture and household goods, local and imported. Not surprising really, since the building belonged to the Modernista artist Ramon Casas.

Bd Ediciones de Diseño (Map 2; ☎ 93 458 69 09; Carrer de Mallorca 291) is worth a look, even if you have left your credit cards at home. Here you will find a collection of pieces for the home by some of Barcelona's leading designers. Opened in 1972, this prize-winning store is located in a Modernista house built by Domènech i Montaner.

Artquitect (Map 6; ☎ 93 268 23 86; Carrer del Comerç 31) is interesting for enthusiasts of building design.

FOOD & DRINK

Serious champagne sippers should pop by **Xampany** (Map 4; ☎ 610 84 50 11; Carrer de València 200). It stocks over 100 types and brands of cava and all the associated drinking utensils. For a completely modern and international approach to wine, try **La Vinia** (Map 3; ☎ 93 363 44 45; w www.lavinia.es; Avinguda Diagonal 605; open 10am-9pm Mon-Sat). This mega wine store has fine drops from around the country and abroad.

Need some cheese? A couple of spots are worth seeking out. **Formatgeria La Seu** (Map 6; ☎ 93 412 65 48; Carrer de la Daguería 16) has a nice selection on display, and you can taste a few morsels with a drop of wine for €2.

If coffee is more your tipple, head for **El Magnífico** (Map 6; ☎ 93 319 60 81; Carrer de l'Argenteria 64). These guys have been roasting all sorts of coffee for most of this century.

Nuts to you at **Casa Gispert** (Map 6; ☎ 93 319 75 35; Carrer dels Sombrerers 23), where they've been toasting almonds and selling all manner of dried fruit since 1851.

L'Ametller (Map 6; ☎ 93 319 64 91; Carrer dels Banys Vells 7) is a tiny little place stacked to the rafters with all sorts of interesting local food and drink products, lots of them with a sweet side.

Xocolateria Valor (Map 2; ☎ 93 487 62 46; Rambla de Catalunya 46) has for more than 100 years been responsible for tooth decay in countless willing victims in Alicante. It opened in Barcelona a few years back. You can buy to takeaway or try anything from ice cream to milk shakes on the spot.

FURNITURE

You probably won't be buying, but drop into **La Maison Coloniale** (Map 4; ☎ 93 443 22 22; Carrer de Sant Antoni Abat 61) anyway. The colonial-style furniture is exquisite, and so is the setting – what remains of the 15th-century Gothic Església de Sant Antoni Abat, largely destroyed in the civil war.

JEWELLERY

Joyería Bagués (Map 2; ☎ 93 216 01 74; Passeig de Gràcia 41), in Casa Amatller, is a reliable name in high-quality rocks. If you want to check out a more international name, try **Cartier** (Map 2; ☎ 93 488 00 62; Carrer del Consell de Cent 351). For gold jewellery, **Vasari** (Map 2; Passeig de Gràcia 73) is reliable.

Tous (Map 2; ☎ 93 488 15 58; Passeig de Gràcia 75) aims its more light-hearted jewellery at young customers and offers other accessories ranging from original perfumes to stylish sunglasses.

If you wander down along the museum trail on Carrer de Montcada, you'll find several silver specialists on the same street. Carrer del Call is lined with little jewellery stores, a lot of them dedicated to cheaper costume stuff.

LATE-NIGHT STORES

The concept of the 24-hour general store has yet to reach Barcelona, but an approximation is **VIPS** (Map 5; ☎ 93 317 48 05; Rambla de Catalunya; open 9am-3am daily), an import from Madrid. In Madrid the chain thrives, but in Barcelona it hasn't really caught on. Another one to try is **7-Eleven** (Map 2; ☎ 93 318 88 63; Carrer de Roger de Llúria 2; open 7am-3am daily).

Need photocopies or films developed at 5am? Head for **Workcenter** (Map 5; ☎ 902 11 50 11; Carrer de Roger de Llúria 2), a printing and reproduction centre open 24 hours a day, 365 days a year.

LLADRÓ & MAJORICA

These are possibly the two best-known Spanish brand names in the world. Lladró porcelain is coveted as much as the Majorica pearls that compete with it for display space in several stores around Barcelona. **García** (Map 5; ☎ 93 302 69 89; La Rambla 4) is a handy spot to take a look at these products. You will find Majorica pearls in El Corte Inglés department stores, too.

MARKETS

Large **Els Encants Vells** ('the old charms'; Map 1; open 8am-7pm, to 8pm summer), also known as the Fira de Bellcaire, is held every Monday, Wednesday, Friday and Saturday next to Plaça de les Glòries Catalanes. The markets moved here in August 1928 from Avinguda Mistral, near Plaça d'Espanya, because the sight of such a jumble sale did not fit in with the town fathers' visions for the 1929 World Exhibition. For years there has been talk of shifting them again but for the moment they seem set to stay put. You can find everything here – all at *preus de ganga* (bargain-basement prices).

In Barri Gòtic, there's a **crafts market** (Map 6; Plaça de Sant Josep Oriol) on Thursday and Friday, an **antiques market** (Map 6; Plaça Nova) on Thursday, and a **coin and stamp collectors' market** (Map 6; Plaça Reial) on Sunday morning. On the western edge of El Raval, **Mercat de Sant Antoni** (Map 4; metro Sant Antoni) dedicates Sunday morning to old maps, stamps, books and cards.

MASKS & NOVELTIES

El Ingenio (Map 6; ☎ 93 317 71 38; Carrer d'En Rauric 6) is a whimsical fantasy store where you will discover giant Carnival masks, costumes, theatre accessories and other fun things.

MUSIC

One of the biggest record stores is **Planet Music** (Map 2; ☎ 93 451 42 88; Carrer de Mallorca 214), with more than 50,000 CDs at its main store. It has other branches

SHOPPING

around town. FNAC (see Department Stores earlier) is another good outlet.

Several small shops specialising in indie and other niche music can be found on or around Carrer de Sitges and especially on Carrer dels Tallers (El Raval), which boasts a dozen music stores. **Castelló** *(Maps 4 & 6; ☎ 93 318 20 41)*, at Nos 3 (classical music), 7 and 79, is a large family business that has been going since 1935; it is said to account for a fifth of the retail record business in Catalunya. **Rock & Blues** *(Map 6; ☎ 93 412 59 86; Carrer dels Tallers 10)* is a haven for vinyl and rare records. **CD-Drome** *(Map 4; ☎ 93 317 46 46; Carrer de Valldonzella 3)*, nearby, specialises in house, hip-hop, trip-hop and other hops. **Daily Record** *(Map 6; ☎ 93 301 77 55; Carrer de Sitges 9)* is another interesting outlet.

MUSICAL INSTRUMENTS
New-Phono *(Map 6; ☎ 93 315 12 04; Carrer Ample 37)*, in Barri Gòtic, has been selling instruments under one name or another since 1834. The shop is housed in what was once the stables of a noble family.

PEARLS & PORCELAIN
See Lladró & Majorica earlier in this chapter.

PERFUME
Regia *(Map 2; ☎ 93 216 01 21; Passeig de Gràcia 39)* is reputed to be one of the best perfume stores in the city.

PHOTOGRAPHY
Arpi *(Map 6; ☎ 93 301 74 04; La Rambla 38)* has five floors given over to all things photographic (still, video and cinema). It is a standard port of call for professional snappers. For a good second-hand collection of cameras, try **Casanova** *(Map 4; ☎ 93 302 73 63; Carrer de Pelai 18)*.

SHOES
There's a gaggle of relatively economical shoe shops on Avinguda del Portal de l'Àngel (Map 6), which is just off Plaça de Catalunya.

Camper *(Map 2; ☎ 93 215 63 90; Carrer de València 249)*, something of a classic shoe merchant in Spain, has a good range.

SOUVENIRS
If you're in the mood for a little kitsch, the easiest thing to do is head for La Rambla. The place is lined with shops that will sell you all sorts of junk. However, before you flash your cash at the merchants, have a look inside Barcelona Original, the souvenir boutique in the building of the **Oficina d'Informació de Turisme de Barcelona** *(Map 6; ☎ 906 30 12 82; Plaça de Catalunya 17)*. It has an interesting range of quality stuff, including ceramics, watches, art prints, coffee-table books and the like. Most of the major museums and art galleries have shops attached where you can 'buy the T-shirt' and other more substantial gifts.

SHOPPING

Excursions

Catalunya, the autonomous region of which Barcelona is the capital, offers a little of everything: tacky package coastal resorts and remote cliff-side beaches; skiing and trekking; a plethora of towns and villages boasting jewels of Romanesque and Gothic art and architecture; ancient ruins to the north and south of Barcelona; and one of Europe's top gay party towns. What appears in this chapter is merely a taste of what is accessible on day trips out of Barcelona. Lonely Planet's *Catalunya & the Costa Brava* contains many more hints on heading further afield.

The costs of train journeys given in this chapter are for 2nd-class, one-way fares, unless otherwise stated.

ACCOMMODATION

This chapter is designed for the day-tripper, so no accommodation information is provided. If you plan to do overnight trips, approach each town's tourist office for accommodation listings.

For the record, the 41 member hostels of Catalunya's official youth hostel network, **Xarxa d'Albergs de Catalunya**, share a central booking service at **Turisme Juvenil de Catalunya** (Map 4; ☎ 93 483 83 63, fax 93 483 83 50; W www.tujuca.com; Carrer de Rocafort 116-122, Barcelona).

At Xarxa hostels you need a Hostelling International (HI) card. Prices vary but the basic structure is as follows: if you're aged under 26 or have an ISIC, B&B costs €14.57/15.93/18.03 in the low/mid/high season; otherwise it's €18.63/20.43/22.24, respectively. In some hostels it is almost always high season. Lunch or dinner costs €4.81 and sheets €2.10 (towels cost the same). For €2.70 you can stay in the hostel during the day.

Catalunya has a wide network of *cases de pagès*. These are farmhouses and other rural lodgings that often provide good and economical accommodation in country areas. You can pick up a complete guide to them at the regional tourist office in the Palau Robert on Passeig de Gràcia 107 in Barcelona.

NORTH OF BARCELONA
Girona
postcode 17080 • pop 71,850
Northern Catalunya's largest city, Girona (Gerona), sits in a valley 36km inland from the Costa Brava. Its impressive medieval centre seems to struggle uphill above the Riu Onyar (Onyar River).

The Roman town of Gerunda lay on the Via Augusta, the highway from Rome to Cádiz (Carrer de la Força in Girona's old town follows it in part). Taken from the Muslims by the Franks in AD 797, Girona became the capital of one of Catalunya's most important counties, falling under the sway of Barcelona in the late 9th century.

Information The **tourist office** (☎ 972 22 65 75; Rambla de la Llibertat 1; open 8am-8pm Mon-Fri, 8am-2pm & 4pm-8pm Sat, 9am-2pm Sun) is towards the southern end of the old town.

Catedral The fine baroque facade of the cathedral stands at the head of a majestic flight of steps rising from Plaça de la Catedral. Most of the building, however, is much older. Repeatedly rebuilt and altered down the centuries, it has Europe's widest Gothic nave (23m). The cathedral's **museum** (☎ 972 21 44 26; admission €3; open 10am-2pm & 4pm-7pm Tues-Sat, to 6pm Oct-Apr, 10am-2pm Sun & holidays), through the door marked 'Claustre Tresor', contains the masterly Romanesque *Tapís de la Creació* (Tapestry of the Creation). The admission for the museum also admits you to the beautiful 12th-century Romanesque cloister.

Other Things to See Next door to the cathedral, in the 12th- to 16th-century Palau Episcopal, the collection of the **Museu d'Art** (☎ 972 20 95 36; Plaça de la Catedral 12; admission €2; open 10am-6pm Tues-Sat

Oct-Apr, to 7pm May-Sept, 10am-2pm Sun & holidays) ranges from Romanesque wood-carvings through to early 20th-century painting.

Girona's second great church, **Església de Sant Feliu**, stands downhill from the cathedral. The 17th-century main facade, with its landmark single tower, is on Plaça de Sant Feliu, but the entrance is at the side. The nave has 13th-century Romanesque arches but 14th- to 16th-century Gothic upper levels.

The **Banys Àrabs** *(Arab baths; ☎ 972 21 32 62; Carrer de Ferran Catòlic; admission €1.50; open 10am-7pm Tues-Sat, 10am-2pm Sun & holidays May-Sept, 10am-2pm Tues-Sun rest of year)* are actually a Christian af-fair from the 12th century in Romanesque style, although they're modelled on earlier Muslim and Roman bathhouses.

Across the street from the Banys Àrabs, steps lead up into lovely gardens that follow the city walls up to the 18th-century Portal de Sant Cristòfol, from which you can walk back down to the cathedral. This quick cir-cuit is known as the **Passeig Arqueològic**.

Down across the little Riu Galligants, the Monestir de Sant Pere de Galligants – an 11th- and 12th-century Romanesque mon-astery – has a lovely cloister. It houses Girona's **Museu Arqueològic** *(admission €1.80; open 10.30am-1.30pm & 4pm-7pm Tues-Sat May-Sept, to 6pm Oct-Apr, 10am-2pm Sun & holidays)*, with items ranging from prehistoric to medieval times.

Until 1492, Girona was the home to Catalunya's second-most important medi-eval Jewish community (after Barcelona), and its Jewish quarter, the Call, centred on Carrer de la Força. For an idea of medieval Jewish life and culture, visit the **Museu d'Història dels Jueus de Girona** *(☎ 972 21 67 61; admission €2; open 10am-8pm Mon-Sat, to 6pm Oct-Apr, 10am-3pm Sun & holidays)*, aka the Centre Bonastruc Ça Porta. Named after Jewish Girona's most illustrious figure, a 13th-century Cabbalist philosopher and mystic, the centre – a war-ren of rooms and stairways around a court-yard – hosts limited exhibitions and is a focal point for studies of Jewish Spain.

You can walk along a good length of the top of the city walls, **Passeig de la Muralla**, from Plaça de Josep Ferrater i Mora, just south of the Universitat de Girona building at the highest point of the old town, down to Plaça del General Marvà, near Plaça de Catalunya.

Places to Eat For vegetarian goodies, try **La Polenta** *(☎ 972 20 93 74; Carrer de la Cort Reial 6; set lunch menu €11.50; open Mon-Sat)*.

Zanpanzar *(☎ 972 21 28 43; Carrer de la Cort Reial 10-12; meals about €25; open Tues-Sun)* is a great little Basque tavern and restaurant. It's usually packed with locals, and offers *pintxos* (Basque tapas) and some fine meat dishes. Round off with *goxua in-txaursaltsarekin*, a Basque tart consisting of biscuit, apple and an amazing nut sauce.

La Crêperie Bretonne *(☎ 972 21 81 20; Carrer de la Cort Reial 14; crepes €3-6.50; open to midnight Mon-Sat)* has tempting savoury and sweet crepes. This is the local branch of a popular eatery in Perpignan (southern France).

Café Le Bistrot *(☎ 972 21 88 03; Pujada de Sant Domènec 4; meals €12-15)*, located high up one of the medieval centre's most picturesque stairways, is a treat. Vaguely bo-hemian, it serves up salads, *pizzes de pagès* (little bread-based pizzas) and full meals.

Restaurant Albereda *(☎ 972 22 60 02; Carrer de l'Albereda 9; meals €35-40; open Tues-Sat, & Mon lunch)* is the town's senior restaurant, serving classic Catalan cuisine with some twists, such as frog's legs.

Getting There & Away You can take **Barcelona Bus** *(☎ 972 20 24 32)* between Barcelona's Estació del Nord (€9.20, 1¼ hours) and Figueres (€3.70, one hour) three to six times daily. **Sarfa** *(☎ 972 20 17 96)* runs buses to most parts of the Costa Brava.

Girona is on the railway line between Barcelona, Figueres and Portbou on the French border. There are more than 20 trains per day to Figueres (€2.05 to €2.40, 30 to 40 minutes) and Barcelona (€4.90 to €5.65, 1½ hours), and about €15 to Portbou and/or Cerbère (€3.20 to €3.70).

EXCURSIONS

EXCURSIONS

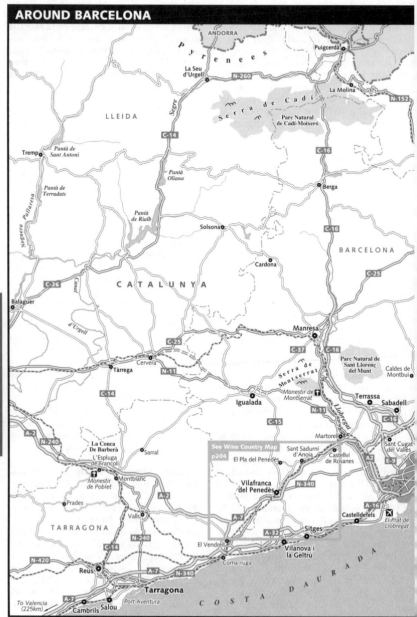

AROUND BARCELONA

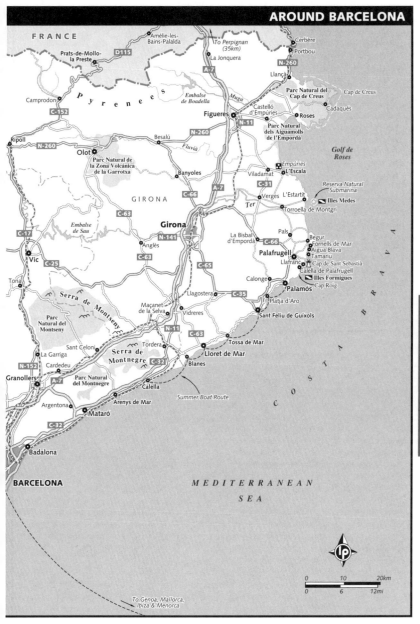

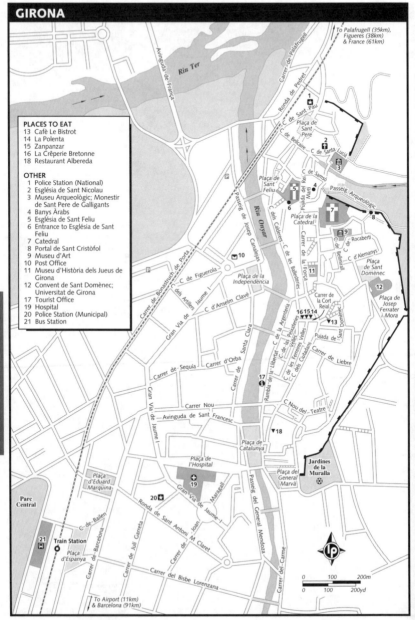

GIRONA

To Palafrugell (35km),
Figueres (38km)
& France (61km)

PLACES TO EAT
13 Cafè Le Bistrot
14 La Polenta
15 Zanpanzar
16 La Crêperie Bretonne
18 Restaurant Albereda

OTHER
1 Police Station (National)
2 Església de Sant Nicolau
3 Museu Arqueològic; Monestir de Sant Pere de Galligants
4 Banys Àrabs
5 Església de Sant Feliu
6 Entrance to Església de Sant Feliu
7 Catedral
8 Portal de Sant Cristòfol
9 Museu d'Art
10 Post Office
11 Museu d'Història dels Jueus de Girona
12 Convent de Sant Domènec; Universitat de Girona
17 Tourist Office
19 Hospital
20 Police Station (Municipal)
21 Bus Station

Riu Ter

Riu Onyar

Plaça de Sant Pere

Plaça de Sant Feliu

Plaça de la Catedral

Plaça de Sant Domènec

Plaça de Josep Ferrater i Mora

Plaça de la Independència

Carrer de la Cort Reial

Plaça de Catalunya

Plaça de l'Hospital

Jardines de la Muralla

Plaça del General Marvà

Plaça d'Eduard Marquina

Parc Central

Plaça d'Espanya

Train Station

To Airport (11km)
& Barcelona (91km)

0   100   200m
0   100   200yd

Figueres
postcode 17600 • pop 33,600

Another 40km north from Girona along the A-7 *autopista*, or by train, is Figueres (Figueras), a bit of a dive with a one-man show – Salvador Dalí. In the 1960s and '70s he created the extraordinary Teatre-Museu Dalí here, the town of his birth.

Information Figueres' **tourist office** (☎ 972 50 31 55; Plaça del Sol; open 9am-9pm Mon-Sat, 9am-3pm Sun June–mid-Sept, 9am-2pm & 4.30pm-8pm Mon-Fri, 10am-2pm & 3.30pm-6.30pm Sat, 10am-2pm Sun mid-Sept–May) can help with information.

Teatre-Museu Dalí Salvador Dalí was born in Figueres in 1904 and went to school here. Although his career took him for spells to Madrid, Barcelona, Paris and the USA, he remained true to his roots and lived well over half his adult life at Port Lligat, near Cadaqués on the coast east of Figueres. Between 1961 and 1974 Dalí converted Figueres' former municipal theatre, ruined by a fire at the end of the civil war in 1939, into the Teatre-Museu Dalí (☎ 972 67 75 09; adult/student €9/6.50 day sessions, €8 night sessions; open 9am-7.15pm daily July-Sept, 10.30am-5.15pm Oct-June, night sessions 10pm-12.30am most of summer).

Even on the outside, the building aims to surprise, from the collection of bizarre sculptures at the entrance on Plaça de Gala i Salvador Dalí to the pink wall along Pujada del Castell, topped by a row of Dalí's trademark egg shapes and what appear to be a female version of the Oscars.

Inside, the ground floor (Level 1) includes a semicircular garden area on the site of the original theatre stalls. In its centre is a classic piece of weirdness called *Taxi Plujós* (Rainy Taxi), composed of an early Cadillac – said to have belonged to Al Capone – and a pile of tractor tyres, both surmounted by statues, with a fishing boat balanced precariously above the tyres. Put a coin in the slot and water washes all over the inside of the car. The Sala de Peixateries (Fish Shop Room) off here holds a collection of Dalí oils, including the famous

Autoretrat Tou amb Tall de Bacon Fregit (Self-Portrait with Fried Bacon) and *Retrat de Picasso* (Portrait of Picasso). Beneath the former stage of the theatre is the crypt, with Dalí's plain tomb.

The stage area (Level 2), topped by a glass geodesic dome, was conceived of as Dalí's Sistine Chapel. The large backdrop of egg, head, breasts, rocks and trees was part of a ballet set, one of Dalí's many ventures into the performing arts. If proof were needed of Dalí's acute sense of the absurd, the painting *Gala Mirando el Mar Mediterráneo* (Gala Looking at the Mediterranean Sea) appears, from the other end of the room, with the help of coin-operated viewfinders, to be a portrait of Abraham Lincoln.

One floor up (Level 3) you come across the Sala de Mae West, a living-room whose components, viewed from the right spot, make up a portrait of Ms West – a sofa for her lips, two fireplaces for nostrils, two impressionist paintings of Paris for eyes.

In 2001 a new section of the museum was opened to house the Owen Cheatham collection of 37 jewels designed by Dalí. Entrance to **Dalí Joies** (Dalí Jewels; adult/student €4.50/3.50) is by a separate door.

Other Things to See Combining archaeological finds from Greek, Roman and medieval times with a sizable collection of art is the **Museu de l'Empordà** (☎ 972 50 23 05; La Rambla 2; admission €2; open 11am-7pm Tues-Sat, 10am-2pm Sun & holidays).

Museu de Joguets (☎ 972 50 45 85; La Rambla 10; adult/student €4.50/3.60; open 10am-1pm & 4pm-7pm Mon & Wed-Sat, 11am-1.30pm Sun & holidays Mar-June & Oct–mid-Jan, 10am-1pm & 4pm-7pm Mon & Wed-Sat, 11am-1.30pm & 5pm-7pm Sun & holidays July-Sept), Spain's only toy museum, has more than 3500 Catalunya- and Valencia-made toys from the pre-Barbie 19th and early 20th centuries. The price of admission is rather hefty.

You can also visit the enormous 18th-century **Castell de Sant Ferran** (☎ 972 50 60 94; admission €2; open 10.30am-8pm daily July–mid-Sept, 10.30am-2pm Nov-Feb, 10.30am-2pm & 4pm-6pm rest of year), on a

EXCURSIONS

FIGUERES

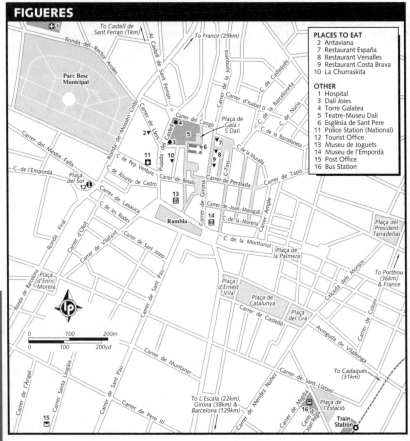

PLACES TO EAT
2 Antaviana
7 Restaurant España
8 Restaurant Versalles
9 Restaurant Costa Brava
10 La Churraskita

OTHER
1 Hospital
3 Dalí Joies
4 Torre Galatea
5 Teatre-Museu Dalí
6 Església de Sant Pere
11 Police Station (National)
12 Tourist Office
13 Museu de Joguets
14 Museu de l'Empordà
15 Post Office
16 Bus Station

low hill 1km northwest of the centre. Still owned by the army, it is one of the biggest such forts in Spain, but it saw almost no serious military action.

Places to Eat Carrer de la Jonquera, just down the steps east of the Teatre-Museu Dalí, is lined with cheap restaurants, among them **Restaurant España** (☎ 972 50 08 69; Carrer de la Jonquera 20), **Restaurant Versalles** (☎ 972 50 00 02; Carrer de la Jonquera 18) and **Restaurant Costa Brava** (Carrer de la Jonquera 10), offering basic three-course menús from €9.

Antaviana (☎ 972 51 03 77; Carrer de Llers 5; meals €25), just to the west of Teatre-Museu Dalí, specialises in a mix of Mediterranean cooking, with some good seafood and light meals.

La Churraskita (☎ 972 50 15 52; Carrer Magre 5; meals €15; open Tues-Sun), on the other hand, is a nice place if you like slabs of Argentinian meat.

Getting There & Away The bus station is southeast of town, near the train station. **Barcelona Bus** (☎ 972 50 50 29) runs seven daily services to/from Girona (€3.70, one hour) with six going on to Barcelona (€11.90, 2¼ hours).

Figueres is on the railway line between Barcelona, Girona and Portbou on the French border, and there are regular connections to Girona (€2.05 to €2.40, 30 to 40 minutes) and Barcelona (€7.05 to €8.05, 2¼ hours).

Costa Brava

The rugged Costa Brava stretches from Blanes (about 60km northeast of Barcelona) up to the French border. Although parts of the coast are truly awful holiday resorts that are jam-packed with the cheap charter–air fare crowd in search of sand, sun and drinks (Lloret de Mar is a prime example of what to avoid), there are some equally spectacular locations.

If you're driving, it is quite possible to choose a spot anywhere along the coast for a day trip. Those relying on public transport will find it a stretch and should plan on staying over at least one night. In the peak months of July and August, finding some lodgings can be difficult.

Tossa de Mar Marc Chagall called it Blue Paradise. A small white village backing onto a curved bay that ends in a headland protected by medieval walls and towers, Tossa is the first truly pleasant stop on the road north along the Costa Brava. In summer, boats with glass bottoms will take you to some enchanting little coves and beaches to the south and north of the main beach, Platja Gran.

The bus station is just off Plaça de les Nacions sense Estat (Stateless Nations Plaza). The **tourist office** (☎ 972 34 01 08; Avinguda del Pelegrí 25) is almost next door.

Beside the church in the old town, **Restaurant Marina** (☎ 972 34 07 57; Carrer de Tarull 6; menú around €10) offers a fairly good set meal menú and opens daily.

Restaurant Bahía (☎ 972 34 03 22; Passeig de Mar 19; full meals €20; opens daily but closed on winter evenings) is a classic on the Tossa coast and has been doing business for decades under various names. Expect good seafood here.

Sarfa (☎ 972 34 09 03) runs to/from Barcelona's Estació del Nord up to 10 times daily (€7.55, 1¼ hours). In summer you could get a *rodalies* train to Blanes (see the Getting Around chapter) and pick up a boat for Tossa. **Crucetours** (☎ 972 37 26 92), **Viajes Marítimos** (☎ 972 36 90 95) and **Dolfi-Jet** (☎ 972 37 19 39) run boats.

Palafrugell & Around One of the most spectacular coastlines on the Costa Brava is that around Palafrugell and there are several low-key beach resorts that truly warrant some effort to get to. A little way inland, Palafrugell is the local transport hub. From there you can fan out to Calella de Palafrugell, Llafranc, Tamariu, Aigua Blava and Fornells de Mar.

Getting There & Away From Barcelona's Estació del Nord, **Sarfa** (☎ 972 30 06 23) runs a bus service to Palafrugell up to 13 times daily (€11.40, two hours). Or you can go to Girona first and switch buses there.

In summer, half-hourly buses link Palafrugell to Calella and Llafranc. Only three or four buses daily run to Tamariu.

For the remaining beaches, you need to get to Begur first. Three of the Barcelona-Palafrugell services continue 10 minutes on to Begur (€12.10).

A Bus Platges (beach bus) service runs from Plaça de Forgas in Begur to Fornells and Aigua Blava from late June to mid-September.

L'Escala & Empúries A pleasant medium-sized resort on the southern shore of the Golf de Roses, L'Escala is close to the ancient town of Empúries (Ampurias in Castilian).

Empúries (☎ 972 77 02 08; adult/student €2.40/1.80; site open 10am-8pm June-Sept, to 6pm Oct-May), founded around 600 BC, was probably the first, and certainly one of the most important, Greek colonies in Iberia. The colony came to be called Emporion (literally, market). In 218 BC, Roman legions set foot on the peninsula here to cut off Hannibal's supply lines during the Second Punic War. By the early 1st century AD, the Roman and Greek settlements had merged. Emporiae, as the place was then known, was abandoned in the late 3rd century after raids by Germanic tribes. Later, an early Christian basilica and cemetery stood on the site of the Greek town. Then, after over a millennium of use, the whole place disappeared altogether, to be rediscovered by archaeologists at the turn of the 20th century.

Many of the ancient stones now laid bare don't rise more than knee high. You need a little imagination – and perhaps the aid of a taped commentary (€1.50 from the ticket office) – to make the most of this site.

There's a pedestrian entrance from the seafront promenade in front of the ruins – just follow the coast from L'Escala to reach it. From October to May the only way in is the vehicle approach from the Figueres road, about 1km from central L'Escala.

L'Escala is famous for its *anchoas* (anchovies) and good fresh local fish, both of which are likely to crop up on menus. The seafront restaurants are mostly expensive but, if your wallet is fat enough, try **Els Pescadors** (☎ 972 77 07 28; Port d'En Perris 5; meals €20-25) on the next bay west from La Platja (five-minutes' walk), which does superb baked and grilled seafood, *suquet* (seafood stew) and rice dishes. **L'Olla** and **Volanti**, also on Port d'En Perris, do pizzas for around €5 to €8.

Sarfa has one bus from Barcelona (via Palafrugell) on weekdays (€13.55, up to 2¾ hours), rising to three hours on Sunday.

Cadaqués The northern end of the Costa Brava is more barren and, for some tastes, more startling than the coast further south. The sprawling white village of Cadaqués is one of the highlights of the entire coast. Salvador Dalí spent a lot of time here and in nearby Port Lligat, attracting a stream of celebs to the place.

The pretty town centre is well worth a stroll, and you'll also find a couple of art museums cashing in on the Dalí theme. About a 20-minutes' walk from Cadaqués is the **Casa Museu Dalí** (☎ 972 25 10 15; adult/student & senior €8/5; open 10.30am-

9pm mid-June–mid-Sept, 10.30am-6pm Tues-Sun mid-Sept–mid-Jan & mid-Mar–mid-June) in Port Lligat. Visits here must be booked and you are allowed a grand total of only around 30 minutes inside as you are guided through.

Casa Nun (☎ 972 25 88 56; Plaça del Port Ditxos 6; meals €25-30; open Thur-Mon) has a cute little upstairs dining area and a few tables outside that overlook the port. Try out the *lluç farcit de gambes* (hake stuffed with prawns).

Restaurant Es Racó (☎ 972 15 94 80; Carrer del Dr Callis 3) does a fine *parrillada de pescado* (mixed seafood grill) for around €15 per person. Its balcony, overlooking the western half of the beach, catches some pleasant breeze.

Sarfa (☎ 972 25 87 13) has buses to/from Barcelona (€15.20, 2¼ hours) two times daily (sometimes more frequently in July and August).

WEST & SOUTH OF BARCELONA
Montserrat

Montserrat (Serrated Mountain), 50km northwest of Barcelona, is a 1236m-high mountain of truly weird rock pillars, shaped by wind, rain and frost from a conglomeration of limestone, pebbles and sand that once lay under the sea. With the historic Benedictine Monestir de Montserrat, one of Catalunya's most important shrines, soaring at 725m on its side, it makes a great outing from Barcelona.

The most dramatic approach is by the cable car that swings high across the Llobregat valley from Montserrat-Aeri station, served by regular trains from Barcelona.

From the mountain, on a clear day, you can see as far as the Pyrenees, Barcelona's Tibidabo and even, if you're lucky, Mallorca. Be aware, though; it can be a lot colder up on Montserrat than in Barcelona.

Orientation & Information The cable car from Montserrat-Aeri arrives on the mountain just below the monastery. Just above the cable-car station is an **information office** (☎ 93 877 77 77; open 9am-6pm daily), with a good free leaflet-map on the mountain and monastery. Past here, a minor road doubles back up to the left to the lower station of the Funicular de Sant Joan. The main road curves around and up to the right, passing the blocks of *Cel.les* (where it is possible to stay overnight), to enter Plaça de Santa Maria at the centre of the monastery complex.

Monestir de Montserrat The monastery was founded in 1025 to commemorate an apparition of the Virgin on the mountain. Wrecked by Napoleon's troops in 1811, then abandoned as a result of anticlerical legislation in the 1830s, it was rebuilt from 1858 onwards. Today, a community of about 80 monks lives here. Pilgrims come from far and wide to venerate the monastery's Black Virgin (La Moreneta), a 12th-century Romanesque wooden sculpture of Mary with the infant Jesus. La Moreneta has been Catalunya's official patron since 1881 (for more information see the boxed text 'Black & White').

The two-part **Museu de Montserrat** *(Plaça de Santa Maria; admission €4.50; open 10am-6pm Mon-Fri, 10am-7pm Sat-Sun)* has an excellent collection, ranging from an Egyptian mummy and Gothic altarpieces to art by El Greco, Monet, Degas and Picasso.

From Plaça de Santa Maria you enter the courtyard of the 16th-century **basilica** *(open*

Black & White

In 2001 researchers discovered that *La Moreneta*, the Black Virgin venerated by Catalans for centuries, is actually white. The Romanesque figure, it appears, was painted black in the early 19th century, partly because over the centuries candle smoke and dust had darkened the virgin's original pallid 'skin tone'. According to the tradition, the statuette had been black – an unusual choice of colour in Christian iconography for the Virgin Mary – since it was made in the 12th century. So much for that piece of tradition. Church authorities have decided to let her be as she is – black on the outside and white on the inside.

8am-8.15pm July-Sept, earlier closing Oct-June), the monastery's church. The basilica's facade, with its carvings of Christ and the Twelve Apostles, dates from 1900, despite its 16th-century plateresque style. When you enter you can file past the image of the Black Virgin high above the basilica's main altar. Follow the signs to the Cambril de la Mare de Déu, to the right of the main basilica entrance.

The **Montserrat Boys' Choir**, or Escolania, reckoned to be Europe's oldest music school, sings in the basilica at 1pm and 7pm Monday to Saturday and 1pm only on Sunday, except in July. The church fills up quickly so try to arrive early. It is a rare treat as the choir does not often perform outside Montserrat – five concerts per year and a world tour every two years.

On your way out have a look in the room across the courtyard from the basilica entrance, filled with gifts and thank-you messages to the Montserrat Virgin from people who give her the credit for all manner of happy events. The souvenirs range from plaster casts to wedding dresses.

If you want to see where the holy image of the Virgin was discovered, take the Santa Cova funicular (€1.60/2.50 one way/return) down from the main area.

The Mountain You can explore the mountain above the monastery on a web of paths leading to some of the peaks and to 13 empty and rather dilapidated hermitages. The **Funicular de Sant Joan** (€3.80/6.10 one way/return) will carry you up the first 250m from the monastery. If you prefer to walk, the road past the funicular's bottom station will lead you up and around to its top station in about one hour (3km).

From the Sant Joan top station, it's a 20-minute stroll (signposted) to the **Sant Joan hermitage**, with fine westward views. More exciting is the one-hour walk northwest, along a path marked with occasional blobs of yellow paint, to Montserrat's highest peak, **Sant Jeroni**, from where there's an awesome sheer drop on the northern side. The walk takes you across the upper part of the mountain, with a close-up experience of some of

EXCURSIONS

the weird rock pillars. Many have names: On your way to Sant Jeroni look over to the right for La Prenyada (the pregnant woman), La Mòmia (the mummy), L'Elefant (the elephant), the phallic Cavall Bernat, and El Cap de Mort (the death's head).

Getting There & Away There's a daily bus with **Julià Tours** *(Map 4; ☎ 93 317 64 54; Ronda de l'Universitat 5)* to the monastery from Barça at 9.30am (returning at 2.30pm) for €41.

The alternative is a trip by train and cable car (information on ☎ 93 205 15 15). FGC trains run from Plaça d'Espanya station in Barcelona to Montserrat-Aeri up to 18 times daily starting at 8.36am. Get the R5 train. Return tickets for €11.70 include the cable car between Montserrat-Aeri station and the monastery. The cable car goes about every 15 minutes from 9.25am to 1.45pm and 3pm to 6.45pm, Monday to Saturday. The whole trip takes a little over an hour. It is planned to reintroduce a cog-wheel *(cremallera)* train from Montserrat-Aeri up to the monastery by the end of 2002.

FGC offers various all-in-one tickets. TransMontserrat tickets (€19.50) include the train, cable car to/from Montserrat-Aeri, two metro rides and unlimited use of the funiculars. For €34 you can have all this, plus museum entrance and a modest dinner at the self-service restaurant.

Probably the most straightforward route by car from Barcelona is by Avinguda Diagonal, then Via Augusta, the Túnel de Vallvidrera and the C-16. Turn on to the BP-1213, just past Terrassa, and follow it 18km northwest to the C-55. Then head 2km south on this road to Monistrol de Montserrat, from where a road snakes about 7km up the mountain.

Penedès Wine Country

Some of Spain's best wines come from the Alt Penedès area centred on the towns of Sant Sadurní d'Anoia and Vilafranca del Penedès. Sant Sadurní d'Anoia, a half-hour train ride west of Barcelona, is the capital of *cava*, Spanish `Champagne'. Vilafranca del Penedès, 12km down the track, is the heart of

the Penedès DO, which produces noteworthy light still whites. A number of wineries open their doors to visitors (see the listing later in this section) and there'll often be a free glass included in the tour, and plenty more for sale. It's a little ad hoc and often you need to call ahead to arrange a visit.

Simply touring around the area in the hope of bumping into wineries is unlikely to yield results. See the Vilafranca del Penedès entry later in this section for tips on where to gather information before embarking on a wine excursion.

Sant Sadurní d'Anoia One hundred or so wineries around Sant Sadurní produce 140 million bottles of *cava* per year – something like 85% of the national output. *Cava* is made by the same method as French Champagne and is gaining ground in international markets. If you happen to be in town in October, you may catch the Mostra de Caves i Gastronomia, a *cava*- and food-tasting fest that has been held annually since 1997 – this is an opportunity to taste the products of a lot of competing wineries.

Vilafranca del Penedès Vilafranca is larger than Sant Sadurní and is a much more interesting town. The **tourist office** *(☎ 93 892 03 58; Plaça de la Vila; open 9am-1pm & 4pm-7pm Tues-Fri, 10am-1pm Sat & 4pm-7pm Mon)* is a good place to look for information on the local wineries. The tourist office staff can direct you to several places aside from the big boys so you can see how wine and *cava* are made and get a glass or two at the end.

A good place to get a handle on the area's wines is **La Botiga del Celler** *(☎ 93 817 10 35; Carrer del Ateneu 9)*. This wonderful store, which sells a fine selection of local wines and gourmet-food products, is about a five-minute walk from the tourist office.

One block north of the tourist office, the mainly Gothic **Basilica de Santa Maria** faces the combined **Museu de Vilafranca** and **Museu del Vi** *(Wine Museum; ☎ 93 890 05 82; adult/child €3/0.90; open 10am-2pm & 4pm-7pm Tues-Sat, 10am-2pm Sun & holidays)* across Plaça de Jaume I. In the combined museum you learn a little about the town and its wine traditions.

For further information on wineries and wines in the area, you could approach **Penedès Denominació d'Origen** (☎ 93 890 48 11, fax 93 890 47 54; *Plaça de l'Agora*). Located near the A-7 motorway on the way to Tarragona, this is an association of all DO wineries in the region.

Visiting Wineries To do a tour of the area you will need your own transport. As already hinted, you should not expect to wander into any old winery you pass. Many open their doors to the public, if at all, only at limited times during the weekend. The more enthusiastic ones will show you around the place, give you an idea of how wines and/or *cava* are made and finish off with a glass or two. Since *cava* is the area's

single biggest product, it stands to reason that many of the wineries that open to the public specialise in bubbly rather than in still wines. The following list is by no means exhaustive but should get you started:

Blancher (☎ 93 818 32 86) Plaça del Pont Romà 5, Sant Sadurní d'Anoia. Just off the town's main road, La Rambla de la Generalitat, this rather huge place has been going since 1955. There are hourly tours from 9.30am to 12.30pm on Saturday and 9.30am to 1.30pm on Sunday. Visits will lead you around the plant and there is also a small museum. During the week you need to call ahead. If you want to picnic on the grounds, they like you to buy a bottle of their *cava*.

Cava Martín Soler (☎ 93 898 82 20) Located in an attractive farmhouse surrounded by vineyards, at Puigdàlber, 8km north of Vilafranca. This winery only makes various kinds of *cava*. It opens for visits 9am to 1pm and 3pm to 7pm

What's in a Label?

LPP

If your bottle is labelled DO *(denominación de origen)*, you can be sure of reasonable quality. DO refers to those areas that have maintained a consistently high quality of wine over a long period. To qualify, the wine-maker must respect a series of norms on production, choice and mix of grape types. In Catalunya there are nine DO wine areas. Only some wines from Spain's premier wine-growing region, La Rioja, go one better – DOC, or *denominación de origen calificada*.

Other categories of wine, in descending order, are: *denominación de origen provisional* (DOp), *vino de la tierra*, *vino comarcal* and *vino de mesa* (ordinary table wine). The last of these categories can be deceiving. As is happening in Tuscany and some regions of France, some vintners wanting greater flexibility in how they produce their wines are opting out of the DO label and producing magnificent drops that go simply by the label of 'table wine'.

Vino joven is wine made for immediate drinking while *vino de crianza* has to have been stored for certain minimum periods. *Reserva* requires storage of at least three years for reds and two years for whites and rosás. *Gran reserva* is a title permitted for particularly good vintages. These wines must have spent at least two calendar years in storage and three in the bottle. They're mostly reds.

In Catalunya, the 10 DO wines come from points all over the region but the bulk are from the Penedès area, which pumps out almost two million hectolitres per year. The other eight DO wine-growing areas, spread as far apart as the Empordà area around Figueres in the north and the Terra Alta zone around Gandesa in the southwest, together have an output of about half that produced in Penedès.

A new regional qualification is also near to being implemented: DO Catalunya. Quality wines that respect certain norms in terms of grape type and production but do not fall within any specific DO area will come under this new umbrella qualification.

For online information about Catalan wines and *cava*, visit **W** www.interceller.com (in Catalan and Castilian only). From here, there are plenty of links to related subjects and individual wineries.

EXCURSIONS

WINE COUNTRY (ALT PENEDÈS)

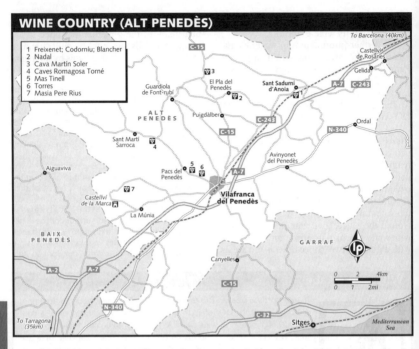

1 Freixenet; Codorníu; Blancher
2 Nadal
3 Cava Martín Soler
4 Caves Romagosa Torné
5 Mas Tinell
6 Torres
7 Masia Pere Rius

Monday to Friday, and 10am to 2pm weekends and holidays.

Caves Romagosa Torné (☎ 93 899 13 53) This winery at Finca La Serra is on the road to Sant Martí Sarroca. Again, although it produces other wines, *cava* is the star. It opens 9am to 1pm and 4pm to 8pm Monday to Saturday, 11am to 1pm on Sunday and holidays. By the way, if you get here, try to move on to the charming little town of Sant Martí Sarroca.

Codorníu (☎ 93 818 32 32; W www.codorniu.es) Bottling *cava* since 1872, it remains one of the best wineries around. The Codorníu headquarters, a modernist building at the entry to Sant Sadurní town by road from Barcelona, opens for free visits 9am to 5pm Monday to Friday, and 9am to 1pm Saturday and Sunday.

Freixenet (☎ 93 891 70 00; W www.freixenet.es) This is the best-known *cava* company (although not everyone agrees its bubbly is the best), based next to the train station in Sant Sadurní d'Anoia at Carrer de Joan Sala 2. It is one of about 20 wineries in Sant Sadurní itself that open, at times, to visitors, although many require you to book ahead. Free tours are given at 9am, 10am, 11.30am, 3.30pm and 5pm Mon-

day to Thursday (also Friday mornings, Saturday and Sunday in December).

Mas Tinell (☎ 93 817 05 86) Here is a good drop that ended up on the table for the Infanta Cristina's wedding. Mas Tinell, northwest of Vilafranca, also does some still wines and technically opens to visitors 9am to noon and 3pm to 6pm Monday to Friday, and 10am to 1pm Saturday, although it's best to call ahead.

Masia Pere Rius (☎ 93 891 82 74) This cute little farmhouse lies just outside La Múnia on the B-212 about 5km southwest of Vilafranca. Here staff show how *cava* is made and will invite you to taste some of the wines as well as the bubbly. It opens 10am to 1pm and 3pm to 8pm Monday to Friday, 10am to 3pm weekends and holidays.

Nadal (☎ 93 898 80 11) Nadal, just outside the hamlet of El Pla del Penedès, has been producing *cava* since 1943. The centrepiece of the place is a fine *masia* (or Catalan country farmhouse), where you can join organised visits in order to become acquainted with the whole process of producing the sparkling wine, including vine-growing and harvesting. A tasting will round off the visit. You can join in at 11.30am, 4pm and

5.30pm Monday to Friday, 11.30am only on Saturday and 10am, 11am, noon and 1pm (this last session in November and December only) on Sunday and holidays.

Torres (☎ 93 817 74 87; W www.torres.es) Three kilometres northwest of the town centre of Vilafranca on the BP-2121 road near Pacs del Penedès, this is the area's premier winery. The Torres family tradition dates from the 17th century, but the family company, in its present form, was founded in 1870. It revolutionised Spanish winemaking back in the 1960s by introducing new temperature-controlled stainless-steel technology and French grape varieties that helped produce much lighter wines than the traditional heavy Spanish plonk. One of the biggest names in the wine world, the Torres enterprise also has wineries in California and Chile. It produces an enormous array of red and white wines of all qualities, using many grape varieties including: Chardonnay, Sauvignon Blanc, Merlot, Cabernet Sauvignon, Pinot Noir and more locally specific ones such as Parellada, Garnacha and Tempranillo. Torres opens for visits 9am to 5pm Monday to Saturday, and 9am to 1pm Sunday and holidays.

Getting There & Away Up to three rodalies trains an hour run from Barcelona Sants to Sant Sadurní (€2.15, 40 minutes) and Vilafranca (€2.65, 50 minutes). By car, take the A-2, then the A-7 and then follow the exit signs.

Conca de Barberà

This hilly, green back-country district comes as a refreshing surprise in the otherwise drab flatlands of southwestern Catalunya. Vineyards and woods succeed one another across rolling green hills, studded with occasional medieval villages and monasteries. The main attraction of the area, however, is the Monestir de Poblet.

If you have time, you should explore the surrounding area, particularly the walled town of **Montblanc**, 8km southeast of the monastery.

Monestir de Poblet The walls of this abbey (☎ 977 87 02 54; adult/student €4.20/2.40; open 10am-12.30pm & 3pm-6pm summer, 10am-12.30pm & 3pm-5.30pm winter) devoted to Santa Maria, as well as being a defensive measure, also symbolised the

An Old Oak Tree

When, way back in 1498, Javier Codorníu bought the land that he would turn into the first vineyards of Sant Sadurní d'Anoia, the single greatest feature of his purchase was a hundred-year-old oak tree.

In the following centuries, a good number of the surrounding country's business deals were solemnly sworn in the shade of the grand old tree. They say that in those days a witnessed handshake was as cast iron a guarantee as anyone could expect.

By the time the first *cava* was bottled in 1872, the tree had become the symbol of the Raventós i Blanc family that ran the winery, and also of the Can Codorníu farm. For Manuel Raventós, the grandson of the original producer of the farm's *cava*, protecting the ancient oak has taken priority even over the business of winemaking. After around 600 years, the grand old oak tree of Can Codorníu is not only in good health, it's even growing!

monks' isolation from the vanities of the outside world. A gate gives access to a long, uneven square, the Plaça Major, flanked by several dependencies including the small Romanesque **Capella de Santa Caterina**. The nearby Porta Daurada is so called because its bronze panels were overlaid with gold to suitably impress the visiting Emperor Felipe II in 1564.

Once inside the **Porta Reial** (Royal Gate), flanked by hefty octagonal towers, you will be led through a worn Romanesque entrance to the grand cloister of Romanesque origins, but largely Gothic in style. With its peaceful fountain and pavilion, the two-level cloister is a marvellous haven. You will be led from the cloister to the head of the church, itself a typically tall and austere Cistercian Gothic creation, to witness the sculptural glory in alabaster that is the **retablo** (altarpiece) and Panteón de los Reyes (Kings Pantheon). The raised alabaster coffins, restored by Frederic Marès (see details on the museum dedicated to him in the Things to See & Do chapter), contain such

EXCURSIONS

greats such as Jaume I (the conqueror of Mallorca and Valencia) and Pere III.

One-hour guided tours of this Unesco World Heritage Site (in Catalan and/or Spanish) start every 15 to 30 minutes. You'll find a **tourist information office** (☎ 977 87 12 47) in the compound.

Getting There & Away Regular trains from Barcelona (Ca4 Regional line) stop at Montblanc (€5.35) and L'Espluga de Francolí (€5.85) – the monastery is a 40-minute walk from the latter.

Sitges
postcode 08870 • pop 17,600
Sitges attracts everyone from jet-setters to young travellers, honeymooners to weekending families, Barcelona night owls to an international gay crowd – anyone after a good time. The beach is long and sandy, the nightlife thumps until breakfast and there are lots of groovy boutiques if you need to spruce up your wardrobe. In winter, Sitges can be quite dead but it wakes up with a vengeance for *carnaval*, when the gay crowd puts on an outrageous show.

Sitges has been fashionable in one way or another since the 1890s, when it became an avant-garde, art-world hang-out. It has been one of Spain's most anticonventional, anything-goes resorts since the 1960s.

Orientation & Information The main landmark is the Església de Sant Bartomeu i Santa Tecla atop a rocky elevation that separates the 2km-long main beach to the southwest from the smaller, quieter Platja de Sant Sebastià to the northeast. The old part of town climbs gently inland from the church, with the train station 500m back, at the top of Avinguda d'Artur Carbonell.

The main **tourist office** (☎ 93 894 42 51, fax 93 894 43 05; ⓦ www.sitgestur.com; Carrer de Sínia Morera 1; open 9am-9pm daily July-Sept, 9am-2pm & 4pm-6.30pm Mon-Fri, 10am-1pm Sat Oct-June) can provide you with information.

Museums There are three museums (☎ 93 894 03 64; admission to each museum €3, to

all museums €5.41; all open 10am-1.30pm & 3pm-6.30pm Tues-Fri, 10am-7pm Sat, 10am-3pm Sun Oct-June, 10am-2pm & 5pm-9pm Tues-Sun July-Sept). The **Museu Cau Ferrat** (Carrer de Fonollar) was built in the 1890s as a house-cum-studio by Santiago Rusiñol – a co-founder of Els Quatre Gats in Barcelona, and the man who attracted the art world to Sitges.

Next door is the **Museu Maricel del Mar**, with art and artistry from the Middle Ages to the 20th century. The museum is part of the Palau Maricel, a stylistic fantasy built around 1910 by Miquel Utrillo. The **Museu Romàntic** (Carrer de Sant Gaudenci 1) re-creates the lifestyle of a 19th-century Catalan land-owning family and contains a collection of several hundred antique dolls.

Beaches The main beach is divided by a series of breakwaters into sections with different names. A pedestrian promenade runs its whole length. Sitges also has two nudist beaches – one exclusively gay – about a 20-minutes' walk beyond Hotel Terramar at the far end of the main beach.

Places to Eat Sprawling and noisy **Los Vikingos** (☎ 93 894 96 87; Carrer del Marques de Montroig 7-9; dishes from €6-8) is a self-service eatery in the thick of the action that does tolerable pasta, pizza and seafood.

Eguzki (☎ 93 811 03 20; Carrer de Sant Pau 3; meals €15) is one of a string of restaurants on Carrer de Sant Pau. This Basque eatery has good tapas and a mixed menu of seafood and meat mains.

Restaurante El Velero (☎ 93 894 20 51; Passeig de la Ribera 38; most mains €30-35; open Thur-Sat, Mon-Tues, & Sun lunch) is a classic glass-fronted fish and seafood joint that's just across from the beach. It's one of several such places.

For real seaside dining you could munch away on expensive tapas at the two **chiringuitos** located on the beach side of Passeig de la Ribera.

El Greco (☎ 93 894 20 51; Passeig de la Ribera 70; meals €40-50; open Thur-Mon & Wed evening) is the most expensive of the

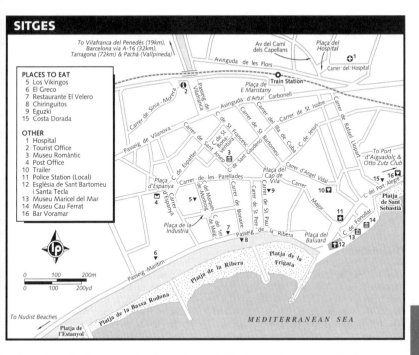

SITGES

To Vilafranca del Penedès (19km),
Barcelona via A-16 (32km),
Tarragona (72km) & Pachá (Vallpineda)

Av del Camí
dels Capellans

Plaça del
Hospital

Avinguda de les Flors

Carrer del Hospital

PLACES TO EAT
5 Los Vikingos
6 El Greco
7 Restaurante El Velero
8 Chiringuitos
9 Eguzki
15 Costa Dorada

OTHER
1 Hospital
2 Tourist Office
3 Museu Romàntic
4 Post Office
10 Trailer
11 Police Station (Local)
12 Església de Sant Bartomeu
i Santa Tecla
13 Museu Maricel del Mar
14 Museu Cau Ferrat
16 Bar Voramar

Train Station

Plaça de
E Maristany

Avinguda d'Artur Carbonell

Carrer de Sinia-Morera

Passeig de Vilanova

Carrer de Vilanova

Passeig de Valfranca

Carrer de Espalter

Plaça
d'Espanya

Carrer
d'Espanya

Carrer de Sant Joseph

C. de St.
Bonaventura

C. de St. Francesc

Carrer de St. Bartomeu

Carrer de illa de Cuba

C. de Sant Gaudenci

Carrer de St Isidre

C. de Jesus

Carrer de St. Pau

Carrer de Rafael Llopart

Plaça del
Cap de
Vila

Carrer d'Angel Vidal

To Port
d'Aiguadolç &
Otto Zutz Club

Carrer de St Pere

Carrer de St Joan

Carrer de les Parellades

Carrer
de Montroig

C. del Marquès
de Maig

C. del 1er
de Maig

Plaça de la
Industria

Carrer de Bonaire

Passeig de la Ribera

Plaça del
Baluard

Carrer

Major

Plaça de
Sant Sebastià

Platja
de Sant
Sebastià

C. del Port Alegre

C. de Fonollar

Passeig-Maritim

Platja de la Ribera

Platja de la Bassa Rodona

Platja de la
Frigata

MEDITERRANEAN SEA

To Nudist Beaches

Platja de
l'Estanyol

0   100   200m
0   100   200yd

---

series of seafood restaurants along the waterfront.

Costa Dorada (☎ 93 894 35 43; Carrer del Port Alegre 27; meals €30; open Fri-Wed) is an old-time classic on this quieter side of town. Old-world service in the 1970s atmosphere (lots of tiles and bottles of wine on display) and reliable standards make it a safe bet, especially for seafood, paella and *fideuá*.

Entertainment Much of Sitges' nightlife happens on one short pedestrian strip packed with humanity right through the night in summer: Carrer del 1er de Maig, Plaça de la Industria and Carrer del Marques de Montroig – all in a short line off the seafront Passeig de la Ribera. Carrer del 1er de Maig – or Calle del Pecado (Sin Street) – vibrates to the volume of 10 or so disco-bars all trying to outdo each other in decibels.

If you're in need of a change of location, head around the corner to either Carrer de les Parellades, Carrer de Bonaire or Carrer de Sant Pere, where you will find even more of the same.

Bar Voramar (Carrer del Port Alegre 55), on Platja de Sant Sebastiá, is a '60s throwback with nautical decoration and good music. Check it out for live jazz sessions.

Carrer de Sant Bonaventura, near Museu Romàntic, has a string of gay bars, mostly behind closed doors. **Trailer** (Carrer d'Àngel Vidal 36) is a very popular gay disco.

Some distance from the centre of town are some of the big discos, such as **Pachá** (☎ 93 894 22 98), in Vallpineda, and the local branch of Barcelona's **Otto Zutz Club** in Port d'Aiguadolç, where you will also find other bars along the waterfront.

Getting There & Away From about 6am to 10pm, four rodalies trains per hour run from Barcelona Sants to Sitges (€2.15, 30 minutes). The best road from Barcelona to Sitges is the A-16 tollway. You can call taxis on either ☎ 93 894 35 94 or ☎ 93 894 13 29.

Tarragona
postcode 43080 • pop 112,800

The Romans raised their base of Tarraco in 218 BC, probably on the site of an earlier Celtiberian settlement. In 27 BC Emperor Augustus made it the capital of his new Tarraconensis province – most of what is now Spain – and lived here until 25 BC while directing campaigns in Cantabria and Asturias. It would not have been long afterwards that Tarragona's most famous son, Pontius Pilate, was supposedly born here. Tarragona was abandoned when the Muslims arrived in AD 714, but reborn as the seat of a Christian archbishopric in 1089. Today it's a mainly modern city, but its rich Roman remains and fine medieval cathedral make it an absorbing place.

Orientation & Information The main street is Rambla Nova, which runs roughly northwest from a cliff top overlooking the Mediterranean. A couple of blocks to the east, and parallel, is Rambla Vella, which marks the beginning of the old town and which follows the line of the Via Augusta, the Roman road from Rome to Cádiz.

The train station is 500m southwest of Rambla Nova, near the seafront, and the bus station is about 2km inland, on Plaça Imperial de Tàrraco.

The **main tourist office** (☎ 977 24 50 64; Carrer Major 39; open 10am-2pm & 4pm-7pm Mon-Sat, 10am-2pm Sun & holidays) is open extra hours July to September.

Catedral Tarragona's cathedral (☎ 977 23 86 85; Pla de la Seu; admission €2.40; open 10am-7pm Mon-Sat July–mid-Oct, 10am-1pm & 4pm-7pm mid-Mar–June, 10am-5pm mid-Oct–mid-Nov, 10am-2pm mid-Nov–mid-Mar, closed Sun & holidays) is a treasure house. Built between 1171 and 1331 on the site of the Roman city's temple, it combines Romanesque and Gothic features, as typified by the main facade on Plaça de la Seu. The entrance is by the cloister on the northwestern side of the building.

The cloister has Gothic vaulting and Romanesque carved capitals. Rooms off the cloister house the Museu Diocesà, with an extensive collection extending from Roman hairpins to some lovely 12th- to 14th-century polychrome woodcarvings of a breast-feeding Virgin.

The interior of the cathedral, over 100m long, is Romanesque at the northeastern end and Gothic at the southwestern end.

The admission includes a detailed booklet.

Museu d'Història de Tarragona This museum (admission to each site €1.87; sites open 9am or 10am-9pm Tues-Sat, 9am-3pm Sun Easter-Sept, 9am-5pm Tues-Sat, 10am-3pm Sun & holidays Oct-Easter) comprises four separate Roman sites and the 14th-century noble mansion, which now serves as the **Museu Casa Castellarnau** (☎ 977 24 27 52; Carrer dels Cavallers 14).

Start with the **Pretori i Circ Romans** (☎ 977 24 19 52; Plaça del Rei), which includes part of the vaults of the Roman circus where chariot races were held. The circus, 300m long, stretched from here to beyond Plaça de la Font. Close to the beach is the well-preserved **Amfiteatre Romà**, where gladiators battled each other, or wild animals, to the death. In its arena are the remains of 6th- and 12th-century churches built to commemorate the martyrdom of the Christian bishop Fructuosus and two deacons, whom they say were burnt alive here in 259.

By Carrer del Lleida are remains of the **Fòrum Romà**, dominated by several imposing columns. The northwestern half of this site was occupied by a judicial basilica (where legal disputes were settled), from which the rest of the forum stretched downhill to the southwest. Linked to the site by a footbridge is another excavated area with a stretch of a Roman street. This forum was the hub of public life for the Roman town but was less important, and much smaller, than the provincial forum, the navel of all Tarraconensis province.

The Passeig Arqueològic is a peaceful walk around part of the perimeter of the old town between two lines of city walls; the inner ones are mainly Roman while the outer ones were put up by the British in the War of the Spanish Succession.

1e Amfiteatre Romà (top left) and other ancient buildings (bottom) at Tarragona on the Costa Daurada ive stunning coastal backdrops. Inland, follow the winding road beneath the towering peaks of ontserrat, the 'serrated mountain'.

SITGES
AIXÒ ÉS VIDA

Detail of Christ and the Twelve Apostles facade at the Monestir de Montserrat (top left); the church and castle of Sant Martí (top right); sample the sights of Sitges (middle); river scene in Girona (botto right); Dalí's trademark eggs, part of the Teatre-Museu Dalí, Figueres (bottom left)

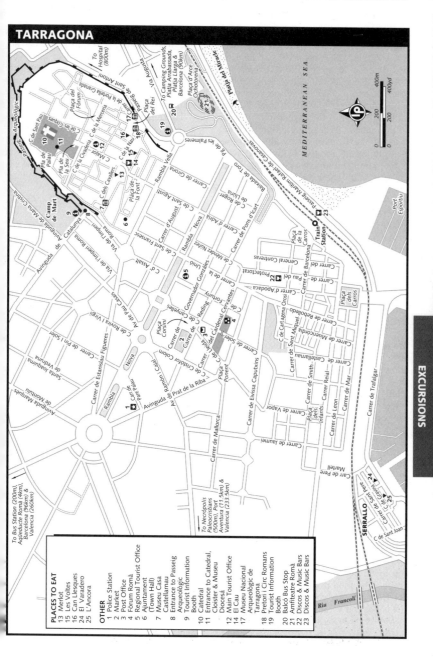

TARRAGONA

PLACES TO EAT
13 Merlot
15 Les Voltes
16 Can Llesques
24 El Varadero
25 L'Ancora

OTHER
1   Police Station
2   Market
3   Post Office
4   Fòrum Romà
5   Regional Tourist Office
6   Ajuntament
    (Town Hall)
7   Museu Casa
    Castellarnau
8   Entrance to Passeig
    Arqueologic
9   Tourist Information
    Booth
10 Catedral
11 Entrance to Catedral,
    Cloister & Museu
    Diocesà
12 Main Tourist Office
14 El Cau
17 Museu Nacional
    Arqueologic de
    Tarragona
18 Pretori i Circ Romans
19 Tourist Information
    Booth
20 Balcó Bus Stop
21 Amfiteatre Romà
22 Discos & Music Bars
23 Discos & Music Bars

Museu Nacional Arqueològic de Tarragona This carefully presented museum (☎ 977 23 62 09; Plaça del Rei 5; admission €2.40; open 10am-8pm Tues-Sat June-Sept, 10am-1.30pm & 4pm-7pm Tues-Sat Oct-May, 10am-2pm Sun & holidays year-round) gives further insight into Roman Tarraco, although most of the explanatory material is in Catalan or Castilian. Exhibits include part of the Roman city walls, frescoes, sculpture and pottery. A highlight is the large, almost complete *Mosaic de Peixos de la Pineda* showing fish and sea creatures. In the section on everyday arts you can admire ancient fertility aids including an outsized stone penis, the symbol of the god Priapus.

Admission entitles you to enter the museum at the **Necròpolis Paleocristians**. This large Christian cemetery of late Roman and Visigothic times is on Passeig de la Independència on the western edge of town and boasts some surprisingly elaborate tombs. Unfortunately only its small museum is open at present.

Beaches The town beach, **Platja del Miracle**, is reasonably clean but can get terribly crowded. **Platja Arrabassada**, 1km northeast across the headland, is longer, and **Platja Llarga**, beginning 2km further out, stretches for about 3km. Bus Nos 1 and 9 from the Balcó stop on Via Augusta go to both (€1). You can get the same buses along Rambla Vella and Rambla Nova.

Places to Eat Looking onto Plaça del Rei, **Can Llesques** (☎ 977 22 29 06; Carrer de Natzaret 6) is a pleasant spot. It offers a cheese platter *(taula de formatges)* for €7 as well as a lot of other dishes, too.

Les Voltes (☎ 977 23 06 51; Carrer de Trinquet Vell 12; menú del día around €10) will appeal if you'd like to eat under the vaults of the former Roman circus. It has set out its dining area on a couple of different levels. The food itself is a little overpriced for what you are served, but the menú del día is not bad value.

Merlot (☎ 977 22 06 52; Carrer dels Cavallers 6; open Tues-Sat, & Mon dinner; meals around €35) is an understated eatery that is one of Tarragona's seriously classy addresses. All sorts of inventive dishes, starting with Catalan classics as a base, are served in this refreshing place. The heavy exposed stone walls are lightened by some paintings and other decoration.

The quintessential Tarragona seafood experience can only be had in the Serrallo, the town's fishing port. About a dozen bars and restaurants here sell the day's catch and on summer weekends in particular the place is packed. Most of the restaurants close their kitchens fairly early – by 10.30pm. Undoubtedly the places to go are **L'Ancora** (☎ 977 24 28 06; Carrer de Trafalgar 25) and its sister establishment **El Varadero** (☎ 977 24 28 06; Carrer de Trafalgar 13). Run by the same people, the places brim with mouthwatering seafood. Go for a selection of dishes (they're all good) at around €7 or less each and wash these down with house white. You can sit inside or, in the summer, take up a seat at the outdoor tables. On weekends and other busy days their kitchens keep running until 2am. Their renown has spread far and wide, with queues of an hour being not unheard of at, say, midnight. Bus No 2 runs here from Rambla Nova.

Entertainment In a Roman circus vault, **El Cau** (Carrer de Trinquet Vell) is a cool hang-out. Otherwise the main concentration of nightlife is along the waterfront behind the train station, and in some of the streets in front of it, such as along Carrer de la Pau del Protectorat.

Getting There & Away Up to 50 regional and long-distance trains per day run to/from Barcelona Passeig de Gràcia via Estació Sants. The cheapest fare costs €4.15 and the journey takes one to 1½ hours. Long-distance trains are faster but more expensive than the regional ones. There are buses too but the train is more convenient.

Port Aventura

Spain's biggest and best funfair-adventure park, Port Aventura (☎ 902 20 22 20;

W *www.portaventura.es; adult/child 5-12 yrs & senior €31/23, night tickets €22; open 10am-7pm, to 10pm weekends 15 Mar-4 Nov & 23 Dec-6 Jan, 10am-midnight mid-June–mid-Sept, 10am-7pm weekends only 4 Nov-23 Dec)* is 7km west of Tarragona. If you have money to spare, it makes an amusing day out, especially if you have ankle-biters in tow. Since Universal bought the park in 1998, Woody Woodpecker has become the park mascot. The park has plenty of spine-tingling rides and other attractions. The big new addition in 2001 was the Temple del Foc (Temple of Fire). Night tickets are valid between 7pm to midnight and are available 22 June to 15 September.

In 2002, Universal opened up an extraordinary leisure centre, Universal Mediterranea (with two theme hotels) next to Port Aventura. In addition came **Universal Costa Caribe** *(adult/child & senior €14/10.50)*, a waterworld with all sorts of wet rides.

Trains run to Port Aventura's own station, about 1km walk from the site, several times a day from Tarragona and Barcelona. Combined rail and entrance tickets from Barcelona cost €33.90/25.40 (adult/child) to Port Aventura or €19.50/14.80 to Universal Costa Caribe. Only a couple of trains run during the week but up to five on Sunday.

By road, take exit 35 from the A-7, or the N-340 from Tarragona.

EXCURSIONS

Language

Barcelona is a bilingual city, with both the local Catalan and Spanish (more accurately Castilian – *castellano*) spoken by just about everyone. Indeed, for every Catalan intent on speaking the local tongue there seems to be another who'll favour Castilian. It *is* true that the signs and menus you read will more often than not be in Catalan.

Foreigners will encounter no ill-feeling for muddling through in Castilian – that in itself is appreciated. If you go the whole hog and try your hand at Catalan, you should earn extra brownie points. It's worth the effort to try at least one local language, as English is not as widely spoken as many travellers seem to expect.

Castilian Spanish

Pronunciation
Vowels
Unlike English, each vowel has a uniform, unvarying pronunciation. For example, the letter 'a' has one pronunciation rather than the numerous ones we find in English, such as in 'cake', 'care', 'cat', 'cart' and 'call'. Many words have a written accent. This acute accent (as in *días*) indicates a stressed syllable; it does not change the sound of the vowel. Vowels are pronounced clearly even if they are in unstressed positions or at the end of a word.

a   somewhere between the 'a' in 'cat' and the 'a' in 'cart'
e   as in 'met'
i   somewhere between the 'i' in 'marine' and the 'i' in 'flip'
o   similar to the 'o' in 'hot'
u   as in 'put'

Consonants
Some consonants are the same as their English counterparts. The pronunciation of other consonants varies according to which vowel follows. The Spanish alphabet also contains the letter ñ, which is not found in the English alphabet. Until recently, the clusters **ch** and **ll** were also officially separate consonants, and you'll most likely encounter many situations – eg, in lists and dictionaries – in which they are still treated that way.

b   soft, as the 'v' in 'van'; also (less commonly) as in 'book' when word-initial or when preceded by a nasal such as 'm' or 'n'
c   as the 'th' in 'thin'
ch as in 'choose'
d   as in 'dog' when word-initial; elsewhere as the 'th' in 'thin'
g   as in 'go' when word-initial or before 'a', 'o' or 'u'; elsewhere much softer. Before 'e' or 'i' it's a harsh, breathy sound, a bit like 'ch' in Scottish *loch*.
h   always silent
j   a harsh, guttural sound similar to the 'ch' in Scottish *loch*
ll similar to the 'y' in 'yellow'
ñ   a nasal sound like the 'ni' in 'onion' or the 'ny' in 'canyon'
q   always followed by a silent 'u' and either 'e' (as in *que*) or 'i' (as in *aquí*); the combined sound of 'qu' is like the 'k' in 'kick'
r   a rolled 'r' sound; longer and stronger when initial or doubled
s   as in 'send'
v   same as 'b'
x   as the 'x' in 'taxi' when between two vowels; as the 's' in 'say' before a consonant
z   as the 'th' in 'thin'

Greetings & Civilities
Hello.	¡Hola!
Goodbye.	¡Adiós!
Yes.	Sí.
No.	No.
Please.	Por favor.

Thank you.	*Gracias.*
You're welcome.	*De nada.*
Excuse me.	*Perdón/Perdone.*
Sorry/Excuse me.	*Lo siento/Discúlpeme.*

Language Difficulties

Do you speak English?	*¿Habla inglés?*
Does anyone speak English?	*¿Hay alguien que hable inglés?*
I (don't) understand.	*(No) Entiendo.*
Just a minute.	*Un momento.*
Could you write it down, please?	*¿Puede escribirlo, por favor?*

Getting Around

What time does the ... leave/arrive?	*¿A qué hora sale/ llega el ...?*
boat	*barco*
bus (city)	*autobús/bus*
bus (intercity)	*autocar*
train	*tren*
metro/ underground	*metro*

next	*próximo*
first	*primer*
last	*último*
1st class	*primera clase*
2nd class	*segunda clase*

I'd like a ... ticket.	*Quisiera un billete ...*
one-way	*sencillo*
return	*de ida y vuelta*

Where is the bus stop?	*¿Dónde está la parada de autobús?*
I want to go to ...	*Quiero ir a ...*
Can you show me (on the map)?	*¿Me puede indicar (en el mapa)?*
Go straight ahead.	*Siga/Vaya todo derecho.*
Turn left.	*Gire a la izquierda.*
Turn right.	*Gire a la derecha.*
here	*aquí*
there	*allí*
near	*cerca*
far	*lejos*

Around Town

I'm looking for ...	*Estoy buscando ...*
a bank	*un banco*
the city centre	*el centro de la ciudad*
the embassy	*la embajada*
my hotel	*mi hotel*
the market	*el mercado*
the police	*la policía*
the post office	*los correos*
public toilets	*los aseos públicos*
a telephone	*un teléfono*
the tourist office	*la oficina de turismo*

the beach	*la playa*
the bridge	*el puente*
the castle	*el castillo*
the cathedral	*la catedral*
the church	*la iglesia*
the hospital	*el hospital*
the lake	*el lago*
the main square	*la plaza mayor*
the mosque	*la mezquita*
the old city	*la ciudad antigua*
the palace	*el palacio*
the ruins	*las ruinas*
the sea	*el mar*
the square	*la plaza*
the tower	*el torre*

Accommodation

Where is a cheap hotel?	*¿Dónde hay un hotel barato?*
What's the address?	*¿Cuál es la dirección?*
Could you write it down, please?	*¿Puede escribirla, por favor?*
Do you have any rooms available?	*¿Tiene habitaciones libres?*

I'd like ...	*Quisiera ...*
a bed	*una cama*
a single room	*una habitación individual*
a double room	*una habitación doble*
a room with a bathroom	*una habitación con baño*
to share a dorm	*compartir un dormitorio*

How much is it ...? *¿Cuánto cuesta ...?*
  per night   *por noche*
  per person   *por persona*

Can I see it?   *¿Puedo verla?*
Where is the   *¿Dónde está el baño?*
  bathroom?

Food
breakfast   *desayuno*
lunch   *almuerzo/comida*
dinner   *cena*

I'd like the set   *Quisiera el menú*
  lunch.   *del día.*
Is service included? *¿El servicio está*
                   incluido?
I'm a vegetarian. *Soy vegetariano/*
                   vegetariana. (m/f)

Time & Dates
What time is it?   *¿Qué hora es?*
today   *hoy*
tomorrow   *mañana*
yesterday   *ayer*
in the morning   *de la mañana*
in the afternoon   *de la tarde*
in the evening   *de la noche*

Monday   *lunes*
Tuesday   *martes*
Wednesday   *miércoles*
Thursday   *jueves*
Friday   *viernes*
Saturday   *sábado*
Sunday   *domingo*

January   *enero*
February   *febrero*
March   *marzo*
April   *abril*
May   *mayo*
June   *junio*
July   *julio*
August   *agosto*
September   *setiembre/septiembre*
October   *octubre*
November   *noviembre*
December   *diciembre*

Emergencies – Spanish

Help!	*¡Socorro!/¡Auxilio!*
Call a doctor!	*¡Llame a un doctor!*
Call the police!	*¡Llame a la policía!*
Where are the toilets?	*¿Dónde están los servicios?*
Go away!	*¡Váyase!*
I'm lost.	*Estoy perdido/a.* (m/f)

Health
I'm ...   *Soy ...*
  diabetic   *diabético/a* (m/f)
  epileptic   *epiléptico/a* (m/f)
  asthmatic   *asmático/a* (m/f)

I'm allergic to ... *Soy alérgico/alérgica*
                   a ... (m/f)
  antibiotics   *los antibióticos*
  penicillin   *la penicilina*

antiseptic   *antiséptico*
aspirin   *aspirina*
condoms   *preservativos/*
                   condones
contraceptive   *anticonceptivo*
diarrhoea   *diarrea*
medicine   *medicamento*
nausea   *náusea*
sunblock cream   *crema protectora*
                   contra el sol
tampons   *tampones*

Numbers
0	*cero*	
1	*uno, una*	
2	*dos*	
3	*tres*	
4	*cuatro*	
5	*cinco*	
6	*seis*	
7	*siete*	
8	*ocho*	
9	*nueve*	
10	*diez*	
11	*once*	
12	*doce*	
13	*trece*	
14	*catorce*	
15	*quince*	
16	*dieciséis*	

17	*diecisiete*
18	*dieciocho*
19	*diecinueve*
20	*veinte*
21	*veintiuno*
22	*veintidós*
23	*veintitrés*
30	*treinta*
31	*treinta y uno*
40	*cuarenta*
50	*cincuenta*
60	*sesenta*
70	*setenta*
80	*ochenta*
90	*noventa*
100	*cien/ciento*
1000	*mil*

one million   *un millón*

Catalan

Pronunciation

Catalan sounds are not hard for an English-speaker to pronounce. You should, however, note that vowels will vary according to whether they occur in stressed or unstressed syllables.

Vowels

a   when stressed, as the 'a' in 'father'; when unstressed, as in 'about'
e   when stressed, as in 'pet'; when unstressed, as in 'open'
i   as the 'i' in 'machine'
o   when stressed, as in 'pot'; when unstressed, as the 'oo' in 'zoo'
u   as the 'u' in 'humid'

Consonants

b   pronounced 'p' at the end of a word
c   hard before 'a', 'o' and 'u' and at the end of a word; soft before 'e' and 'i'
ç   like 'ss'
d   pronounced 't' at the end of a word
g   hard before 'a', 'o' and 'u'; as the 's' in measure before 'e' and 'i'
h   silent
j   as the 's' in 'pleasure'
r   as in English in the middle of a word; silent at the end of a word
rr the roll of the tongue 'r', at the beginning of a word, or a doubled 'rr' in the middle of a word
s   as in 'so' at the beginning of a word; as 'z' in the middle of a word
v   as a 'b' in Barcelona; pronounced 'v' in some other areas
x   mostly as in English; sometimes 'sh'

Other letters are approximately as in English. There are a few odd combinations:

l.l repeat the 'l'
tx   like 'ch'
qu   like 'k'

Greetings & Civilities

Hello.	*Hola.*
Goodbye.	*Adéu.*
Yes.	*Sí.*
No.	*No.*
Please.	*Sisplau/Si us plau.*
Thank you (very much).	*(Moltes) gràcies.*
You're welcome.	*De res.*
Excuse me.	*Perdoni.*
May I?/Do you mind?	*Puc?/Em permet?*
Sorry. (forgive me)	*Ho sento/Perdoni.*
What's your name?	*Com et dius?* (inf)
	Com es diu? (pol)
My name's ...	*Em dic ...*
Where are you from?	*D'on ets?*

Language Difficulties

Do you speak English?	*Parla anglès?*
Could you speak in Castilian please?	*Pot parlar castellà sisplau?*
I (don't) understand.	*(No) ho entenc.*
Could you repeat that?	*Pot repetir-ho?*
Could you please write that down?	*Pot escriure-ho, sisplau?*
How do you say ... in Catalan?	*Com es diu ... en català?*

Getting Around

What time does the ... leave?	A quina hora surt ... ?
bus	l'autobús
flight	le vol
train	le tren

I'd like a ... ticket.	Voldria un bitllet ...
one-way	d'anada
return	d'anar i tornar

Where is (the) ...?	On és ...?
bus station	l'estació d'autobusos
train station	l'estació de tren
subway station	la parada de metro

How do I get to ...?	Com puc arribar a ...?
I want to go to ...	Vull anar a ...
Please tell me when we get to ...?	Pot avisar-me quan arribem a ...?

baggage claim	recollida d'equipatges
departures	sortides
exchange	canvi
platform	andana

Turn left.	Giri a mà esquerra.
Turn right.	Giri a mà dreta.
here	aquí
there	allà
near	a prop
far	lluny de

Around Town

I'm looking for ...	Estic buscant ...
a bank	un banc
the city centre	el centre de la ciutat
the market	el mercat
the police	la policia
the post office	el correus
a public toilet	els lavabos públics
a restaurant	un restaurant
the telephone centre	la central telefònica
the tourist office	l'oficina de turisme

What time does it open/close?	A quina hora obren/tanquen?

I want to change ...	Voldria canviar ...
some money	diners
travellers cheques	txecs de viatge

Accommodation

Is there a camp site/ hotel near here?	Hi ha algun càmping/ hotel a prop d'aquí?
Do you have any rooms available?	Hi ha habitacions lliures?

I'd like ...	Voldria ...
a single room	una habitació individual
a double room	una habitació doble
to share a dorm	compartir un dormitori

I want a room with a ...	Vull una habitació amb ...
bathroom	cambra de bany
double bed	llit de matrimoni
shower	dutxa

How much is it per night/person?	Quant val per nit/persona?
Does it include breakfast?	Inclou l'esmorzar?
Are there any cheaper rooms?	Hi ha habitacions més barates?
I'm going to stay for (one week).	Em quedaré (una setmana).
I'm leaving now.	Me'n vaig ara.

Shopping

Where can I buy ...?	On puc comprar ...?

Where is the nearest ...?	On és ...més propera/proper? (m/f)
bookshop	la llibreria
camera shop	el botiga de fotos
department store	el gran magatzem
greengrocer	el botiga de verdures (or la fruiteria)
launderette	la bugaderia
market	el mercat
newsagency	el quiosc
pharmacy	la farmàcia
supermarket	el supermercat
travel agency	la agència de viatges

open	obert
closed	tancat
more	més
less	menys

condoms	*preservatius/condons*	Monday	*dilluns*
deodorant	*desodorant*	Tuesday	*dimarts*
razor blades	*fulles d'afaitar*	Wednesday	*dimecres*
sanitary napkins	*compreses*	Thursday	*dijous*
shampoo	*xampú*	Friday	*divendres*
shaving cream	*crema d'afaitar*	Saturday	*dissabte*
soap	*sabó*	Sunday	*diumenge*
sunblock cream	*crema solar*		
tampons	*tampons*	January	*gener*
tissues	*mocadors de paper*	February	*febrer*
toilet paper	*paper higiènic*	March	*març*
toothbrush	*raspall de dents*	April	*abril*
toothpaste	*pasta de dents*	May	*maig*
		June	*juny*
magazines	*revistes*	July	*juliol*
newspapers	*diaris*	August	*agost*
postcards	*postals*	September	*setembre*
envelope	*sobre*	October	*octubre*
map	*mapa*	November	*novembre*
pen (ballpoint)	*bolígraf*	December	*desembre*
stamp	*segell*		

Health

I'm allergic to ...	*Soc al.lèrgi a ...*
antibiotics	*antibiòtics*
penicillin	*penicil.lina*

Time & Dates

What time is it?	*Quina hora és?*
It's one o'clock.	*És la una.*
It's two o'clock.	*Són les dues.*
It's quarter past six.	*És un quart de set.*
It's half past eight.	*Són dos quarts de nou.*

One thing to remember when asking about times in Catalan: minutes past the hour (eg quarter past, twenty-five past) are referred to as being before the next hour. Thus:

2.30 becomes *dos quarts de tres* (two quarters of three, or 30 of 3)

9.20 becomes *un quart i cinc de deu* (one quarter and five minutes of ten, or 20 of 10)

9.40 becomes *tres quarts menys cinc de deu* (three quarters minus five minutes of ten, or 40 of 10)

4.50 becomes *tres quarts i cinc de cinc* (three quarters and five minutes of five, or 50 of 5).

Numbers

0	*zero*
1	*un, una*
2	*dos, dues*
3	*tres*
4	*quatre*
5	*cinc*
6	*sis*
7	*set*
8	*vuit*
9	*nou*
10	*deu*
11	*onze*
12	*dotze*
13	*tretze*
14	*catorze*
15	*quinze*
16	*setze*
17	*disset*
18	*divuit*
19	*dinou*
20	*vint*
30	*trenta*
40	*quaranta*
50	*cinquanta*
60	*seixanta*
70	*setanta*
80	*vuitanta*
90	*noranta*
100	*cent*
1000	*mil*

Food

breakfast	*esmorzar*
lunch	*dinar*
dinner	*sopar*

May I see the menu please?	*Puc veure el menú, sisplau?*
I'm a vegetarian.	*Soc vegetarià/ vegetariana.* (m/f)
Bon appétit/Cheers!	*Bon profit!/Salut!*

I'd like ... please	*Voldria ... sisplau*
the set lunch	*el menú del dia*
the bill	*el compte*
another bottle	*una ampolla més*
more bread	*més pa*
salt and pepper	*sal i pebre*
an ashtray	*un cendrer*

cutlery	*coberts*
dessert	*postres*
a drink	*una beguda*

Some Popular Catalan Dishes

allioli – garlic sauce

amanida Catalana – Catalan salad; almost any mix of lettuce, olives, tomatoes, hard-boiled eggs, onion, chicory, celery, green pepper and garlic, with fish, ham or sausage, and mayonnaise or an oil-and-vinegar dressing

arròs a la cassola or *arròs a la Catalana* – Catalan paella, cooked in an earthenware pot, without saffron

arròs negre – rice cooked in cuttlefish ink; quite black. It sounds awful but it tastes very good

bacallà a la llauna – salted cod baked in tomato, garlic, parsley, paprika and wine

botifarra amb mongetes – pork sausage with fried white beans

calçots amb romesco – *calçots* are a type of long onion, delicious as a starter with romesco sauce. Catalans sometimes get together for a *calçotada*, the local version of a BBQ!

cargols – snails, almost a religion in parts of Catalunya; often stewed with *conill* (rabbit) and chilli

coca – a dense, flat pastry, especially popular during St Joan (John) celebrations, when the pastry is decorated with candied peel or pine nuts

crema Catalana – a crème caramel with a burnt toffee sauce

ensaimada mallorquina – a sweet Mallorcan pastry

escalivada – red peppers and aubergines (sometimes onions and tomatoes as well), grilled, cooled, peeled, sliced and served with an olive oil, salt and garlic dressing

escudella – a meat, sausage and vegetable stew, the liquid of which is mixed with noodles or rice and served as a soup, followed by the rest served as a main course known as *carn d'olla*. It's generally available in winter only

espinacas a la Catalana – spinach with raisins and pine kernels

esqueixada – salad of shredded salted cod (*bacallà*) with tomato, red pepper, onion, white beans, olives, olive oil and vinegar

fideuá – similar to paella but using vermicelli noodles as the base, it is usually served with tomato and meat/sausage or with fish

fricandó – a pork and vegetable stew

fuet – a thin dried pork sausage, native to Catalunya

mandonguilles amb sipia – meatballs with cuttlefish, a subtly flavoured land-sea combination

mel i mató – honey and fresh cream cheese; simple but delicious

mongetes seques i botifarra – haricot beans with thick pork sausage

music – a serving of dried fruits and nuts, sometimes mixed with ice cream or a sweetish cream cheese and served with a glass of sweet muscatel wine

Food for Thought

Although, in some restaurants, the menus (cartas) are available in English, French and one or two other languages, the choices in most places will be Catalan and Castilian only, with an emphasis on the former. The following decoder will help steer you through some of the labyrinth.

pa amb tomàquet (i pernil) – crusty bread rubbed with ripe tomatoes, garlic and olive oil, often topped with cured ham

paella – dish made of rice, chicken and shellfish. Remember, paella is Valencian in origin – if you only have it once, try to have it in Valencia

pollastre amb escamerlans – chicken with shrimps, another amphibious event

sarsuela (zarzuela) – mixed seafood cooked in *sofregit* with seasonings – a Barcelona invention

sobrassada – a spreadable red sausage; a speciality in Mallorca

suquet de peix – fish, potato and tomato soup

tortilla de botifarra – sausage omelette

Food Decoder

Here are more words (with, where they differ, their Castilian equivalents) to help you with Catalan-only menus:

ametller (almendra) – almond
anyell (cordero) – lamb (see *xai*)
bacallà (bacalao) – salted cod
bou (buey) – beef
caldereta – a seafood stew
carxofe (alcachofa) – artichoke
castanya (castaña) – chestnut
ceba (cebolla) – onion
costella (chuleta) – cutlet
cranc (cangrejo/centello) – crab
entrepà (bocadillo) – bread roll with filling
farcit (relleno) – stuffed
formatge (queso) – cheese
fregit (frito) – fried
gelat (helado) – ice cream
llagosta (langosta) – lobster
llenties (lentejas) – lentils
llet (leche) – milk
llonganissa (longaniza) – pork sausage
oli (aceite) – oil
ostra – oyster
ous (huevos) – eggs
pastís (pastel) – cake/pie

pebre (pimienta) – pepper
peix (pescado) – fish
pernil de la comarca – country-cured ham
pop (pulpo) – octopus
rap (rape) – monkfish
suquet – stew (like a French bouillabaisse)
torrada (tostada) – open toasted sandwich
trucha – trout
truita (trucha) – omelette/tortilla; trout
xai – lamb

Drinks

tiger-nut drink	*orxata*
fruit juice	*suc*
mineral water (plain, no gas)	*aigua mineral (sense gas)*
tap water	*aigua de l'aixeta*
soft drinks	*refrescos*
coffee ...	*cafè ...*
with liquer	*carajillo (cigaló* in northern Catalunya)
with a little milk	*tallat*
with milk	*amb llet*
black coffee	*cafè sol*
long black	*doble*
iced coffee	*cafè gelat*
decaffeinated coffee	*cafè descafeinat*
tea	*te*

Catalunya is famous for its *cava*, the region's 'champagne'.

a beer	*una cervesa*
a champagne	*un cava*
a rum	*un rom*
a whisky	*un whisky*
muscatel	*moscatell*
ratafia (liquer)	*ratafia*
a glass of ... wine	*un vi ...*
red	*negre*
rosé	*rosat*
sparkling	*d'agulla*
white	*blanc*

Glossary

Items listed below are in Catalan/Castilian (Spanish) where they start with the same letter. Where the two terms start with different letters, they have their own entry – identified as Catalan (C) or Spanish (S). Identified in the same way are words given in only one or the other language, either because that term is predominantly used by all, or because the word is the same in both languages. In a few other cases, the Spanish alone is given as the only distinction from the Catalan is the addition of accents. For a detailed listing of popular Catalan dishes, see the language chapter.

abierto – (S) open
aigua/agua – water
ajuntament/ayuntamiento – city or town hall
alberg de joventut/albergue juvenil – youth hostel; not to be confused with *hostal*
alcalde – (C & S) mayor
allioli – (C) sauce of garlic and olive oil, occasionally with egg yolk
altar major/mayor – high altar
amanides – (C) salads
anyell – (C) lamb
apartat de correus/apartado de correos – post office box
arribada – (C) arrival
arròs/arroz – rice
artesonado – (S) *Mudéjar* wooden ceiling with interlaced beams leaving a pattern of spaces for decoration
autonomía – (S) autonomous community or region; Spain's 50 *provincias* are grouped into 17 of these, one of which is Catalunya
autopista – (C & S) tollway
autovía – (S) toll-free dual carriageway

...lao – (S) ear-splitting Spanish ...c (not to be confused with ...lted cod)
...) bathroom

Barcelonin – (C) inhabitant/native of Barcelona
barri/barrio – district, quarter of Barcelona
BCN – an abbreviation for Barcelona
biblioteca – (C & S) library
bikini – (C) toasted ham and cheese sandwich
bocadillo – (S) filled roll
bodega – (S) literally, a cellar (especially a wine cellar); also means a winery, or a traditional wine bar likely to serve wine from the barrel
botiga – (S) shop
bústia/buzón – postbox

caixer automàtic/cajero automático – automated teller machine (ATM)
call – (C) Jewish quarter in medieval Barcelona (and other Catalan towns)
canvi/cambio – in general, change; also currency exchange
canya/caña – a small beer in a glass
cap de setmana – (C) weekend
capella major/capilla mayor – chapel containing the high altar of a church
capella/capilla – chapel
capgròs – (C) huge-headed figure seen in traditional Catalan festivals
carn/carne – meat
Carnestoltes/Carnaval – carnival; the period of fancy-dress parades and merry-making ending on the Tuesday 47 days before Easter Sunday
carrer/calle – street
carretera – (C & S) highway
carta – (C & S) menu
casa de pagès/casa rural – a village or country house or farmstead with rooms to let
castellers – (C) human castle builders
catedral – (C & S) cathedral
cava – Catalan version of champagne
celler – (C) see *bodega*
cena – (S) dinner
cercanías – (S) local trains serving

Barcelona's airport, suburbs and some
outlying towns

cerdo – (S) pork

cerrado – (S) closed

cerveseria/cervezería – beer bar

chiringuito – (S) covered beach bar

churros con chocolate – (S) deep-fried
pastry with hot chocolate

claustre/claustro – cloister

comarca – (C & S) district, a grouping of
municipalities

comedor – (S) dining room, sit-down
restaurant

comida – (S) lunch, food

comissaria/comisaría – police station

compte/cuenta – bill (check)

comte/conde – count

consigna – (C & S) left-luggage office or
lockers

copes/copas – drinks (literally, glasses);
anar de copes/ir de copas is to go out for
a few drinks

cor/coro – choir (part of a church,
usually in the middle)

cordero – (S) lamb

correfoc – (C) fire-running, a part of
many Catalan *festes* where people run
about the streets chased by fire-breathing
dragons and the like

**Correus i Telègrafs/Correos y
Telégrafos** – post office

costa – (C & S) coast

desayuno – (S) breakfast

dinar – (C) lunch

ensalada – (S) salad

entera – (S) whole

entrada – (C & S) entrance

entremeses – (S) hors d'oeuvres

entrepans – (C) filled rolls

església – (C) church

esmorzar – (C) breakfast

**estació d'autobusos/estación de
autobuses** – bus station

estancs/estancos – tobacconist shops
that also sell stamps

ferrocarril – (C & S) railway

festa/fiesta – festival, public holiday or
party

FGC – (C) Ferrocarrils de la Generalitat
de Catalunya; local trains operating alongside the metro in Barcelona

fin de semana – (S) weekend

fira/feria – (trade) fair

flamenc/flamenco – means flamingo
and Flemish as well as flamenco music
and dance

Frankfurt – no, not the name of a bar but
a generic (if bizarre) name for bars that
traditionally serve *entrepans* (see earlier)

futbol – (S) football

futbolín – (S) table football

Generalitat – regional government

garum – (Latin) a spicy, vitamin-rich
sauce made from fish entrails found
throughout the former Roman Empire,
including Barcelona

gegant – (C) a huge figure, usually
representing kings, queens and other
historical figures, often seen parading
around at *festes*

gelats – (C) ice cream

gitano – (C & S) the Roma people,
formerly called Gypsies

granissat/granizado – iced-fruit crush

guapa – (S) beautiful

havaneres – (C) nostalgic songs and sea
shanties

helados – (S) ice cream

horchata – (S) tiger-nut drink

hostal – (C & S) commercial establishment providing accommodation in the one-
to three-star category; not to be confused
with *alberg de joventut/albergue juvenil*

huevos – (S) eggs

iglesia – (S) church

infusión de hierbas – (S) herbal tea

IVA – *impost sobre el valor afegit/im-
puesto sobre el valor añadido*, or value-
added tax (VAT)

llegada – (S) arrival

llet/leche – milk

llibreria or llibreteria/librería –
bookshop

llista de correus/lista de correos –
poste restante

llitera/litera – couchette or sleeping carriage

mariscs/mariscos – seafood
marisquería – (S) seafood eatery
marxa/marcha – action, life, 'the scene'
masia – (C) Catalan country farmhouse
media – (S) half
menjador – (C) dining room, sit-down restaurant
menú – (S) short form of menú del día; not to be confused with *carta*
menú del día – (S) fixed-price meal available at lunchtime, sometimes in the evening too
mercat/mercado – market
mesón – (S) literally 'big table', a modest eatery
Modernisme – (C) modernism; the architectural and artistic style, influenced by Art Nouveau and sometimes known as Catalan modernism, whose leading practitioner was Antoni Gaudí
Modernista – (C & S) an exponent of Modernisme
moll/muelle – wharf or pier
Mudéjar – (S) a Muslim living under Christian rule in medieval Spain; also refers to their decorative style of architecture
museu/museo – museum

obert – (C) open
oca – (S) goose
oficina de turisme/turismo – tourist office
orxata – (C) tiger-nut drink
ous – (C) eggs

paella – (S) rice, seafood and meat dish
parrillada de pescado – (S) mixed seafood grill
peix/pescados – fish
penya/peña – a club, usually of flamenco or football fans
pica pica – (C) snacks/snacking
picada – (C) sauce of ground almonds, ~~rsley~~, pine nuts and breadcrumbs
~~)sh~~
~~chos~~ – Basque for *tapes*/tapas
~~C & S~~) swimming pool

plaça/plaza – plaza
plaça de braus/plaza de toros – bullring
plat combinat/plato combinado – literally 'combined plate', a large serving of meat/seafood/omelette with trimmings
platja/playa – beach
poble/pueblo – village
pollastre/pollo – chicken
pont/puente – bridge; also means the extra day or two off that many people take when a holiday falls close to a weekend
porc – (C) pork
porta/puerta – gate or door
porto/puerto – port
potable – (S) fit to drink
provincia – (C & S) province; Spain is divided into 50 of them

ración – (S) a larger portion of a tapa dish
REAJ – (S) Red Española de Albergues Juveniles, the Spanish HI youth hostel network
Realisme – artistic movement in mid-19th-century Catalunya in which artists sought to reflect in painting what they saw in real life
Reconquista – the Christian reconquest of the Iberian Peninsula from the Muslims (8th to 15th centuries)
refrescs/refrescos – soft drinks
refugi/refugio – shelter or refuge, especially a mountain refuge with basic accommodation for walkers
Renaixença – Renaissance period during the second half of the 19th century. There was a revival in all things Catalan and the Catalan language was readopted by the middle and upper classes
Renfe – (S) Red Nacional de los Ferrocarriles Españoles, the national rail network
retaula/retablo – retable, or altarpiece
riu/río – river
rodalies – (C) see *cercanías*
romesco – (C) sauce of almonds, tomato olive oil, garlic and vinegar
rovellons – (S) mushrooms

s/n – (S) *sin número* (without number)

saló – (S) hall
samfaina – (C) sauce of fried onion, tomato and garlic with red pepper and aubergine or courgette
sandwich mixto – (S) toasted ham and cheese sandwich
sardana – (C) traditional Catalan folk dance
serra/sierra – mountain range
Setmana Santa/Semana Santa – Holy Week, the week leading up to Easter Sunday
SIDA – (C & S) AIDS
sidrería – (S) cider bar
sofregit – (C) sauce of fried onion, tomato and garlic
sopa – soup
sopar – (C) dinner
sortida/salida – exit or departure

tancat – (C) closed
tapes/tapas – bar snacks traditionally served on a saucer or lid (tapa)
taquilla – (C & S) ticket window
targeta de crèdit/tarjeta de crédito – credit card
tarjeta telefónica – (S) phonecard
tascas – (S) snack bars
tavernes/tabernas – taverns
ternera – (S) beef

terrassa/terraza – terrace; often means a café or bar's outdoor tables
tienda – (S) shop
torero – (S) bullfighter
torrada – (C) open toasted sandwich
torre – (S) tower
tostada – (S) buttered toast
turisme/turismo – means both tourism and saloon car; *el turismo* can also mean the tourist office
turrón – (S) nougat

urbanització/urbanización – suburban housing development

v.o. – *versión original*, a foreign-language film subtitled in Spanish
vall/valle – valley
vedella – (C) beef
vella – (C) old
venta de localidades – (S) ticket office
verdures/verduras – vegetables
vi/vino – wine

Xarxa d'Albergs de Catalunya – (C) umbrella organisation for youth hostels in Catalunya
xocolata – (C) chocolate
xurros amb xocolata – (C) deep-fried pastry with hot chocolate

Lonely Planet Guides by Region

Lonely Planet is known worldwide for publishing practical, reliable and no-nonsense travel information in our guides and on our Web site. The Lonely Planet list covers just about every accessible part of the world. Currently there are 16 series: Travel guides, Shoestring guides, Condensed guides, Phrasebooks, Read This First, Healthy Travel, Walking guides, Cycling guides, Watching Wildlife guides, Pisces Diving & Snorkeling guides, City Maps, Road Atlases, Out to Eat, World Food, Journeys travel literature and Pictorials.

AFRICA Africa on a shoestring • Botswana • Cairo • Cairo City Map • Cape Town • Cape Town City Map • East Africa • Egypt • Egyptian Arabic phrasebook • Ethiopia, Eritrea & Djibouti • Ethiopian Amharic phrasebook • The Gambia & Senegal • Healthy Travel Africa • Kenya • Malawi • Morocco • Moroccan Arabic phrasebook • Mozambique • Namibia • Read This First: Africa • South Africa, Lesotho & Swaziland • Southern Africa • Southern Africa Road Atlas • Swahili phrasebook • Tanzania, Zanzibar & Pemba • Trekking in East Africa • Tunisia • Watching Wildlife East Africa • Watching Wildlife Southern Africa • West Africa • World Food Morocco • Zambia • Zimbabwe, Botswana & Namibia
Travel Literature: Mali Blues: Traveling to an African Beat • The Rainbird: A Central African Journey • Songs to an African Sunset: A Zimbabwean Story

AUSTRALIA & THE PACIFIC Aboriginal Australia & the Torres Strait Islands •Auckland • Australia • Australian phrasebook • Australia Road Atlas • Cycling Australia • Cycling New Zealand • Fiji • Fijian phrasebook • Healthy Travel Australia, NZ & the Pacific • Islands of Australia's Great Barrier Reef • Melbourne • Melbourne City Map • Micronesia • New Caledonia • New South Wales • New Zealand • Northern Territory • Outback Australia • Out to Eat – Melbourne • Out to Eat – Sydney • Papua New Guinea • Pidgin phrasebook • Queensland • Rarotonga & the Cook Islands • Samoa • Solomon Islands • South Australia • South Pacific • South Pacific phrasebook • Sydney • Sydney City Map • Sydney Condensed • Tahiti & French Polynesia • Tasmania • Tonga • Tramping in New Zealand • Vanuatu • Victoria • Walking in Australia • Watching Wildlife Australia • Western Australia
Travel Literature: Islands in the Clouds: Travels in the Highlands of New Guinea • Kiwi Tracks: A New Zealand Journey • Sean & David's Long Drive

CENTRAL AMERICA & THE CARIBBEAN Bahamas, Turks & Caicos • Baja California • Belize, Guatemala & Yucatán • Bermuda • Central America on a shoestring • Costa Rica • Costa Rica Spanish phrasebook • Cuba • Cycling Cuba • Dominican Republic & Haiti • Eastern Caribbean • Guatemala • Havana • Healthy Travel Central & South America • Jamaica • Mexico • Mexico City • Panama • Puerto Rico • Read This First: Central & South America • Virgin Islands • World Food Caribbean • World Food Mexico • Yucatán
Travel Literature: Green Dreams: Travels in Central America

EUROPE Amsterdam • Amsterdam City Map • Amsterdam Condensed • Andalucía • Athens • Austria • Baltic States phrasebook • Barcelona • Barcelona City Map • Belgium & Luxembourg • Berlin • Berlin City Map • Britain • British phrasebook • Brussels, Bruges & Antwerp • Brussels City Map • Budapest • Budapest City Map • Canary Islands • Catalunya & the Costa Brava • Central Europe • Central Europe phrasebook • Copenhagen • Corfu & the Ionians • Corsica • Crete • Crete Condensed • Croatia • Cycling Britain • Cycling France • Cyprus • Czech & Slovak Republics • Czech phrasebook • Denmark • Dublin • Dublin City Map • Dublin Condensed • Eastern Europe • Eastern Europe phrasebook • Edinburgh • Edinburgh City Map • England • Estonia, Latvia & Lithuania • Europe on a shoestring • Europe phrasebook • Finland • Florence • Florence City Map • France • Frankfurt City Map • Frankfurt Condensed • French phrasebook • Georgia, Armenia & Azerbaijan • Germany • German phrasebook • Greece • Greek Islands • Greek phrasebook • Hungary • Iceland, Greenland & the Faroe Islands • Ireland • Italian phrasebook • Italy • Kraków • Lisbon • The Loire • London • London City Map • London Condensed • Madrid • Madrid City Map • Malta • Mediterranean Europe • Milan, Turin & Genoa • Moscow • Munich • Netherlands • Normandy • Norway • Out to Eat – London • Out to Eat – Paris • Paris • Paris City Map • Paris Condensed • Poland • Polish phrasebook • Portugal • Portuguese phrasebook • Prague • Prague City Map • Provence & the Côte d'Azur • Read This First: Europe • Rhodes & the Dodecanese • Romania & Moldova • Rome • Rome City Map • Rome Condensed • Russia, Ukraine & Belarus • Russian phrasebook • Scandinavian & Baltic Europe • Scandinavian phrasebook • Scotland • Sicily • Slovenia • South-West France • Spain • Spanish phrasebook • Stockholm • St Petersburg • St Petersburg City Map • Sweden • ᵈland • Tuscany • Ukrainian phrasebook • Venice • Vienna • Wales • Walking in Britain • Walking in ᵍ in Ireland • Walking in Italy • Walking in Scotland • Walking in Spain • Walking in Switzer-ᵢ Europe • World Food France • World Food Greece • World Food Ireland • World Food Italy • pain **Travel Literature:** After Yugoslavia • Love and War in the Apennines • The Olive Grove: ᵉece • On the Shores of the Mediterranean • Round Ireland in Low Gear • A Small Place in Italy

Lonely Planet Mail Order

Lonely Planet products are distributed worldwide. They are also available by mail order from Lonely Planet, so if you have difficulty finding a title please write to us. North and South American residents should write to 150 Linden St, Oakland, CA 94607, USA; European and African residents should write to 10a Spring Place, London NW5 3BH, UK; and residents of other countries to Locked Bag 1, Footscray, Victoria 3011, Australia.

INDIAN SUBCONTINENT & THE INDIAN OCEAN Bangladesh • Bengali phrasebook • Bhutan • Delhi • Goa • Healthy Travel Asia & India • Hindi & Urdu phrasebook • India • India & Bangladesh City Map • Indian Himalaya • Karakoram Highway • Kathmandu City Map • Kerala • Madagascar • Maldives • Mauritius, Réunion & Seychelles • Mumbai (Bombay) • Nepal • Nepali phrasebook • North India • Pakistan • Rajasthan • Read This First: Asia & India • South India • Sri Lanka • Sri Lanka phrasebook • Tibet • Tibetan phrasebook • Trekking in the Indian Himalaya • Trekking in the Karakoram & Hindukush • Trekking in the Nepal Himalaya • World Food India **Travel Literature:** The Age of Kali: Indian Travels and Encounters • Hello Goodnight: A Life of Goa • In Rajasthan • Maverick in Madagascar • A Season in Heaven: True Tales from the Road to Kathmandu • Shopping for Buddhas • A Short Walk in the Hindu Kush • Slowly Down the Ganges

MIDDLE EAST & CENTRAL ASIA Bahrain, Kuwait & Qatar • Central Asia • Central Asia phrasebook • Dubai • Farsi (Persian) phrasebook • Hebrew phrasebook • Iran • Israel & the Palestinian Territories • Istanbul • Istanbul City Map • Istanbul to Cairo • Istanbul to Kathmandu • Jerusalem • Jerusalem City Map • Jordan • Lebanon • Middle East • Oman & the United Arab Emirates • Syria • Turkey • Turkish phrasebook • World Food Turkey • Yemen **Travel Literature:** Black on Black: Iran Revisited • Breaking Ranks: Turbulent Travels in the Promised Land • The Gates of Damascus • Kingdom of the Film Stars: Journey into Jordan

NORTH AMERICA Alaska • Boston • Boston City Map • Boston Condensed • British Columbia • California & Nevada • California Condensed • Canada • Chicago • Chicago City Map • Chicago Condensed • Florida • Georgia & the Carolinas • Great Lakes • Hawaii • Hiking in Alaska • Hiking in the USA • Honolulu & Oahu City Map • Las Vegas • Los Angeles • Los Angeles City Map • Louisiana & the Deep South • Miami • Miami City Map • Montreal • New England • New Orleans • New Orleans City Map • New York City • New York City City Map • New York City Condensed • New York, New Jersey & Pennsylvania • Oahu • Out to Eat – San Francisco • Pacific Northwest • Rocky Mountains • San Diego & Tijuana • San Francisco • San Francisco City Map • Seattle • Seattle City Map • Southwest • Texas • Toronto • USA • USA phrasebook • Vancouver • Vancouver City Map • Virginia & the Capital Region • Washington, DC • Washington, DC City Map • World Food New Orleans **Travel Literature**: Caught Inside: A Surfer's Year on the California Coast • Drive Thru America

NORTH-EAST ASIA Beijing • Beijing City Map • Cantonese phrasebook • China • Hiking in Japan • Hong Kong & Macau • Hong Kong City Map • Hong Kong Condensed • Japan • Japanese phrasebook • Korea • Korean phrasebook • Kyoto • Mandarin phrasebook • Mongolia • Mongolian phrasebook • Seoul • Shanghai • South-West China • Taiwan • Tokyo • Tokyo Condensed • World Food Hong Kong • World Food Japan **Travel Literature:** In Xanadu: A Quest • Lost Japan

SOUTH AMERICA Argentina, Uruguay & Paraguay • Bolivia • Brazil • Brazilian phrasebook • Buenos Aires • Buenos Aires City Map • Chile & Easter Island • Colombia • Ecuador & the Galapagos Islands • Healthy Travel Central & South America • Latin American Spanish phrasebook • Peru • Quechua phrasebook • Read This First: Central & South America • Rio de Janeiro • Rio de Janeiro City Map • Santiago de Chile • South America on a shoestring • Trekking in the Patagonian Andes • Venezuela **Travel Literature**: Full Circle: A South American Journey

SOUTH-EAST ASIA Bali & Lombok • Bangkok • Bangkok City Map • Burmese phrasebook • Cambodia • Cycling Vietnam, Laos & Cambodia • East Timor phrasebook • Hanoi • Healthy Travel Asia & India • Hill Tribes phrasebook • Ho Chi Minh City (Saigon) • Indonesia • Indonesian phrasebook • Indonesia's Eastern Islands • Java • Lao phrasebook • Laos • Malay phrasebook • Malaysia, Singapore & Brunei • Myanmar (Burma) • Philippines • Pilipino (Tagalog) phrasebook • Read This First: Asia & India • Singapore • Singapore City Map • South-East Asia on a shoestring • South-East Asia phrasebook • Thailand • Thailand's Islands & Beaches • Thailand, Vietnam, Laos & Cambodia Road Atlas • Thai phrasebook • Vietnam • Vietnamese phrasebook • World Food Indonesia • World Food Thailand • World Food Vietnam

ALSO AVAILABLE: Antarctica • The Arctic • The Blue Man: Tales of Travel, Love and Coffee • Brief Encounters: Stories of Love, Sex & Travel • Buddhist Stupas in Asia: The Shape of Perfection • Chasing Rickshaws • The Last Grain Race • Lonely Planet … On the Edge: Adventurous Escapades from Around the World • Lonely Planet Unpacked • Lonely Planet Unpacked Again • Not the Only Planet: Science Fiction Travel Stories • Ports of Call: A Journey by Sea • Sacred India • Travel Photography: A Guide to Taking Better Pictures • Travel with Children • Tuvalu: Portrait of an Island Nation

LONELY PLANET

You already know that Lonely Planet produces more than this one guidebook, but you might not be aware of the other products we have on this region. Here is a selection of titles that you may want to check out as well:

Barcelona Map
ISBN 1 86450 174 X
US$5.99 • UK£3.99

Madrid Map
ISBN 1 74059 322 7
US$5.99 • UK£3.99

Spanish phrasebook
ISBN 0 86442 475 2
US$5.95 • UK£3.99

Spain
ISBN 1 86450 192 8
US$24.99 • UK£14.99

Madrid
ISBN 1 74059 174 7
US$14.99 • UK£8.99

World Food Spain
ISBN 1 86450 025 5
US$12.95 • UK£7.99

Andalucia
ISBN 1 74059 279 4
US$17.99 • UK£10.99

Catalunya & the Costa Brava
ISBN 1 86450 315 7
US$17.99 • UK£11.99

Valencia & the Costa Blanca
ISBN 1 74059 032 5
US$17.99 • UK£11.99

Canary Islands
ISBN 1 86450 310 6
US$15.99 • UK£9.99

Mediterranean Europe
ISBN 1 74059 302 2
US$27.99 • UK£16.99

Walking in Spain
ISBN 0 86442 543 0
US$17.95 • UK£11.99

Available wherever books are sold

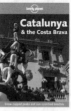
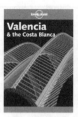

Index

Text

Bold indicates maps.

Boxed Asides

Places to Stay

Bold indicates maps.

Places to Eat

Ham for sale, Mercat de la Boqueria

A café window shows its wares

Advertising for a bullfight

Playing dominos on La Barceloneta beach

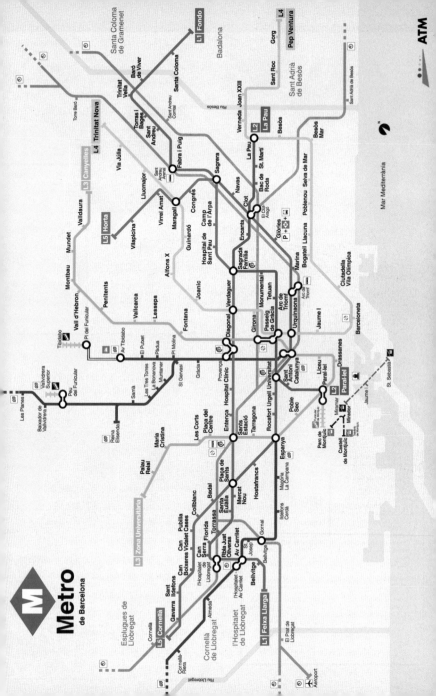

MAP 1 – BARCELONA

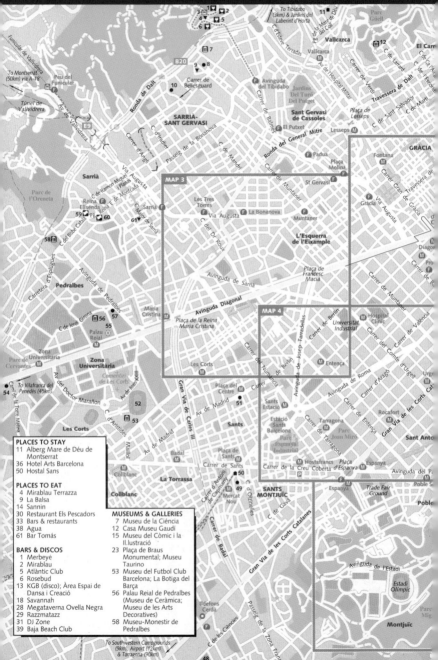

PLACES TO STAY
11 Alberg Mare de Déu de Montserrat
36 Hotel Arts Barcelona
50 Hostal Sans

PLACES TO EAT
4 Mirablau Terrazza
9 La Balsa
14 Sannin
30 Restaurant Els Pescadors
33 Bars & restaurants
38 Agua
61 Bar Tomás

BARS & DISCOS
1 Merbeyé
2 Mirablau
5 Atlàntic Club
6 Rosebud
13 KGB (disco); Àrea Espai de Dansa i Creació
18 Savannah
28 Megataverna Ovella Negra
29 Razzmatazz
31 DJ Zone
39 Baja Beach Club

MUSEUMS & GALLERIES
7 Museu de la Ciència
12 Casa Museu Gaudí
15 Museu del Còmic i la Il.lustració
23 Plaça de Braus Monumental; Museu Taurino
53 Museu del Futbol Club Barcelona; La Botiga del Barça
56 Palau Reial de Pedralbes (Museu de Ceràmica; Museu de les Arts Decoratives)
58 Museu-Monestir de Pedralbes

To Southwestern Campgrounds (9km); Airport (12km) & Tarragona (90km)

48

OTHER
3 Tibidabo Funicular Estació Inferior (Lower Station)
8 Universitat Ramon Llull
10 Bellesguard
16 Hospital de la Santa Creu i de Sant Pau; Biblioteca de Catalunya
17 Hospital Creu Roja
19 Barcelona Activa
20 Centre Comercial de les Glòries
21 Els Encants Vells Flea Market
22 Institut Municipal de Persones amb Disminució & Centre Municipal d'Informació i Recursos per a les Dones
24 Teatre Nacional de Catalunya
25 L'Auditori

26 Estació del Nord (Bus Station)
27 Palau de Justica
32 Yelmo Cineplex Icària
34 Torre Mapfre
35 Gran Casino de Barcelona
37 Peix Sculpture
40 Banys Sant Sebastiá
41 Torre de Sant Sebastiá & Torre d'Alta Mar
42 World Trade Center & Grand Marina Hotel
43 Torre de Jaume I
44 Ferry Terminal (Trasmediterránea & Turbocat)
45 Trasmediterránea fast ferry dock
46 Trasmediterránea Ferry Terminal
47 Barcelona-Genoa Ferry Dock
48 Fira de Barcelona - Complex 2
49 Coordinadora Gai-Lesbiana
51 Farmàcia Saltó
52 Camp Nou
54 RACC
56 Parc del Palau Reial
57 Finca Güell Gate
59 Canadian Consulate
60 US Consulate

Walk 1 p96
Walk 2 p98
Walk 3 pp100-01

0 250 500m
0 250 500yd

MAP 2 – GRÀCIA & CENTRAL L'EIXAMPLE

Plaça de
la Torre

Carrer de Torrent de l'Olla

Plaça de
la Virreina

Plaça de
Sant Lluís

To Plaça de
Rovira i Trias (400m)

Cajal

Plaça del
Diamant

Carrer de l'Or

Carrer de Verdi

Carrer de la Perla

GRÀCIA

Carrer de Montmany

Carrer de Ramon y

Carrer de Balèn

Avinguda del Príncep d'Astúries

Carrer de los Carolines

Carrer d'Astúries

Carrer de Torrijos

Fontana

Carrer de Milà i Fontanals

Carrer de Montseny

Plaça de
la Revolució
de Setembre
de 1868

Food
Market

Carrer de Puigmartí

Carrer de Siracusa

Plaça de
Raspall

Carrer de Ros de Olano

Plaça del
Sol

Carrer del Planeta

Carrer de Maspons

Carrer de Pere Serafí

Carrer de Siguès de Valls

Travessera de Gràcia

Carrer de Lincoln

Carrer Gran de Gràcia

Plaça de Rius
i Taulet

Carrer de Torrent de l'Olla

Carrer del Perill

Carrer de Laforja

Plaça de la
Llibertat

Carrer de Martínez de la Rosa

Carrer de Còrse

Gràcia

Via Augusta

Carrer de Regàs

Carrer de Vic

Carrer de la Riera Sant Miquel

Carrer Maria

Carrer de Francisco Giner

Carrer de Mozart

Carrer de Bonavista

Travessera de Gràcia

Carrer de la Granada del Penedés

Carrer de Sèneca

Plaça
de Joan
Carlos I

Carrer de Pau

MAP 3

Carrer de Tuset

Carrer de Balmes

Diagonal

Passeig de Gràcia

Carrer d'Arbau

Carrer de Moià

Avinguda Diagonal

Diagonal

Carrer de Còrsega

Carrer de Londres

Carrer de París

Carrer d'Enric
Granados

Carrer de Balmes

Provença

Carrer de Muntaner

Carrer d'Enric Granados

Carrer de Provença

Rambla de Catalunya

Carrer de Casanova

Carrer de Còrsega

Carrer del Rosselló

Carrer de Mallorca

Carrer de València

Carrer de Ar

Hospital Clínic
i Provincial

Plaça del
Doctor Ferrer
i Cajigal

Carrer d'Arbau

0   100   200m

0   100   200yd

MAP 4

La Sagrada
Família

Avinguda de Gaudí

Plaça de
Gaudí

Carrer de Lepant

Carrer de Sant Antoni Maria Claret

Carrer de la Indústria

Carrer de Roger de Flor

Carrer de Nàpols

Carrer de Sicília

Sagrada
Família
M

26

Carrer de Marina

Passeig de Sant Joan

Carrer de Grassot

Carrer de Còrsega

Carrer de Rosselló

Carrer de Provença

Carrer de Roger de Flor

Plaça de
la Sagrada
Família

Carrer de Sardenya

27

Carrer de València

25

Carrer de Mallorca

Carrer d'Aragó

Carrer de Bailèn

Carrer de Rosselló

Passeig de Sant Joan

Verdaguer
M

Plaça Mossèn
Jacint
Verdaguer

Avinguda   Diagonal

Carrer d'Aragó

Carrer del Consell de Cent

Verdaguer
M

29

Avinguda   Diagonal

28

Carrer de la Diputació

Passeig de Sant Joan

Carrer de Provença

Carrer de Mallorca

Carrer d'Aragó

45

Carrer d'Aragó

L'EIXAMPLE

Carrer de Girona

Carrer de Bailèn

Tetuan
M

63

Carrer de València

Carrer del Bruc

Girona
M

Plaça
de Tetuan

64

65

66

67

88

Carrer d'Aragó

Passeig de Mèndez Vigo

Carrer de Roger de Llúria

Carrer de la Diputació

87

86

89

90

92

Carrer de les Corts Catalanes

Carrer de Casp

114

116

117

91

Passeig de Gràcia
M

93

115

Gran Via de les Corts Catalanes

Carrer del Bruc

Carrer de Girona

Carrer d'Ausiàs Marc

97

Mançana de la
Discòrdia

112

113

Carrer del Consell de Cent

Carrer de Pau Claris

118

98

99

100

101

110

111

Carrer de Roger de Llúria

Carrer de Casp

102

108

MAP 6

103

105

107

109

Passeig de Gràcia

104

106

119

120

122

121

123

124

125

Ronda de Sant Pere

MAP 5

MAP 2 – GRÀCIA & CENTRAL L'EIXAMPLE

PLACES TO STAY
15 Hostal San Medín
18 Pensión Norma
65 Hotel Claris
69 Comtes de Barcelona Hotel; Vasari; Tous
79 Hotel Balmes
82 Hotel Regente
85 Hotel Majèstic & Drolma restaurant
104 Hostal Neutral
107 Hostal Oliva; Adolfo Domínguez
111 St Moritz Hotel
118 Hotel Ritz
121 Hotel Gran Via

PLACES TO EAT
7 Dionisos
11 Cal Juanito
19 Botafumeiro
20 Sol Soler
21 The Bagel Shop
22 La Singular
38 Restaurant Roig Robí
54 La Dama (Casa Sayrach)
59 El Japonés
60 Tragaluz
67 FrescCo
68 Centro Asturiano
70 Principal
71 Pans & Company
75 El Racó d'en Baltà
80 Cerveseria Catalana
81 Bocatta
89 L'Hostal de Rita
93 Restaurant Madrid Barcelona
94 Cafè Torino
99 Pans & Company
108 Swan
110 Thai Gardens
120 Quasi Queviures (Qu Qu)

BARS & DISCOS
3 Café la Virreina
4 Café Salambó
9 Buda
14 Café del Sol
16 Otto Zutz

23 Gusto
25 Michael Collins Pub
30 Sala Cibeles
31 Sabor Cubano
32 Bar Musical Zimbabwe
33 Alfa
34 Maria
35 Café de la Calle
36 Martin's
37 Bahía
39 Member's
51 The Sutton Club
53 Luz de Gas
56 Velvet
72 La Bodegueta
73 Nick Havanna
76 La Fira
115 Fuse

MUSEUMS & GALLERIES
86 Museu Egipci
87 Fundación Francisco Godia
96 Fundació Antoni Tàpies

HISTORIC BUILDINGS
1 Casa Vicenç
2 Església de Sant Josep
26 Sagrada Família; Museu Gaudí
29 Casa de les Punxes (Casa Terrades)
43 Casa Comalat
44 Palau Quadras (former Museu de la Música)
61 La Pedrera (Casa Milà)
84 Casa Enric Batlló
97 Casa Batlló
98 Casa Amatller; Joyería Bagués
100 Regia; Museu del Parfum
101 Casa Lleó Morera; Cartier; Loewe

OTHER
5 Verdi Park
6 Verdi
8 Teatre Lliure
10 Teatreneu
12 Wash'N Dry Launderette

13 Laundry
17 Mercat de la Llibertat
24 Artenbrut
27 Inetcorner
28 Hertz
40 Cambra Oficial de Comerç, Indústria i Navegació
41 Casablanca
42 German Consulate
45 Bd Ediciones de Diseño
46 Vinçon
47 American Express
48 Palau Robert (Regional Tourist Office)
49 Calvin Klein
50 Giorgio Armani
52 Institut Français de Barcelona
55 Gucci
57 Alitalia
58 Avis
62 Farmàcia Castells (24 hours)
63 Swedish Consulate
64 Italian Consulate
66 La Casa Elizalde
74 Galeria Victor Saavedra
77 Come In Bookshop
78 Planet Music
83 Camper
88 Conéctate
90 Istituto Italiano di Cultura
91 Post Office
92 Casa del Libro
95 Bulevard Rosa; Centre Català d'Artesania
102 Antonio Miró
103 Xocolateria Valor
105 Natura Selection
106 Max Mara
109 Iberia
112 Halcón Viatges
113 Café Interlight
114 Belgian Consulate
116 Pullmantur
117 Europcar
119 Farmàcia Álvarez (24-hours)
122 Laie Bookshop
123 Ca la Dona
124 7-Eleven
125 Workcenter

MAP 3 – WESTERN L'EIXAMPLE

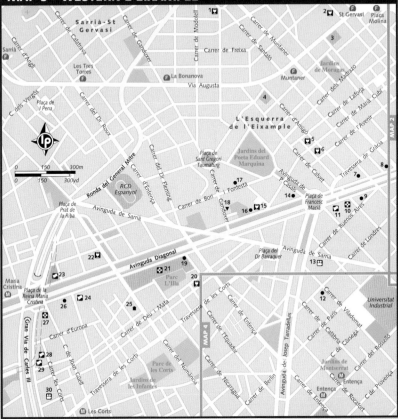

MAP 3 – WESTERN L'EIXAMPLE

PLACES TO STAY & EAT
18 Via Veneto
25 Alberg Pere Tarrès

BARS & DISCOS
1 Cova del Drac
2 La Rosa
5 Universal
6 Mas i Mas
15 Vlad; Lolita
20 Bikini
22 Up & Down

OTHER
3 Institute for North
    American Studies
4 British Council
7 Zara
8 Loewe
9 Jean Pierre Bua
10 El Corte Inglés
11 British Consulate;
    La Boîte
12 Vanguard
13 Filmoteca

14 Gianni Versace
16 Giorgio Armani
17 Ortiga
19 FNAC
21 L'Illa del Diagonal
23 Japanese Consulate
24 Dutch Consulate
26 La Vinia
27 El Corte Inglés
28 Australian Consulate
29 Swiss Consulate
30 Renoir-Les Corts

MAP 4 – WEST OF CIUTAT VELLA

PLACES TO STAY
13 Pensión Aribau
23 Hostal Australia &
   Hostal Central
25 Hotel Lleó
27 Hotel Inglaterra
30 Hotel Mesón de Castilla
47 Hotel AB Viladomat
50 Hostal Sofia

PLACES TO EAT
1 Yamadory
4 Gargantúa i Pantagruel
14 Restaurant de l'Escola de
   Restauració I Hostalatge
20 Bar Estudiantil
24 Pans & Company
40 Tress I No Res
41 Horchatería Sirvent
53 Kohenoor
54 Shellfish

BARS & DISCOS
5 Arena
6 Arena Clasic
8 Arena VIP; Arena Dandy
12 Satanassa
15 Àtame
16 Dietrich
17 Punto BCN
32 Metro
34 La Paloma
35 Imprevist
38 Jazz Si Club

OTHER
2 Xampany
3 Farmàcia Torres (24 hours)
7 Danish Consulate
9 Altäir Bookshop
10 Alibri Bookshop
11 University Information
   Office (Informació)
18 Méliès Cinemes
19 National/Atesa
21 Viatgi
22 Julià Tours
26 Casanova
28 Castelló
29 CD-Drome
31 Centre de Cultura
   Contemporània
   de Barcelona (CCCB)
33 ECOM
36 Renoir Floridablanca
37 ONCE
39 La Maison Coloniale
42 Goethe Institut
43 Aerobus Stop to Airport
44 The English Bookshop
45 Turisme Juvenil de
   Catalunya; Xarxa
   d'Albergs de Catalunya
   & usit Unlimited
46 Punt d'Informació Juvenil
48 Dona i Ocell Sculpture
49 Julià Car
51 Estació d'Autobusos de Sants
52 Aerobus Stop to Airport

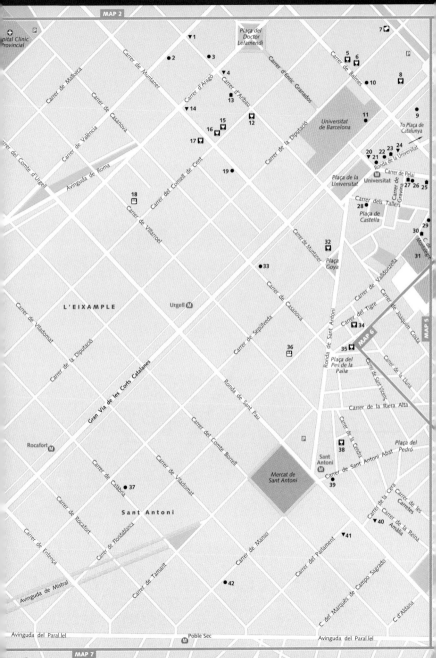

MAP 5 – CENTRAL BARCELONA

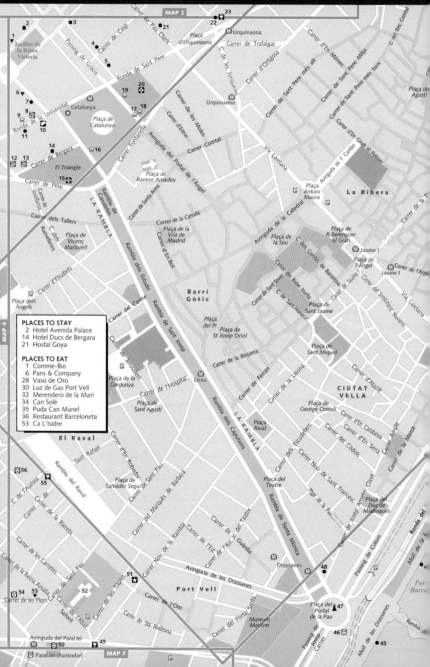

PLACES TO STAY
- 2 Hotel Avenida Palace
- 14 Hotel Ducs de Bergara
- 21 Hostal Goya

PLACES TO EAT
- 1 Comme-Bio
- 6 Pans & Company
- 28 Vaso de Oro
- 30 Luz de Gas Port Vell
- 32 Merendero de la Mari
- 34 Can Solé
- 35 Puda Can Manel
- 36 Restaurant Barceloneta
- 53 Ca L'Isidre

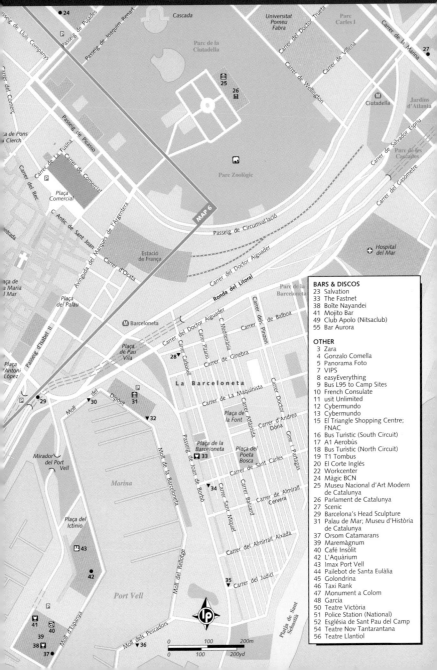

Cascada

Universitat Pompeu Fabra

Parc Carles I

Parc de la Ciutadella

Carrer del Doctor Trueta

Carrer de la Marina

Passeig de Lluís Companys

Passeig de Pujades

24

Passeig de Joaquim Renart

27

Carrer del Comerç

Passeig de Picasso

Carrer de Vilena

Carrer de Wellington

Ciutadella

Jardins d'Atlanta

25

26

Carrer de Salvador Espriu

Parc de les Cascades

Carrer del Rec

Carrer de la Fusina

Carrer de Comercial

Plaça Comercial

Parc Zoològic

Carrer del Gasòmetre

a de Pons

Clerch

C Antic de Sant Joan

Avinguda del Marquès de l'Argentera

Passeig de Circumval·lació

Estació de França

Carrer d'Ocata

Carrer del Doctor Aiguader

MAP 6

Hospital del Mar

a de

a Maria

l Mar

Plaça del Palau

Carrer del Doctor Aiguader

Ronda del Litoral

Parc de la Barceloneta

Passeig d'Isabel II

Barceloneta

Carrer dels Pescadors...

Plaça Antoni López

29

Moll

30

Dipòsit

31

32

Carrer Pizarro

Carrer Cabanes

Carrer de Ginebra

Carrer de La Maquinista

La Barceloneta

Carrer de La Maquinista

Carrer Atlàntida

Carrer Doctor

Carrer dels Pinzon

Mediterrània

Carrer dels Balboa

28

Plaça de Pau Vila

Plaça de la Font

Carrer d'Andrea Dòria

Cine i Pertalges

Carrer de Sant Carles

Mirador del Port Vell

Marina

Plaça del Ictineo

42

Port Vell

Passeig de Joan de Borbó

Plaça de la Barceloneta

33

34

Plaça del Poeta Bosca

Carrer de Sant Carles

Carrer Sant Miquel

Carrer Baluard

Carrer de Almirall Cervera

Moll del Rellotge

35

Carrer del Judici

Carrer del Almirall Aixàda

43

Moll d'Espanya

41

40

39

38

37

Moll dels Pescadors

36

Platja de Sant Sebastià

0   100   200m

0   100   200yd

MAP 6 – CIUTAT VELLA

MAP 6 – CIUTAT VELLA

PLACES TO STAY
1 Hostal Gat Raval
16 Pensión Noya
23 Hotel Nouvel
25 Hotel Continental
32 Hostal Fontanella
40 Hostal Lausanne; Zara
42 Hostal Campi
45 Le Meridien
53 Hostal-Residencia Rembrandt
56 Hotel Colón
59 Alberg Hostel Itaca
86 Hotel Racó del Pi
87 Hostal Galerias Maldà; Maldà Cinema
93 Hotel Jardi
105 Alberg Center Rambles
107 Hotel Principal
108 Hotel Joventut
109 Hostal La Terrassa
111 Hotel San Agustín
112 Hotel Peninsular
113 Hostal Residencia Opera
114 Hostal Mare Nostrum
118 Hotel Call
128 Hotel Suizo
130 Hotel Rey Don Jaime I
138 Pensión Fernando
141 Pensión Bienestar
147 Hotel España; Fonda Espanya
148 Ideal Youth Hostel
157 Hotel Oriente
158 Pensión Villanueva
172 Hostal Levante
180 Hotel Roma Reial
184 Youth Hostel Kabul
196 Hotel Cuatro Naciones
197 Hotel Comercio
198 Hotel Barcelona House
202 Casa Huéspedes Mari-Luz
203 Alberg Juvenil Palau
210 Hotel Banys Orientals; Senyor Parellada
280 Hostal El Cantón
281 Hostal Nilo

PLACES TO EAT
5 Pla dels Angels
10 Elisabets
11 Buenas Migas
14 Bar Kasparo
15 Café Zurich
21 Pans & Company
22 Bocatta
24 Self-Naturista
29 Hard Rock Cafe
35 Bocatta
38 Els Quatre Gats
39 Betawi
41 The Bagel Shop
44 Champion Supermarket
46 Biocenter
47 Lupino
48 Ra
52 Bar Jardi
54 Pans & Company
57 Bar Els Hispanos
58 Shunka
62 Glüh
65 Restaurant L'Econòmic
67 Espai Sucre
70 Pla de la Garsa
71 Bunga Raya
73 Comme-Bio (La Botiga)
85 Croissanterie del Pi
88 Granja La Pallaresa
92 Xocolateria La Xicra
96 Irati
99 Juicy Jones
103 Casa Leopoldo
104 Restaurant El Cafetí
110 Rita Blue
119 Salterio
123 Santa Clara
124 Bon Mercat
127 Il Caffè di Roma
129 La Colmena
134 Bocatta
142 Sushi-Ya
143 Maoz
144 Cafè de l'Òpera
149 Restaurante Pollo Rico
150 Kashmir Restaurant Tandoori
161 Les Quinze Nits
163 Pans & Company
166 Restaurant Agut d'Avignon
168 El Gran Café
170 La Cereria
173 Superservis supermarket
179 Santamonica
199 Los Caracoles
200 La Verónica
204 Venus Delicatessen
209 Cometacinc
211 La Carassa
213 Habana Vieja
228 Little Italy
231 Centre Cultural Euskal Etxea
235 El Xampanyet
237 El Pebre Blau
238 L'Ou Com Balla
239 La Flauta Mágica
243 Hofmann
255 Restaurante Estrella
256 Ábac
257 Cal Pep
258 Gades
260 Estrella de Plata
261 Coses de Menjar
268 Restaurant Pitarra
269 Mastroqué
282 Ristorante Il Mercante di Venezia
283 El Paraguayo
284 Margarita Blue
287 Bar Celta
288 Restaurant Set Portes
289 Can Paixano

BARS & DISCOS
2 Benidorm
3 Granja de Gavà
4 Casa Almirall
7 Café Que Pone Muebles Navarro
12 L'Ovella Negra
20 Boadas
68 El Foro
89 Segundo Acto
90 Bar Roca
94 Bar del Pi
115 Travel Bar
121 Del Paradis
139 Schilling
151 Bar Marsella
152 The Quiet Man
153 London Bar
154 Milk House Café
155 Salsitas
159 Barcelona Pipa Club
160 Glaciar
162 Sidecar
164 Bar Malpaso
175 Al Limón Negro
176 Shanghai
177 Zoo
178 Thiossan
181 Karma
182 Sala Tarantos
183 Jamboree
188 Enfants
189 Bar La Concha
192 Panams
205 Harlem Jazz Club
208 Bodega la Palma
212 El Nus
221 Luz de Luna
224 Gimlet
225 Borneo
229 El Copetín
230 Miramelindo
240 Va de Vi
244 Abaixadors 10
245 La Vinya del Senyor
248 La Tinaja
249 Magic
252 Suborn
253 Repùblica
259 Mudanzas
265 Parnasse
267 Síncopa
270 Dot

MAP 6 – CIUTAT VELLA

271 Moog
272 Kentucky
273 Bar Pastís
285 Antinous

MUSEUMS & GALLERIES
9 Museu d'Art Contemporani de Barcelona (Macba)
66 Museu de Zoologia & Castell dels Tres Dragons
69 Museu de la Xocolata
78 Museu Frederic Marès
84 Museu del Calçat
100 Museu de l'Eròtica
125 Museu d'Història de la Ciutat (Casa Padellàs)
215 Museu Tèxtil i d'Indumentària; Museu Barbier-Mueller d'Art Precolombí
220 Museu Picasso
222 Museu de Geologia
274 Centre d'Art Santa Mònica
276 Museu Marítim
279 Museu de Cera

HISTORIC BUILDINGS
8 Convent dels Àngels
34 Palau de la Música Catalana
43 Roman Tombs
49 Palau de la Virreina
50 Llibreria & Informaciò Cultural de la Generalitat de Catalunya; Casa de Comillas
72 Capella d'En Marcús
74 Capella Reial de Santa Àgata
75 Palau del Lloctinent
76 Saló del Tinell
77 Mirador del Rei Martí
79 Casa de la Pia Almoina; Museu Diocesà
80 Casa de l'Ardiaca
81 Capella de Santa Llúcia
82 Església de Sant Sever
83 Palau Episcopal
101 Antiga Casa Figueras
120 Palau de la Generalitat
122 Temple Romà d'Agustí

133 Església de Sants Just i Pastor
136 Ajuntament (Town Hall); Information
171 Casa Centelles
185 Palau Güell
206 Casa Gualbes
233 Palau de Dalmases
246 Església de Santa Maria del Mar

OTHER
6 Cheap Rate Phone Office
13 Daily Record
17 Rock & Blues
18 Castelló
19 Castelló
26 Drinking Fountain
27 Asatej
28 Taxi Rank
30 Banco de España
31 Oficina d'Informació de Turisme de Barcelona
33 International House
36 Ceràmiques í Terrisses Cadí
37 Ceramica
51 Institut Català de la Dona
55 Col.legi de Arquitectes
60 Casa Bonnemaison
61 Casal Lambda
63 Arc de Triomf
64 easyCar
91 Quera Bookshop
95 Estamperia d'Art
97 Farmàcia Clapès (24 hours)
98 Documenta Bookshop
102 Antic Hospital de la Santa Creu; Biblioteca de Catalunya
106 Teatre Romea
116 La Condoneria
117 Casa Miranda
126 Cereria Subirà
131 Pròleg Bookshop
132 Formatgeria La Seu
135 Centre d'Informació Turisme de Barcelona
137 Obach
140 Jeanne Weiss

145 American Express
146 Gran Teatre del Liceu
156 Police Station (Guàrdia Urbana)
165 Sestienda
167 CIAJ
169 La Cafetera de l'Esbart Català de Dansaires
174 Loft Avignon
186 Wash'N Dry laundrette
187 Centre Cívic Drassanes
190 Escola Oficial d'Idiomes de Barcelona
191 Teatre Principal
193 easyEverything
194 Tablao Cordobés
195 Arpi
201 Cómplices Bookshop
207 Objectes Perduts (lost property)
214 Bcnet
216 Galleria Africa Negra
217 L'Ametller
218 Sala Montcada of the Fundació La Caixa; Galeria Beaskoa
219 Galeria Surrealista
223 Teatre Malic
226 Ètnia
227 Aspectes
232 Galeria Maeght
234 Galeria Montcada
236 Casa Gispert
241 BCN Bike
242 El Magnífico
247 Un Cotxe Menys
250 Bicycle hire places
251 Park Entrance
254 Artquitect
262 Lavomatic
263 Servei d'Atenció a la Víctima
264 Main Post Office
266 New Phono
275 El Gat Sculpture
277 Universitat Pompeu Fabra
278 Lavomatic
286 Universitat Pompeu Fabra

Fantastic tile detail, Parc Güell

DALE BUCKTON

MAP 7 – MONTJUÏC

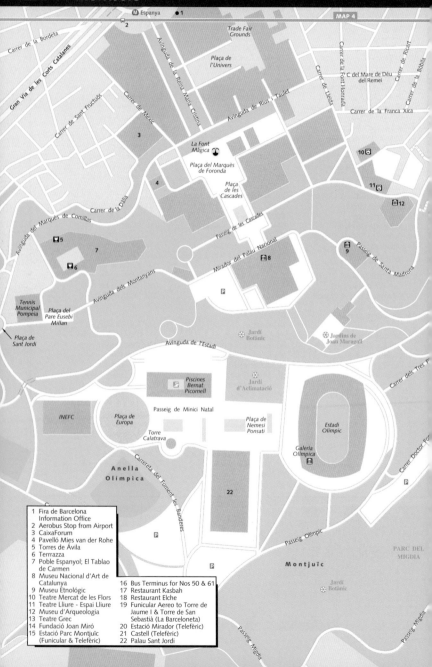

M Espanya ● 1

MAP 4

Carrer de la Bordeta

Gran Via de les Corts Catalanes

Carrer de Sant Fructuós

Carrer de Mèxic

Avinguda de la Reina Maria Cristina

Trade Fair Grounds

Plaça de l'Univers

Carrer de la Font Honrada

Carrer de Lleida

Carrer de Rius i Taulet

Avinguda de Rius i Taulet

C del Mare de Déu del Remei

Carrer de Ricart

Carrer de la Bòbila

Carrer de la Franca Xica

3

La Font Màgica

Plaça del Marquès de Foronda

10

4

Plaça de les Cascades

11

Avinguda del Marquès de Comillas

Carrer de la Dàlia

Passeig de les Cascades

12

5

7

6

Mirador del Palau Nacional

8

9

Passeig de Santa Madrona

Avinguda dels Montanyans

Tennis Municipal Pompeia

Plaça del Pare Eusebi Millan

Plaça de Sant Jordi

P

Jardí Botànic

Jardins de Joan Maragall

Carrer dels Tres P

Avinguda de l'Estadi

Piscines Bernat Picornell

Jardí d'Aclimatació

Passeig de Minici Natal

Plaça de Nemesi Ponsati

Estadi Olímpic

Carrer Doctor For

INEFC

Plaça de Europa

Torre Calatrava

Galeria Olímpica

Anella Olímpica

Carretera del Foment les Banderes

22

Passeig Olímpic

P

PARC DEL MIGDIA

P

Montjuïc

Jardí Botànic

P

Passeig Migdia

Passeig Migdia

1 Fira de Barcelona Information Office
2 Aerobus Stop from Airport
3 CaixaForum
4 Pavelló Mies van der Rohe
5 Torres de Ávila
6 Terrrazza
7 Poble Espanyol; El Tablao de Carmen
8 Museu Nacional d'Art de Catalunya
9 Museu Etnológic
10 Teatre Mercat de les Flors
11 Teatre Lliure - Espai Lliure
12 Museu d'Arqueologia
13 Teatre Grec
14 Fundació Joan Miró
15 Estació Parc Montjuïc (Funicular & Telefèric)

16 Bus Terminus for Nos 50 & 61
17 Restaurant Kasbah
18 Restaurant Elche
19 Funicular Aereo to Torre de Jaume I & Torre de San Sebastià (La Barceloneta)
20 Estació Mirador (Telefèric)
21 Castell (Telefèric)
22 Palau Sant Jordi

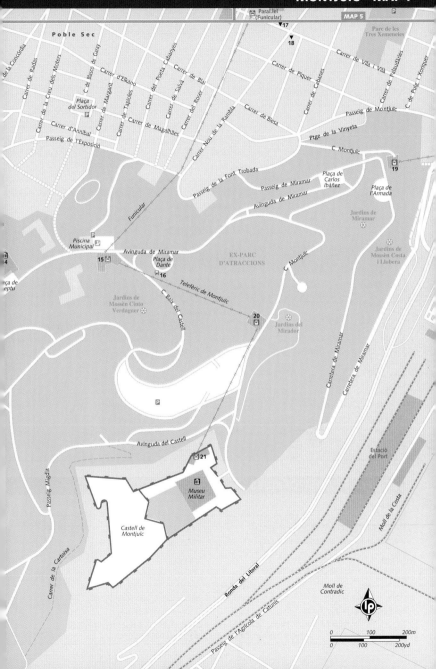

Paral.lel
(Funicular)

MAP 5

▼17

▼
18

Poble Sec

Parc de les
Tres Xemeneies

Carrer de la Concòrdia

Carrer de Radàs

Carrer de la Creu dels Molers

C de Blasco de Garay

Carrer d'Elkano

Carrer de Margarit

Carrer del Poeta Cabanyes

Carrer de Tapioles

Carrer de Blai

Carrer de Piquer

Carrer de Cabanes

Carrer de Vila i Vilà

Carrer de Palaudàries

C. de Puig i Xoriguer

Plaça del Sortidor

Carrer del Roser

Carrer de Salvà

Carrer Nou de la Rambla

Carrer de Blesa

Passeig de Montjuïc

Carrer d'Annibal

Carrer de Carrer de Magalhães

Passeig de l'Exposició

Ptge. de la Vinyeta

C. Montjuïc

19

Passeig de la Font Trobada

Passeig de Miramar

Plaça de Carlos Ibàñez

Plaça de l'Armada

Avinguda de Miramar

Jardins de Miramar

Funicular

Jardins de Mossèn Costa i Llobera

Piscina Municipal

Avinguda de Miramar

Plaça de Dante

15

EX-PARC D'ATRACCIONS

C. Montjuïc

Plaça de Neptu

4

16

Telefèric de Montjuïc

Jardins de Mossèn Cinto Verdaguer

C. Baix del Castell

20

Jardins del Mirador

Carretera de Miramar

Carretera de Miramar

Avinguda del Castell

21

Estació del Port

Museu Militar

Castell de Montjuïc

Passeig Migdia

Moll de la Costa

Carrer de la Cartoixa

Ronda del Litoral

Moll de Contradic

Passeig de l'Agricola de Catlunis

0   100   200m
0   100   200yd

MAP LEGEND

CITY ROUTES

Freeway .... Freeway
Highway .... Primary Road
Road .... Secondary Road
Street .... Street
Lane .... Lane
.... On/Off Ramp

---- ---- .... Unsealed Road
----→---- .... One Way Street
.... Pedestrian Street
.... Stepped Street
)= = = ... Tunnel
.... Footbridge

REGIONAL ROUTES

.... Tollway, Freeway
.... Primary Road
.... Secondary Road
.... Minor Road

BOUNDARIES

—·—·— .... International
—··—·· .... State
— — — .... Disputed
▬▬▬ .... Fortified Wall

HYDROGRAPHY

.... River, Creek
.... Canal
.... Lake

.... Dry Lake; Salt Lake
.... Spring; Rapids
.... Waterfalls

TRANSPORT ROUTES & STATIONS

●─── .... Train
●───── .... Underground Train
Ⓟ─Ⓜ .... FGC/Metro Station
.... Tramway
├─☐── .... Cable Car, Funicular

----☐ .... Ferry
----·---- .... Walking Trail
· · · · · · .... Walking Tour
.... Path
.... Pier or Jetty

AREA FEATURES

.... Beach
.... Building
.... Cemetery
.... Forest
.... Hotel
.... Market
.... Park, Gardens
.... Rocks

POPULATION SYMBOLS

○ **CAPITAL** .... National Capital
◉ **CAPITAL** .... State Capital

● **CITY** .... City
○ **Town** .... Town

● Village .... Village
.... Urban Area

MAP SYMBOLS

■ .... Place to Stay
☒ .... Airport
◔ .... Bank
🚏 🚉 .... Bus Stop/Station
🅰 .... Camping Area
🚐 .... Caravan Park
✝ 🕌 .... Cathedral/Church
🎬 .... Cinema
🤿 .... Dive Site

▼ .... Place to Eat
🖂 .... Embassy, Consulate
♨ .... Fountain
✚ .... Hospital
🛈 .... Information
🖥 .... Internet Café
🗼 .... Lighthouse
☼ .... Lookout
⚑ .... Monument

● .... Point of Interest
🗻 .... Mountain Range
🏛 .... Museum, Gallery
Ⓟ .... Parking
✚ .... Police Station
✉ .... Post Office
🍺 .... Pub, Club, Bar
⚑ .... Ruins
🛒 .... Shopping Centre

🏠 .... Stately Home
🏊 .... Swimming Pool
🚕 .... Taxi
☎ .... Telephone
🏛 .... Temple
🎭 .... Theatre
🍷 .... Winery
🦁 .... Zoo

Note: not all symbols displayed above appear in this book

LONELY PLANET OFFICES

Australia
Locked Bag 1, Footscray, Victoria 3011
☎ 03 8379 8000 fax 03 8379 8111
email: talk2us@lonelyplanet.com.au

USA
150 Linden St, Oakland, CA 94607
☎ 510 893 8555 TOLL FREE: 800 275 8555
fax 510 893 8572
email: info@lonelyplanet.com

UK
10a Spring Place, London NW5 3BH
☎ 020 7428 4800 fax 020 7428 4828
email: go@lonelyplanet.co.uk

France
1 rue du Dahomey, 75011 Paris
☎ 01 55 25 33 00 fax 01 55 25 33 01
email: bip@lonelyplanet.fr
www.lonelyplanet.fr

World Wide Web: www.lonelyplanet.com *or* AOL keyword: lp
Lonely Planet Images: lpi@lonelyplanet.com.au